Handbook of Reconfigurable Computing

Volume II

Handbook of Reconfigurable Computing
Volume II

Edited by **Akira Hanako**

CLANRYE INTERNATIONAL

New Jersey

Published by Clanrye International,
55 Van Reypen Street,
Jersey City, NJ 07306, USA
www.clanryeinternational.com

Handbook of Reconfigurable Computing: Volume II
Edited by Akira Hanako

International Standard Book Number: 978-1-63240-289-9 (Hardback)

Contents

Preface

A reconfigurable system is any system whose sub-system configurations can be changed or modified after fabrication. Reconfigurable computing is generally used to allocate computers whose memory units, processing elements, and interconnections can transform function and spatial configuration after manufacturing and fabrication, before or during the run-time of a particular program or as part of such a program. This field uses the knowledge of computer architecture combined with the high performance of hardware and the flexibility of software by processing with very flexible high speed computing fabrics. One can say that its prime feature is the ability to execute computations in hardware to increase performance, while retaining most of the flexibility of software solution at the same time. In the late 20th century, one can see that there was resurgence in this area of research with many proposed future reconfigurable architectures developed in industrial and academic arenas. Reconfigurable computing has now fast established itself as a major technical discipline that encompasses numerous subjects including computing science and electronic engineering. There is vast potential in reconfigurable computing with the chance to greatly speed up a wide variety of applications. This ensures that reconfigurable computing has become the focus of a great deal of research.

This book is an attempt to compile and collate all available research on reconfigurable computing under one cover. I am grateful to those who put their hard work, effort and expertise into these research projects as well as those who were supportive in this endeavor.

Editor

Adaptive Multiclient Network-on-Chip Memory Core: Hardware Architecture, Software Abstraction Layer, and Application Exploration

Diana Göhringer,[1,2] **Lukas Meder,**[3] **Stephan Werner,**[3]
Oliver Oey,[3] **Jürgen Becker,**[3] **and Michael Hübner**[4]

[1] Institute for Data Processing and Electronics, Karlsruhe Institute of Technology, 76344 Eggenstein-Leopoldshafen, Germany
[2] Object Recognition Department, Fraunhofer IOSB, 76275 Ettlingen, Germany
[3] Institute for Information Processing Technology, Karlsruhe Institute of Technology, 76128 Karlsruhe, Germany
[4] Chair for Embedded Systems in Information Technology, Ruhr-University of Bochum, 44780 Bochum, Germany

Correspondence should be addressed to Diana Göhringer, diana.goehringer@kit.edu

Academic Editor: René Cumplido

This paper presents the hardware architecture and the software abstraction layer of an adaptive multiclient Network-on-Chip (NoC) memory core. The memory core supports the flexibility of a heterogeneous FPGA-based runtime adaptive multiprocessor system called RAMPSoC. The processing elements, also called clients, can access the memory core via the Network-on-Chip (NoC). The memory core supports a dynamic mapping of an address space for the different clients as well as different data transfer modes, such as variable burst sizes. Therefore, two main limitations of FPGA-based multiprocessor systems, the restricted on-chip memory resources and that usually only one physical channel to an off-chip memory exists, are leveraged. Furthermore, a software abstraction layer is introduced, which hides the complexity of the memory core architecture and which provides an easy to use interface for the application programmer. Finally, the advantages of the novel memory core in terms of performance, flexibility, and user friendliness are shown using a real-world image processing application.

1. Introduction and Motivation

Due to the increasing number of available logic blocks on today's Field Programmable Gate Arrays (FPGAs), complete multiprocessor systems can be realized on FPGA. Compared to traditional application specific integrated circuit (ASIC) solutions these FPGA-based Multiprocessor Systems-on-Chip (MPSoCs) can be realized-with lower costs and a shorter (re)design cycle, due to the flexible hardware architecture of the FPGA, which can be adapted to the needs of the application.

However, the major limitations of these FPGA-based MPSoCs are the limited on-chip memory resources as well as the limited physical connection to an off-chip memory. A possible solution would be to connect each processing element to its own external memory. However, this would result in a very specific board design and reduce the flexibility of such an FPGA-based solution. Moreover, due to different application scenarios, the memory requirements of a processor can vary at design and runtime. This is in particular the case, if runtime adaptive MPSoCs, such as RAMPSoC [1], are considered, which support the modification of the MPSoC hardware architecture (number and type of processing elements, communication infrastructure, etc.) as well as the runtime adaptation of the software.

To resolve the memory bottleneck for FPGA-based MPSoCs, an adaptive multiclient Network-on-Chip (NoC) memory core has been developed [2]. This intelligent memory core can support between 1 and 16 processing cores, so-called clients, via an NoC. The clients and their memory allocation are managed dynamically. This is an important feature for adaptive MPSoCs, such as RAMPSoC, which use dynamic and partial reconfiguration for runtime adaptation of both hardware and software. An additional benefit of this dynamic memory allocation is the support of the so-called "virtual-data transfers" by mapping very fast larger memory blocks from one client to another. For the data transfer a priority-based scheduling approach is used to guarantee the access with a negotiated delay. At runtime the priorities can be adapted dynamically, for example, due to application requirements or for example, due to the fact that the data have to be transferred periodically from a source (image sensor).

To hide the complexity of the adaptive multi-client NoC memory core, a software abstraction layer has been developed and integrated. This software abstraction layer provides a user-friendly interface to all the aforementioned features and is based on the well-known message passing interface (MPI) programming model [3].

The benefits of this intelligent memory core are evaluated for executing an image processing application on RAMP-SoC. Performance results with and without the software abstraction layer are shown and compared against a standard connection to external memory by using the processor local bus (PLB) [4] and the Xilinx MultiPort Memory Controller (MPMC) [5].

The paper is organized as follows. Related work is presented in Section 2. RAMPSoC is briefly introduced in Section 3. In Section 4 and its subsections, the functionality and the hardware architecture of the adaptive multi-client NoC memory core are presented. In Section 5 the software abstraction layer is introduced. The image processing application used for the evaluation is presented in Section 6. In Section 7 the integration of the adaptive memory core and the software abstraction layer into the RAMPSoC approach together with measured performance results are given. Finally, the paper is closed by presenting the conclusions and future work in Section 8.

2. Related Work

This work exploits the Multi-Port Memory Controller (MPMC) from Xilinx [5], which supports from 1 up to 8 channels connected to one memory block. The core itself supports multiple connection standards which are tailored to the processors used in Xilinx-based designs (Microblaze, Power PC). Furthermore, low-level direct access ports to the memory called Native Port Interface (NPI) are supported which were used for the core described in this paper.

The idea to connect a memory via a network node in an NoC was also used in the heterogeneous multicore System-on-Chip MORPHEUS [6]. The controller enabled a data transfer to and from an ARM9 processor as well as to different reconfigurable hardware blocks. As in the MORPHEUS project an ASIC was developed, the area optimization like it is required in FPGA-based designs was not that critical. Furthermore, in MORPHEUS, the clients in the NoC were fixed and not adaptive in that extent, as in the here presented NoC.

Intelligent memory controllers were successfully realized in previous research works. Intelligence had been integrated into the memory itself, so that it is able to process data without the host processor and therefore results in a higher performance (see [7, 8]). Especially, FlexRAM and Self-Aware Memory (SAM) were developed for this purpose and the decentral management of large memory. The approach presented in this paper benefits definitely from the excellent ideas in these works, but targets directly the support of a runtime adaptive FPGA-based MPSoC and an NoC built especially for this purpose. Additionally, the focus of this work is not to increase the performance of a processor through a memory internal data manipulation, but rather to enable the flexible access of an FPGA-based system to an external memory block.

A good example for scheduling algorithms for multiport memory controllers is given in Dai and Zhu [9]. They propose a quality of service guaranteed scheduling algorithm which is based on a combination of weighted round robin, credit borrow, and repay and residual bandwidth calculation. The approach is very interesting, but the dynamic change of clients due to dynamic and partial reconfiguration of the MPSoC at runtime is not supported by the algorithm. Also a connection to this MPMC via an NoC is not considered.

Redsharc [10] presents a software API based on the stream model for hiding the complexity of accessing on- and off-chip memory via their proprietary Block Switch NoC (BSN) and the Xilinx MPMC controller. However, also in this work runtime adaptation of the system is not supported.

In summary, the major contributions of this work compared to related works are the combination of a flexible multiclient NoC memory core with an MPI-based software abstraction layer for a runtime adaptive MPSoC.

The approach presented in this paper, can efficiently be integrated into the Aethereal NoC (see [11]), which has a high importance in current research projects such as Flex-Tiles (see [12]). The Aethereal NoC is used in the FlexTiles project, to establish the intertile communication and for the data transfer from and to the on-chip and external memory blocks. The adaptive multi-client Network-on-Chip memory core presented in this paper can be efficiently exploited for this innovative multicore architecture.

The concept and its efficient realization are described in the following sections.

3. Runtime Adaptive MPSoC: RAMPSoC

RAMPSoC [1] is an FPGA-based heterogeneous MPSoC consisting of different types of processors and hardware accelerators which communicate with each other and with the environment over the Star-Wheels Network-on-Chip [1]. The Star-Wheels NoC has a heterogeneous topology consisting of three different kinds of switches: *subswitch*, *superswitch*, and *rootswitch*. Each processing element is connected via a network interface (NI) to a subswitch. For this purpose, a unified NI based on the Xilinx FIFO-based Fast Simplex Links (FSL, [13]) is used. The super- and the rootswitch are used as central network nodes. The superswitch connects up to seven subswitches into a so-called subnet. The rootswitch is used as the central node for

Adaptive Multiclient Network-on-Chip Memory Core: Hardware Architecture, Software Abstraction Layer, and
Application Exploration

3

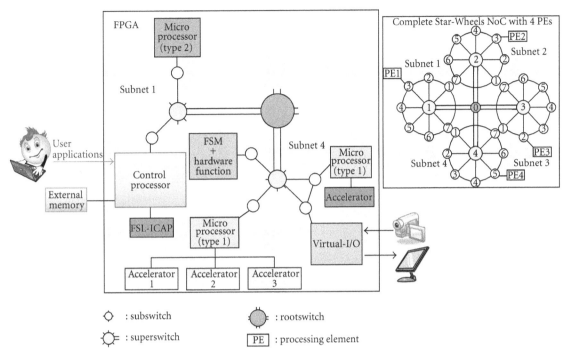

FIGURE 1: Example RAMPSoC system at one point in time connected over the Star-Wheels Network-on-Chip.

connecting up to four subnets with each other. The Star-Wheels NoC provides both a packet- and a circuit-switching communication protocol using separate ports for each protocol. The packet-switching communication protocol is used for control purposes, such as establishing/freeing a circuit-switching communication, and for small data transfers. Per packet 16 bits of data can be transferred. For high data volumes the circuit-switching communication protocol is preferred, as it has a lower latency and supports a data width of 32 bits.

Using dynamic and partial reconfiguration, the MPSoC can be adapted at runtime to the application requirements, for example, changing the number and type of processors and accelerators, modifying the communication infrastructure or changing the software executables. In Figure 1, an example RAMPSoC architecture at one point in time is shown.

To hide the complex heterogeneous MPSoC architecture from the user, a virtualization layer has been developed (for details see [14]). It consists of an embedded Linux server, which is responsible for scheduling and mapping of the software and hardware adaptations. It furthermore acts as a user interface. This Linux server communicates and controls the slave processors. The slave processors execute a special purpose operating system called ELEX-OS (ELF executing operating system). Both ELEX-OS and the embedded Linux operating system include proprietary communication libraries based on MPI to facilitate the communication over the Star-Wheels NoC and to hide the low level communication protocol routines.

4. Functionality and Structure of the Adaptive Memory Core

The main goal when designing the runtime adaptive memory core was to make it adaptable to both changing conditions from the information's point of view and to changes at the component's interfaces.

In more detail, the memory core should on the one hand be flexible to support the following:

(i) priority based scheduling of the processor accesses;

(ii) adapting the priorities of the processors on demand;

(iii) dynamic management of varying numbers of processors, several requests at the same time, and different memory requirements due to changing applications;

(iv) up to 16 distinct processor peripherals which are provided overlap-free virtual memory resources which are dynamically managed.

On the other hand, the memory core should have a modular structure supporting a high portability to be independent from the NoC as well as from the number and types of off-chip memory cores. Therefore, the adaptive memory core is connected via FSL [13] to the Star-Wheels NI and therefore to the Star-Wheels NoC. As most of these functionalities are handled by the NI the memory core is this way decoupled from the Star-Wheels NoC. Also the memory core's complexity at the packet evaluation stage is reduced because it only receives the packets and data which are meant for it. It is linked to the MPMC via two NPI ports

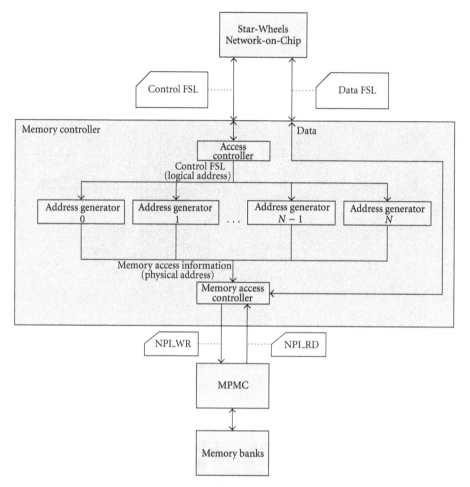

FIGURE 2: Overview of the adaptive memory core.

(one to write and one to read) which is the native interface to the manufacturer's memory controller. The MPMC can be configured for a variety of different types of off-chip memory and it is frequently updated by Xilinx to support the newest memory types. Currently the MPMC core provides 8 ports which support a variety of bus standards.

In Figure 2, the structure of the adaptive memory core and its interfaces to the off-chip memory and the Star-Wheels NoC is depicted.

Both routing protocols supplied by the Star-Wheels NoC are supported. The memory core is connected to the packet-switching lines via the *control-FSL* which is solely used for control purposes such as memory de- and allocation or changing the priority of a processor. Reading or writing data from/to the external memory is done using the faster circuit-switching communication protocol via the parallel *data-FSL* port. The reason for using only the circuit-switching communication for the data exchange is on the one side the wider data width of 32 bits compared to 16 bits of the packet-switching protocol. On the other side, the overhead for accessing external memory is higher than accessing local on-chip memory and should therefore be only used for exchanging high amount of data, which is faster via the circuit-switching protocol due to the low latency.

The aforementioned capability to manage 16 distinct processors by one memory core was selected according to the maximum number of devices which can be connected to the NoC (see the right part of Figure 1). With growing numbers of devices to be managed, the required logic resources, and the communication load at the network node the memory core is connected to do also increase. Thus, 16 supported processors were found as a good tradeoff between the required area and the flexibility of the memory core.

In order to reduce latency, simplify the design and increase portability; the control and data paths are decoupled. The paths are separated at the NI and are reunited at the memory access controller. As can be seen in Figure 2, there is no intermediate processing of the data path that would add latency or deteriorate the throughput of the high speed data transmission.

Internally the adaptive memory core consists of three main components: *access controller*, 1 to 16 *address generators*, and the *memory access controller*. These components are explained in detail in the following subsections.

4.1. Access Controller. The access controller is the administrating component that evaluates priority and memory allocation requests, registers devices, and decides in resource assignments to the address generators.

Adaptive Multiclient Network-on-Chip Memory Core: Hardware Architecture, Software Abstraction Layer, and
Application Exploration

5

Prior to storing or reading data to/from a memory location of the external memory that is connected to the memory core, memory regions need to be allocated to the processors. The memory allocation is based on blocks with a fixed number and size. For the implementations and results 64 blocks at 64 kbytes each were selected. 64 kbytes were chosen as a minimal block size, because for smaller amounts of bytes the FPGA has sufficient on-chip resources, which can be accessed faster than the external memory. Also, this selection allows providing the needed flexibility by keeping the complexity and therefore the area requirements of the adaptive memory core low. Both parameters can be adapted to the users need at design time. Each time a processor allocates memory blocks, the access controller informs the respective address generator about the corresponding block numbers. These block numbers are then later used by the address generators to translate the logical addresses of the processor requests into the physical addresses of the MPMC controller.

The access controller stores internally the index of the *current block* and the index of the *next free block*. On the allocation or deallocation of a block both indexes are increased or decreased, respectively.

For the deallocation process a simple, yet effective, scheme for block-based allocation is applied. The basic idea is to store the block numbers of deallocated blocks in a so-called *deallocation array*. If an allocated block is freed by a processor, the block number is copied to the top position of the deallocation array and the indexes of the current/next block are decreased by one. When the allocation of a block is requested, first it is checked, if the deallocation array holds a block number. If this is the case, this block is reused and both indexes are left unchanged, if not, a new block is allocated by increasing both indexes. Like this, fragmentation is avoided and the required memory resources are minimized.

Illegal deallocation or allocation requests are denied by the access controller by sending a not OK (NOK) packet. Such deallocations or allocations are defined as requests where a processor wants to deallocate a nonexistent block or allocate a block when all blocks are being used. On the other hand, if an allocation/deallocation was successful the associated address generators reply by sending an OK packet to the requesting processor.

In order to reduce network traffic it is allowed to allocate/deallocate multiple blocks at a time. This is done by setting the lower six bits of the allocation packet to the desired number of blocks. Here the address generator always answers such packets with an OK packet which contains the number of allocated blocks. It is then in the processors' responsibility to check, if the requested number of blocks was allocated. If the number of allocated blocks was too low, the remaining blocks could not be allocated, because all blocks were in use when the request was being processed.

In the process of memory allocation the address generators only play a minor role. The computed number of a newly allocated memory block is forwarded to the assigned address generator on a memory allocation. When a block needs to be deallocated the number of the last allocated block is obtained from the address generator and added to the deallocation array.

The access controller has an assignment table, in which the address of each processor is assigned to one address generator. New processors will be assigned to the next free address generator. In case of 16 address generators up to 16 processors can access the memory core. No dedicated control packet is required for the registration of a processor because every control packet contains the processor's unique address in the NoC as defined by the communication protocol. Through this scheme the memory core behaves as a coherent module hiding the information about the internal details from connected devices.

Packets related to memory accesses or for establishing and freeing a circuit-switching channel are directly forwarded to the respective address generator.

In addition, the access controller is responsible for updating the priorities of the address generators based on the requests of the assigned processors. In order to keep the priority encoder simple and to assure that each address generator is assigned to a single priority and vice versa, the processors can only request to increase/decrease the current priority of their address generator by 1. If, for example, the priority of one address generator has to be increased by 1, the access controller searches in its internal *priority table* for the address generator which has currently the desired priority. Then the priorities of these two address generators are switched. Due to this switch, it occurs that the priority of an address generator is changed by the priority change request of a different processor. Therefore, each processor can send a so-called *get-priority-packet* to the access controller before accessing the memory, in order to request its current priority level and to decide if it will be necessary to increase the own priority before accessing the memory.

For all memory accesses and transfers via the control-FSL, the access controller assigns available resources to the address generators based on a priority table. The requesting address generator which has currently the highest priority gets the access to the component. If all resources of a kind are being used, the remaining requests are postponed until the next time one of the required resources is released by an address generator. In order to guarantee high throughput for different processors in data-driven applications, the idle time between assignments of the connections to the memory access controller has to be kept at a small value. Thus a second interface to both the NoC and the memory controller was introduced as presented in Section 4.5.

To be able to evaluate requests for a change of priorities during memory accesses or allocations and to avoid resource sharing problems during these processes, a second priority table is introduced that stores these changes. If a priority change has to be applied new resource assignments are postponed and the contents of the second priority table are copied to the first one as soon as all resources have been released.

4.2. Address Generator. Each processor is assigned to an address generator. The address generators receive the packets, which have been sent by the processors via the packet-switching communication protocol and which include either information about the desired memory access or information for establishing or freeing a circuit-switching communication channel for the requested data transfer.

The address generators work independently from each other and primarily serve the processors on handling requested memory accesses and controlling the establishment and freeing of the circuit-switching channels required for the data transmission to or from the MPMC core. However, for addressing a specific block of the allocated off-chip memory space the logical address of the request needs to be translated into a physical memory address. For this reason, the address generator is equipped with an *allocation array* that stores the numbers of the allocated blocks which are forwarded from the access controller to the address generator. By evaluating the validity of incoming requests, the address generator guarantees that only these requests may be executed which are allowed due to restrictions of the memory access controller and which will not cause any corruption of data of other address generators' address space. Requests which are evaluated as invalid are directly rejected (NOK packet).

The computation of the physical addresses has to be performed by the address generator because the memory access controller itself has no information about the allocated block numbers of each address generator. Thus the physical addresses are generated as follows.

First, the address generator controls if the address is a multiple of 32 bits (=4 bytes). This address alignment is selected because of the minimum portion of data (4 bytes) that can be transferred through the FSL connection between the memory core and the processor. Due to the 32-bit width of the FSL interface, an address which is not a multiple of 4 bytes would not be beneficial as parts of the data word would need to remain free in the first and in the last transmitted packet.

Second, the address generator checks if the number of bytes to be transferred is also a multiple of 4 and therefore a multiple of 32 bits. If this is not the case, the number of bytes is rounded up to the next multiple of 4 bytes.

Third, the address generator verifies, if sufficient memory blocks have been allocated for the respective memory access. This means, it assures that both the start address and the total transfer size are within the allocated address space of this address generator. If not or if the address is not a multiple of 4 bytes, a NOK packet will be sent to the processor. For all other cases, the address generator checks, if the requested memory transfer crosses the block boundary. This is important, as two successive logical blocks are not necessarily mapped to two successive physical memory blocks. In case the physical blocks are not successive the requested memory transfer is split into two transfers. The address of the physical block ap required for these checks is calculated by dividing the address of the access request ar by the block size b and multiplying the block number of the allocated block at the position "ar div b" of the allocation array by the block size b. The physical address is finally obtained by adding the rest of the division r as an offset to the base address of the physical block. The information for all transfers is then forwarded to the memory access controller. The maximum number of transfers per memory access is two, as the maximum access request is 4 kbytes based on the structure of the control packets as described in Section 4.4. As each block has 64 kbytes, only one block boundary can be crossed by a memory access resulting in a maximum of two transfers.

Conflicts of different address generators trying to access the memory access controller or the control-FSL to send back packets to the processors at the same time must be avoided. Thus a shared access to these resources is applied. This scheme is implemented by assigning every address generator a specific priority, that is, a bijective transform is used. By guaranteeing unique priorities during the whole runtime, a simple encoder can be designed that decides which currently requesting address generator has the highest priority and grants access to the resource due to this decision. For the priorities a cooperative method with dynamic priorities and no preemption is used. Because of the bijectivity of the priority → address generator relation, the tasks of priority decision and priority update of the access controller can be eased by storing the inverse relation in the second priority table instead of a direct copy of the first one.

4.3. Memory Access Controller. The memory access controller receives the information for the transfer (physical memory address, number of bytes, read, or write) from the address generators and it handles the memory accesses by arbitrating and communicating with the MPMC controller.

It translates the number of bytes to be transferred into the number of 64-bit words, because it accesses the MPMC via a 64-bit NPI interface. To minimize the communication load for the MPMC, all supported NPI transfer sizes will be used by preferring the maximum possible one based on the address alignment: 2, 4, 8, 16, 32, and 64 word transfers.

If none of the chosen transfer sizes fits the address alignment and no smaller transfers have been computed during the initial phase, larger transfers have to be subdivided. Here, the smallest remaining transfer, which is larger than the transfer whose address alignment requirement would fit the circumstances, is consecutively divided into smaller transfers. An example is shown in Figure 3.

Here one 64-word and one 32-word transfer is available but the address is aligned to an address boundary that would fit 8-word transfers only. In the proposed scheme, the 32-word transfer is divided first into two 16-word transfers and afterwards one 16-word transfer is divided into two 8-word transfers. After one of the smallest transfers has been finished, step by step the address alignment allows larger transfer sizes. Due to this strategy the number of needed transfers and therefore the load on the MPMC are minimized.

The memory access controller has a direct access to the circuit-switching communication ports of the Star-Wheels NI via the data-FSL component, as can be seen in Figure 2. Only the memory access controller is dependent on the MPMC controller. In case a different memory controller shall be used or in case Xilinx will stop the support of the MPMC and will offer a different memory controller, only the memory access controller needs to be adapted. All other components of the adaptive memory core are independent of the selected memory controller. This way,

Adaptive Multiclient Network-on-Chip Memory Core: Hardware Architecture, Software Abstraction Layer, and
Application Exploration

7

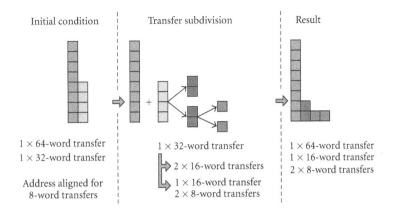

Figure 3: Transfer subdivision example.

a higher performance compared to a single NPI port can be achieved by slightly increasing the number of required FPGA resources.

4.4. Structure and Types of Control Packets. The basic structure of the control packets used for the memory core is shown in Figure 4. It is based on the so-called flexible packet [14] and uses the corresponding header. The flexible packets are provided by the Star-Wheels NoC to add user defined packets. The header is then followed by the destination address and the source address.

The following four bits are used for the memory core header. This header allows differentiating between the different packets required for the functionality of the memory core. These are the following packets:

Get-priority,

Decrease-priority,

Increase-priority,

Deallocate-block,

Allocate-block,

NOK (Not OK),

OK,

Write-flexible 1 (address part 1),

Write-flexible 2 (address part 2),

Write-flexible 3 (number of bytes),

Read-flexible 1 (address part 1),

Read-flexible 2 (address part 2),

Read-flexible 3 (number of bytes).

The 12 bits of data are used to transfer the required address, split in two parts (e.g., Write-flexible-packet 1 and 2), to transfer the number of bytes (e.g., Write-flexible-packet 3) or to specify, how many blocks to allocate/deallocate.

The protocol for a memory access is composed of an access information phase and a channel handling phase using packet-switched routing and a data transmission phase using circuit-switched routing, see Figure 5.

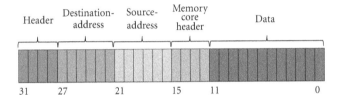

Figure 4: Basic structure of the control packets used for the memory core.

In the access information phase only a packet with Write/Read-flexible 3 header is mandatory. If the first two packets of the information phase are omitted, the address of the last read or write access, respectively, is used.

4.5. Extension with Two Star-Wheels Network Interfaces. For very memory-intensive applications, where several processors have to frequently access the memory core, an extended version with two Star-Wheels NI ports and four NPI ports has been developed. An overview of this memory core version is shown in Figure 6.

With this extended memory core version, two write and two read accesses can be processed simultaneously. To prevent waiting cycles, the memory access controller and the finite state machine of the access controller have been duplicated: one for each additional port. This results in a higher performance, but also in higher area requirements. For even more memory-intensive scenarios or to be able to access more memory space, the address space of the memory core can be modified by an offset at a design time to support more than one instance of the memory core in an NoC system.

5. Software Abstraction Layer

5.1. Motivation. Using the memory core in a C-program is not very simple. There are a lot of things which have to receive attention. For instance, for reading or writing data from or to the external memory using the memory core, a sequence of three low level commands for initializing the hardware must be used. Additionally, the buildup and release

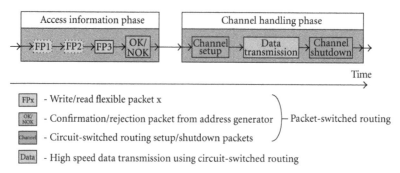

FIGURE 5: Memory access protocol.

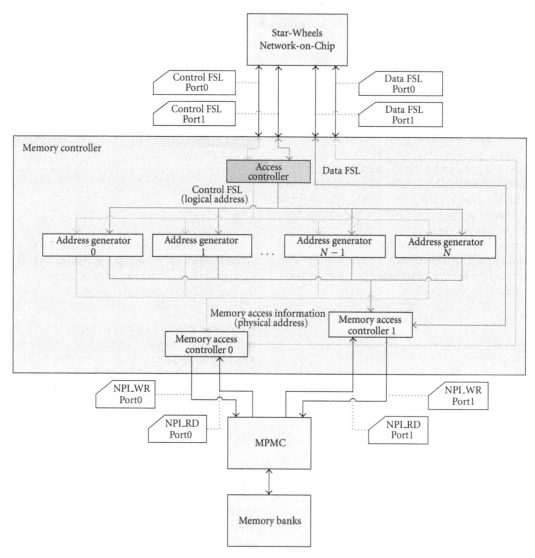

FIGURE 6: Overview of the adaptive memory core with four NPIs and two Star-Wheels NI ports.

of a communication channel must be handled. Furthermore, the programmer must calculate the amount of bytes to be transferred. For allocating memory with the memory core, the number of blocks of 64 kbytes, which is needed for this number of bytes, must be computed. After calculating this, the programmer has to keep in mind that the argument, specifying the number of blocks to allocate, must be

decreased by one. So "0" must be passed for allocating 1 block of 64 kbytes in external memory. Later, this number of blocks must be used for releasing the memory.

To ease the usage of the memory core, some functions of the Message Passing Interface protocol (MPI) were implemented in the MPI library of RAMPSoC. Furthermore, the ELEX-OS running on the Microblazes connected to

Adaptive Multiclient Network-on-Chip Memory Core: Hardware Architecture, Software Abstraction Layer, and
Application Exploration

9

TABLE 1: MPI functitons used for accessing the adaptive memory core.

int MPI_Alloc_mem (MPI_Aint size, MPI_Info info, void *baseptr)	
MPI_Aint size	Size of memory to be allocated in byte
MPI_Info info	Usage depends on implementation; only the value 0 must be supported
void* baseptr	Pointer to the allocated memory
int MPI_Put (void *origin_addr, int origin_count, MPI_Datatype origin_datatype, int target_rank, MPI Aint target_disp, int target_count, MPI Datatype_target datatype, MPI_Win win)	
origin_*	Defines which data shall be sent to the target node
target_*	Defines where the data are to be sent: the node (by rank), in which local memory address (target_disp) and the amount of data
win	Defines the memory window on target
int MPI_Get (void *origin_addr, int origin_count, MPI_Datatype origin_datatype, int target_rank, MPI_Aint target_disp, int target_count, MPI_Datatype target_datatype, MPI_Win win)	
origin_*	Defines where the data which are read from target shall be stored
target_*	Defines which data shall be read: from which node (by rank), from which local memory address (target_disp), and the amount of data
win	Defines the memory window on target
int MPI_Free_mem(void *base)	
void *base	Pointer to the memory that was allocated with MPI_Alloc_mem

the NoC was extended for handling the access to the memory core. Additionally, ELEX-OS provides a special memory management to handle the needs for allocating and freeing local and external memory using the corresponding MPI functions. Implementing the new MPI functions in the library, we are aware to support the MPI standard as much as possible, but because of the special features and restrictions of the embedded architecture some modification are needed.

5.2. Normal Use of the MPI Functions. Before describing the adaptations, it is explained how the usage of the functions listed in Table 1 is defined in the standard of MPI. The function MPI_Alloc_mem() allocates storage in memory and returns a pointer to it. This pointer is stored in the third argument *"baseptr"* of the function. The second argument *"info"* of the function is not standardized. The meaning and the accepted values for "info" depend on the implementation of the MPI library. The standard only defines that the value MPI_INFO_NULL (=0) must be accepted always. The function MPI_Free_mem() is then used for freeing this memory again.

In MPI, there is a possibility for transferring data between the memories of several nodes in the same communicator. For this purpose the corresponding nodes must allow each task in the intracommunicator group to access their local memory. Therefore the nodes must specify a *"window"* in their memory that is accessible by remote tasks. For this purpose the function MPI_Win_create() is used. To free this window again, the function MPI_Win_free() is called. After defining a window, the nodes within one communicator can exchange data with each other using the functions MPI_Get() and MPI_Put(). Both functions have the same arguments specifying the target and source node, the addresses in the corresponding memory window of the nodes, and the amount of data to transfer. The command MPI_Put() is used

to send data from the origin task to the given address in a window of the target task. The function MPI_Get() transfers data from the target node to the origin node.

5.3. Implementation and Its Adaptations. Since the Message Passing Interface (MPI) was originally developed for high-performance computing (HPC), there are some modifications needed in our implementation of the MPI library. One thing is that the memory core cannot know which area in memory it must share with other nodes. Furthermore, it should provide exclusive access to a memory region only for one explicit node in the network. So the memory core is not able to allow access to a specific window in memory for an intracommunicator group. In contrast, it is needed that one node which requires external memory must communicate it to the memory core. For this, the function MPI_Alloc_mem() is used in this implementation of MPI. The only restriction here is that the value MPI_INFO_NULL (=0) must be supported. So this argument is used for defining the amount of memory that should be allocated in the remote memory in bytes. If it is zero, no area in external memory is allocated. The argument *"size"* still defines how many bytes are to be allocated in the local memory of the current node. So you are able to allocate more bytes in external memory than are available as local memory. The function returns a pointer to the position of the allocated local memory. The memory management in local memory is done by the ELEX-OS running on the node. The MPI function determines how many 64 kB-blocks must be allocated by the memory core to provide the count of bytes demanded with *"info."* MPI_Alloc_mem() returns MPI_SUCCESS if the allocation in both memories was successful, MPI_ERR_NO_MEM otherwise.

This implementation of the MPI library is not using windows to specify the area that is allocated in external memory. Due to this fact, the corresponding argument of the functions MPI_Put() and MPI_Get() is ignored, if the target_rank defines the rank of the memory core. This information will be given to the ELEX-OS on the node during the boot process. The other arguments of the two functions MPI_Put() and MPI_Get() are almost used like defined in the standard. The arguments named *origin_** specify the local address and the amount of data on the node calling the MPI function. The arguments named *target_** specify the memory address in the remote node. If the "*target_rank*" corresponds to the rank of the memory core then these arguments define the address and data size within the 64 kB blocks which were allocated by the calling node previously.

The function MPI_Free_mem() is used to free the memory which previously was allocated with MPI_Alloc_mem(). So it frees the memory in local and in external memory. The only restriction for using MPI_Free_mem() and MPI_Alloc_mem() comes from the fact that the memory core is working with the FILO policy ("First In Last Out") when allocating and freeing memory. So you have to use the functions in inverse order. For instance, when allocating region 1 and then region 2 you have first to free region 2 and after that region 1. Freeing the external and local memory is done by a collaboration of the memory management in ELEX-OS and the MPI library.

5.4. Collaboration of MPI Library and ELEX-OS. In this section the collaboration between the MPI library and the ELEX-OS running on the Microblaze nodes in the Star-Wheels Network-on-Chip (NoC) is described. For handling the allocation in local and external memory, a special memory management is implemented in ELEX-OS. It provides the information which the MPI library needs for freeing the blocks in external memory. Additionally it manages the allocation and release of storage in local memory. So it is possible to work with different sizes in local and external memory. Furthermore the memory management controls that no parts of the executable file or ELEX-OS itself are overwritten when allocating memory dynamically.

In Figure 7, the usage of the functions for allocating and freeing memory is shown. When the user application calls the function MPI_Alloc_mem() with the shown arguments, there will be allocated 40 bytes of local memory by a collaboration of ELEX-OS and the MPI library at first (step 1). After the allocation the pointer "A" is assigned with this area. Then the library calculates the number of 64 kB blocks which are needed to store the asked 100.000 bytes. Afterwards it sends a corresponding request to the memory core and goes sleeping (step 2).

The memory core handles the request, allocates the demanded 2 blocks, and sends back an answer to the sender of the request (step 3). When the reply arrives at the processor running the user application, an interrupt occurs which is handled by the "Interrupt Service Routine" (ISR) of ELEX-OS. After that the MPI library sends a signal (step 4) to the user application and it continues working.

In order to release the allocated memory, the user application calls MPI_Free_mem(). Therefore the pointer which

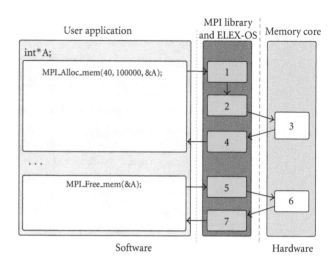

FIGURE 7: Application flow for allocating and releasing external memory with the memory core using MPI.

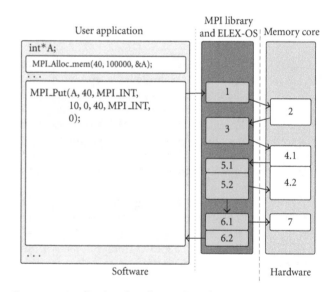

FIGURE 8: Application flow for sending data to the memory core using MPI_Put.

was set using MPI_Allocate_mem() must be used as argument (see Figure 7). Then the MPI library asks the memory core for releasing the amount of blocks that are assigned with this pointer (step 5). The memory core handles the command, frees the blocks in external memory, and sends an acknowledgment to the sender (step 6). When the reply arrives, the ISR of ELEX-OS handles the reply, releases the local memory, and sends a signal to the user application (step 7).

When external memory is allocated, the two functions MPI_Put() and MPI_Get() can be used to transfer data between the local and the external memory. Since the activities of both functions are very similar, here it will be described only with MPI_Put(). The application flow is shown in Figure 8.

Adaptive Multiclient Network-on-Chip Memory Core: Hardware Architecture, Software Abstraction Layer, and Application Exploration

11

When the user application calls the function MPI_Put(), the MPI library sends the command sequence for a write access to the memory core (step 1). Therefore, the amount of bytes is calculated by the library using the arguments for data type and count of values to write. The memory core handles the request and checks if the access is permitted (step 2). ELEX-OS then handles the answer of the memory core and sends a request for building up a channel (step 3). The memory core handles this request and acknowledges it (step 4.1). Then the memory core starts waiting for data. When ELEX-OS receives this acknowledgment, it sends a signal to the MPI library (step 5.1) which then begins sending the data over the channel (step 5.2). Simultaneously the memory core receives the data and writes them into the external memory (step 4.2). After all data is sent, the MPI library sends an "End-of-Communication"-command (EoC) to the memory core to release the channel (step 6.1). When this command is handled (step 7) by the Star-Wheels NoC the channel is released. At last, the MPI library sends a signal to the user application saying that all data is transmitted (step 6.2).

MPI_Get() works very similar, but here the MPI library sends the command sequence for a reading access and then waits for a signal from ELEX-OS to indicate a channel is built up and data can be received. Therefore, the ISR of ELEX-OS handles the request for a channel from the memory core. Then the MPI library reads the data from the channel and writes it in the receive buffer of the user application. When the memory core has transmitted all data, it sends the EoC command to release the channel. Since the amount of data to read is known by the MPI library, it does not have to wait for this and sends a signal to the user application immediately after receiving all data it has expected. The EoC command is only handled internally by ELEX-OS to recognize that the channel resources have been released.

6. Application Exploration

To explore the benefits of the novel memory core, the Scale Invariant Feature Transform (SIFT, [15]), a complex and very computational intensive image processing algorithm, has been used. This algorithm finds interesting points in an image and describes them as features (so-called descriptors). These descriptors have the advantage that they are invariant to scaling and orientation as well as partially invariant to distortion and illumination changes. These properties make them beneficial for object recognition applications.

The algorithm has been implemented following the description in [15]. Through blurring and resampling of the input image, several intermediate images are created. The differences between the generated images deliver minima and maxima, which are taken as so-called keypoints. Out of these the best are used as descriptors. The found descriptors are then marked as red circles in the output image, as can be seen in Figure 9.

For parallelization, the input image can be divided into several tiles which can be processed independently. To allow all processors access to the input image, a global shared memory is necessary. All intermediate images of the

FIGURE 9: SIFT descriptors marked in output image.

same tile are kept in the local memories of the processors as more calculations are done with them.

7. Integration and Results

The test system is implemented on a Xilinx Virtex-5 LX110 FPGA and uses two Xilinx Microblaze softcore processors for the computation. Each one of them has 128KB of local block RAM. The input image is received over a video graphics array (VGA) connection and written directly into the DDR2 memory by the use of the Xilinx IPCores vga_in, de_gen, and video_to_vfbc. There, the data can be accessed by the processors through the memory controller. As only a specific part of the memory is assigned to a processor, this leads to the image segmentation, where one processor has access to the upper part of the image and the other has access to the lower part of the image.

For the output the module Xilinx xps_tft is used. It uses a given memory area as a framebuffer and outputs it over digital visual interface (DVI) as an image on an external display. To speed up the calculation a hardware accelerated finite response filter was added to the system. It allows faster calculation of Gaussian filtered images. The complete system can be seen in Figure 10.

With the help of the memory core, the image input and output can be handled as seen in Figure 11. Each processor can read data from the input image as well as write data to the XPS TFT address range to output the results on the external display.

At first, the performance overhead of the new MPI layer was evaluated. The achieved throughput was compared to the values of [2]. In addition to that, tests were run using the MPI layer with PLB access to the memory. The results can be seen in Figure 12 for writes and in Figure 13 for reads.

The write throughput of the memory core access with more than 128 bytes is reduced to about 55% when using the MPI layer. With more than 128 bytes transferred, it is faster than PLB with the MPI layer and with more than 256 bytes transferred it is even faster than direct PLB access.

Reading data is not as much affected as writing and still manages to achieve more than 80% of the throughput at a higher number of bytes. Both PLB accesses are outperformed when more than 64 bytes are transferred to the DDR memory.

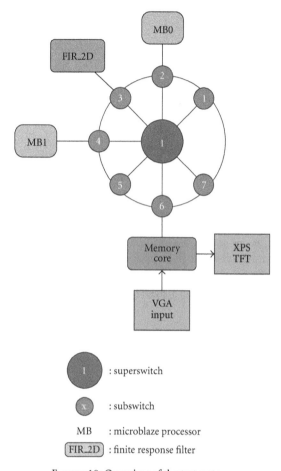

FIGURE 10: Overview of the test system.

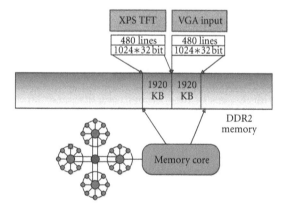

FIGURE 11: Memory core as Framebuffer.

For the SIFT algorithm an input image with a resolution of 640×480 pixels is used. Each pixel uses 32 bits of data and to ease the addressing of single lines 1024 pixels per line are saved in the memory. All pixels not belonging to the image are forced to the value 0. Thus one image in the memory needs 1920 KB of space. For the memory core access this means the allocation of 15 blocks per processor for the input and 15 blocks per processor for the output of data.

TABLE 2: Resource utilization of the individual components.

Component	Number of Virtex 5 LUTs	Percentage of whole system
Microblaze	1746	4.9
Accelerator	7470	21.0
Memory core	5206	14.7
MPMC	4835	13.6
Video I/O	2039	5.7
On-chip communication	11873	33.5

A segment size of 64×120 pixels was chosen. As the image is read line by line, a good read throughput of more than 30 MB/s can be achieved this way. Bigger segments would allow even higher throughput rates but are limited by the size of the local memory of the processors. Getting a new image segment from the shared memory is about 3-times faster when using the memory core: 2.79 ms with PLB access versus 0.89 ms with memory core access.

As a result the found descriptors are marked in the output image. One pixel would be enough but for better highlighting a circle around the found pixel is used. This scenario does not really fit the memory access through the memory core because only small amounts of data need to be transferred. In this case writing one single pixel takes $3.42\,\mu s$ against $0.63\,\mu s$ with PLB access. With a circle for better emphasis, the times increase to $58.14\,\mu s$ and $10.71\,\mu s$, respectively.

In Table 2 the resource utilization of the individual components can be seen. The memory core with two address generators needs only around 1% more look-up tables (LUTs) than the MPMC. The processing elements (Microblaze and accelerator) take up about one-third of the whole resources as does the on-chip communication. Components concerning the memory system need a little less than 30 percent and the rest of the resources is shared between the video I/O modules as well as the general parts such as clock and reset generation.

8. Conclusions and Outlook

In this paper the hardware architecture and the software abstraction layer of an adaptive multiclient Network-on-Chip memory core have been presented. The memory core dynamically manages the varying number of processing elements within a reconfigurable MPSoC and the therefore varying memory requirements. For the memory access a scheduling algorithm based on dynamic priorities is used. Due to its modular structure resource requirements can be adapted to achieve a good tradeoff between performance and area based on the application requirements, for example, by selecting the appropriate number of address generators. Furthermore, the memory core can easily be modified to support other NoCs or to be ported to other FPGAs, such as Altera.

The software abstraction layer introduced in this paper is based on MPI. It eases the use of the memory core by hiding the complexity and therefore the low-level commands for accessing the memory core.

Adaptive Multiclient Network-on-Chip Memory Core: Hardware Architecture, Software Abstraction Layer, and
Application Exploration

13

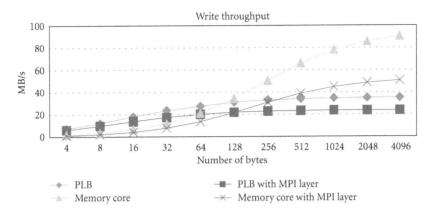

FIGURE 12: Comparison of the achievable write throughput in MB/s at 125 Mhz: Star-Wheels NoC and adaptive memory core versus PLB
and Xilinx MPMC controller, both with and without MPI layer.

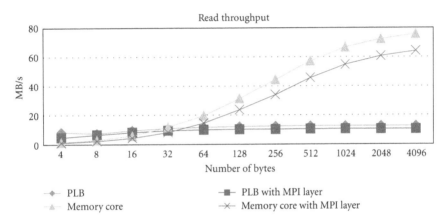

FIGURE 13: Comparison of the achievable read throughput in MB/s at 125 Mhz: Star-Wheels NoC and adaptive memory core versus PLB
and Xilinx MPMC controller, both with and without MPI layer.

The correct functionality of the memory core was explored using a complex image processing application. Performance results were measured on a Virtex-5 FPGA. It was shown that for higher amounts of data, as needed for example, in image processing applications, the adaptive memory core provides a higher throughput compared to using the MPMC controller via the standard PLB interface provided by Xilinx. Furthermore, it supports up to 16 processor cores, while the MPMC only allows up to 8 connections. Even with the overhead of the software abstraction layer a higher performance for higher amounts of data was achieved compared to accessing the MPMC via the PLB interface.

Future work is to develop an administrative subcomponent or separate controller whose functionality goes beyond the capabilities of the access controller. This component will make it possible to monitor the allocated blocks of the different address generators and allow the allocation of shared memory regions to support the above-mentioned MPI feature to define windows to work on the same data set with several processors.

Acknowledgments

The authors would like to thank Andreas Stuckert from Fraunhofer IOSB for supporting them with the SIFT algorithm. This work received financial support by Fraunhofer IOSB and by the Concept for the Future of the Karlsruhe Institute of Technology (KIT) within the framework of the German Excellence Initiative.

References

[1] D. Göhringer, *Flexible design and dynamic utilization of adaptive scalable multi-core systems [Ph.D. thesis]*, Dr. Hut München, 2011.

[2] D. Göhringer, L. Meder, M. Hübner, and J. Becker, "Adaptive multi-client network-on-chip memory," in *Proceedings of the International Conference on ReConFigurable Computing and FPGAs (ReConFig '11)*, pp. 7–12, Cancun, Mexico, 2011.

[3] MPI, "A message-passing interface standard," Version 2.2, Message Passing Interface Forum, September 2009, http://www.mpi-forum.org/.

[4] Xilinx, "LogiCORE IP Processor Local Bus (PLB) v4.6 (v1.05a)," DS531, September 2010, http://www.xilinx.com/.

[5] Xilinx, "LogiCORE IP Multi-Port Memory Controller (MPMC) (v6.01.a)," DS643, July 2010, http://www.xilinx.com/.

[6] N. Voros, A. Rosti, and M. Hübner, *Dynamic System Reconfiguration in Heterogeneous Platforms: The MORPHEUS Approach*, Springer, 2009.

[7] B. B. Fraguela, J. Renau, P. Feautrier, D. Padua, and J. Torrellas, "Programming the FlexRAM parallel intelligent memory system," in *Proceedings of the 9th ACM SIGPLAN Symposium on Principles and Practice of Parallel Programming (PPoPP '03)*, pp. 49–60, New York, NY, USA, June 2003.

[8] R. Buchty, O. Mattes, and W. Karl, "Self-aware memory: managing distributed memory in an autonomous multi-master environment," in *Proceedings of the 21st International Conference on Architecture of Computing Systems (ARCS '08)*, pp. 98–116, Dresden, Germany, February 2008.

[9] Z. Dai and J. Zhu, "A bursty multi-port memory controller with quality-of-service guarantees," in *Proceedings of the 9th International Conference on Hardware/Software Codesign and System Synthesis (CODES+ISSS 111)*, pp. 21–28, Taipei, Taiwan, October 2011.

[10] W. Kritikos, A. Schmidt, R. Sass, E. K. Anderson, and M. French, "Redsharc: a programming model and on-chip network for multi-core systems on a programmable chip," *International Journal of Reconfigurable Computing*, vol. 2012, Article ID 872610, 11 pages, 2012.

[11] K. Goossens, J. Dielissen, and A. Rădulescu, "Æthereal network on chip: concepts, architectures, and implementations," *IEEE Design and Test of Computers*, vol. 22, no. 5, pp. 414–421, 2005.

[12] F. Lemonnier, P. Millet, G. M. Almeida et al., "Towards future adaptive multiprocessor systems-on-chip: an innovative approach for flexible architectures," in *Proceedings of the International Conference on Embedded Computer Systems: Architectures, Modeling, and Simulation (SAMOS XII)*, Samos, Greece, July 2012.

[13] Xilinx, "Fast Simplex Link (FSL) Bus (v2.11a)," DS449, June 2007, http://www.xilinx.com/.

[14] S. Werner, O. Oey, D. Göhringer, M. Hübner, and J. Becker, "Virtualized on-chip distributed computing for heterogeneous reconfigurable multi-core systems," in *Proceedings of the Design, Automation & Test in Europe (DATE '12)*, pp. 280–283, Dresden, Germany, March 2012.

[15] D. G. Lowe, "Distinctive image features from scale-invariant keypoints," *International Journal of Computer Vision*, vol. 60, no. 2, pp. 91–110, 2004.

2

Transparent Runtime Migration of Loop-Based Traces of Processor Instructions to Reconfigurable Processing Units

João Bispo,[1] **Nuno Paulino,**[2] **João M. P. Cardoso,**[1] **and João Canas Ferreira**[2]

[1] Departamento de Engenharia Informática, Faculdade de Engenharia, Universidade do Porto, Rua Dr. Roberto Frias s/n, 4200-465 Porto, Portugal
[2] INESC TEC, Faculdade de Engenharia, Universidade do Porto, Rua Dr. Roberto Frias s/n, 4200-465 Porto, Portugal

Correspondence should be addressed to João Canas Ferreira; jcf@fe.up.pt

Academic Editor: René Cumplido

The ability to map instructions running in a microprocessor to a reconfigurable processing unit (RPU), acting as a coprocessor, enables the runtime acceleration of applications and ensures code and possibly performance portability. In this work, we focus on the mapping of loop-based instruction traces (called Megablocks) to RPUs. The proposed approach considers offline partitioning and mapping stages without ignoring their future runtime applicability. We present a toolchain that automatically extracts specific trace-based loops, called Megablocks, from MicroBlaze instruction traces and generates an RPU for executing those loops. Our hardware infrastructure is able to move loop execution from the microprocessor to the RPU transparently, at runtime, and without changing the executable binaries. The toolchain and the system are fully operational. Three FPGA implementations of the system, differing in the hardware interfaces used, were tested and evaluated with a set of 15 application kernels. Speedups ranging from 1.26× to 3.69× were achieved for the best alternative using a MicroBlaze processor with local memory.

1. Introduction

The performance of an embedded application running on a general-purpose processor (GPP) can be enhanced by moving the computationally intensive parts to specialized hardware units and/or to Reconfigurable Processing Units (RPUs) acting as acceleration coprocessors of the GPP [1, 2]. This is a common practice in embedded systems. However, doing so, manually or automatically, usually implies a hardware/software partitioning step over the input source code [3]. This step is static, requires the source code of the application, and does not promote code and performance portability as the hardware/software components are obtained for a specific target architecture. Dynamic partitioning and mapping of computations (hereafter simply referred as dynamic partitioning) [4–6] is a promising technique able to move computations from an GPP to the coprocessor in a transparent and flexible way, and may become an important

contribution for the future reconfigurable embedded computing systems.

In this paper, we present a system which can automatically map loops, detected by running a MicroBlaze executable binary, to an RPU. We focus on a special kind of trace-based loop, named Megablock [7], and transform Megablocks into graph representations which are then used to generate Megablock-tailored RPUs. Megablocks are repeating patterns of elementary units of the trace (e.g., basic blocks) in the instruction stream of the program being executed. The RPU is runtime reconfigurable and can use several configurations during program execution.

In our current implementation, Megablocks are detected offline through cycle-accurate simulation of running applications [8, 9]. The synthesis of the RPU is also done offline, while reconfiguration of the RPU is done online. The migration of the application execution between hardware and software is done online, without changes in the binary code of the application to be executed.

This paper makes the following main contributions:

(i) with respect to our previous work [8, 9], it proposes a more efficient use of an RPU for transparent binary acceleration by using lower-overhead interface schemes between RPU and GPP.

(ii) It presents implementations of three distinct system architectures and their system components to allow transparent migration of sections of GPP execution traces to the RPU, which includes reconfiguration of the RPU and runtime insertion of communication primitives.

(iii) It analyses the runtime overhead of the partitioning and mapping stages (currently performed by offline tools) and it presents a dedicated hardware detector circuit to accelerate the runtime identification of Megablocks bearing in mind a future runtime implementation.

(iv) It includes an extensive experimental evaluation of the proposed approaches with a set of 17 benchmarks (15 kernels and 2 examples of multiple executions of kernels in the same RPU).

The rest of this paper is organized as follows. Section 2 introduces the Megablock, the type of loop considered for mapping to the RPU. Sections 3 and 4 describe the proposed hardware/software system and the RPU architectures used, respectively. Section 5 explains the toolchain of our current approach, and Section 6 presents experimental results obtained for the three prototyped hardware/software implementations using an RPU coupled to a microprocessor. Section 7 presents related work, and Section 8 concludes the paper.

2. Megablocks

The architecture of the RPU was heavily influenced by the kind of repetitive patterns we are mapping, the Megablocks [7]. A Megablock is a pattern of instructions in the execution trace of a program and is extracted from execution instruction traces. Figure 1 shows a portion of the trace of a *count* kernel. In this case, when the kernel enters a loop, the trace repeats the same sequence of six instructions until the loop is finished.

The Megablock concept [7] was proposed in the context of dynamic partitioning, that is, deciding at runtime which instruction sequences executing on an GPP should be moved to dedicated hardware. We consider four steps for dynamic partitioning: detection, translation, identification, and migration. *Detection* determines which sections of the application instruction traces are candidates for dedicated hardware execution; *translation* transforms the detected instruction traces into equivalent hardware representations (i.e., RPU resources and corresponding configurations); *identification* finds, during program execution, the sections that were previously detected; *migration* is the mechanism that shifts the execution between the GPP and the RPU.

. . .		
0×188	addk	r6, r6, r3
0×174	bsra	r3, r5, r4
0×178	addik	r4, r4, 1
0×17C	andi	r3, r3, 1
0×180	xori	r18, r4, 8
0×184	bneid	r18, −16
0×188	addk	r6, r6, r3
0×174	bsra	r3, r5, r4
0×178	addik	r4, r4, 1
0×17C	andi	r3, r3, 1
0×180	xori	r18, r4, 8
0×184	bneid	r18, −16
0×188	addk	r6, r6, r3
0×174	bsra	r3, r5, r4
. . .		

FIGURE 1: Example of a repeating pattern of instructions in the trace of a 8-bit *count* kernel.

In a full online approach, all the above steps would be executed online. In the current prototypes, detection and translation are done offline (Section 5), while identification and migration are done online (Section 3.4). This approach has been also used by Faes et al. [16], which manually partitions code at the method level and proposes a framework which can, at runtime, intercept arbitrary method calls and pass control to previously designed hardware modules.

A Megablock represents a single, recurring path of a loop across several basic blocks. For every instruction which can change the control flow (e.g., branches), the Megablock considers a new exit point which can end the loop if the path of the Megablock is not followed. Since we are considering only a single path, the control-flow of a Megablock is very simple and we do not need to use decompilation techniques which extract higher-level constructions such as loops and *if* structures. And unlike other instruction blocks (e.g., Superblock and Hyperblock [17]), a Megablock specifically represents a loop.

For Megablocks to be useful, they must represent a significant part of the execution of a program. Previous work [7] shows that for many benchmarks, Megablocks can have coverage similar or greater than other runtime detection methods, such as monitoring short backward branches (the approach used by Warp [10]).

Megablocks are found by detecting a pattern in the instruction addresses being accessed. For instance, Figure 1 shows a pattern of size 6 (0x174, 0x178, 0x17C, 0x180, 0x184, and 0x188). In [7], it is shown how the detection of Megablocks can be done in an efficient way.

In the mapping approach described in this paper, each Megablock is first transformed into a graph representation. Because of the repetitive nature of the Megablock, we can select any of the addresses in the Megablock to be the start address. However, the start address can influence optimizations which use only a single pass. The start address is also used in our system architecture as the identifier of the Megablock during the identification step and must define the start of the Megablock unambiguously. We use the following heuristic to choose the start address: choose the lowest address of the Megablock which appears only once.

For the example in Figure 1, the start address according to this heuristic is 0x174. Since two or more Megablocks can start at the same memory address, but the current identification procedure only supports one Megablock for each start address, we synthesize the Megablock which has the highest coverage as determined in the detection phase.

2.1. Detecting Megablocks. There are several parameters we need to take into account when detecting Megablocks. For instance, the unit of the pattern can be coarser than a single instruction (e.g., a basic block). We impose an upper limit on the size of the patterns that can be detected (e.g., patterns can have at most 32 units). We define a threshold for the minimum number of instructions executed by the Megablock (i.e., only consider Megablocks which execute at least a given number of instructions). We can detect only inner loops, or decide to unroll them, creating larger Megablocks.

The values chosen for these parameters are dependent on the size and kind of Megablocks we want to detect.

2.2. Hardware for Megablock Detection. The problem of detecting a Megablock is similar to an instance of the problem of detecting repeated substrings, for example, xx, with x being a substring containing one or more elements. This is also known as *squares*, or tandem repeats [18]. In our case, substring x is equivalent to the previous sequence of instructions and represents a single iteration of a loop. Although we want to find patterns with many repetitions (a square strictly represents only two repetitions), we observed that if a sequence of instructions forms a square, it is likely that more x elements will follow (e.g., $xxxx \dots$). The detection method considers that two repetitions are enough to signal the detection of a Megablock.

Figure 2 presents a hardware solution for Megablock detection when using basic blocks as the detection unit. It has three main modules: the *Basic Block Detector* reads the instructions executed by the processor and detects which instructions correspond to the beginning of basic blocks. It outputs the instruction addresses corresponding to the beginning of basic blocks (*BB_address*), and a flag which indicates if the current instruction is the beginning of the basic block (*is_BB_address*).

The *Megablock Detector* receives pattern elements, which in this case are the first addresses of basic blocks. It outputs the size of the current pattern, or zero if no pattern is detected (*pattern_size*), and a control signal indicating the current state of the detector (*pattern_state*).

The module *Trace Buffer* is a memory that, when Megablock detection is active (i.e., the module is currently looking for Megablocks), stores the last instructions executed by the processor, their corresponding addresses, and a flag which indicates if the instruction corresponds to a pattern element of the Megablock (e.g., the start of a basic block). After a Megablock is detected, the *Trace Buffer* stops storing executed instructions and can be used to retrieve the detected Megablock.

Figure 3 presents the general diagram for the *Megablock Detector*. The *Squares Detector* finds patterns of squares. It

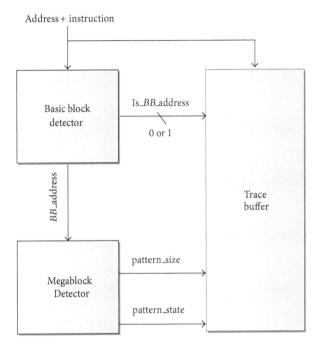

FIGURE 2: Hardware solution for Megablock detection.

receives pattern elements and detects squares of size one up to a maximum and outputs one flag per detected square size (*pattern_of_size_X*).

A pattern element can trigger one or more square sizes. The module *Pattern Size Arbiter & Encoder* receives the individual *pattern_of_size_X* flags, chooses which pattern size should be given priority, and encodes the chosen size into a binary string. For instance, when detecting only inner loops, this module can be implemented as a priority encoder. The module *Pattern State* is a state machine which indicates the current state of the pattern, and can have one of five values: *Pattern_Started*, *Pattern_Stopped*, *Pattern_Changed_Sizes*, *Pattern_Unchanged*, and *No_Pattern*.

Figure 4 presents the block diagram for a hardware implementation of the *Squares Detector*. It shows the first three modules, which correspond to detectors for sizes 1 up to 3. The additional modules follow the same structure. The *pattern_element* signal corresponds to a basic block start address. Each detector for a specific square size (with exception of the detector for size one) uses an FIFO. When FIFOs have a reset signal they are usually implemented in hardware using Flip-Flops (FFs), becoming relatively expensive. However, if it is not necessary to access the intermediate values of *FIFOs*, they can be implemented with considerably less resources (e.g., if an FPGA has primitives for shift registers available). When using such *FIFOs*, the reduction factor in resources can be as high as 16× and 32× [19] (e.g., when using the primitives SRL16 and SLR32 in Xilinx FPGAs, resp.).

3. Target System Architectures

We consider three prototype implementations of the target system: DDR-PLB (Arch. 1, illustrated in Figure 5), LMB-PLB (Arch. 2, presented in Figure 6), and LMB-FSL (Arch.

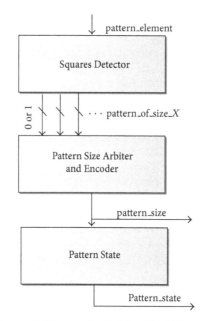

FIGURE 3: Diagram for the Megablock Detector.

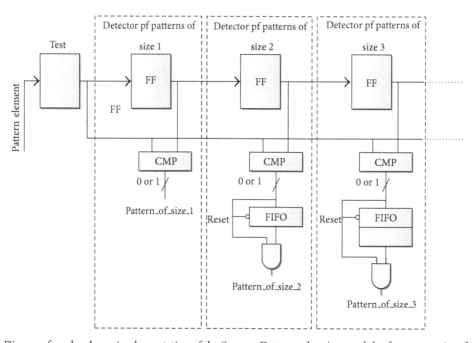

FIGURE 4: Diagram for a hardware implementation of the Squares Detector showing modules for pattern sizes from 1 to 3.

3, illustrated in Figure 7). All three implementations consist of an GPP executing a target application, an RPU used to accelerate execution of Megablocks, and additional hardware (the Injector) to support online identification and migration of Megablocks. The three system architectures share similar hardware modules, the main difference being their interfaces and arrangements. The prototypes were designed for an FPGA environment: instead of proposing a single all-purpose RPU, we developed a toolchain which generates the HDL (hardware description language) files of an RPU tailored for a set of Megablocks detected in the application to be run on the system. This step is done offline and automatically, as detailed in Section 5.

All versions use the same RPU architecture. This module is reconfigured in runtime to execute any of the supported Megablocks. To identify Megablock start addresses an auxiliary system module, named Injector (e.g., Processor Local Bus (PLB) Injector in Figure 5), is placed on the instruction bus between the GPP and its instruction memory. The Injector monitors the program execution and determines when to switch to/from execution on the RPU, by comparing the current Program Counter (PC) to a table containing the

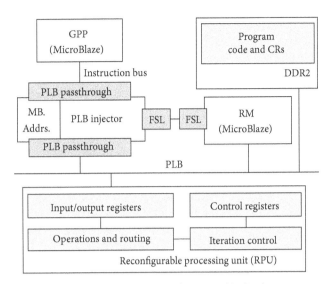

FIGURE 5: DDR-PLB architecture (Arch. 1).

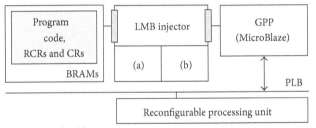

(a) Megablock addrs.

(b) CR and RCR addrs.

FIGURE 6: LMB-PLB architecture (Arch. 2).

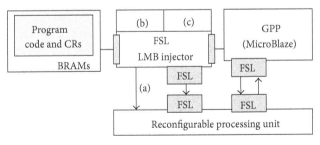

(a) Start

(b) Megablock addrs.

(c) RPU configurations

FIGURE 7: LMB-FSL architecture (Arch. 3).

start addresses of the Megablocks previously detected from the instruction traces. Once a Megablock is identified, the Injector executes the migration step.

The Injector is capable of controlling the execution of the GPP, by modifying the contents of the instruction bus and injecting arbitrary instructions. Thus, the Injector changes the behavior of the program running on the GPP in a transparent way, avoiding modifications to the GPP hardware and to the program binary stored in the memory.

All three architectures use a similar Injector module, adapted to the memory and RPU interfaces. Specific details on the different interfaces and behavior of the system are given in the following sections.

3.1. Architecture 1: External Memory and Processor Bus. Figure 5 shows the first system architecture, the DDR-PLB variant (Arch.1). The program code is located in external DDR memory and the interface between the GPP and the RPU is done via the Processor Local Bus (PLB).

Arch.1 consists of the GPP, a loosely coupled RPU, the PLB version of the Injector module, and an auxiliary reconfiguration module (RM), currently implemented as a second MicroBlaze. In addition to the program to be executed on the main GPP, the external memory also contains automatically generated communication routines (CRs), which are later explained in detail in Section 5.

The system operates as follows: during boot, the GPP copies the program code from flash (not shown in Figure 5) to the DDR, while the RM copies the instructions of the CRs, which are initially within its own local memories (not shown in Figure 5), to predefined DDR positions, so they can be later accessed by the GPP. During execution, the Injector monitors the PC of the GPP and stalls the system (by placing a branch to PC + 0 on its instruction bus) if the current PC matches any entry in an internal table of Megablock start addresses. Then, the Injector indicates to the RM, via its point-to-point Fast Simplex Link (FSL) [20] connection, which Megablock was identified. The RM reconfigures the RPU for the detected Megablock (this step is skipped if the RPU is already configured for that Megablock). When done, the RM responds to the Injector with a memory address, which is the start address of an CR stored in DDR memory, specific for the detected Megablock. The Injector then inserts a branch operation to that address in the GPP's instruction bus.

From this point on, the Injector and the RM no longer interfere, and the GPP executes the CR, which contains microprocessor instructions to load operands to the RPU from its register file, to start computation, to wait for completion (by polling an RPU status register), and to retrieve results, as well as a branch back to original program code. Once the GPP returns to program code, the Megablock code executed on the RPU is skipped in software, and the execution continues normally. If the PC of the GPP reaches another address known to the Injector, the process is repeated and the RPU is reconfigured if necessary.

Currently, the RM is used to reconfigure the RPU and to return the address of the corresponding CR. In the case of a fully online approach, the RM can be used to perform Megablock detection and generation of new configurations for the RPU, that is, translation, at runtime. Section 6.4 presents execution times for the partitioning tools running on an ARM processor, considering mapping to a general-purpose RPU architecture [15].

In our current mixed offline/online approach, the RM and the loosely coupled interfaces are superfluous, and the remaining two architectures were developed with this in mind. The DDR-PLB case is still being used to analyze the viability for a later expansion for fully online operation.

3.2. Architecture 2-Local Memory and Peripheral Bus. Using external memory introduces a large communication overhead, due to the access latency, both when accessing the original code and the CRs which have to be executed in order to use the RPU. The alternative system (Arch. 2), shown in Figure 6, reduces this latency by having the program code in local memories. In this case, the PLB Injector is replaced by the Local Memory Bus (LMB) Injector. The LMB is used by the GPP to access local, low-latency memories (Block RAMs—BRAMs). The use of these memories reduces execution time for both the CRs and the regions of program not mapped to the RPU, thus reducing global execution time. In this architecture, the RPU structure and interface are the same as the ones presented in the previous section. Also, as the GPP to RPU interface is the same, the CRs do not change.

In this approach, we removed the RM and moved its functionality to the Injector. The Injector now includes a table that maps Megablock addresses to CR start addresses (where one Megablock start address corresponds to one target CR address). The method to reconfigure the RPU was also changed: in addition to CRs there are also reconfiguration routines (RCRs) which load immediate 32-bit values to the RPUs configuration registers (explained later). RCRs are also placed in the same local memories and the LMB Injector keeps an additional table with their start addresses. Thus, when a Megablock address is identified, the Injector causes the GPP to branch to either an RCR or an CR, based on whether or not the RPU is already configured for the detected Megablock. If an RCR is executed, its last instruction is a branch to its corresponding CR. For the GPP, there is no distinction between the two situations (the only difference

is the overhead introduced in the communication with the RPU).

3.3. Architecture 3: Local Memory and Point-to-Point. Despite the reduction in overhead due to the use of local memories, the PLB access latency still introduces a significant overhead when sending/retrieving operands/results to/from the RPU. In the architecture shown in Figure 7 (Arch. 3), both the Injector and the GPP communicate with the RPU via FSL. In the previous scenarios, RCRs and CRs contain MicroBlaze load/store instructions that place configuration values or inputs on the RPU through the PLB. In this case, these instructions (whose latency was measured to be as high as 9 to 12 bus clock cycles in some cases, depending on bus arbitration) are replaced by one-cycle *put/get* instructions [21] per value sent/received.

In this case, the RPU reconfiguration is handled by the Injector itself. Configurations are held in a dedicated memory for the Injector (not shown in Figure 7), whose contents are defined at synthesis time. When a Megablock is identified, the Injector performs two tasks: it causes the GPP to branch to the corresponding CR and sends configuration data to the RPU via an FSL connection. While this last task is being done, the GPP is sending the operands to the RPU. The CRs mostly consist of *get* and *put* instructions. The GPP executes *put* instructions to load operands and then, since the *get* instructions are performed blocking, the GPP automatically stalls until data are placed on the RPU's output FSL (i.e., until the computation is finished).

The RPU only starts computing when it receives a start signal from the Injector, which indicates that all configurations have been written, and that the GPP is now stalled by the blocking *get*. The latter situation is detected by the Injector, which in this setup monitors both the instruction *opcode* and the instruction address.

3.4. Injector Architecture. Figure 8 shows the architecture of the PLB Injector, which is responsible for interfacing the GPP with the rest of the system in Arch.1 (Figure 5), as well as for starting the reconfiguration process by identifying Megablocks. The PLB, LMB, and FSL variants of the LMB Injector vary slightly in structure due to the buses they interface with. The LMB version does not implement communication with other modules. With respect to the DDR version, both PLB-LMB and FSL-LMB versions (Figure 7) require different control logic due to different latencies at which instructions can be fetched by the GPP (1 clock cycle for the LMB bus and as many as 23 clock cycles for the external DDR memory, as measured using ChipScope Analyzer [22], a runtime bus monitor).

The Injector monitors the instruction address bus of the GPP. It reacts to instruction addresses which correspond to the start of Megablocks and acts as a passthrough for all other instructions. If the PC matches a table of addresses, the Injector stalls the GPP and execution is switched from software to hardware, as already explained. This means the system can be enabled or disabled through a single modification of the instruction bus. The current PLB Injector

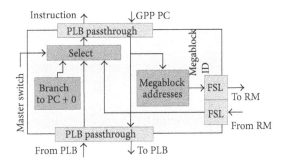

FIGURE 8: PLB injector architecture.

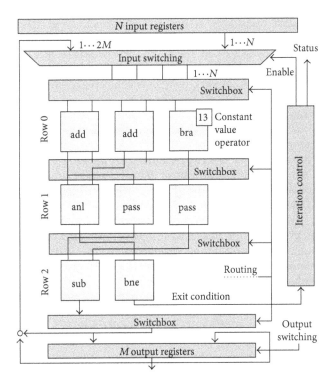

FIGURE 9: Array of FUs.

for the DDR-PLB system does not allow the use of cache. When using external memories with cache, the MicroBlaze uses a dedicated cache bus to the external memory, and an enhanced PLB Injector would be required to interface with that bus. This will be addressed in our future work.

Although the Injectors alter the instruction stream in order to modify runtime behavior, they cannot do so indiscriminately. The Injector can only interfere in order to keep the GPP from executing code that can now be executed on the RPU, but the possibility of false positives exists, due to the instruction fetch behavior of processor pipelines: the processor is performing a *fetch* during the *execute* stage of a previous instruction. If a Megablock start address comes after a branch instruction and the branch is taken, then the GPP will still fetch the instruction from the Megablock's start address, even though it will not be executed. To solve this problem, the Injector inserts a single stall (branch to PC + 0) after a Megablock address is identified, replacing the first instruction of the Megablock. If the next requested address is different from the address following the Megablock start address, it means that the initial branch was taken. In this case, the inserted branch is discarded by the GPP, and execution continues normally; otherwise the initial branch was not taken and the GPP would actually enter the corresponding region of code. The inserted branch will cause the Megablock address to repeat, and on this second occurrence, the Injector can safely cause the GPP to branch to the CR. This verification introduces a short delay equivalent to eight processor instructions. For the PLB case, this corresponds to approximately 184 clock cycles (considering an average external memory access latency of 23 clock cycles, through the PLB). For the LMB case, 8 clock cycles are required since BRAM latency is 1 clock cycle.

Another issue is caused by the fact that some instruction sequences must execute atomically in the MicroBlaze ISA. For instance, the IMM instruction loads a special register with a 16 bit immediate value. The following instruction combines these upper 16 bits with its own lower 16 bits to generate a 32 bit immediate operand. An instruction must not be injected after an IMMinstruction. As expected, the identified Megablocks do not start after IMM instructions.

4. RPU Architecture

The RPU is generated offline and is based on a parameterized HDL description. Modifying the parameterization at

synthesis time produces a single RPU which can execute a particular set of Megablocks, with the required layout and number of functional units (FUs). The RPU specification is generated automatically by our toolchain, based on the Megablocks found in the detection step. Interfaces and control logic remain the same regardless of the supported set of Megablocks. According to a particular online configuration, the RPU performs calculations equivalent to one of the Megablocks it was tailored for.

4.1. FU Array. Figure 9 illustrates a possible array of FUs for an RPU. The array is organized in rows with variable number of single-operation FUs. The number and width of rows are variable according to parameterization. The first row receives inputs from the input registers, which are written to by the GPP by executing a CR. The values placed in these registers originate from the GPP's register file. Likewise, values read from the output registers of the RPU are placed in the GPP's register file.

Some Megablocks produce the same result onto two or more GPP registers. Instead of having a duplicated output register, we handle this by adding equivalent value assignment instructions in CRs. Other Megablocks always produce one or more constants values onto the register file. In this case, since the Megablock detection tool optimizes the Megablock graph representation and removes such operations, we also add these constant value attributions to registers as CR instructions.

Each row contains operations that have no data dependencies and can execute in parallel, and results are then propagated to following rows. Each row of FUs is registered and data propagates at one row per clock cycle. If an operation has a constant input, the RPU generation process tailors the FU to that input (e.g., *bra* FU in Figure 9). The current implementation supports arithmetic and logic operations with integers, as well as comparison operations and operations producing or receiving carry. Carry can be retrieved by the GPP in both PLB and FSL scenarios. FUs on the array may have different number of inputs/outputs amongst themselves. The carry from additions is an example of a second output of an FU. Another is the upper 32-bit result of a multiplication. Any output of an FU can be used as an input of FUs in the following row. One or more inputs of an FU may be constant, synthesis-time-specified values.

Crossbar-type connections (switchboxes in Figure 9) are used between adjacent rows to perform this operand routing, and are runtime reconfigurable. The switchboxes automatically adapt to the width of the associated row during synthesis and can direct any of their inputs to any number of outputs. Connections spanning more than one row are established by passthrough FUs (pass FUs in Figure 9).

The RPU architecture was specifically designed to run loops with one path and multiple exits, and does not need logic for multiple paths (e.g., predicated hardware). The number of iterations of the loop does not need to be known before execution: the RPU keeps track of the possible exits (e.g., *bne* FU in Figure 9) of the loop and signals when an exit occurs (via a status register). If the number of iterations is constant in software, this is built into the array as a constant value operator. In order to terminate execution, the RPU always has at least one exit condition.

Only atomic Megablock iterations are supported. That is, either a Megablock iteration completes or is discarded. Support for nonatomic iterations would require discriminating which exit condition triggered, recovering the correct set of outputs and returning to a particular software address. Thus, when an exit occurs, the current iteration is discarded, and execution resumes in the GPP at the beginning of the Megablock. This means that the last iteration will be performed in software, allowing the GPP to follow whichever branch operation triggered an exit, maintaining the integrity of the control flow. In the current version of the RPU, all operations complete within one clock cycle and each iteration takes as many clock cycles as the number of rows (depth) of the RPU.

In the first iteration, the array is input with values from the input registers. After the first iteration is completed, control logic enables the first switchbox, and results from the previous iteration(s) are used to compute the subsequent one(s). This means that, although rows are registered, the execution is not pipelined. The RPU can keep the output values of the previous iteration and these values can be routed back to the output registers so as to change positions in order to mimic the software behavior of register assignments present in some loops. This feature is used when a Megablock includes code that places into a GPP register the value of another GPP register in a previous iteration. Along with the values produced in the current iteration, these previous values can also be routed back into the first row to be reused. Thus, the input switching *mux* takes $N + 2M$ values and

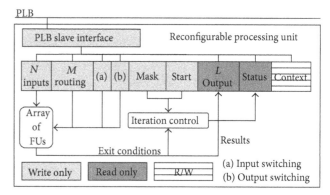

FIGURE 10: RPU architecture overview, with PLB interface.

produces N values. Since some input values are constant for all iterations of a call of the RPU, each of the N outputs either maintains its initial value found in the input register, or they are assigned one of the $2M$ values produced. This is followed by another switchbox that can route any of these N values to any number of FU inputs in the first row (the sequence of 2 multiplexers was kept for simplicity of implementation).

4.2. RPU Interface. RPU configuration is performed by writing to configuration registers. These registers control the routing of the operands through the switchboxes and indicate which exit conditions should be active. Figure 10 presents the main components of the RPU, detailing the PLB interface. The PLB interface RPU uses the bus interface to feed operands and retrieve results through 32-bit, memory-mapped registers. The FSL interface is composed simply of three FSL ports, two being inputs (for configuration and operands) and one output (for results). Apart from these interface level differences, the array of FUs and other internal aspects of the RPU remain the same in all three architectures.

Depending on the specification of the RPU, the number of input (N), output (L), and configuration (M) registers may vary. The remaining registers are implementation independent. Values written at runtime to the *routing*, *input/output switching*, and *mask* registers are generated offline.

Input and *output* registers contain operands/results of computations, and there are as many input/output registers as the maximum number of operands/results found in the set of Megablocks implemented by the RPU. The *routing*, *input switching*, and *output switching* registers configure the switchbox connections between rows, the routing of results back to the first row (i.e., feedback) and the routing of output register values to different positions of said output register bank (i.e., managing results from the previous iteration). Both the *input* and *output switching* are handled by a single 32-bit register. This was done for simplicity of design and limits the number of input and output registers of the RPU. For instance, if there are 4 output registers, a total of 9 values (current and previous results plus one initial value from the input register) can be chosen. This requires 4 bits to represent this selection range, which limits the number of input registers to 8 in order to use a maximum of 32 bits.

The number of routing registers is a function of the width and depth of the RPU. In our implementation, the largest number of outputs between all rows determines the minimum number of bits used to perform a selection and a single register may hold routing information for more than one row. For instance, in Figure 9 (where $N = 2$ and $M = 1$), the maximum width is 5 (row 1). Three bits are required to represent this range, and since the total number of inputs is 18 (input to FUs and number of output registers), a total of 54 routing bits are required (2 registers). The synthesis time parameterization selects and wires the proper number and groups of bits from the registers into the switchboxes of the array.

The *mask* register determines which exit conditions can trigger the end of computation. If more than one Megablock is mapped to the RPU, different exit conditions may exist on the array. Since data propagates through all the FUs during execution, even though FUs that are not part of the Megablock the RPU is configured for, an exit condition may trigger incorrectly unless disabled. The *mask* register performs a bit masking of the exit conditions. This limits the number of exits allowed on the RPU to 32. However, no observed combination of Megablocks in our benchmarks exceeded this value. In the FSL case, these configuration registers have the same function, but they have to be written to in a specific sequence.

The *start* register signals the RPU to initiate computations, and is written to by the GPP as part of the CRs, after all operands have been loaded. In the FSL scenario, the start signal is directly sent by the Injector. The *status* register contains information on the current status of the RPU. A *busy* bit on this register is the value the GPP polls for completion. A *first fail* bit indicates if the execution terminated during the first iteration. This is a special case in which no results need to be recovered from the RPU. The two *context* registers are used as scratchpad memories during the execution of Reconfiguration Routines (RCRs) and Communication Routines (CRs). During execution of these routines, one or two GPP registers must be used as auxiliary registers to load/store values. In the case of a *first fail* the used GPP registers recover their original values from the *context* registers.

The iteration control enables the propagation of data to output registers after a number of clock cycles equal to the depth of the RPU, monitors the exit conditions according to the applied mask, and sets the *status* register.

5. Toolchain for Offline Megablock Detection and Translation

5.1. Tool Flow Overview. We developed a tool suite to detect Megablocks and generate an RPU and its configuration bits. The tool flow is summarized in Figure 11. We feed the executable file (i.e., ELF file) to the Megablock Extractor tool [8] which detects the Megablocks. This tool uses a cycle-accurate MicroBlaze simulator to monitor execution traces. Although this step is performed offline, it is not a typical static code analysis.

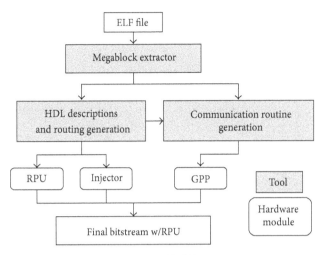

FIGURE 11: Tool flow.

For translation, Megablocks are processed by two tools: one generates the HDL (Verilog) descriptions for the RPU and the Injector, and the other generates the CRs for the GPP. The HDL description generation tool parses Megablock information, determines FU sharing across Megablock graph representations, assigns FUs to rows, adds passthrough units, and generate a file containing the placement of FUs. FUs are shared between different Megablocks, since at any given time there is only one Megablock executing in the RPU. The tool also generates routing information to be used at runtime (configuration of the interrow switches), as well as the data required for Megablock identification.

5.2. Generating the RPU Description. The RPU description generation tool produces an HDL header file that specifies the number of input/output and routing registers, the number of rows and columns of the RPU, the placement of FUs, constant value operators of the FUs, if any, and other auxiliary parameters that enable the use of the Verilog based generate constructs that instantiate the RPU. Inputs to this tool are Extractor outputs regarding the sequence of operations in the Megablock, their scheduling on the equivalent graph representation and connections between them. Figure 12 shows an excerpt of a generated HDL header that fully characterizes the RPU, along with the input Megablock information. The parameter array *ROW_OPS* specifies the layout of the RPU. The *INPUT_TYPES* array configures the *A_BRA* (arithmetic barrel shift right) to have its second input as a constant value, while all other accept 2 variable inputs.

In order to generate a combined RPU description for several Megablocks, the tool maintains information between calls. Each call treats a single Megablock. The Extractor transforms the MicroBlaze ISA into an abstract instruction set. Each operation in the Megablock is then mapped to a single FU. Different instructions can be mapped to the same FU type. For instance, a distinction between an *add* and *addi* exists only in the context of the MicroBlaze ISA. This decoupling means the toolchain and RPU could easily be expanded to any other processor ISA. Supporting new

Extractor input:	HDL output:
(· · ·) OP:1 operation:bsrli level:1 numInputs:2 inputType:livein inputValue:r5 inputType:constant inputValue:13 OP:2 operation:andi level:2 numInputs:2 inputType:internalValue inputValue:3, 0 inputType:internalValue inputValue:4, 0 (· · ·)	parameter NUM_IREGS = 32'd5; parameter NUM_OREGS = 32'd1; parameter NUM_COLS = 32'd3; parameter NUM_ROWS = 32'd3; parameter NUM_ROUTEREGS = 32'd2; parameter [0 : (32 ∗ NUM_ROWS ∗ NUM_COLS)-1] ROW_OPS = { `A_ADD,    `A_ADD, `A_BRA,          `L_ADD, `PASS,    `PASS, `L_SUB,    `B_NEQ, `NULL}; parameter [0 : (32 ∗ NUM_ROWS ∗ NUM_COLS)-1]  INPUT_TYPES = { `INPUT, `INPUT,   `CONSTB, `INPUT,   `INPUT, `INPUT, `INPUT, `INPUT,   `NULL};

FIGURE 12: RPU HDL header excerpt.

types of FUs would be equally straightforward, as each is an individual hardware module.

After this mapping, FU placement is performed. Since connections between rows are crossbar-like, horizontal placement is unrestricted, and rows are filled from left to right. During this placement phase, the arrays current status is checked to reuse already mapped FUs, if possible, to reduce resources (this also reduces the number of required routing bits). Only operations, from two distinct Megablocks, that occur on the same row and map to the same type of FU may reuse the same FU between them. After placement of operation FUs, passthroughs are placed. Rows are checked bottom to top so as to propagate passthroughs upwards. If an FU requires as an input, an output originating from an FU that spans more than one row, a passthrough is inserted. If two FUs require the same operand that originates several rows above, the same chain of passthroughs is used. This repeats until all connection spans equal 1. Due to the nature of the Megablock graphs, passes tend to be created in an inverted pyramid fashion. As this behavior repeats from Megablock to Megablock, passthroughs are heavily reused between them.

Values for routing and configuration registers are then generated and saved to files. As explained, routing information is concatenated across all routing registers, and selection values depend on the width of the RPU rows. As a consequence, already generated routing information must be regenerated if the depth and/or width of the RPU vary. If the depth increases, passthroughs need to be inserted for Megablocks of smaller depth. This implies that Megablocks of a smaller depth will suffer a delay (in clock cycles per iteration) equal to the difference between their depth and the maximum depth of the RPU.

5.3. *Generating the Communication Routines.* Megablock Extractor outputs also detail which GPP registers contain RPU inputs and which are destinations of RPU outputs. An additional file provided by the RPU generation tool (after translating the Megablock) includes the routing and configuration register values and associations between each GPP register in the Megablock and an RPU register. The Communication Routine generation tool either generates a PLB CR or an FSL CR, along with a HDL header containing the Megablock addresses. This file also contains the addresses of communication routines if generated for Arch. 2 (RCRs and CRs) or Arch. 3 (CRs).

For all three architectures, the routines are executed by the GPP, and they are located in the GPP's program memory, along with the program itself. The generated RCRs and CRs are placed in *C*-code structures (arrays), which are then compiled together with the application. This does not imply altering application code. These instructions are merely linked to tool predefined memory positions (defined in the linker script), which are known by the Injector.

Figure 13 shows the PLB and FSL CRs for the *reverse* benchmark. Not only is the FSL CR shorter, the instruction latencies are also smaller than those of the PLB case. The tool attempts to optimize CRs by using relative load/stores and immediate value assignments to registers (which occur in the RCRs). Relative instructions may shorten the length of the CR, depending on the number of values to send/receive. If such instructions are used, the RPUs scratchpad registers are used to store the original values of the GPP registers used by the instructions at the start of the routine.

For the PLB, CR operands are loaded (one is automatically saved into one *context register* when writing to the first input register), a start signal is written and the RPU is polled

PLB CR

Load live-ins:

0×1d40: imm -15136

0×1d44: swi r5, r0, 0

0×1d48: imm -15136

0×1d4c: swi r4, r0, 8

0×1d50: imm -15136

0×1d54: swi r6, r0, 4

Send start signal:

0×1d58: addi r5, r0, −1

0×1d5c: imm -15136

0×1d60: swi r5, r0, 36

Wait for fabric:

0×1d64: imm -15136

0×1d68: lwi r5, r0, 64

0×1d6c: andi r5, r5, 4

0×1d70: bnei r5, −12

Check for exit status:

0×1d74: imm -15136

0×1d78: lwi r5, r0, 64

0×1d7c: andi r5, r5, 32

0×1d80: beqi r5, 16

Return if First fail true:

0×1d84: imm -15136

0×1d88: lwi r5, r0, 68

0×1d8c: brki r0, 440

Restore live-outs:

Set address offset:

0×1d90: imm -15136

0×1d94: addi r6, r0, 0

0×1d98: lwi r18, r6, 40

0×1d9c: lwi r3, r6, 52

0×1da0: lwi r4, r6, 56

0×1da4: lwi r5, r6, 60

Recovering carry:

0×1da8: imm -15136

0×1dac: lwi r6, r0, 44

0×1db0: bnei r6, 12

0×1db4: msrclr r6, 4

0×1db8: bri 8

0×1dbc: msrset r6, 4

Recovering last live-out:

0×1dc0: imm -15136

0×1dc4: lwi r6, r0, 48

Return Jump:

0×1dc8: brki r0, 440

FSL CR

Putting live-ins:

0×1e00: nput r4, rfsl0

0×1e04: nput r6, rfsl0

0×1e08: nput r5, rfsl0

Getting control:

0×1e0c: get r5, rfsl0

0×1e10: beqi r5, 12

0×1e14: get r5, rfsl0

0×1e18: brki r0, 440

Getting live-outs:

0×1e1c: get r18, rfsl0

Getting carry:

0×1e20: msrclr r6, 4

0×1e24: get r6, rfsl0

0×1e28: beqi r6, 8

0×1e2c: msrset r6, 4

Remaining live-outs:

0×1e30: get r6, rfsl0

0×1e34: get r3, rfsl0

0×1e38: get r4, rfsl0

0×1e3c: get r5, rfsl0

Return Jump:

0×1e40: brki r0, 440

FIGURE 13: Comparison between PLB- and FSL-based CRs for the *reverse* benchmark.

for a done signal; once done, the status register is checked for the *first fail* bit. If set, values are recovered from the context registers, and execution immediately returns to software. If not, results are retrieved (in this case using relative loads), including the set/clear of the GPP carry bit according to the respective RPU result and execution returns to software. For the FSL CR, each operand is sent with a nonblocking *put* instruction. The *get* instructions are blocking until the output FSL contains data; the first output sent by the RPU is the status register. If a *first fail* occurs, the GPP reads another value. This value restores the content of the GPP register used to perform the *first fail* check. If this situation does not occur, results are recovered, including carry, and a branch back to software is taken.

For the benchmarks used in this paper, PLB-based CRs consist of 32 instructions on average. Arch. 2 (see Figure 6) also uses RCRs to reconfigure de RPU. Their average length is 28 instructions. For the case of Arch. 2, a maximum average length of 61 instructions for communication may occur if reconfiguration of the RPU is required at every call. For the FSL case, the average number of instructions is only 16, with reconfiguration occurring in parallel, if required.

5.4. Example. Figure 14 exemplifies the behavior of the system for the reverse benchmark. The outlined addresses (1b8 to 1d0, where 1b8 is the start address) constitute the Megablock, which iterates 32 times. This totals 255 clock cycles to execute this kernel. Considering the latency of each instruction (labeled on the right) and the number of instructions, the IPC (number of instructions per clock cycle) of this kernel is 0.89. When the Injector triggers at address 1b8, the execution of these instructions is replaced with the steps outlined in Figure 14. The first part of the CR (sending operands) takes place. Then execution proceeds on the RPU, and since the array depth is 3 and the number of iterations is 32, a total of 107 cycles are required. The RPU executes eight instructions in 3 clock cycles and achieves an IPC of 2.67. The last iteration must be performed in software for 7 cycles (the bneid branch is not taken, reducing its latency to 1). Results are then retrieved during 15 cycles. The resulting reduction in cycles provides an execution speedup of 1.97.

6. Experimental Results

The proposed architectures and tools were tested and evaluated with 15 code kernels. All kernels work on 32-bit values. Each individual benchmark calls the corresponding kernel N times. The reported results were obtained for $N = 500$.

Two additional tests (merge1 and merge2) group together six kernels in order to evaluate the case where an RPU is

Original program: Megablock execution in RPU + CR:

⟨reverse⟩:   cycles   ⟨reverse⟩:
1b0: addk r6, r0 , r0   1b0: addk r6, r0, r0
1b4: addk r4, r6, r0   1b4: addk r4, r6, r0
1b8: andi r3, r5, 1   1   1b8: Replaced by:
1bc: or r3, r3, r6   1   Injector delay: = 8
1c0: addik r4, r4, 1   1   + 3 CR cycles   = 11
1c4: addk r6, r3, r3   1   + 3 cycles per iteration:
1c8: xori r18, r4, 32   1   11 +3 * 32   = 107
1cc: bneid r18, − 20   2   + 15 CR cycles   = 122
1d0: sra r5, r5   1   + last iteration in software
1d4: rtsd r15, 8   122 + (8 − 1)   = 129
1d8: addk r3, r6, r0   1d4: rtsd 15, 8
                                      1d8: addk r3, r6, r0
Total cycles per iteration: 8
Total cycles: 8 * 32 − 1 = 255   delta = 255 − 129 = 126 → Speedup

FIGURE 14: Cycle reduction for the *reverse* kernel, for a LMB-FSL system.

generated from several Megablocks. The RPUs generated for these cases have six possible configurations. The *merge1* benchmark contains *count, even_ones, fibonacci, hamming, popcount32,* and *reverse*. Benchmark *merge2* includes *compress1, divlu, expand, gcd2, isqrt2,* and *maxstr*. For these cases, we evaluate the scenario where the calls to each kernel are alternated (for $N = 500$, the total number of RPU configuration changes during kernel execution is equal to 500 × 6 = 3,000). This is the worst-case scenario, which requires RPU reconfiguration between each kernel execution. We also consider an additional scenario where each kernel is called N times in sequence without intermediate reconfiguration (*merge1/2 n/s*).

The loops of most kernels have a constant number of iterations (16 or 32). Five kernels iterate a variable number of times per call, according to the inputs. The number of iterations of *fibonacci*, for instance, is an arithmetic progression of the input value. In all benchmarks, the current iteration count (between 0 and $N − 1$) is used as an input.

6.1. Setup. We used the Megablock Extractor tool to do an offline detection of the Megablocks from execution traces. For the detection we disabled inner loop unrolling (except in the *popcount3* case, where we map the Megablock of an unrolled inner loop), used basic blocks as the elementary pattern unit, set the maximum pattern size to 32, and rejected any Megablock which executed less than 100 instructions. For each kernel (except for *merge1/2*), we implemented only one Megablock. The majority of the computation was spent in the selected Megablock, the average coverage being 91.59% of the executed instructions.

Each kernel was compiled with *mb-gcc* 4.1.2 using the −O2 flag and additional flags which enable specific units of the MicroBlaze processor (e.g., -mxl-barrel-shift for barrel shifter instructions). The MicroBlaze version used was v8.00a.

The prototype was implemented on a Digilent Atlys board with a Xilinx Spartan-6 LX45 FPGA and DDR2 memory. We used Xilinx EDK 12.3 for system synthesis and bitstream generation. All benchmarks run at 66 MHz except *merge1/2* and *usqrt*, which run at 33 MHz. In most cases, the RPU achieved higher operating clock frequencies than the 66 MHz used for the MicroBlaze processor. Since we use the same clock signal for all the modules of the system, including the RPU, speedups can be computed from measurements given in number of clock cycles, and are therefore, independent of the actual system frequency. To count clock cycles, we used a timer peripheral attached to the PLB.

6.2. Megablocks and RPUs. Table 1 summarizes the characteristics of the Megablocks used in the evaluation. The average number of instructions per call of the Megablock is a product of the number of instructions per iteration and the average number of iterations. Table 1 includes values for maximum instruction level parallelism (ILP), percentage of instructions covered by the Megablocks versus the total executed instructions, and instructions per cycle achieved in software (SW IPC). IPC was computed considering the number of clock cycles required to complete one iteration over the number of instructions. As all Megablocks include branch operations, which have a 2 cycle latency, the SW IPC is always below 1 instruction per clock cycle. The SW IPC values shown assume a latency of 1 clock cycle for instruction fetch, which is not the case for the DDR-PLB architecture, but is valid for LMB-based architectures. Since all implemented operations in the tested benchmarks have one clock cycle of latency, the critical path length (CPL) has a value equal to the depth of the RPU (see Table 2, RPU characteristics). For the *merge1/2* cases, the values presented are the averages of the values of the individual kernels implemented in each case.

Table 2 summarizes the characteristics of the RPU for each kernel. The *#OP. FUs* column presents the number of FUs used as operations (i.e., not passthroughs). Due to the interconnection scheme used, passthroughs often outnumber operation FUs. However, the resulting RPUs were relatively small. Due to FU sharing, the *merge1/2* cases use about 35.44% and 50.43% of the total number of FUs for the individual Megablocks. This is equivalent to 51 and 58 reused FUs between kernels (including operations and passthroughs). Since passthroughs occur frequently in all kernels, they are reused more often; *merge1* reuses passthrough FUs 41 times and *merge2* 104 times. This is equivalent to reducing a total

TABLE 1: Detected Megablock characteristics.

| Kernels | Megablock characteristics | | | |
	Avg. Inst. Executed p/call	Max. ILP	Coverage (%)	SW IPC
count	192	2	94.9	0.857
even_ones	192	3	94.0	0.857
fibonacci	1,497	2	99.4	0.857
ham_dist	192	3	94.0	0.857
pop_cnt32	256	3	97.2	0.889
reverse	224	3	95.6	0.875
compress	138	3	89.7	0.889
divlu	155	2	90.5	0.833
expand	138	3	89.7	0.889
gcd	330	2	98.8	0.889
isqrt	96	3	84.0	0.857
maxstr	120	2	88.1	0.800
popcount3	15500	3	85.4	0.912
mpegcrc	465	4	87.6	0.934
usqrt	288	6	84.9	0.947
merge1	444	2.7	N/A	0.865
merge2	166	2.5	N/A	0.860

TABLE 2: RPU characteristics.

| Kernels | RPU characteristics | | | | |
	#OP. FUs	# Pass. FUs	Max. row depth	Depth	HW IPC
count	6	6	5	3	2.00
even_ones	5	4	7	3	1.67
fibonacci	4	6	4	3	1.33
ham_dist	6	11	6	3	2.00
pop_cnt32	8	7	8	3	2.67
reverse	7	9	7	3	2.33
compress	8	21	8	4	2.00
divlu	5	4	5	3	1.67
expand	8	21	8	4	2.00
gcd	8	17	8	6	1.33
isqrt	6	9	6	3	2.00
maxstr	4	6	4	3	1.33
popcount3	18	33	18	9	2.00
mpegcrc	14	32	14	7	2.00
usqrt	17	42	17	8	2.13
merge1	16	12	16	3	1.65
merge2	24	35	24	6	1.07

of 43 passthroughs to 12, for *merge1*, and reducing a total of 78 pass–throughs to 35, for *merge2*.

The maximum ILP achieved by each RPU is the same as the maximum ILP shown for each Megablock in Table 1. The average ILP is 2.93 (*merge1/2* excluded) and the highest value occurs for *usqrt* (6 instructions in parallel). The IPC achieved

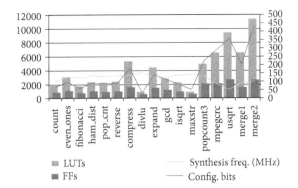

FIGURE 15: FPGA resources, synthesis frequency, and required configuration bits for each RPU with a PLB interface (LUTs and FFs shown on the left axis).

by an RPU depends on the total number of operations it performs per iteration and its depth. Each RPU contains, at most, as many operations as the Megablock it implements. Due to graph-level optimizations such as register assignment simplification and constant propagation, the actual number of operations can be lower (e.g., *popcount3*, requires only 18 operations to implement its original 31 assembly instructions). *IMM* instructions [23] are an example of instructions that do not need an additional FU. If ILP is high and depth of the RPU is low, this results in a higher IPC. Ignoring any overheads, speedups are obtained when the RPU IPC is larger than software IPC.

Figure 15 shows the implementation characteristics of the individual RPUs for the PLB interface case (it is very similar to the FSL case). The reported synthesis maximum clock frequencies of the RPUs ranged from 52 MHz to 154 MHz. Except for the minimum case (which occurs for *usqrt*), all RPU frequencies are higher than the clock frequency of the MicroBlaze. The largest RPU uses 34.57% (9,433) of the LUTs and 4.91% (2,680) of the FFs. The average usage for these resources is 12.62% and 2.32%, respectively. Due to the reuse of FUs performed by the tools, the RPUs for *merge1/2* require a number of LUTs and FFs that is smaller than the sum of LUTs and FFs of the RPUs for the individual kernels they implement. The *merge1* RPU uses about 47% of the LUTs and 27% of the FFs. For the *merge2* RPU, these values are 68% and 40%. In both cases, the RPU frequency is above the GPP frequency, being 94 MHz and 102.6 MHz, respectively. Since the RPU only reconfigures interconnections and not FUs, the number of configuration bits for each RPU is relatively low, with an average of 133 bits for the RPUs of individual kernels (i.e., excluding *merge1/2*).

6.3. Speedups. Figure 16 presents speedups for all architectures. In the DDR-PLB scenario, the MicroBlaze has a 23-cycle penalty for each instruction (note that this scenario does not use caches), while execution of a single row of the RPU takes 1 clock cycle. So, most of the achieved speedup comes from executing operations on the RPU instead of executing the original instructions in the GPP. However, for each call to the RPU, the GPP executes an CR and since the CRs are in

TABLE 3: Communication overhead.

| Kernels | Communication overhead | | | | |
	#Inst. of PLB CR	#Inst. of FSL CR	DDR-PLB (%)	LMB-PLB (%)	LMB-FSL (%)
count	27	12	92.4	56.39	26.22
even_ones	34	18	92.1	62.25	30.49
fibonacci	27	14	63.2	15.58	4.22
ham_dist	35	17	91.8	61.18	29.98
pop_cnt32	35	17	92.1	61.34	30.49
reverse	35	17	92.3	61.34	30.49
compress	35	19	95.0	71.82	39.97
divlu	25	10	92.2	53.79	26.83
expand	35	19	95.0	71.76	40.75
gcd	32	15	77.3	34.51	12.81
isqrt	34	16	96.2	74.77	45.52
maxstr	25	10	92.5	55.25	26.89
popcount3	37	18	46.97	8.16	2.77
mpegcrc	36	20	85.5	47.00	21.69
usqrt	31	18	89.9	59.56	28.93
merge1	56.3	22.5	87.0	58.14	17.07
merge1 (n/s)	32.17	15.8	N/A	41.94	16.13
merge2	57	22.0	89.6	70.32	24.43
merge2 (n/s)	31	14.8	N/A	48.04	21.26

DDR, they also suffer of the DDR access latency. In fact, the DDR access latency is the main contributor to the very high overhead of this scenario (Table 3). The situation is aggravated by the relatively low number of instructions executed per call (Table 1). The overhead includes the detection of the Megablock, configuration of the RPU, and execution of the CR. Since the RM fetches instructions from local memories, a large part of the overhead comes from executing the CRs afterwards. It is noticeable that, for a greater number of iterations, the overhead becomes less significant, as is the case of *fibonacci* and *popcount3*. The speedups measured for the DDR scenario include all overheads and range from 2.25× (*isqrt*) to 43.37× (*popcount3*). Speedups in this no-cache scenario do not show the best case for sequential software execution. However, it demonstrates the architecture concept and is a starting point for future work on cache support.

For the LMB-PLB case, slowdowns still occur frequently since the number of iterations and operations found in many of the kernels is still relatively small, and the possible parallelism is not enough to compensate for the overhead. Since program code is now in local memories, GPP execution is not hindered by high memory latencies due to the lack of cache support. However, access to the RPU still suffers from PLB latency, which in this case results in an average overhead of 52.98%. For *merge1/2*, the overhead introduced by reconfiguration is noticeable in the resulting speedup. In these benchmarks, the kernels are executed alternately: every time the RPU is called, it has to be reconfigured. The speedup of *merge1/2* is lower than that of *merge1/2 n/s* due to reconfiguration overhead. Speedups for *merge1/2* are equal to

57% and 72% of the speedups for *merge1/2 n/s*, respectively. This is equivalent to reconfiguration overheads of 27.8% and 42.9%, respectively.

For the LMB-FSL case, the average overhead for individual kernels is 26.54%. Performing the RPU reconfiguration in parallel with the transfer of input operands reduces the effect of reconfiguration overhead. For *merge1*, reconfiguring the RPU at every call introduces negligible additional overhead when compared to *merge1 n/s*, since the number of operands is close, on average, to the number of reconfiguration values. This is not the case for *merge2*, which requires over twice as much configuration values. This means compact RPUs with many configurations and implementing Megablocks with many inputs can be done by switching between configurations within the operand transfer time, that is, without suffering from additional overhead. The overhead introduced by reconfiguration in this case is near zero for *merge1* and 4.03% for *merge2*.

The effect of different overheads is visible in Figure 16, where the speedup trend across benchmarks is consistent, and where the LMB-FSL case is the one closest to the maximum possible speedups. This maximum was computed assuming a software instruction fetch latency of 1 clock cycle (implying IPC = 1), which does not hold true for the DDR case. Table 3 shows the overhead for each scenario along with the number of instructions in the communication routines (CRs) for each interface type. The average number of cycles for an FSL CR, for these kernels, is 17, and the average number of instructions is 16. Since reconfiguration occurs in parallel in this architecture, if necessary, the time required to start computation depends on the maximum between the number of operands to send and the number of configuration values to send. Considering this, the average number of cycles for a complete communication with the RPU in this architecture can be as high as 23.5, for *merge1*, and 31, for *merge2*.

For PLB-based CRs, the averages are 129.2 cycles and 32.2 instructions. For reconfiguration routines (RCRs), which are used in the LMB-PLB architecture, these averages are 110.9 and 28.73, respectively. In the worst-case scenario for this architecture, in which reconfiguration has to be performed at every call, the sequence of RCR and CR takes an average of 239.47 cycles and totals an average of 60.93 instructions. Since generating an RPU for several kernels will increase the number of configuration registers, the RCRs for each kernel in a combined RPU will differ (as the structure of the RPU differs). For *merge1*, the average number of cycles in an RCR is 138.83 and the average number of instructions is 32.8. For *merge2*, the averages are 223.2 and 52.2, respectively. Since the RPU for *merge2* is larger (higher depth and width), it requires more configuration information and the RCRs increase in size.

The gain, in cycles, of using the RPU, as shown in the example of Figure 14, must exceed these communication cycles, in order for a speedup to still be possible. Speedup is a direct function of the ratio between SW IPC and HW IPC, as shown in (1), and is valid for all three architectures (the fetch latency of the DDR-PLB case is accounted for in the IPC_{SW} factor). In (1), N_{rSW} represents the number of assembly instructions per iteration of a Megablock in

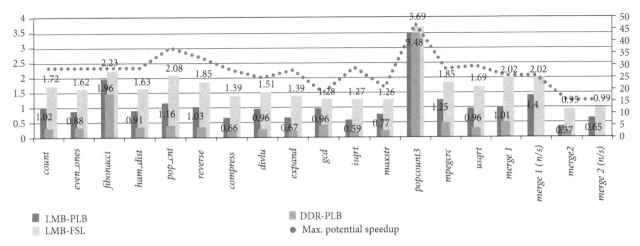

FIGURE 16: Speedups for all three architectures. Results for DDR-PLB architecture (Arch. 1) use the axis on the right. Bar labels show the results for the LMB-PLB (Arch. 2) and LMB-FSL (Arch. 3) architectures (axis on the left). The maximum possible speedups (dotted line relative to the left axis) are estimations calculated using (1), assuming an instruction fetch latency of 1 cycle. A trend can be observed for all three cases. The different overheads dictate the relative scales of the attained speedups.

software, N_{rHW} represents the number of operations per iteration in the RPU (these values are not necessarily the same since some operations can be optimized during translation), OH_c represents the number of clock cycles due to overhead (in which the communication routine, injector delay and last iteration cycles are accounted for), and N_{it} is the number of iterations of the Megablock:

$$\text{Speedup} \cong \frac{N_{rSW}}{N_{rHW}} \times \frac{IPC_{SW}^{-1}}{IPC_{HW}^{-1} + OH_c/\left(N_{it} \times N_{rHW}\right)}. \quad (1)$$

There is a 2.0% difference for the LMB-FSL case and 1.5% for the LMB-PLB between the values given by (1) and actual measured speedup values; deviations occur due to additional clock cycles. These correspond to instructions that are executed between the activation and deactivation of the timer and are not part of the Megablock. The speedup estimates have been corrected for these effects. The FSL case is less precise because measurement errors become more significant as the measurements become finer (i.e., smaller number of cycles).

The maximum speedup would be the direct ratio of both IPCs, if there were no overhead cycles. The overhead effect can be reduced when there are many iterations and/or instructions mapped on the RPU. See for example the following equation for the *reverse* kernel in the LMB-FSL architecture:

$$\text{Speedup} \cong \frac{7}{7} \times \frac{1.143}{0.429 + 38/\left(32 \times 7\right)} = 1.91. \quad (2)$$

6.4. *Hardware Module for Megablock Detection.* We developed a proof-of-concept HDL generator which outputs

VHDL for a Megablock Detection hardware module, as depicted in Figure 3 in Section 2. Figure 17 presents the resources needed to implement the module when varying some of the parameters accepted by the generator (maximum pattern size and the bit width of the pattern element).

For the explored parameter ranges, the number of LUTs and FFs increases linearly with the increase of the maximum pattern size. Higher bit widths generally represent a higher number of used resources, although the increase is more significant for FFs than for LUTs. The shape of the LUT resources used is more irregular than the shape of the FFs. We attribute this to the way the synthesis tool maps certain FPGA primitives (e.g., SRLs), used in the HDL code.

For the base case with a maximum pattern size of 24 elements, and considering an address space for instructions of 20 bits, the module needs 455 LUTs and 636 FFs, which represent around 1% of the targeted FPGA (a Xilinx Spartan-6 LX45). These values include the encoder and the state machine for determining the current state of the detector. The decrease of the maximum clock frequency with the increase of the maximum pattern size was expected, as higher values for the maximum pattern size implies more complex logic paths in some parts of the Megablock Detection module (e.g., the comparison between the current pattern element and all the positions in the FIFO).

However, the current implementation working frequencies are sufficient for the considered scenarios. For instance, considering the base case of a maximum pattern size of 24 elements, the maximum estimated clock frequency is between 134 MHz and 147 MHz (depending on the bit width of the elements), which is enough to meet the clock frequency of the MicroBlaze softcore for the targeted FPGA. Higher bit widths generally produce designs with lower clock frequencies, although the impact is relatively small. The maximum impact of the bit width on the clock frequency is on average 14% for the cases studied.

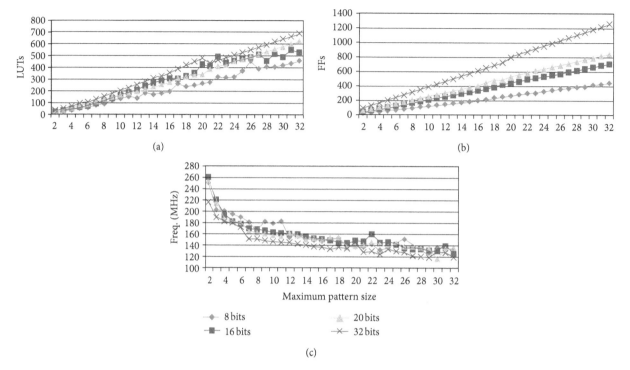

FIGURE 17: LUTs, FFs, and estimated maximum frequencies for Megablock Detector hardware designs.

TABLE 4: Execution times for several implementations of the pattern detector for megablocks.

# Addrs	Execution times (ms)			Speedup (HM versus MB/HM versus A8)
	HM@50 MHz	MB@50 MHz	Cortex-A8@1 GHz	
12	0.0002	2.7	0.6	11,251/2,500
24	0.0005	5.7	1.3	11,963/2,708
48	0.0010	14.0	2.8	14,594/2,917
96	0.0019	30.8	5.9	16,036/3,073
192	0.0038	64.3	12.5	16,757/3,255
384	0.0077	131.5	24.8	17,118/3,229
768	0.0154	265.7	78.7	17,298/5,124

Table 4 contains execution times for three implementations of the pattern detector used to detect Megablocks, executing on different targets. The execution times represent the time each implementation needed to process the given number of addresses (column #*Addresses*). The given addresses are repetitions of the 6 address sequence of the *fir* Megablock. The values in the column *HM@50 MHz* correspond to an implementation of the architecture described in Section 2.2, clocked at 50 MHz. It can process one address every clock cycle. The column *MM@50 MHz* represents a C implementation of the equivalent detection functionality running directly on a MicroBlaze processor clocked at 50 MHz. Column *Cortex-A8@1 GHz* corresponds to an implementation in Java, running on a Cortex-A8 clocked at 1 GHz, over the Android 2.2 platform.

Generally, the execution times grow linearly with the input (doubling the size of the input doubles the execution time). There is an exception in the Cortex case, where going from 384 addresses to 768 addresses tripled the execution time, instead of doubling. We think this is due to calls from the system to the garbage collector, during execution of the detector.

When comparing execution speeds, the hardware module for Megablock detection is much faster than the software implementations of the same functionality: around 3,000x faster than the Cortex case and around 16,000x faster than the MicroBlaze case. This difference can be explained by the highly parallel design of the hardware module, and by the software version not being fully optimized for the target platforms.

Table 5 shows average execution times for the several phases needed to perform the translation step, when running their Java implementation on the Cortex-A8, and considering a Megablock of the *fir* loop. The translation step took, on average, about 79 ms to transform the assembly code of the Megablock into a mapping configuration for a general purpose RPU architecture [15]. The most expensive operation is the conversion from assembly code to the graph intermediate representation, which needs 58% of the execution time. The following most expensive operations are Placement and Transform, which take 20% and 12% of the execution time, respectively. The most light-weight steps are Routing and Normalization, each one with 6% and 4% of the total execution time, respectively.

From the values of Table 4, we expect software execution times for the *Translation* phase below 1s (possibly around

TABLE 5: Average execution times in milliseconds of the translation step.

Normalize	Graph generation	Transform	Mapping		Total
			Placement	Routing	
3.03	46.00	9.71	15.45	4.89	79.09

400 ms) when executed in a MicroBlaze at 50 MHz. Our future work will consider a complete software implementation of the tools in order to achieve a fully runtime mapping system. We will then consider the need to accelerate by hardware the most computationally intensive stages of the mapping process.

7. Related Work

There have been a number of research efforts to map computations to RPUs during runtime. Typically, those efforts focused on schemes to execute in the RPU one or more iterative segments of code, that is, loops, in order to reduce execution time.

These systems can be classified based on the level of coupling between the RPU and the GPP, the granularity of the RPU, the capability to support memory operations, and on the type of approach: online or offline. Although there have been many authors focusing on partitioning and compilation of applications to systems consisting of an GPP and an RPU (see, e.g., [24]), we focus here on the approaches that consider runtime efforts. Related to our work are the approaches proposed by Warp [4, 10], AMBER [12, 13], CCA [5, 11], and DIM [6, 14].

The Warp Processor [4, 10] is a runtime reconfigurable system which uses a custom FPGA as a hardware accelerator for a GPP. The system performs all steps at runtime, from binary decompilation to FPGA placement and routing. The running binary code is decompiled into high-level structures, which are then mapped to a custom FPGA fabric with tools developed by the authors. Warp attains good speedups for benchmarks with bit-level operations and is completely transparent. It relies on backward branches to identify small loops in the program.

AMBER [12, 13] uses a profiler alongside a sequencer. The sequencer compares the current Program Counter (PC) with previously stored PC values. If there is a match, it configures the proposed accelerator to execute computations starting at that PC. The accelerator consists of a reconfigurable functional unit (RFU), composed by several levels of homogeneous functional units (FUs) placed in an inverted pyramid shape, with a rich interconnection scheme between the FUs. The RFU is configured whenever a basic block is executed more times than a certain threshold. Further work considered a heterogeneous RFU [12], and introduced a coarser-grained architecture to reduce the configuration overhead. The AMBER approach is intrusive as the RFU is coupled to the GPP's pipeline stages.

The CCA [5, 11] is composed of a reconfigurable array of FUs in an inverted pyramid shape, coupled to an ARM processor. The work addresses the detection of computations

suitable to be mapped to a given CCA, as well as discovering a CCA architecture that best suits a set of detected control-data flow graphs (CDFGs). Initially, the detection was performed during runtime, by using the rePLay framework [25], which identifies large clusters of sequential instructions as atomic frames. The detection was later moved to an offline phase, during compilation [11]. Suitable CCA CDFGs are discovered by trace analysis, and the original binary is modified with custom instructions and rearranged to enable the use of the CCA at runtime.

The DIM reconfigurable system [6, 14] proposes a reconfigurable array of FUs in a multiple-row topology and uses a dynamic binary translation mechanism. The DIM array is composed of uniform columns, each with FUs of the same type. DIM transparently maps single basic blocks from a MIPS processor to the array. DIM also introduced a speculation mechanism which enables the mapping of units composed by up to 3 basic blocks. The system is tightly coupled to the processor, having direct access to the processor's register file.

Table 6 presents the main characteristics of the approaches previously described and of our approach (Megablock column). The main difference between our approach and previous ones is the use of repetitive patterns of machine instructions (Megablocks, in this case) as the partitioning unit [7, 8, 15]. To the best of our knowledge, we have presented the first automated toolchain capable of transparently moving repetitive instruction traces from an GPP to an RPU at runtime without changing the executable binary. Our system is fully operational and all evaluations presented in this paper were actually based on real measurements using an FPGA board. We have shown in greater detail how the hardware system works. Although we previously presented the main concepts, this paper extends them by presenting details for three architectures (two of them implemented for the first time) and an evaluation using a more representative set of benchmarks. Furthermore, three architecture prototypes were implemented and tested on a current commercial FPGA.

8. Conclusion

This paper presented an automated approach to transparently move computations from GPP instruction traces to reconfigurable hardware, without changing the executable binary of the application being run on the GPP. The computations of interest are represented by Megablocks which are patterns of machine instructions that repeat contiguously. Those Megablocks are then mapped to a reconfigurable processing unit implemented with an FPGA.

Using an FPGA board, we evaluated three system architectures that are fully operational. We implemented the detection and translation steps offline to generate RPU descriptions and we introduced an architecture which allows for very fast identification and replacement of Megablocks at runtime. Preparing for a full online approach, we also introduced a hardware module for Megablock detection at runtime.

TABLE 6: Summary of characteristics for the more relevant approaches.

Characteristics		Approaches			
	Warp [4, 10]	CCA [5, 11]	Amber [12, 13]	DIM [6, 14]	Megablock [7, 15]
Partitioning approach	Detect and decompile inner loops, dynamically translate those loops into configurations for a custom FPGA	Detect segments of instructions which are transformed into subgraphs and executed as macroinstructions on the CCA. Migration by modifying the instruction stream	Detection of hot basic blocks by trace analysis, which are translated to DFGs and mapped to mesh-type RPU configurations	Identify as many instructions as possible, inside one or more basic blocks, to be mapped to DIM	Detect repeating patterns of instructions in the execution trace and migrate those loops to an RPU
Coupling	Loose RPU/GPP coupling, shared instruction and data memory	Tight RPU coupling to the GPP pipeline	Tight RPU coupling to the GPP pipeline	Tight RPU coupling to the GPP pipeline	Loose RPU/GPP coupling through bus or dedicated connections
Granularity	Fine-grained RPU (LUTs, MAC)	Coarse-grained RPU (ALUs)	Coarse-grained RPU (ALUs)	Coarse-grained RPU (ALUs)	Coarse-grained RPU (ALUs)
Size of the segment of code to be mapped in a configuration	Inner loops with up to tens of lines of code	From a couple to a dozen of instructions across basic blocks	Up to 1 basic block	(1) A couple to a dozen of instructions inside a basic block or (2) across up to three basic blocks with speculation	Inner and outer loops with up to hundreds of lines of code
Benchmarks	NetBench, MediaBench, EEMBC, Powerstone, and in-house tool ROCM	MediaBench, SPECint, and encryption algorithms	MiBench suite	MiBench suite	Texas DSPLIB and IMGLIB
Target domain	General Embedded systems	General Embedded and General-Purpose Systems	General Embedded and General-Purpose Systems	General Embedded and General-Purpose Systems	General Embedded Systems
GPP	(1) ARM7 at 100 MHz (2) MicroBlaze at 85 MHz	(1) 4-issue superscalar ARM (2) In-order 5-stage pipelined ARM (ARM-926EJ)	4-issue in-order MIPS-based RISC	Minimips softcore based on the MIPS R3000	MicroBlaze
Size of the RPU	14.22 mm^2 with 180 nm library (~852,000 gates)	0.61 mm^2 with 130 nm library	n.a.	>1 million gates	n.a.
Average speedup	(1) 6.3x (2) 5.9x	(1) 1.2x (2) 2.3x	1.25x	(1) 2.0x (2) 2.5x	2.0x
Average energy reduction	(1) 66% (2) 24%–55%	n.a.	n.a.	.7x	n.a.

Our current system is runtime reconfigurable, both in terms of the resources of the RPU and in terms of the insertion of communication and synchronization primitives. The hardware infrastructure for migration is easily adaptable to other GPPs. For the small benchmark kernels used in the evaluation, the speedups are very dependent on communication latencies. In the most favorable scenario for GPP performance (program code in local memory), the present approach achieved speedups in the range from 1.26× to 3.69×. Furthermore, we have shown that the runtime detection and translation of Megablocks on FPGA-based embedded systems is feasible when assisted by a dedicated hardware detector. However, to consider a fully online partition, mapping, and synthesis approach, one needs to consider the migration to specific hardware of the most execution time demanding tasks. Our future work will be focused on providing full support for the dynamic identification and mapping of Megablocks.

Although the results presented in this paper are encouraging, further work is required to process larger kernels, and in particular kernels which contain memory accesses. Future work will also address the support for caches.

Acknowledgments

This work was partially funded by the European Regional Development Fund through the COMPETE Programme (Operational Programme for Competitiveness) and by National Funds (ERDF) through the Fundação para a Ciência e a Tecnologia (FCT) (Portuguese Foundation for Science and Technology) within (project FCOMP-01-0124-FEDER-022701). J. Bispo and N. Paulino acknowledge the support of FCT through Grants SFRH/BD/36735/2007 and SFRH/BD/80225/2011, respectively.

References

[1] J. Henkel, "Low power hardware/software partitioning approach for core-based embedded systems," in *Proceedings of the 36th Annual Design Automation Conference (DAC '99)*, pp. 122–127, June 1999.

[2] L. Jóźwiak, N. Nedjah, and M. Figueroa, "Modern development methods and tools for embedded reconfigurable systems: a survey," *Integration, the VLSI Journal*, vol. 43, no. 1, pp. 1–33, 2010.

[3] T. Wiangtong, P. Y. K. Cheung, and W. Luk, "Hardware/software codesign," *IEEE Signal Processing Magazine*, vol. 22, no. 3, pp. 14–22, 2005.

[4] R. Lysecky and F. Vahid, "Design and implementation of a MicroBlaze-based warp processor," *Transactions on Embedded Computing Systems*, vol. 8, no. 3, article 22, 2009.

[5] N. Clark, J. Blome, M. Chu, S. Mahlke, S. Biles, and K. Flautner, "An architecture framework for transparent instruction set customization in embedded processors," in *Proceedings of the 32nd Interntional Symposium on Computer Architecture (ISCA '05)*, pp. 272–283, June 2005.

[6] A. C. S. Beck, M. B. Rutzig, G. Gaydadjiev, and L. Carro, "Transparent reconfigurable acceleration for heterogeneous embedded applications," in *Proceedings of the Conference on Design,*

Automation and Test in Europe (DATE '08), pp. 1208–1213, Munich, Germany, March 2008.

[7] J. Bispo and J. M. P. Cardoso, "On identifying and optimizing instruction sequences for dynamic compilation," in *Proceedings of the International Conference on Field-Programmable Technology (FPT '10)*, pp. 437–440, Beijing, China, December 2010.

[8] J. Bispo, N. Paulino, J. M. P. Cardoso, and J. C. Ferreira, "From instruction traces to specialized reconfigurable arrays," in *Proceedings of the International Conference on ReConFigurable Computing and FPGAs (ReConFig '11)*, pp. 386–391, Cancun, Mexico, 2011.

[9] J. Bispo, N. Paulino, J. C. Ferreira, and J. M. P. Cardoso, "Transparent trace-based binary acceleration for reconfigurable HW/SW systems," *IEEE Transactions on Industrial Informatics*. In Press.

[10] R. Lysecky, G. Stitt, and F. Vahid, "Warp processors," *ACM Transactions on Design Automation of Electronic Systems*, vol. 11, no. 3, pp. 659–681, 2006.

[11] N. Clark, M. Kudlur, H. Park, S. Mahlke, and K. Flautner, "Application-specific processing on a general-purpose core via transparent instruction set customization," in *Proceedings of the 37th International Symposium on Microarchitecture (MICRO '04)*, pp. 30–40, Portland, Ore, USA, December 2004.

[12] A. Mehdizadeh, B. Ghavami, M. S. Zamani, H. Pedram, and F. Mehdipour, "An efficient heterogeneous reconfigurable functional unit for an adaptive dynamic extensible processor," in *Proceedings of the IFIP International Conference on Very Large Scale Integration (VLSI-SoC '07)*, pp. 151–156, October 2007.

[13] H. Noori, F. Mehdipour, K. Murakami, K. Inoue, and M. S. Zamani, "An architecture framework for an adaptive extensible processor," *Journal of Supercomputing*, vol. 45, no. 3, pp. 313–340, 2008.

[14] A. C. Beck, M. B. Rutzig, G. Gaydadjiev, and L. Carro, "Run-time adaptable architectures for heterogeneous behavior embedded systems," in *Proceedings of the 4th International Workshop Reconfigurable Computing: Architectures, Tools and Applications*, pp. 111–124, 2008.

[15] J. Bispo, *Mapping runtime-detected loops from microprocessors to reconfigurable processing units [Ph.D. thesis]*, Instituto Superior Técnico, 2012.

[16] P. Faes, P. Bertels, J. Van Campenhout, and D. Stroobandt, "Using method interception for hardware/software co-development," *Design Automation for Embedded Systems*, vol. 13, no. 4, pp. 223–243, 2009.

[17] S. A. Mahlke, D. C. Lin, W. Y. Chen, R. E. Hank, and R. A. Bringmann, "Effective compiler support for predicated execution using the hyperblock," in *Proceedings of the 25th Annual International Symposium on Microarchitecture*, pp. 45–54, IEEE Computer Society Press, December 1992.

[18] J. V. Leeuwen, *Handbook of Theoretical Computer Science: Algorithms and Complexity*, MIT Press, 1990.

[19] J. Bispo and J. M. P. Cardoso, "Synthesis of regular expressions for FPGAs," *International Journal of Electronics*, vol. 95, no. 7, pp. 685–704, 2008.

[20] H. P. Rosinger, "Connecting Customized IP to the MicroBlaze Soft Processor Using the Fast Simplex Link (FSL) Channel," XAPP529 (v1. 3), Xilinx2004.

[21] I. Xilinx, "Microblaze processor reference guide v13. 4," reference manual, 2011.

[22] I. Xilinx, "ChipScope pro 11. 1 software and cores user guide (v11. 1)," 2009.

[23] I. Xilinx, "Microblaze software reference guide v2. 2," reference manual, 2002.

[24] Y. Kim, J. Lee, A. Shrivastava, and Y. Paek, "Memory access optimization in compilation for coarse-grained reconfigurable architectures," *ACM Transactions on Design Automation of Electronic Systems (TODAES)*, vol. 16, p. 42, 2011.

[25] S. J. Patel and S. S. Lumetta, "rePLay: a hardware framework for dynamic optimization," *IEEE Transactions on Computers*, vol. 50, no. 6, pp. 590–608, 2001.

3

A Dynamically Reconfigured Multi-FPGA Network Platform for High-Speed Malware Collection

Sascha Mühlbach[1] and Andreas Koch[2]

[1] Secure Things Group, Center for Advanced Security Research Darmstadt, Mornewegstr. 32, 64293 Darmstadt, Germany
[2] Department of Computer Science, Embedded Systems and Applications Group, Technische Universität Darmstadt, Hochschulstr. 10, 64289 Darmstadt, Germany

Correspondence should be addressed to Sascha Mühlbach, sascha.muehlbach@cased.de

Academic Editor: Marco D. Santambrogio

Malicious software has become a major threat to computer users on the Internet today. Security researchers need to gather and analyze large sample sets to develop effective countermeasures. The setting of honeypots, which emulate vulnerable applications, is one method to collect attack code. We have proposed a dedicated hardware architecture for honeypots which allows both high-speed operation at 10 Gb/s and beyond and offers a high resilience against attacks on the honeypot infrastructure itself. In this work, we refine the base NetStage architecture for better management and scalability. Using dynamic partial reconfiguration, we can now update the functionality of the honeypot during operation. To allow the operation of a larger number of vulnerability emulation handlers, the initial single-device architecture is extended to scalable multichip systems. We describe the technical aspects of these modifications and show results evaluating an implementation on a current quad-FPGA reconfigurable computing platform.

1. Introduction

The significant increase of malicious software (malware) in recent years (see [1]) requires security researchers to analyze an ever increasing amount of samples for developing effective prevention mechanisms. One method for collecting a large number of samples is the use of low-interaction honeypots (e.g., [2]). Such dedicated computer systems emulate vulnerabilities in applications and are connected directly to the Internet, spanning large IP address spaces to attract many different attackers. A number of software applications are available helping in building up honeypot systems. But in addition to having performance limitations in high-speed environments (10+ Gb/s), such software systems also suffer from being compromisable themselves (they can be subverted to attack even more hosts). Given the experience of the Nepenthes research project [3], it is extremely hard to realize an attack surface of millions of IP addresses (such as multiple class B networks) with actively communicating service modules running in software on a single server.

In this context, we have proposed MalCoBox, a low-interaction malware-collection honeypot realized entirely in reconfigurable hardware without any software components in [4]. The core of the MalCoBox system is NetStage, a high-speed implementation of the basic Internet communication protocols, attached to several independent vulnerability emulation handlers (VEH), each emulating a specific security flaw of an application (see Figure 1). We have demonstrated the feasibility of that approach by implementing a prototype on a FPGA platform, fully employing the power of dedicated hardware resources to support 10+ Gb/s network traffic.

With NetStage able to sustain above wire-speed throughput, MalCoBox can easily handle the emulation of multiple class B networks in a single system (Honeynet-in-a-Box), thus avoiding the overhead of administering a honeynet distributed across multiple servers. Beyond the performance aspects, in context of the network security domain, a purely hardware-based approach such as ours has the additional advantage that no general-purpose software programmable

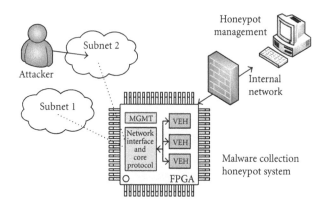

FIGURE 1: Hardware-based malware collection.

processor is present that could be subverted if the honeypot itself is being attacked.

An important issue for potential MalCoBox users is how the platform can be updated during operation with new or improved vulnerability emulation handlers (VEHs) to react to the changing threat landscape. For an FPGA-based system, the hardware functionality can be altered during operation by using partial reconfiguration (PR). This approach has already been used for network routers in [5]. We now employ the technique in a larger scope to flexibly swap-in new VEHs while the rest of the system stays in operation. The initial discussion presented in [6] is expanded in this work.

Another aspect of great practical interest is the number of different vulnerabilities that can be emulated in *parallel*. The original MalCoBox relied on a single-device implementation of NetStage and was limited to ca. 20 VEHs active in the system. This is a gap to software honeypots, where even the low-interaction variants often support 50 · · · 100 different vulnerabilities implemented as scripts in languages such as Perl and Python. While it could be argued that the capacities of individual FPGA chips does increase from each generation to the next (which they do), the larger high-end devices are significantly more expensive per logic cell than the mid-range versions. Thus, it is worthwhile to examine how the MalCoBox capacity can be extended using a multidevice NetStage implementation. This approach has been introduced in [7] and is described in greater detail here.

The paper is organized as follows: Section 2 briefly describes the core architecture components. Section 3 covers details of the ring implementation and elaborates the differences between single-chip and multichip solution. Section 4 continues with a description on the required modifications of the partial reconfiguration strategy. The implementation of the complete system on the BEEcube BEE3 quad-FPGA reconfigurable computing platform [8] is described in Section 5, followed by experimental results given in Section 6. We close with a conclusion and an outlook towards further research in the last Section.

1.1. Related Work. To our knowledge, this is the first implementation of such a honeypot system using pure dedicated hardware blocks. In 2007, Pejović et al [9]. presented an

initial concept for a hardware honeypot with RAM-based state machines for the emulations. Unfortunately, they did not give any detailed results on the achievable performance and the possible parallelism. It is likely, however, that the RAM-based state machines could become a bottleneck in high-speed environments due to limited bandwidth. Thus, our architecture contains only dedicated hardware blocks.

In terms of FPGA-based networking, a popular generic platform for research is the Stanford NetFPGA [10], containing an FPGA, four 1G interfaces, and various memories. The platform is the vehicle for a wide spectrum of research, for example, on accelerated switches, routers, and network monitoring devices. Internally, NetFPGA provides a flexible data-path structure into which custom processing modules can be easily inserted. With the widespread use of NetFPGA, a new version supporting 10 G networks is currently being released.

Another related research project is DynaCORE [11]. It consists of a network-on-chip- (NoC-) oriented architecture for a generic reconfigurable network coprocessor, combining general network processing in software with accelerated functions (e.g., encryption) in hardware units. By using current techniques such as partial reconfiguration, the platform can be adapted to different communication situations.

In [12], the authors present a reconfigurable network processor based on a MicroBlaze softcore-CPU extended with multiple exchangeable hardware accelerators. Partial reconfiguration is used to adapt the system to the current network traffic workload. Partial reconfiguration is also employed in [13] to support network virtualization, realizing multiple virtual routers in hardware on a single FPGA.

In contrast to these often packet-oriented approaches, our own research has always been aiming at higher-level Internet (e.g., TCP and UDP) and application protocols. We, thus, have created NetStage [4] as a novel base architecture for our honeypot appliance. NetStage is built around an all-hardware Internet protocol stack implementation (including TCP operation). We have chosen to follow some of the approaches proven useful with NetFPGA, for example, the capability to insert "plug-in" hardware modules at various points in the processing flow. In contrast to DynaCORE, however, we generate a light-weight application specific interconnect between these modules, instead of using a general-purpose, but larger NoC scheme.

2. Key Architecture Components

Figure 2 shows the base NetStage architecture (discussed in greater detail in [4]), including extensions to support dynamic partial reconfiguration (DPR). The architecture provides module slots (Figure 2(a)) into which the partial VEH bitstreams can be loaded. These VEH slots are loosely interconnected with the core system by buffers, allowing all VEHs to have the same external interface (important for DPR). Thus, any VEH may be configured into any of the slots of the same size, with the buffers limiting the impact of brief VEH-level stalls on the system-level throughput.

VEHs share the underlying implementations of the core protocols (IP, TCP, and UDP) in NetStage. These have

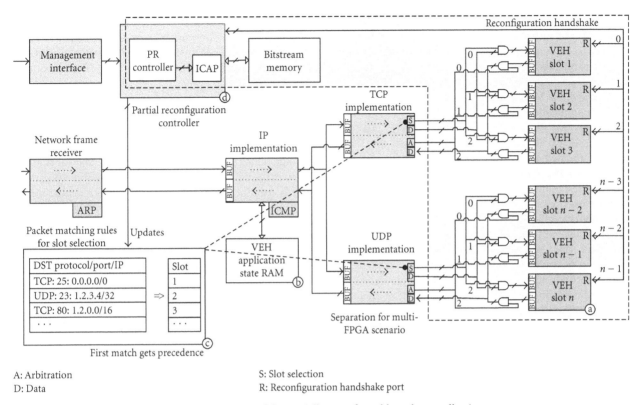

FIGURE 2: Core architecture of the partially reconfigurable malware collection system.

been very carefully optimized to achieve a throughput of at least 10 Gb/s by using pipeline- and task-level parallelism to keep up with the line rate of the 10 Gb/s external network interface.

In some cases, VEHs have to track session state to generate an appropriate response. NetStage provides a central facility for storing per-connection state (Figure 2(b)). When a packet is passing the IP implementation, the globally maintained state information is attached to the packet in a custom control header which accompanies every packet through the system. The VEH can read this information, act on it, and update the value if necessary. The modified header is written back to the state memory when a response packet (or an empty state write packet) passes the IP implementation on the transmit path. Such a centralized storage is more efficient than attempting to store state in each VEH (which would fragment the capacity of the on-chip memories).

The global VEH application state memory can also be used to save/restore VEH state during reconfiguration to allow the seamless swapping-in of newer (but state-compatible) versions of a VEH.

2.1. Vulnerability Emulation Handler.
When a packet has passed through the NetStage core, it will be forwarded to the responsible slot, where the VEH performs the actual malware detection and extraction. Packets are routed to the appropriate slots by means of a routing table (Figure 2(c)) that holds matching rules for the different vulnerability emulations currently active in the system. The table is

writable to allow dynamic modification of the actual VEHs used. A basic set of matching rules includes the destination port, destination IP and netmask. The latter allows us to set up separate IP address ranges which use VEHs for different vulnerabilities on the same port (e.g., many handlers will listen on the HTTP port 80).

With the processing speed achievable using reconfigurable hardware, these basic rules could also be extended to directly match packet contents instead of just header fields. Dedicated matching units could search the payloads of packets being forwarded through the NetStage layers and have the matching results available in time for the slot routing decision. However, this would require dynamic reconfiguration of the actual matching units together with the VEHs when they change instead of just writing new values into registers (as in the basic header-only matcher). Since all our current VEHs are selected just based on protocol and port (independently of the payload), we can continue to use the simpler basic approach.

2.2. Management Section.
The partial dynamic reconfiguration of VEHs is managed by the partial reconfiguration controller (PRC, Figure 2(d)), which is connected to the FPGAs internal configuration access port (ICAP). On the application side, the PRC is connected to the MalCoBox management interface (either by a PCI express endpoint or a dedicated network link, depending on the selected deployment mode of the system). The PRC is also connected to the individual VEH slots by a number of handshake signals to inform the VEHs about their impending reconfiguration

(for a clean shutdown, etc.) and to check whether the VEH is idle. An attached bitstream memory can hold several partial bitstreams to allow the system to be reconfigured independently of the management station in future implementations.

2.3. Reconfigurable VEHs. The VEHs are dedicated to emulate known application vulnerabilities that may be exploited by malware. As malware is evolving quickly and new vulnerabilities are detected on a regular basis, the VEHs need to be updated as well. For example, when the system is used for research purposes, multiple updates per day would commonly be required if a researcher would like to react to current observations in the network traffic.

In a conventional software-based system, such changes could generally be handled quickly by altering a few lines of code in a script language. However, when using dedicate hardware, even minor changes of the functionality require full logic synthesis, mapping, and place-and-route steps. This effort can be significantly reduced by employing dynamic partial reconfiguration (DPR) to recompile just those VEHs actually affected by the change.

As a secondary effect, DPR also allows the arbitrary combination of VEHs in the system. Otherwise, each specific set of selected VEHs would need to be compiled into its own static configuration.

To support independent partial reconfiguration of any of the VEH slots within the architecture, a wrapper encapsulates the actual VEH implementation module (see Figure 3). This wrapper includes glue logic controlled by the partial reconfiguration controller to disconnect/reconnect all inputs and outputs of the VEH module. This clean separation is essential to avoid introducing errors in the rest of the system when reconfiguring.

The wrapper also contains the send and receive buffers for each module as well as the corresponding buffer management logic. As all the handlers share the same buffer structure, it is more efficient to keep it static than configure it with each VEH. The inputs and outputs of the wrapper are directly connected to the MalCoBox core (see Figure 2).

3. Multidevice Architecture

To extend our system to multiple FPGAs, we will draw the boundaries between the static NetStage core (basic Ethernet and Internet protocol functions) and the dynamically exchangeable VEH slots (see the dotted line in Figure 2). One FPGA acting as Master node holds the network core and the network interfaces, and the remaining other FPGAs, called VEH nodes, contain the individual emulation blocks. The BEE3 platform supports a number of interdevice interconnection schemes. For future scalability independently of the BEE3 architecture, we decided to implement a ring structure. Such rings have already proven useful in multichip systems internally using NoCs [14].

For extending the NetStage-based MalCoBox to multiple devices, a unidirectional ring suffices (Figure 4). The unidirectional ring needs fewer I/O pins on the FPGAs and avoids the increased latency of the bus-turnaround cycles that would be required when running a bidirectional bus over the same pins. Also note that in contrast to the implementations in discussed in prior work, the one described here is using the external SDRAM instead of the internal BlockRAM to temporarily store bitstreams, conserving FPGA resources to allow more VEHs.

3.1. Ring Communication. For the communication on the ring, we use 66 of the 72 available inter-FPGA data lines on the BEE3 which are run in DDR mode, resulting in 132 bits of data per clock cycle [7]. Four bits are reserved for status bits, the remaining 128 form the data transmission word. As data words are sent continuously on the ring for synchronization purposes (even if not actual data needs to be transmitted), a valid flag is used to indicate words holding actual message data. For the separation of individual messages, we use two flags to signal the first and the last word of a message. As the actual byte size of the message is already stored within the internal control header (ICH, see Figure 8) used by NetStage (prefixed to the message body), no special-case processing is required for unused bytes in the last data word of a message. A final flag is used to denote special ring control messages used, for example, to control the DPR process (see next section). In a future extension, this could also be used, for example, to enumerate the ring nodes automatically during initialization. Currently, the destination addresses of the available FPGAs inside the ring are set during compile time.

The ICH-prefixed message is prefixed yet again with a 128 b ring control header (RCH) when it is transmitted between devices. The RCH carries the type information of the message and the destination FPGA. The remaining bits are reserved to implement further control functions in the future.

Since we want to maintain a high bandwidth and low latency even when distributing the architecture across multiple devices, we want to operate the interdevice links at maximum speed. To this end, we use the BEE3-provided global clock to all FPGAs as the ring clock. However, due to different trace lengths and other board-level signal integrity effects, reliable operation at our target frequency of 250 MHz requires a training of the individual FPGAs to the link characteristics. This is done using the technique proposed in [15]. A known training sequence is transmitted between adjacent FPGAs, and the receiver adjusts its delay until it receives a stable pattern from the transmitter.

Two additional signals are required to realize training procedure (see Figures 5 and 6). The Master starts the process by asserting a Sync signal, which is routed around the entire ring. It is used to both initiate training between neighboring FPGAs and to test whether the nodes did configure correctly on start-up (an error is indicated if the Sync sent out by the Master does not match the incoming Sync passed around the ring). Once the receiving FPGA of a synchronization pair has locked on to the training pattern, it asserts its internal Ready signal, which is ANDed with the Ready incoming from its transmitting partner before being output to its receiving partner (the next device on the ring). Once the Master has received an asserted Ready signal passed around the entire

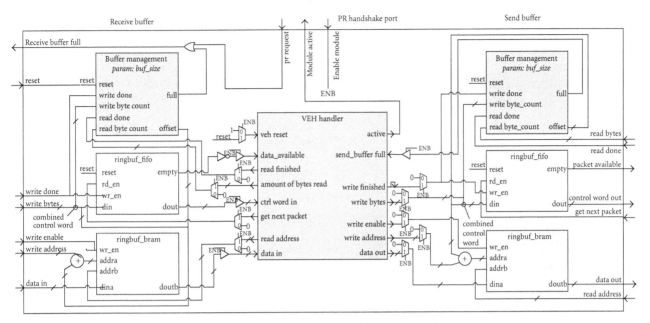

FIGURE 3: Wrapper encapsulating a vulnerability emulation handler slot.

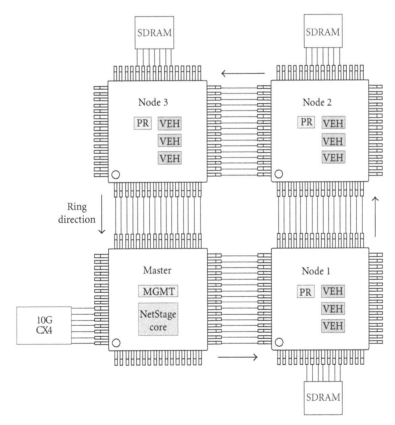

FIGURE 4: Multi-FPGA network processor in ring topology.

ring, it stops training and releases the ring into normal operation.

The ring thus achieves a transfer rate of 32 Gb/s between nodes, more than sufficient for our current 10 Gb/s network environment. For simplicity, and since we did not experience any data integrity issues in our practical experiments once training completed, we do not perform error detection/correction on the ring communications. However, for long-term production use, CRC/ECC facilities could be added here. As there are still data lines available on the BEE3, this could be easily implemented without affecting the base architecture.

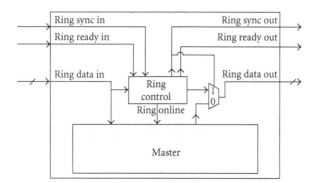

FIGURE 5: Schematic overview of the master.

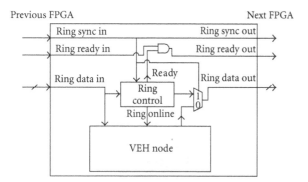

FIGURE 6: Schematic overview of the nodes.

3.2. Master Node. Beyond the network core and the management section that was already present in the single-chip NetStage implementation, the Master node (see Figure 7) now contains additional logic (Figure 7(a)) to handle the ring communication. In particular, this includes send and receive interface modules as well as the FPGA addressing logic. Note that we do not place any VEHs in the Master node and the currently unused space is intended to be used for future extensions of the NetStage core (e.g., to IPv6). Thus, the Master itself will not be dynamically reconfigured and does not require an internal ICAP controller. However, the Master is responsible for initiating the reconfiguration of the VEH nodes. Thus, the management section in the Master and the configuration controllers in the VEH nodes interact, which is achieved by specialized ring control messages.

The payload data traffic around the ring is organized on two levels. The 32B ICH (see Figure 8) replaces the original protocol headers for a packet with a more compact representation. It also carries the packet-to-handler routing information of a message on the ring in the form of a destination VEH node ID and the VEH slot on that node. Since the destination node ID is already specified in the RCH, this might be seen as redundant. However, the RCH is present only while a packet is transmitted between nodes and stripped from it for node-internal processing. Since we want to give VEHs the ability to transparently forward packets to other VEHs which might also reside on other nodes, they can read/write that destination data in the ICH instead (which, due to alignment reasons, is not efficient for performing ring-level routing).

As we now have multiple destination FPGAs, the Master routing table, which associated packets just with the responsible VEH slot in the single-chip version, needs be extended to hold the destination node ID as well (Figure 7(b)). This is used to build the RCH when the packet is sent out over the ring. To reduce the latency, the process to look up the destination address (Figure 7(c)) is pipelined between the core and the Ring Send module. This can be easily done as packets are not reordered between the two modules.

The Master will silently discard packets not matching any rule in its routing table to conserve bandwidth on the ring links. Furthermore, core IP protocols such as ARP and ICMP are usually handled with low-latency entirely inside the Master, and do not cause ring traffic, either.

3.3. VEH Node. The individual VEHs are housed in the VEH nodes (see Figure 9). For communication with the rest of the system, the VEH nodes need the same ring interface modules (Figure 9(a)) as the Master node. Furthermore, a node-local packet distributor and aggregator (Figure 9(b)) emulate the single-chip NetStage core interface so that VEHs can be attached directly connected to the network core of the single-chip implementation. VEHs are thus portable between the single- and multichip versions.

In contrast to the Master node, the VEH are actually dynamically reconfigured to exchange VEHs. Thus, they do need a PR controller and access to the ICAP. The details of this are described in greater detail in the next section.

The ring receive module in each VEH node checks the type of an incoming ring message and its destination address field and either forwards the packet to the local distributor module, a reconfiguration message to the local PR controller, or immediately inserts the message into the forwarding queue if is intended for another node. VEH response network packets are picked up by the packet aggregator and inserted into an output queue, passing it on around the ring until it reaches the external network connection at the Master node.

4. Partial Reconfiguration

Partial bitstream data is transferred from the management station (usually an external PC or server) to the MalCoBox via the management interface. As the MalCoBox should be able to run as an appliance under remote management, we implemented a stand-alone on-chip reconfiguration interface instead of using the JTAG port together with a software programmer on a host PC.

The underlying protocol used to transmit the bitstream to the MalCoBox consists of the raw bitstream prefixed by a reconfiguration header (see Figure 10). The header contains the bitstream size, the FPGA slot location information, and the rules for the Master node routing table to direct packets to the newly configure VEH.

In contrast to the single-chip implementation [6], in the multidevice scenario, the management interface housed in the Master does not have a direct connection to the partial reconfiguration controller (PRC). Instead, the bitstream is transferred over the ring to the destination VEH node

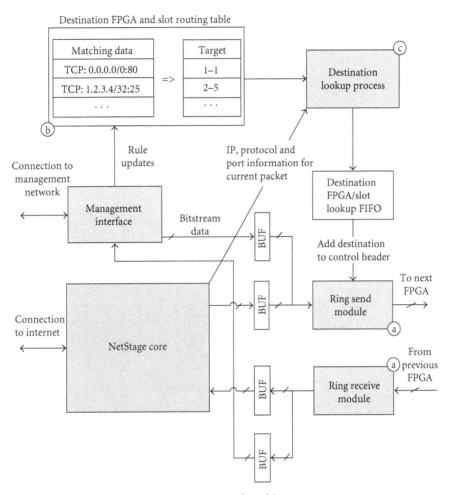

FIGURE 7: Master node architecture.

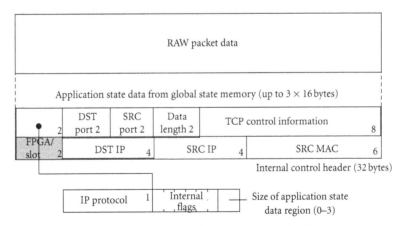

FIGURE 8: Structure of the internal control header.

FPGA, but the routing rules table still remains inside the Master node. The management interface, therefore, extracts the header information from incoming reconfiguration data requests and updates the routing table, while the raw bitstream data is forwarded to the FPGA specified in the reconfiguration header (see also Figure 7). As the partial reconfiguration process is now distributed across multiple devices, the time between the Master-local routing rule update and the activation of new VEH in a remote node is longer than on the single-chip system. Thus, to avoid misrouting of packets, the new routing rule is explicitly disabled until the VEH is actually ready to accept traffic.

In a VEH node, an incoming bitstream is stored in node-local external DDR-SDRAM memory. One an actual

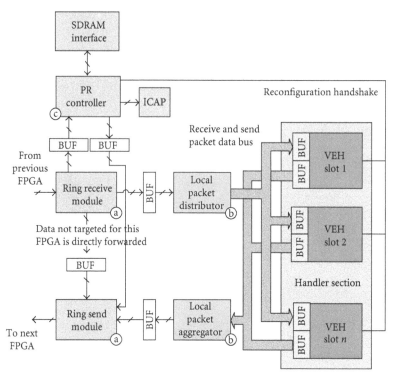

FIGURE 9: VEH node architecture.

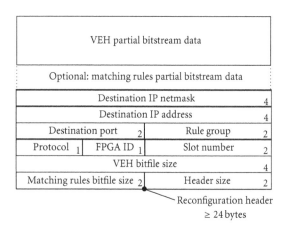

FIGURE 10: Custom PR header and bitstream data.

reconfiguration is requested, a fast DMA unit retrieves the bitstream data from memory and transfers it at maximum speed to the ICAP configuration interface. This two-step approach could also be used in a later extension to, for example, integrity-check the bitstream for communication errors, or to accept only signed bitstreams [16, 17]. Since the ring communication has proven reliable in our tests, and the management console is trusted, the current prototype does not implement these facilities.

4.1. Partial Reconfiguration Process. The distributed reconfiguration process is performed in the following order.

(1) The rule header of incoming bitstream data is extracted, and the rule table is updated with the new

rule (eventually replacing an existing one), having the active flag set to zero.

(2) Incoming bitstream data is forwarded to the corresponding VEH node.

(3) After complete reception of bitstream data, the PRC in the VEH node starts the reconfiguration process.

(4) After completion of reconfiguration, the PRC sends a DONE status to the Master as a ring control message.

(5) The Master management interface receives the message and activates the routing rule so that packets will actually be forwarded.

Network packets and reconfiguration messages (including the bitstream data) share the ring. However, since reconfiguration management is crucial for the reliable operation of the system, these ring control messages receive priority over regular packet transmissions.

Internally, the reconfiguration process in the VEH nodes follows the approach implemented for the single-chip solution [6]. When the node-local PRC receives a reconfiguration request, it initially informs the wrapper of the target slot that the slot is about to be reconfigured. This will stop the receive buffer of the VEH from accepting new packets. The VEH is allowed to process all of the packets held in the buffer at this time, asserting a signal to the PRC on completion. The PRC then deactivates the VEH, and the now inactive VEH is disconnected from the slot wrapper. The actual bitstream data is then read from the DDR-SDRAM and fed into the ICAP. Once reconfiguration is completed, the PRC re-enables the VEH-wrapper connections and allows the new VEH to wake up in its reset state.

5. Implementation

The MalCoBox running on the multidevice NetStage architecture has been implemented on the BEEcube BEE3 FPGA-based reconfigurable computing platform, which is equipped with eight 10 Gb/s network interfaces and four Xilinx Virtex 5 FPGAs (2x LX155T, 2x LX95T). The Master node is realized as one of the smaller SX95Ts to have both of the larger LX155T devices available for VEHs.

Network connectivity is provided by the Xilinx XAUI and 10 G MAC IPs. The network core in the Master runs at the speed of the 156.25 MHz clock of the 10 G network interface. Together with the internal bus width of 128 bit, this leads to a maximum core throughput of 20 Gb/s. This overprovisioning allows us to react to brief stalls in the data flow. These could occur if complex VEHs needed extra time to process a packet (e.g., perform a DRAM lookup) and could not guarantee a steady 10 Gb/s throughput. The 20 Gb/s throughput supported by NetStage thus allows handlers to "catch up" with the normal 10 Gb/s traffic by burst-processing the data accumulated in the buffers at double speed.

To allow for greater design flexibility and allow the execution of more complex VEHs having longer combinational paths, the clock rates of the Master and VEH Nodes can be set independently. Currently, we run the VEH Nodes at 125 MHz, thus supporting burst processing at a rate of 16 Gb/s. This can be easily altered (sped up or slowed down) to match the complexity (delay) of the required VEHs, as long as the 10 Gb/s minimum throughput is always achieved.

The ICAP is operated at 32 b data width and driven by a separate clock to support variable reconfiguration speeds (and thus support experiments with overclocking the ICAP). Management access is implemented as dedicated network interface with a unique MAC address, directly connected to a standard desktop PC or server. The management interface receives bitstream data and control operations over the network using a custom protocol. Perl scripts are used to assemble the appropriate network packets. The DDR2-SDRAM interface in the VEH nodes is realized by a Xilinx MIG core and fully uses the DDR2-SDRAM bandwidth.

The size of all intermodule and slot buffers is set to 4 kB (to hold 2 packets with a maximum size of 1500 B), which is sufficient to assure stall-free operation as the modules generally consume the data at a minimum rate of 10 Gb/s). If many variable-latency VEHs requiring burst processing are employed, the buffer size will need to be increased correspondingly. This has already been done for the ring receive buffers, which are set to 16 kB to provide sufficient headroom to receive bursts of packets on the ring. The size of the global application state memory in the Master node is currently set to 1 Mb of BRAM, which is sufficient to manage the short running sessions (only a few seconds each) that we expect in the honeypot use case. By session, we mean the time interval the attacker needs to check whether the target is vulnerable until the reception of the attack code. For applications requiring more state storage, the data could also be stored in the per-node DDR2-SDRAM available on the BEE3. This would incur longer access latencies, though.

These could be avoided on newer hardware platforms by using low-latency external memory technologies such as Bandwidth Engine [18] or Hybrid Memory Cube [19].

5.1. Destination Lookup. The rules that control the message routing to VEHs in different nodes are stored in the destination routing table (see Figure 11) inside the Master node. This table is implemented as BRAM (currently with a size of 1024 rules), to achieve high lookup speeds and flexible scaling. In addition to the routing information, each rule entry contains a rule ID that is used for management purposes and an active flag used during the reconfiguration process. The table supports multiple rules for the same destination VEH (e.g., to let it respond to different IP addresses).

As the destination routing decision is on the critical path with regard to latency, we use a hierarchical approach for lookups. Rules with the same destination port are represented as a linked list, and a CAM is used to retrieve the BRAM address of the list head for a given port (see Figure 12). Then, the individual rules for this port are searched in list order by following the rules' next pointers. Beyond quick lookups, this also ensure that rules with the longest IP address prefix will be matched first. The management process ensures that rules are inserted in the correct order.

For efficiency, we have restricted the CAM size to 256 entries, reasoning that 256 different active ports should be sufficient for most cases. Since the CAM has an 8b wide output, the heads of the per-port rule lists always start in the bottom 256 addresses of the routing table BRAM.

5.2. Example VEHs. To test the system, we have created a number of VEHs emulating different vulnerabilities and applications. In addition to controlling FSMs, the VEHs contain additional logic to perform tasks such as fast parallel pattern matching.

(1) *SIP.* The SIP VEH looks for packets exploiting a vulnerability of the software SIP SDK sipXtapi [20]. The exploit uses a buffer overflow occurring if a SIP INVITE packet contains a CSeq field value exceeding 24 bytes in length. This VEH is based on the UDP protocol.

(2) *MSSQL.* Another UDP-based VEH has a similar structure and is emulating a vulnerable MSSQL 2000 server looking for exploits targeting the resolution service [21]. This exploit was used in the past by, for example, the Slammer worm.

(3) *Web Server.* As a VEH for a further popular application, we implemented a simple web server emulation that contains a ROM with predefined HTML pages to be served to clients. The HTTP headers needed for response generation are also stored inside the ROM. An FSM checks the URL of incoming requests and fetches the corresponding output data to be sent from the ROM. This VEH can be flexibly used, for example, to emulate a login page for a company intranet and monitor

Target FPGA and slot selection table (BRAM)									
Addr.	Protocol	Target	Target	Port	Netmask	IP addr.	Rule ID	Rule	Next
		FPGA	Slot					Act.	Rule
(10 b)	(8 b)	(8 b)	(8 b)	(16 b)	(32 b)	(32 b)	(16 b)	(1 b)	(10 b)
0	0x06	1	0	80	0x00000000	0x00000000	13	0	0
1	0x06	1	1	25	0xFFFFFFFF	0x53251021	25	1	256
...	...	...	...	...	...	...	...	...	...
256	0x11	2	3	25	0xFFFFFF00	0x10102500	47	1	257
257	0x06	1	1	25	0xFFFFFF00	0x32122500	69	1	0
...	...	...	...	...	...	...	...	...	...

$\longrightarrow$ Linked list to speed up lookups and to maintain IP/netmask prefix order for matching

FIGURE 11: Layout of the destination lookup table.

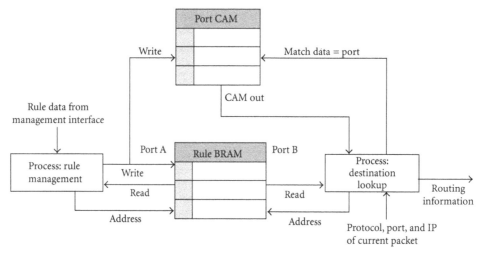

FIGURE 12: Implementation of the destination lookup process.

attack attempts (e.g., brute force logins) or attacks to the web server itself.

(4) *Mail Server.* As spam is amongst the widespread distribution techniques for malware, we implemented a mail server VEH that accepts incoming mails and pretends to be an open relay server. It contains a FSM that implements the basic SMTP dialog for the reception of mails.

6. Results

The design was synthesized and mapped using Xilinx ISE 12.4, targeting a SX95T for the Master node and both SX95T and the LX155T devices as VEH nodes. Partial reconfiguration was implemented using the latest partial reconfiguration flow available in PlanAhead 12.4 [22]. Each VEH node was configured to include 24 slots. The VEH module slots were placed manually on the FPGA and sized based on the resource usage trends shown by the sample VEH synthesis results. The resulting layout can be seen in Figure 13. To support VEHs with different resource needs (BRAM vs. LUTs), four kinds of slots, differing in the number and types of contained resources (see Table 5), are provided.

As techniques to dynamically relocate bitstreams on the FPGA matrix are not yet production ready, and even research versions have significant limitations (e.g., only support for outdated device families), we have to create separate bitstreams for the all of the different slots a VEH can be placed. In addition to requiring more storage, this also necessitates to run the place-and-route tools multiple times with different area constraints. Each run produces the partial bitfile for a specific VEH-slot combination. However, due to using partial reconfiguration, bitfile sets for different VEHs can be created and used independently, for example, exploiting a multicore server by executing many tool runs in parallel.

System tests were performed by simulation as well as on an actual BEE3 machine connected to a quad-XEON Linux server, sending data to the VEHs at 10 Gb/s. Partial reconfiguration was performed under operator control, loading in new bitstreams via network from the management station.

6.1. Synthesis Results. The synthesis results for all components are given in Tables 1 and 2. For the VEH nodes, we show results only for the LX155T, as the results for the SX95T are very similar (in terms of resource requirements).

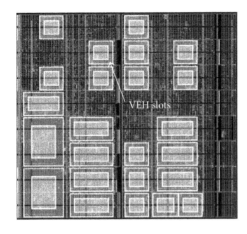

FIGURE 13: FPGA layout for 24 VEH slots.

TABLE 1: Synthesis results for Master node components.

Module	LUT	Reg. bits	BRAM
Network core incl. management	12,297	8,884	93
Ring interface	788	1,489	16
Mapped incl. MAC, XAUI and clocks	16,532	13,526	117
In % of SX95T	28	22	47

TABLE 2: Synthesis results for VEH node components.

Module	LUT	Reg. bits	BRAM
Ring interface	976	2,048	20
PR controller	722	544	4
VEH section with 24 slots (w/o VEHs)	15,494	6,426	120
Total incl. MIG, without VEHs	19,540	12,428	150
In % of LX155T	20	12	70

TABLE 3: Synthesis results for the VEHs.

Module	LUT	Reg. bits
SIP VEH	1082	358
MSSQL VEH	875	562
Web server VEH	1026	586
Mail server VEH	741	362

The NetStage core on the SX95T Master node requires around 20% of the LUTs and 38% of the BRAMs. The high number of BRAMs is due to several buffers and the global application state memory. The mapped design including IP blocks occupies around 28% of the LUT and 47% of the BRAM resources distributed amongst 50% of the slices. This still leaves sufficient area unoccupied on the SX95T to allow for further extension of the Master node functionality.

The number of available BRAMs is crucial for our platform (due to the multiple buffers). As the SX95T and the LX155T have nearly the same number of BRAMs, these mapping results confirm our decision to put the Master node into the SX95T and leave the large number of LUTs inside the LX155T available for VEHs.

In the VEH node, the ring interface, the partial reconfiguration controller, and the VEH slot interfaces occupy around 20% of the FPGA. This leaves nearly 80% of the LUT resources available for the actual VEH implementations. In practice, the total number of slots per FPGA is limited by the number of BRAMs available to implement the slot buffers (five BRAMs are needed per slot). From these results, we conclude that we could theoretically support up to 36 VEH slots per FPGA on both the LX155T and SX95T.

In comparison to our single-chip implementation, which could hold 20 VEHs together with the NetStage core on a single LX155T device, the multi-FPGA approach is a significant improvement of the total processing power of our platform. When using all three VEH node FPGAs to their full extent, the system supports the parallel operation of 100 VEHs (depending on module size), which should suffice even for very complex honeypot use cases.

6.2. VEHs. Table 3 summarizes the area requirements for the various VEH modules. They are only showing little variation, which is advantageous for putting them into different slots on the FPGA. Amongst them, the SIP VEH requires the most LUTs, as it contains the most complex pattern matching algorithm. Overall, the VEHs are relatively small compared to the device capacity, thus we are confident that our slot numbers are realistic.

6.3. Performance. The actual response time depends on the latency of the platform and the speed of the VEHs. As these numbers are, in turn, highly dependent on the implemented functionality, and the distribution of incoming network traffic, we show numbers for the upper and lower limits. For these experiments, we consider different fill levels of the buffers inside the NetStage core and the ring: all buffers empty (the best case), nearly half full (average case), and nearly full (worst case). For simplicity, we assume that all buffers in the system have the same fill level and that the VEHs are able to actually sustain a speed of 10 Gb/s (possible using the sample VEHs described above).

Table 4 lists the total round-trip times (RTTs) for a 1000 byte request packet that generates a 1000 byte response packet. As the packets have the same size, the time is independent of the ring location of the device holding the measured VEH.

Obviously, the fill level of the buffers inside the ring nodes has a severe impact on the latency, inducing a 10x increase in latency between empty and nearly full buffers. However, as we are currently feeding the system with only one 10 G interface, and the VEHs are all designed for high-speed operation, the buffers should not fill up in practice. We thus expect the average latency of the current system to be between 10–20 μs.

TABLE 4: Round-Trip Time for a 1000 B packet: overall and per system component.

Buffer Fill Level	Round-Trip Time	Core	Ring	VEH
Empty	5.5 μs	3.6 μs	1.4 μs	0.5 μs
Half	28.7 μs	9.8 μs	17.4 μs	1.5 μs
Full	51.9 μs	16 μs	33.4 μs	2.5 μs

6.4. Partial Reconfiguration Results. Table 5 lists the local reconfiguration time and the total time needed to update a VEH. The local reconfiguration time is measured from the beginning of the DMA transfer between node-local DDR2-SDRAM and ICAP and the end of the reconfiguration process. The remote update time is measured from the first reception of a bitstream packet request at the management interface until the DONE message sent by the node PRC has been received at the Master. This time includes all data transfers of bitstream data from the management station to the system using the dedicated management network interface, sending bitstream messages on the ring from Master to the VEH node and the actual device configuration time. The measurements were made using a 10G Ethernet link at 80% utilization as the management interface. The table lists the theoretical optimum time (assuming raw transmission speeds) as well as the actual measured time on the prototype machine (by using tcpdump).

We also distinguish two cases for when looking at the local reconfiguration times. On a clean shutdown (labeled "w/ SD"), an outgoing VEH is allowed to fully process the packets already present in its input queue. Without a clean shutdown ("w/o SD"), the enqueued packets are discarded when the slot is reconfigured. For the clean shutdown measurement, we assume that the receive buffer of the VEH to be replaced is half full and that the VEH is able to process data at 10 Gb/s (being conservative, since all of our current VEHs can actually handle more).

The time required for cleanly shutting down the outgoing VEH is negligible. Most of the reconfiguration time is actually taken by feeding the bitstream into the ICAP, which limits the overall reconfiguration speed. Thus, a small size of the VEHs is important for fast reconfiguration (see also Section 6.5) and justifies our approach of heterogeneously sized VEH slots (we can configure the 14 smaller VEH slots much faster than the 4 + 4 + 2 larger ones).

When looking at the total reconfiguration time including transfer of the bitstreams from the management station, the use of a 10 Gb/s management link theoretically adds only about 40% of overhead to the raw device reconfiguration time. Even in practice, the actually measured time for reconfiguring the bitstream for the largest VEH slot over the network was just 2.3 ms. Thus, the MalCoBox can be very quickly adapted to changing attack behavior even if the bitstreams are not already present in the node-local DDR2-SDRAM, but have to be fetched from the remote management station.

In [3], Baecher et al. presented results indicating that in their experiment, the honeypot received an average of 3 requests per second, with a peak of 1300 requests per second. Based on this data, MalCoBox should have sufficient headroom for very dynamic attack scenarios even if we assume that the system manages a larger attack surface (e.g., a million IP addresses). This capability will be studied in the upcoming live test of the MalCoBox system at a central Internet router.

Note that for the more common use-case of infrequent VEH updates, a 1 Gb/s Ethernet link to the management station is quite sufficient.

6.5. Impact of Data Path Width. To evaluate the impact of the 128 b data path on the VEH size, we created 64 b versions of the SIP and the Web Server VEHs and compared them to the original 128 b implementation (Table 6). Data path conversion between the NetStage core and the VEHs can be easily performed by the wrappers at the cost of a reduced throughput for the attached VEH.

The area overhead of the 128 b version is roughly 75% for the SIP VEH and 65% for the Web Server VEH. This was to be expected, since these VEHs mostly read data from the input buffer and write data to the output buffer. The area required is thus strongly related to the bus width. Together with the data path area, the BlockRAM usage is also reduced. With 64 b operation, we can now narrow the buffers and only require three BlockRAMs per wrapper instead of five for 128 b VEHs.

Given these results, the number of parallel VEHs in the system could be increased even further by using the smaller datapath width, but only at a loss of per-VEH throughput (8 Gb/s with 64 b width and 125 MHz VEH node clocks). Assuming a heterogeneous traffic distribution across all VEHs, this would not actually lead to a slow-down, since the NetStage core would keep its 20 Gb/s-capable 128 b data path width and *distribute* the traffic across multiple of the smaller-but-slower VEHs. The bottleneck would only become apparent if all traffic was to be directed at a *single* VEH, which then would not be able to keep up with the 10 Gb/s line rate.

7. Conclusion and Next Steps

With this refinement of our MalCoBox system, we have presented a scalable architecture to build a high-speed hardware-accelerated malware collection solution that offers great flexibility through partial reconfiguration and the distribution of VEHs over multiple FPGAs. In the multidevice scenario, the total amount of VEH processing power is significantly improved in contrast to the single-chip implementation, allowing us to implement even large-scale honeynets with a single appliance. A dedicated management interface allows quick updates or replacements of single vulnerability emulation handlers by loading new partial

TABLE 5: Slot size distribution and reconfiguration time.

Qty.	LUT/BRAM	Bitfile size	Reconfiguration time			
			Local reconfiguration		Remote reconfiguration	
			w/o SD	w/SD	Optimum	Measured
14	1440/0	59 KB	151 μs	154 μs	218 μs	574 μs
4	2304/0	119 KB	305 μs	308 μs	432 μs	1740 μs
4	2304/2	128 KB	328 μs	332 μs	465 μs	1886 μs
2	4864/0	237 KB	607 μs	610 μs	852 μs	2269 μs

TABLE 6: Synthesis results for 128 b and 64 b VEHs.

VEH	LUT	Reg. Bits
SIP 128 Bit	1082	358
SIP 64 Bit	619	278
Web Server 128 Bit	1026	586
Web Server 64 Bit	663	244

bitstreams, without interrupting the operation of the rest of the system.

Enabled by the high performance of the dedicated hardware, the VEHs actually performing the malware detection and extraction can contain a wide range of functionality. They can embed complex regular expression logic as well as simple request-response patterns, while still reaching the required throughput of 10 Gb/s. Furthermore, our hardware approach is resilient against compromising attacks and significantly reduces the risk of operating honeypots in a production environment.

The presented implementation of the multi-FPGA system on the BEEcube BEE3 quad-FPGA reconfigurable computing platform demonstrated the feasibility of the approach. Operators have a great flexibility to adapt the system to their needs: A tradeoff can easily be made between individual VEH complexity and total vulnerability coverage using many different VEHs just by altering the distribution of VEH slots sizes; throughput and area can be traded off by selecting between VEH implementations with 64 b and 128 b processing widths, and the overall system size can be scaled by selecting either the single-chip or the multi-FPGA approach.

We will continue our work in this area. MalCoBox is planned to be stress-tested in a real production environment connected to the Internet (e.g., university or ISP). From this, we expect to gain valuable insights on how to improve the architecture and its parameters in the future. Furthermore, we will combine the multi-FPGA system with our recent work on self-adapting by dynamic partial reconfiguration based on the observed traffic characteristics. We expect to achieve a platform that exploits many of today's cutting-edge technologies in reconfigurable computing to enable a system presenting maximal flexibility, performance, and security to the user.

Acknowledgments

This work was supported by CASED and Xilinx, Inc.

References

[1] "Internet Security Threat Report, Volume XV," Symantec, 2010, http://www.symantec.com/.

[2] "HoneyD," http://www.honeyd.org/.

[3] P. Baecher, M. Koetter, T. Holz, M. Dornseif, and F. Freiling, "The nepenthes platform: an efficient approach to collect malware," in Recent Advances in Intrusion Detection,, vol. 4219 of Lecture Notes in Computer Science, pp. 165–184, Springer, Berlin, Germany, 2006.

[4] S. Mühlbach, M. Brunner, C. Roblee, and A. Koch, "Mal-CoBox: designing a 10 Gb/s malware collection honeypot using reconfigurable technology," in Proceedings of the 20th International Conference on Field Programmable Logic and Applications (FPL '10), pp. 592–595, IEEE Computer Society, 2010.

[5] J. W. Lockwood, N. Naufel, J. S. Turner, and D. E. Taylor, "Reprogrammable network packet processing on the field programmable port extender (FPX)," in Proceedings of the ACM/SIGDA 9th International Symposium on Field Programmable Gate Arrays (FPGA '01), pp. 87–93, ACM, 2001.

[6] S. Mühlbach and A. Koch, "A dynamically reconfigured network platform for high-speed malware collection," in Proceedings of the International Conference on ReConFigurable Computing and FPGAs (ReConFig '10), pp. 79–84, IEEE Computer Society, 2010.

[7] S. Mühlbach and A. Koch, "A scalable multi-FPGA platform for complex networking applications," in Proceedings of the IEEE International Symposium on Field-Programmable Custom Computing Machines (FCCM '11), pp. 81–84, IEEE Computer Society, 2011.

[8] BEEcube, Inc., "BEE3 Hardware User Manual," 2008.

[9] V. Pejović, I. Kovačević, S. Bojanić, C. Leita, J. Popović, and O. Nieto-Taladriz, "Migrating a honeypot to hardware," in Proceedings of the International Conference on Emerging Security Information, Systems, and Technologies (SECURWARE '07), pp. 151–156, 2007.

[10] J. W. Lockwood, N. McKeown, G. Watson et al., "NetFPGA—an open platform for gigabit-rate network switching and routing," in Proceedingsof the IEEE International Conference on Microelectronic Systems Education: Educating Systems Designers for the Global Economy and a Secure World (MSE '07), pp. 160–161, IEEE Computer Society, 2007.

[11] C. Albrecht, R. Koch, and E. Maehle, "DynaCORE: a dynamically reconfigurable coprocessor architecture for network processors," in Proceedings of the 14th Euromicro International Conference on Parallel, Distributed, and Network-Based Processing, pp. 101–108, IEEE Computer Society, 2006.

[12] C. Kachris and S. Vassiliadis, "Analysis of a reconfigurable network processor," in Proceedings of the 20th International Parallel and Distributed Processing Symposium (IPDPS '06), p. 187, IEEE Computer Society, 2006.

[13] D. Yin, D. Unnikrishnan, Y. Liao, L. Gao, and R. Tessier, "Customizing virtual networks with partial FPGA reconfiguration," *ACM SIGCOMM—Computer Communication Review*, vol. 41, pp. 57–64, 2010.

[14] S. Bourduas and Z. Zilic, "A hybrid ring/mesh interconnectfor network-on-chip using hierarchical rings for global routing," in *Proceedings of the 1st International Symposium on Networks-on-Chip (NOCS '07)*, pp. 195–204, IEEE Computer Society, 2007.

[15] C. Thacker, "DDR2 SDRAM Controller for BEE3," Microsoft Research, 2008.

[16] K. v. d. Bok, R. Chaves, G. Kuzmanov, L. Sousa, and A. v. Genderen, "FPGA reconfigurations with run-time region delimitation," in *Proceedings of the 18th Annual Workshopon Circuits, Systems and Signal Processing (ProRISC '07)*, pp. 201–207, 2007.

[17] Y. Hori, A. Satoh, H. Sakane, and K. Toda, "Bitstream encryption and authentication using AES-GCM in dynamically reconfigurable systems," in *Proceedingsof the 3rd International Workshop on Security (IWSEC '08)*, pp. 261–278, Springer, 2008.

[18] M. Miller, "Bandwidth engine serial memory chip breaks 2 billion accesses/sec," in *Proceedings of the 23rd Hot Chips Symposium*, 2011.

[19] J. T. Pawlowski, "Hybrid memory cube: breakthrough DRAM performance with a fundamentally re-architected DRAM subsystem," in *Proceedings of the 23rd Hot Chips Symposium*, 2011.

[20] M. Thumann, "Buffer Overflow in SIP Foundry's SipXtapi," 2006, http://www.securityfocus.com/archive/1/439617.

[21] D. Litchfield, "Microsoft SQL Server 2000 Unauthenticated System Compromise," http://marc.info/?l=bugtraq&m=102760196931518&w=2.

[22] Xilinx, Partial Reconfiguration User Guide, 2010.

4

Blind Cartography for Side Channel Attacks: Cross-Correlation Cartography

Laurent Sauvage, Sylvain Guilley, Florent Flament, Jean-Luc Danger, and Yves Mathieu

Télécom ParisTech, Institut Télécom CNRS LTCI, 46 rue Barrault, F-75634 Paris Cedex 13, France

Correspondence should be addressed to Laurent Sauvage, laurent.sauvage@telecom-paristech.fr

Academic Editor: Kris Gaj

Side channel and fault injection attacks are major threats to cryptographic applications of embedded systems. Best performances for these attacks are achieved by focusing sensors or injectors on the sensible parts of the application, by means of dedicated methods to localise them. Few methods have been proposed in the past, and all of them aim at pinpointing the cryptoprocessor. However it could be interesting to exploit the activity of other parts of the application, in order to increase the attack's efficiency or to bypass its countermeasures. In this paper, we present a localisation method based on cross-correlation, which issues a list of areas of interest within the attacked device. It realizes an exhaustive analysis, since it may localise any module of the device, and not only those which perform cryptographic operations. Moreover, it also does not require a preliminary knowledge about the implementation, whereas some previous cartography methods require that the attacker could choose the cryptoprocessor inputs, which is not always possible. The method is experimentally validated using observations of the electromagnetic near field distribution over a Xilinx Virtex 5 FPGA. The matching between areas of interest and the application layout in the FPGA floorplan is confirmed by correlation analysis.

1. Introduction

Side channel attacks (SCA) and fault injection attacks (FIA) are very efficient techniques to retrieve secret data stored in cryptographic devices such as smartcards. First attacks have been performed globally, for instance by measuring the power consumption (power analysis: PA) [1] of a device under analysis (DUA) or by quickly changing the nominal voltage of its power supply [2]. But best results have then been achieved locally, by using a small EM probe just over the cryptoprocessor (electromagnetic analysis: EMA) [3] or by shooting at it with a laser beam [4, 5]. Indeed, for SCA, such locality permits to solely collect the activity of the cryptoprocessor, instead of gathering the activity of the whole DUA. In the case of FIA, depending on the technology process of the integrated circuit, only one bit of the implementation can be affected. However, the efficiency of these attacks relies on localisation methods which have to pinpoint as accurately as possible the DUA-sensitive areas. Using these localisation methods is mandatory in the case of a cryptographic application embedded in a field Programmable gate array (FPGA) as its regular structure prevents the localisation of sensible modules by optical or electron microscopy. Indeed, the task is easier for most ASICs, where the functional modules stand clearly out from a visual inspection of the layout as rectangular shapes. Some methods have been proposed in the past, illustrated using as observations the near electromagnetic (EM) field radiated by the DUA: an EM probe is moved over the DUA from a position to another one, and for each of them, the temporal variation of the EM field is measured with an oscilloscope. We use once again such cartography procedure in this paper. Furthermore, we note that all previously published localisation methods along with the one in this paper can deal with other physical phenomenons, such as photons emitted by transistors while they commute [6, 7].

Up to now, two strategies have been deployed to locate cryptographic modules within a DUA. They consist in identifying areas where the physical observations vary according to:

(1) the data processed during an encryption [8, 9] or

(2) the operations performed by the cryptographic module [10], even if this latter is protected against SCA [11].

With the first strategy, two observations are collected for two different plaintexts p_1 and p_2, and their fluctuations are assessed either by looking for the maximum difference in their temporal domain [8] or by calculating the incoherence of the frequency spectrum [9]. The larger the difference is or the lower the incoherence is, the closer to the cryptoprocessor the EM probe is. To improve the accuracy of the method, a third observation but of the same plaintext p_1 can be acquired, with a view to reject the measurement noise [8]. These approaches seem to be the most suitable because statistical tools which are then used, the CPA [12] for example, exploit plaintexts or ciphertexts as well. However, they would be optimal only if and only if the differences in the observations are maximal, which requires that all of the transistors making the datapath of the cryptoprocessor commute. This can happen only if the attacker knows the secret data, obviously the key but also the mask values when the DUA is protected by masking [13, 14], which is possible in the framework of an evaluation but not with a real-world application.

Instead of focusing on the same time slot, that of the encryption, and collecting two observations, the techniques of the second strategy need only one plaintext and take advantage of two or more time slots of a single observation. Typically, if the cryptoprocessor is in idle state, none of its transistors commute and the corresponding activity is at a low level. On the contrary, during an encryption, the activity is expected to be at a high level. Thus, the localisation of the cryptoprocessor can be achieved in the temporal domain by evaluating the difference between these activities [10]. To diminish the impact of the measurement noise, the localisation can be performed in the frequency domain: indeed, the succession of these low and high activity levels yields a special signature in the frequency spectrum [10]. As this succession still occurs for some countermeasures, the second strategy remains valid to localise protected cryptoprocessors. This fact is all the more true with protections using dual-rail with precharge logic (DPL [15]): as they alternate between two phases, namely, precharge and evaluation phases, they "oscillate" at the half of the master clock frequency, a frequential component of great interest for the frequency analysis [11].

Both previous strategies require to identify the time slot of some sensible operations, such as the encryption. This information can be extracted from the implementation netlist or by using simple power analysis (SPA) [1] or simple electromagnetic analysis (SEMA). Nonetheless, exploring the full implementation appears to be complex, at least time consuming and forces it to be partial, focused on few targets. In this paper, we propose a method to *exhaustively* locate the information sources of a DUA, *without preliminary knowledge* about it. This method is described in Section 2. Then, its ability to identify areas of interest, and in particular

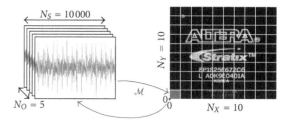

Figure 1: Cartography principle commonly used.

cryptographic modules, is evaluated in Section 3. Finally, Section 4 concludes this paper and presents some future works and perspectives.

2. Cross-Correlation Cartography

Cartography formally consists in monitoring one or more physical phenomenons at N_P positions over a DUA. Generally, these positions form a 2D grid composed of N_X and N_Y points over, respectively, the X and Y axes. N_X and N_Y could have the same value, for instance 10 as in Figure 1. For each of the $N_P = N_X \times N_Y$ positions, identified by their coordinates (x, y), N_O observations $O_{(x,y)}^0$ of N_S samples n are achieved. They constitute an observations set $\mathcal{O}_{(x,y)} = \{O_{(x,y)}^0, O_{(x,y)}^1, \ldots, O_{(x,y)}^{N_O-1}\}$. In the example of Figures 1 and 4 observations of 10,000 samples are collected per position. To build the final 2D map, each set $\mathcal{O}_{(x,y)}$ has to be reduced to a unique scalar $m_{(x,y)}$. The common usage is to apply a function $\mathcal{M}$ to the corresponding observations $O_{(x,y)}^0, O_{(x,y)}^1, \ldots, O_{(x,y)}^{N_O-1}$. From a "graphical" standpoint, the $m_{(x,y)}$ values, real numbers, are then mapped to colors according to a user-defined scale.

The localisation method we propose in this paper is motivated by the fact that the observation of a physical phenomenon depends on the time and on the space. In the SCA topic, the physical phenomenon we consider is the emanation of a digital integrated circuit. As the state of this circuit changes from a synchronization clock cycle to another one, the observations are made of successive peaks. The amplitude of each one of these peaks

(i) varies in the time according to the data manipulated by its source (see for instance Figure 7);

(ii) decreases when the distance between the source and the observation point increases.

In consequence, sources carrying distinct information generate physical phenomenons whose temporal variations look completely different, that is, *uncorrelated*. At the opposite, observations gathered at positions close to each other, and in particular at positions which are themselves close to a source, look very alike. Thus, to locate these sources, we collect a single observation $O_{(x,y)}^0$ per (x, y) position, then estimate the similarity level between all of these observations. While the methods presented in Section 1 consider (through the $\mathcal{M}$ function, see Figure 1) each observations set $\mathcal{O}_{(x,y)}$ independently from the other, we use conjointly all of them.

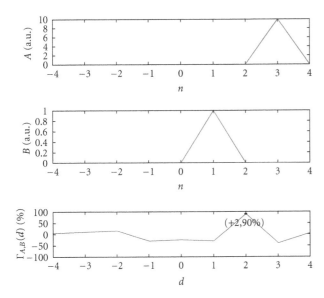

FIGURE 2: From top to bottom: one reference signal A, the same B but with a lower amplitude and delayed by two samples, and their normalized cross-correlation function $\Gamma_{A,B}(d)$.

The first step of our technique consists in taking each observation $O^0_{(x,y)}$ as a reference, then looking for the maximum of normalized cross-correlation (abridged NXC) between this reference and the other observations. The NXC function is defined as

$$\Gamma_{A,B}(d)$$
$$= \frac{\text{cov}(A, B_d)}{\sigma_A \cdot \sigma_B}$$
$$= \frac{\sum_{n=d}^{d+\inf(N_A, N_B)-1} \left(A(n) - \overline{A(n)}\right) \cdot \left(B(n-d) - \overline{B(n)}\right)}{\sqrt{\sum_{n=0}^{N_A-1} \left(A(n) - \overline{A(n)}\right)^2} \cdot \sqrt{\sum_{n=0}^{N_B-1} \left(B(n-d) - \overline{B(n)}\right)^2}}.$$
$$(1)$$

In (1), $\text{cov}(\cdot, \cdot)$ stands for the covariance, A and B are two observations (at two different points), which, respectively, have N_A and N_B temporal samples, whose mean values are $\overline{A(n)}$ and $\overline{B(n)}$, and whose standard deviations are σ_A and σ_B. B_d means that a delay d belonging to the interval from $-(N_B - 1)$ to $N_A - 1$ is applied to B. From a "graphical" standpoint, the waveform of B is shifted to the right along the temporal X-axis, or in other words the origin $n = 0$ of B is moved to $n = m$. We simply abridge A_0 as A and note that $\sigma_{B_d} = \sigma_B$ because the standard deviation is considered over the complete waveform (and is thus independent of the offset d). Figure 2 shows the variations of the NXC function $\Gamma_{A,B}(d)$ according to the d values, when A and B are two signals with an identical shape, but distinct amplitudes, are delayed by two samples. The maximum value of $\Gamma_{A,B}(d)$ indicates that A and B are 90% similar, while the index of this maximum, 2, provides the sample delay between A and B. The value of $\Gamma_{A,B}(d)$ does not reach 100% because of computational side-effects: the X-axis is not infinite but bounds to $[-4; +4]$.

To briefly illustrate the result of such computation, we provide two NXC maps on Figure 3. The first one, (a), has

been obtained considering the center of the map as the reference point. Maximum correlation values are at a very low level, lightly positive in red on the map, or negative in blue, except for the reference point, which by definition is 100% correlated to itself and takes the yellow point in the center. It does not identify a source of interest, because it is insulated. On the second map, (b) of Figure 3, an area of high correlation (in yellow) stands out around the reference point located at $X = -7.90$ mm and $Y = 12.0$ mm and is marked with a white cross. This zone has a size greater than the actual active logic in the FPGA and notably extends outside the silicon chip's boundary, depicted in a white dashed line. The diffusion of the EM field accounts for this extension of a couple of millimeters around the radiating logic. Indeed, in our setup, the distance between the loop sensor and the silicon surface is roughly speaking equal to 2 mm. Above, a second area emerges in blue, with a negative correlation value, as the observations correspond to EM field measurements, these ones, and in turn the correlation values, may be of opposite sign. But in reality, this second blue area contains the same information as the first yellow area does. Therefore, to prevent such artifact, we now consider the *absolute* maximum values of the normalized cross-correlation function.

Each observation gathered at a position of the 2D grid become in turn a reference observation, we finally collect N_P NXC maps. Most of them are alike, as computed at neighbouring points, close to physical sources. The second step of our technique aims at grouping them. For this purpose, we need once again a correlation estimator, but this time, as we manipulate maps, this one should take into account the two dimensions x and y. This bidimensional estimator, namely, $\Gamma^{2D}_{M,N}(p,q)$, is defined as:

$$\Gamma^{2D}_{M,N}(p,q) = \frac{\text{cov}\left(M, N_{(p,q)}\right)}{\sigma_M \cdot \sigma_N}, \qquad (2)$$

where

$$\text{cov}\left(M, N_{(p,q)}\right) = \sum_{x=p}^{x_{\max}} \sum_{y=q}^{y_{\max}} \left(M(x,y) - \overline{M(x,y)}\right)$$
$$\cdot \left(N(x-p, y-q) - \overline{N(x,y)}\right),$$
$$\text{with } x_{\max} = p + \inf(N_{X_M}, N_{X_N}) - 1$$
$$\text{and } y_{\max} = q + \inf(N_{Y_M}, N_{Y_N}) - 1,$$

$$\sigma_M = \sqrt{\sum_{x=0}^{N_{X_M}} \sum_{y=0}^{N_{Y_M}} \left(M(x,y) - \overline{M(x,y)}\right)^2},$$

$$\sigma_N = \sqrt{\sum_{x=0}^{N_{X_N}} \sum_{y=0}^{N_{Y_N}} \left(N(x-p, y-q) - \overline{N(x,y)}\right)^2}.$$
$$(3)$$

In this equation, M and N are two maps, of N_{X_M} and N_{X_N} points on x, N_{Y_M} and N_{Y_N} points on y, whose mean values

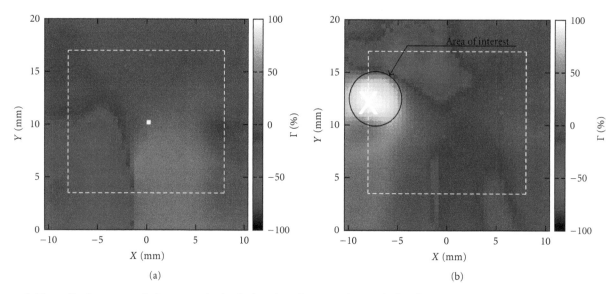

FIGURE 3: Normalized cross-correlation maps obtained when the reference point, marked with a white cross, is useless (a) or of interest (b).

are $\overline{M(x,y)}$ and $\overline{N(x,y)}$ and standard deviations σ_M and σ_N. $N_{(p,q)}$ means that a spacial offset is applied to the map N, so that its origin point $(0,0)$ is moved to (p,q). This offset is useful when the objective is to find the location of a small pattern within a reference map. In this paper, as we compare maps with identical size, p and q are set to zero. As previously, we fix a reference map, then we look for the maximum of the absolute value of $\Gamma^{2D}_{M,N}(p,q)$. If this maximum is greater than a user-defined threshold, maps are considered as identical and grouped in the same list. Every list is called an area of interest.

To finish the analysis, one map per list has to be extracted. It could be randomly chosen, but we suggest to select the map for which the number of points with a value above under, respectively, a user-defined threshold is the greatest. The corresponding map is the one with the widest, nearest area. The full method is summarized by the Algorithm 1. In this algorithm, the selection of areas of interest is represented by a function called "*extract*."

3. Experimental Results

To evaluate the efficiency of our method, we have used it against an FPGA-based cryptoprocessor performing the simple and triple Data Encryption Standard (3DES) [16], and protected by first-order Boolean masking [13, 14]. In practice, we have implemented the same masking scheme as in [17]. We concur this design is obsolete for at least two reasons. First of all, DES has been replaced by the Advanced Encryption Standard (AES) [18] since the year 2001. Second, the employed masking scheme is not robust against High-Order Side Channel Attack (HO-SCA) [17, 19]. Nonetheless, the objective of this section is not to come up with a new attack to break a still considered invulnerable countermeasure, but to experimentally prove that our method identifies areas of interest, and in particular two

sensible 64-bit registers, LR and MASK, carrying respectively the masked value and the mask itself.

To make the experiment easier, we have constrained their placement so that they may fit in rectangular areas, themselves placed at the opposite sides of the FPGA. As depicted by Figure 4, MASK is at the top left hand corner, while LR is at the bottom right hand corner. Splitting these registers in such a way has spread the routing of the 3DES cryptoprocessor datapath all over the FPGA. Therefore, in a view to keep the other components of our implementation visible, for the 3DES datapath, only its logic cells are displayed. They appear as black dots in the upper half part of the floorplan. The KEY scheduling block is at the bottom right of Figure 4, in salmon, while the 3DES CONTROLler, in green, is in the middle, on the left. Close to this latter, we find a 6502 CISC CPU in olive and an UART in turquoise. All previous components share a VCI bus along with its memories, in gold in Figure 4. This real-life application has been programmed into a Xilinx [20] Virtex 5 FPGA, whose metallic lid has been removed with a cutter, as shown in Figure 5. This way, not only we can reduce the analysis area strictly to the FPGA silicon die, but the signal to noise ratio is also greatly improved.

Observations have been acquired using a 2 mm diameter EM probe, a 3 GHz bandwidth 30 dB gain preamplifier, and an Agilent [21] Infiniium 54854 oscilloscope, whose bandwidth and sampling rate have been set up to, respectively, 3 GHz and 10 GSa/s. The EM probe has been moved following a 25×25 points grid, per step of 480 μm along the X-axis, and 400 μm along the Y-axis. The grid is rather rectangular, since we covered the whole silicon die of the Virtex 5 (refer to Figure 5): 12 mm wide and 10 mm high. Then, maps have been grouped together according to a threshold of 90%, that is, two maps whose 2D cross-correlation coefficient is greater than 90% are considered as identical and gathered in the same list. Finally, we have counted for each map the number of points with a correlation level above 90%. From each list,

Require: One observation per point
Ensure: List of identical maps
   For each 2D grid point (x, y) **do** {Fixed reference point A}
     {/* Looping over all fixed reference points A */}
     $x\ ref \leftarrow x$
     $y\ ref \leftarrow y$
     for each 2D grid point (x, y) **do**
       {/* Looping over all mobile points B */}
       $m(x, y) \leftarrow \max_d(|\Gamma_{O(x\ ref, y\ ref), O(x,y)}(d)|)$
     end for
     $map(x\ ref, y\ ref) \leftarrow m$
   end for
   $i \leftarrow 0$ {/* Index of areas of interest */}
   for each 2D grid point (x, y) **do**
     {/* Looping over all fixed reference points A */}
     $x\ ref \leftarrow x$
     $y\ ref \leftarrow y$
     $list[i] \leftarrow map(x\ ref, y\ ref)$
     for each 2D grid point (x, y) **do**
       {/* Looping over all mobile points B */}
       $M_r \leftarrow map(x\ ref, y\ ref)$
       $M_c \leftarrow map(x, y)$
       if $M_c \notin list$ and $\max(|\Gamma_{M_r, M_c}^{2D}(0, 0)|) > threshold$
       then
         $list[i] \leftarrow map(x, y)$
       end if
     end for
     $i \leftarrow i + 1$
   end for
   for $j = 0$ to i **do**
     $area(j) \leftarrow extract\ (list[j])$
   end for

ALGORITHM 1: Algorithm for grouping maps per area of interest.

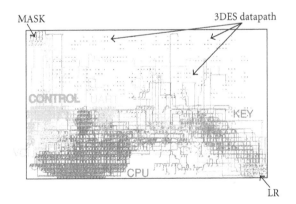

FIGURE 4: Floorplan of the cryptographic application under ISE floorplanner.

FIGURE 5: Photograph of the FPGA chip whose cryptographic modules are to be located by cross-correlation cartography.

we have extracted only the map with the greatest number of such points.

Proceeding this way, we have obtained eleven areas of interest. The nine most significant ones are reported on Figure 6, with a disposition in the page that reflects their location within the FPGA. As in Figure 3, reference points

are marked with a white cross. The maps (a) and (i) pinpoint two areas in the top left hand and bottom right hand corners. At first sight, they correspond to the two sensible registers LR and MASK. To confirm this, we have conducted large acquisition campaigns of 1,000 observations per point, then computed for each of them the CEMA factor, that is, CPA (Correlation Power Analysis) with electromagnetic waves. We denote by ρ this CEMA factor, to distinguish it from Γ, the NXC coefficient defined in (1). Note that we use data

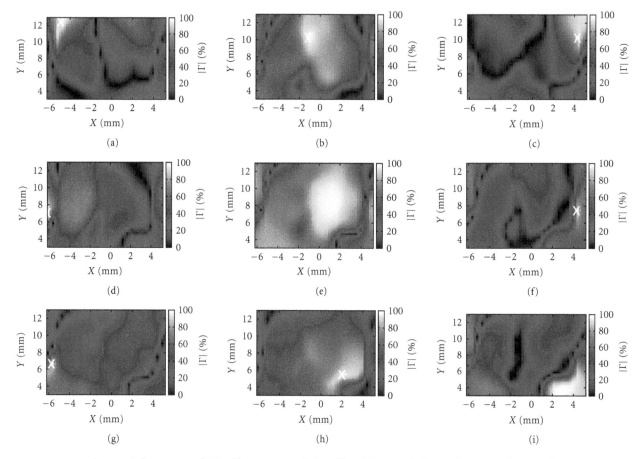

FIGURE 6: Some maps obtained by cross-correlation. The white cross indicates the point of greatest Γ.

normally not accessible to an attacker such as the mask's value: this is, however, possible in an evaluation context. The resulting maps for the MASK and LR registers are depicted by Figure 8. The CEMA clearly identifies that area of interest (a) is correlated with the mask and that area (i) is correlated with the masked data. In these two CEMA maps, the point with the maximum ρ correlation is marked with a white cross. This location coincides almost exactly with that of maximum Γ in the NXC maps. Hence, the proof that the methodology succeeds in insulating areas of consistent activity. Therefore, our main objective has been successfully reached. This result is very precious to continue with a HO-SCA (second order) taking advantage of this spatial diversity: LR is leaking more about the masked data, whereas MASK discloses information more related to the mask. HO-SCA such as those based on correlation reviewed in [22] or the one based on information theory in [23] would advantageously combine observations over these points. Identifying the other areas is not trivial as their shapes do not fit the arrangement of Figure 4. Indeed, EM radiations are generally more likely due to the power grid and the clock tree of the FPGA [10] than to its logic cells and routing paths.

To complement the analysis, Figure 7 delivers the output voltage of the EM probe when this latter is just over the points of interest. Except for the map (f), the 16 rounds of the DES encryption are neatly visible in the right hand part of

the observations. The 16 peaks amplitude varies in time, but not in the same way from a position to another one, which confirms that we observe the activity of distinct elements. We guess that the observation that coincides with the locations:

(i) (e) and/or (h) may be due to the key scheduling;

(ii) (d) and/or (g) to some reads/writes on the VCI bus;

(iii) (b) and/or (c) and/or (f) to some combinatorial functions in the 3DES datapath, such as exclusive logical OR.

We insist that our blind cartography method does not actually distinguish cryptographic blocks from the others. But still, the method has the following interests.

(i) It highlights "equivalent areas" for EMA. Once those areas of interest are localized, the attacker can focus her measurements on them. In our example, this reduces the number of positions from $25 \times 25 = 625$ to only 11.

(ii) Applied to the second-order attack of a first-order masking scheme, the number of combinations to be tested to match the mask and the masked data activity is only $\binom{11}{2} = 55$. Without NXC, the number of couples to test would be equal to $\binom{25 \times 25}{2} \approx 200,000$, which is deterrent for an attacker, but the computational workload is too high.

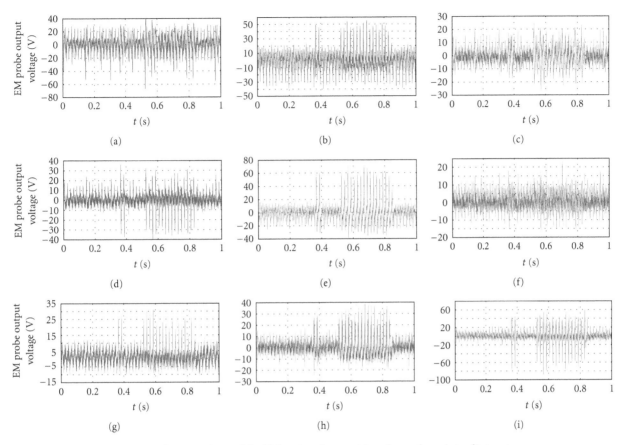

FIGURE 7: Output voltage of the EM probe when positioned over the points of interest.

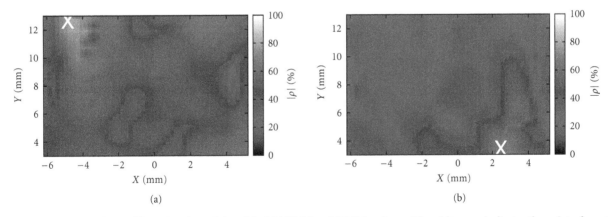

FIGURE 8: CEMA maps obtained knowing the activity of the MASK (a) and LR (b) registers. The white cross indicates the point of greatest ρ.

4. Conclusion and Future Works

Many implementation-level attacks can be enhanced if the floorplan of the application is known by the attacker. For instance, side-channel measurements can be made less noisy if focused on the most leaking zone, and fault injection attacks (by electromagnetic waves or laser shots) have indeed more chance to succeed in perturbing the adequate resource if positioned well in a vicinity of the zone of influence. As far as ASICs are concerned, the location of each module can be guessed by an optical analysis of chip photographs.

Modern ASICs (such as modern smartcards) have their logic dissolved so as to make its analysis intractable. Now, regarding FPGAs, the problem is the same, since the fabric is extremely regular and does not show the location of the user design. In addition, FPGA chips are wider than ASICs, thus the research for sensitive regions is *a priori* more complex.

In this paper, we introduce a novel location method based on cross-correlation of electromagnetic cartographies. It is indeed able to reveal the position of blocks. This shows that the structure of the floorplan shall not be considered confidential in FPGAs, even if the bitstream is confidential (e.g., encrypted). Then, we experimentally demonstrate that the cross-correlation location method is efficient to pinpoint areas of interest in the context of a protected cryptographic application. This methodology illustrates a new aspect of the wealth of the information carried out by the electromagnetic field leaked by electronic devices. The floorplan reverse-engineering method presented in this paper is an algorithm-agnostic preliminary step that enables the further realization of well-focused electromagnetic analysis attacks aiming this time at extracting secrets. We have exemplified this method with the successful localization of the registers that hold the mask and the masked data that are manipulated con-comitantly. Being able to record traces from both locations allows for second-order attacks by combination of the twain measurements [24]. Also, the same method could be used to record traces selectively from one half of separable dual-rail logic styles (such as SDDL [25, Section 3.1], DWDDL [26], divided backend duplication [27], partial DDL [28], or PA-DDL [29]) thereby defeating the complementation property of those "hiding" countermeasures.

References

[1] P. C. Kocher, J. Jaffe, and B. Jun, "Differential power analysis," in *Proceedings of the 19th Annual International Cryptology Conference Advances in Cryptology (CRYPTO '99)*, vol. 1666 of *Lecture Notes in Computer Science*, pp. 388–397, Springer, Santa Barbara, Cali, USA, 1999.

[2] R. Anderson and M. Kuhn, "Tamper resistance—a cautionary note," in *Proceedings of the 2nd USENIX Workshop on Electronic Commerce (WOEC'96)*, pp. 1–11, USENIX Association, Berkeley, Calif, USA, 1996.

[3] K. Gandolfi, C. Mourtel, and F. Olivier, "Electromagnetic analysis: concrete results," in *Proceedings of the 3rd International Workshop Cryptographic Hardware and Embedded Systems (CHES'01)*, C. K. Koc, D. Naccache, and C. Paar, Eds., vol. 2162 of *Lecture Notes in Computer Science*, pp. 251–261, Springer, Paris, France, 2001.

[4] M. Agoyan, J.-M. Dutertre, A.-P. Mirbaha, D. Naccache, A.-L. Ribotta, and A. Tria, "Single-bit DFA using multiple-byte laser fault injection," in *Proceedings of the IEEE International Conference on Technologies for Homeland Security (HST'10)*, pp. 113–119, 2010.

[5] G. Canivet, J. Clédière, J. B. Ferron, F. Valette, M. Renaudin, and R. Leveugle, "Detailed analyses of single laser shot effects in the configuration of a Virtex-II FPGA," in *14th IEEE International On-Line Testing Symposium, (IOLTS '08)*, pp. 289–294, Rhodes, Greece, 2008.

[6] S. P. Skorobogatov, "Using optical emission analysis for estimating contribution to power analysis," in *Proceedings of the 6th International Workshop on Fault Diagnosis and Tolerance in Cryptography (FDTC '09)*, pp. 111–119, IEEE Computer Society, Lausanne, Switzerland, 2009.

[7] J. Di-Battista, J.-C. Courrège, B. Rouzeyre, L. Torres, and P. Perdu, "When failure analysis meets side-channel attacks," in *Proceedings of the 12th International Workshop Cryptographic Hardware and Embedded Systems (CHES '10)*, Santa Barbara, Calif, USA, 2010.

[8] D. Réal, F. Valette, and M. Drissi, "Enhancing correlation electromagnetic attack using planar near-field cartography," in *Proceedings of the Design, Automation and Test in Europe, (DATE '09)*, pp. 628–633, IEEE, Nice, France, April 2009.

[9] A. Dehbaoui, V. Lomne, P. Maurine, and L. Torres, "Magnitude squared incoherence em analysis for integrated cryptographic module localisation," *Electronics Letters*, vol. 45, no. 15, pp. 778–780, 2009.

[10] L. Sauvage, S. Guilley, and Y. Mathieu, "ElectroMagnetic radiations of FPGAs: high spatial resolution cartography and attack of a cryptographic module," *ACM Transactions on Reconfigurable Technology and Systems*, vol. 2, no. 1, pp. 1–24, 2009.

[11] L. Sauvage, S. Guilley, J.-L. Danger, Y. Mathieu, and M. Nassar, "Successful attack on an FPGA-based WDDL DES cryptoprocessor without place and route constraints," in *Proceedings of the Design, Automation and Test in Europe (DATE'09)*, pp. 640–645, IEEE, Nice, France, April, 2009.

[12] É. Brier, C. Clavier, and F. Olivier, "Correlation power analysis with a leakage model," in *Proceedings of the 6th International Workshop Cryptographic Hardware and Embedded Systems (CHES'04)*, vol. 3156 of *Lecture Notes in Computer Science*, pp. 16–29, Springer, Cambridge, Mass, USA, August, 2004.

[13] L. Goubin and J. Patarin, "DES and differential power analysis (The "Duplication" Method)," in *Proceedings of the 1st International Workshop Cryptographic Hardware and Embedded Systems (CHES'99)*, vol. 1717 of *Lecture Notes in Computer Science*, pp. 158–172, Worcester, Mass, USA, August, 1999.

[14] S. Chari, C. S. Jutla, J. R. Rao, and P. Rohatgi, "Towards sound approaches to counteract power-analysis attacks," in *Proceedings of the 19th Annual International Cryptology Conference Advances in Cryptology (CRYPTO '99)*, vol. 1666 of *Lecture Notes in Computer Science*, pp. 398–412, Springer, Santa Barbara, Calif, USA, August, 1999.

[15] J.-L. Danger, S. Guilley, S. Bhasin, and M. Nassar, "Overview of dual rail with precharge logic styles to thwart implementation-level attacks on hardware cryptoprocessors," in *Proceedings of the 3rd International Conference on Signals, Circuits and Systems (SCS'09)*, pp. 1–8, IEEE, Jerba, Tunisia, November 2009.

[16] National Institute of Standards and Technology, "Data Encryption Standard (DES): FIPS PUB 46-3," 1999, http://csrc.nist.gov/publications/fips/fips46-3/fips46-3.pdf. .

[17] E. Peeters, F.-X. Standaert, N. Donckers, and J.-J. Quisquater, "Improved higher-order side-channel attacks with FPGA experiments," in *Proceedings of the 7th International Workshop Cryptographic Hardware and Embedded Systems (CHES '05)*, vol. 3659 of *Lecture Notes in Computer Science*, pp. 309–323, Springer, Edinburgh, UK, 2005.

[18] National Institute of Standards and Technology, "Advanced Encryption Standard (AES): FIPS PUB 197," 2001, http://csrc.nist.gov/publications/fips/fips197/fips-197.pdf.

[19] T. S. Messerges, "Using second-order power analysis to attack DPA resistant software," in *Proceedings of the 2nd International Workshop Cryptographic Hardware and Embedded Systems (CHES'00)*, vol. 1965 of *Lecture Notes in Computer Science*, pp. 238–251, Springer, Worcester, Mass, USA, August, 2000.

[20] "Xilinx FPGA designer," http://www.xilinx.com/.

[21] "Agilent Technologies," http://www.home.agilent.com/.

[22] E. Prouff, M. Rivain, and R. Bévan, "Statistical analysis of second order differential power analysis," *IEEE Transactions on Computers*, vol. 58, no. 6, pp. 799–811, 2009.

[23] B. Gierlichs, L. Batina, B. Preneel, and I. Verbauwhede, "Revisiting higher-order DPA attacks: multivariate mutual information analysis," in *Proceedings of the The Cryptographer's Track at RSA Conference (CT-RSA'10)*, vol. 5985 of *Lecture Notes in Computer Science*, pp. 221–234, Springer, San Francisco, Calif, USA, March 2010.

[24] E. Prouff, M. Rivain, and R. Bévan, "Statistical analysis of second order differential power analysis," *IEEE Transactions on Computers*, vol. 58, no. 6, pp. 799–811, 2009.

[25] K. Tiri and I. Verbauwhede, "A logic level design methodology for a secure DPA resistant ASIC or FPGA implementation," in *Proceedings of the Design, Automation and Test in Europe Conference and Exhibition (DATE'04)*, pp. 246–251, IEEE Computer Society, Paris, France, February 2004.

[26] P. Yu and P. Schaumont, "Secure FPGA circuits using controlled placement and routing," in *Proceedings of the 5th IEEE/ACM international conference on Hardware/software codesign and system synthesis (CODES+ISSS'07)*, pp. 45–50, ACM, New York, NY, USA, 2007.

[27] K. Baddam and M. Zwolinski, "Divided Backend duplication methodology for balanced dual rail routing," in *Proceedings of the Cryptographic Hardware and Embedded Systems (CHES '08)*, vol. 5154 of *Lecture Notes in Computer Science*, pp. 396–410, Springer, Washington, DC, USA, 2008.

[28] J.-P. Kaps and R. Velegalati, "DPA Resistant AES on FPGA Using Partial DDL," in *Proceedings of the 18th IEEE Annual International Symposium on Field-Programmable Custom Computing Machine (FCCM'10)*, pp. 273–280, IEEE Computer Society, Charlotte, NC, USA, May, 2010.

[29] W. He, E. D. L. Torre, and T. Riesgo, "A precharge-absorbed DPL logic for reducing early propagation effects on FPGA implementations," in *Proceedings of the ReConFig*, IEEE Computer Society, Quintana Roo, México, 2011.

5

Object Recognition and Pose Estimation on Embedded Hardware: SURF-Based System Designs Accelerated by FPGA Logic

Michael Schaeferling, Ulrich Hornung, and Gundolf Kiefer

Department of Computer Science, Augsburg University of Applied Sciences, An der Hochschule 1, 86161 Augsburg, Germany

Correspondence should be addressed to Michael Schaeferling, michael.schaeferling@hs-augsburg.de
and Gundolf Kiefer, gundolf.kiefer@hs-augsburg.de

Academic Editor: René Cumplido

State-of-the-art object recognition and pose estimation systems often utilize point feature algorithms, which in turn usually require the computing power of conventional PC hardware. In this paper, we describe two embedded systems for object detection and pose estimation using sophisticated point features. The feature detection step of the "Speeded-up Robust Features (SURF)" algorithm is accelerated by a special IP core. The first system performs object detection and is completely implemented in a single medium-size Virtex-5 FPGA. The second system is an augmented reality platform, which consists of an ARM-based microcontroller and intelligent FPGA-based cameras which support the main system.

1. Introduction

Computer vision (CV) and augmented reality (AR) are growing areas of research with many applications. For example, automotive industry makes use of passive optical sensors in the field of offboard traffic observation and management [1–3]. Onboard systems often utilize CV techniques for driver assistance and traffic sign detection [4, 5]. Turning CV to account, AR enhances real environments by virtual elements and allows manifold applications such as guided order picking or maintenance tasks [6, 7].

Optical object detection and pose estimation are very challenging tasks since they have to deal with problems such as different views of an object, various light conditions, surface reflections, and noise caused by image sensors. Presently available algorithms such as SIFT or SURF can to some extent solve these problems as they compute so-called point features, which are invariant towards scaling and rotation [8–11]. However, these algorithms are computationally complex and require powerful hardware in order to operate in real time. In automotive applications and generally in the field of mobile devices, limited processing power and the demand for low battery power consumption play an important role. Hence, adopting those sophisticated point feature algorithms

to mobile hardware is an ambitious, but also necessary computer engineering task.

This paper describes two embedded systems for SURF-based object recognition and pose estimation. The first system performs feature-based object recognition and has been implemented as a SoC on a single FPGA (Virtex-5 FX70). It can process images at a frame rate of up to five frames per second and (in our experiments) recognize and distinguish 9 different objects at a sensitivity of 91% and a specificity of 100% (no false positives). The second system determines the 3D pose of one or more objects. It features an ARM microcontroller board and is equipped with two FPGA-based cameras which support the main system in the stage of feature detection. As this system is very power efficient, it may be used as a mobile AR system, for example, for educational or training applications.

Among the existing feature detection and description algorithms, SURF is considered to be both robust and efficient [8, 12]. However, it is still very demanding in terms of computational effort and memory bandwidth, especially within the detector stage. One of the core parts of the presented systems is *Flex-SURF+*, a configurable hardware module which accelerates the time-critical part of the SURF detector [13, 14]. It contains an array of *Difference Elements*

(DEs) in order to overcome the irregular memory access behavior exposed by SURF during the computation of image filter responses. A special computing pipeline processes these filter responses and determines the final detection results. Due to its customizable and flexible structure, *Flex-SURF+* allows a tradeoff between area and speed. This flexibility allows to efficiently implement this IP core within high-end FPGAs as well as low-end ones, depending on the application requirements. Besides accelerating the SURF algorithm by means of configurable hardware, lightweight object recognition and pose estimation algorithms have been designed to minimize the computational effort and memory requirements of the software part.

Section 2 gives an overview on related work concerning different implementations of SURF, object recognition, and pose estimation. Section 3 summarizes the SURF algorithm and describes the *Flex-SURF+* hardware module which is used to accelerate the feature detection step of SURF. Section 4 presents the one-chip object recognition system, followed by the pose estimation system in Section 5. The main hardware components and developed software frameworks are disclosed, providing an overview on the algorithms and some implementation details. A conclusion to this work is provided in Section 6.

2. Related Work

With increasing processing power of conventional PC hardware, object recognition nowadays is often based on natural features. These may be global or local features, where global features evaluate the whole image space (e.g., by comprising the image histogram) and local (point) features solely use significant areas of the image to gain scene information [15]. Many application fields greatly benefit from feature recognition techniques. Especially autonomous robot systems as well as automotive systems are popular fields where optical image processing is used to solve manifold problems [16]. Recent publications even deal with safety-related topics such as car recognition, collision avoidance, or traffic and danger sign recognition [1–3, 17, 18]. The impact of very difficult light conditions may be weakened, for example, by applying point feature algorithms to infrared images for pedestrian or vehicle detection [19].

Common algorithms for detecting and describing point features are the Harris Corner Detector [10], SIFT [11], and SURF [9]. Providing local features, both SIFT and SURF actually outperform global features whereby in terms of speed SURF is considered to be ahead of SIFT [8, 12]. These algorithms have been developed with high distinctiveness of features in combination with scale and rotation invariance in mind. As such, they are very demanding in terms of computational power and in their original form need to be implemented on powerful, PC-like hardware [16].

For this reason, it is desirable to speed up these algorithms. This may, for example, be achieved by the use of modern GPU hardware [20, 21]. Other proposals focus on reducing the algorithmic complexity, for example, by combining different approaches in feature recognition and description [22] or software optimizations [23].

An important technique to accelerate feature detection is the use of programmable logic (FPGAs). Application-specific logic allows to implement specific functionality at low power consumption compared to conventional PC and GPU hardware, making it an attractive candidate especially for mobile applications. An overview of several implementations of the SIFT algorithm is given in [24]. FPGA implementations of SURF have been proposed independently in [13, 25, 26]. In contrast to the other two approaches, the architecture of [13] is scalable and does not need any block RAM resources of the FPGA, thus it has been chosen to be integrated in both the object recognition system and the augmented reality framework.

3. Hardware-Accelerated Feature Extraction

The most time-critical components of the presented object recognition and pose estimation systems are the detection and the description of SURF feature points.

In the following subsections, we give a short overview on the SURF algorithm and present an outline of the *Flex-SURF+* module. This module gains speedup by improving memory access behavior and parallelizing arithmetic operations where it is adequate.

3.1. Overview on the SURF Algorithm. *Flex-SURF+* is based on the *OpenSURF* implementation of the original SURF algorithm. (Open)SURF operates in two main stages, namely the *detector* and the *descriptor* stage. The detector analyzes the image and returns a list of center points for prominent features. For each point, the descriptor stage computes a vector characterizing the appearance of the feature. Both stages require an *integral image* to be computed in advance. Figure 1 shows the overall flow of the SURF algorithm.

Integral images can be used to efficiently calculate the sum of pixel values of upright rectangular image areas. Given the original image I, each pixel (x, y) of the integral image I_Σ contains the sum of all image pixel values above and to the left of (x, y):

$$I_\Sigma(x, y) = \sum_{i=0}^{i \leq x} \sum_{j=0}^{j \leq y} I(i, j). \tag{1}$$

After calculating the integral image once, the summation of any rectangular area of the original image can be determined with a constantly low effort by adding/subtracting the four integral image values enclosing the desired rectangle as depicted in Figure 2. In SURF, integral images are used to minimize the incurring memory bandwidth and computational effort when calculating box filter responses in the detector and descriptor stage.

In the detector stage, SURF first filters the entire image using 3 box filter kernels, which are depicted in Figure 3. White, gray, and black pixels refer to a weighting of the corresponding pixel value by 1, 0, and -2 for D_{xx} and D_{yy} filters and 1, 0, and -1 for D_{xy}, respectively. In order to achieve scale invariance, the image is filtered multiple times for different scale levels σ, where the kernel sizes increase with σ (see [9] for details). With the concept of integral

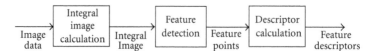

FIGURE 1: Stages of the SURF algorithm.

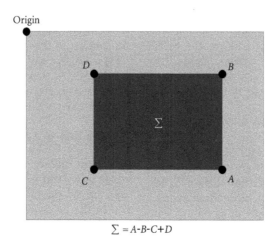

$$\Sigma = A\text{-}B\text{-}C\text{+}D$$

FIGURE 2: Summation calculation of a rectangular image area using an integral image.

images, the number of memory accesses is independent of σ, as only those few pixels marked with a dot in Figure 3 need to be accessed. Figure 4 depicts the combination of all these pixels for two different kernel sizes.

Box filter responses D_{xx}, D_{yy} and D_{xy} represent the entries of the Hessian Matrix H, which are determined for each point coordinate (x, y) and scale level σ. As the used filter kernels are actually approximations of Gaussian filters, a weight factor ω is used to compensate the occurring approximation error:

$$H(x, y, \sigma) = \begin{bmatrix} D_{xx}(x, y, \sigma) & \omega D_{xy}(x, y, \sigma) \\ \omega D_{xy}(x, y, \sigma) & D_{yy}(x, y, \sigma) \end{bmatrix}. \quad (2)$$

In *Flex-SURF+*, a value of $\omega^2 = 0.875$ is used as proposed in [18]. The determinant $\det(H)$ is an indicator for the quality of a feature point candidate:

$$\det(H) = D_{xx}D_{xy} - \omega^2 D_{xy}{}^2. \quad (3)$$

Determinants that fall below a given threshold T or which are not the local maximum within their $3 \times 3 \times 3$ neighborhood around (x, y, σ) are suppressed.

The descriptor stage of SURF calculates a descriptor vector for each feature found by the detector. To this end, Haar wavelets are applied to the pixels within a square window which is centered around the feature point and whose size depends on the features scale σ. To achieve rotation invariance, it optionally can be rotated according to a feature direction. The final result is a 64-dimensional floating point descriptor vector which is commonly used in a subsequent feature matching stage. To speed up the matching process,

feature candidates are partitioned with the help of the sign of the Laplacian lap(H):

$$\text{lap}(H) = \text{sgn}\left(D_{xx} + D_{yy}\right). \quad (4)$$

More details on SURF and *OpenSURF* can be found in [9, 27], respectively.

3.2. Overview of the Flex-SURF+ Module. The design of *Flex-SURF+* uses the concept of *tile-based processing*, as it is introduced in [13] and further developed in [14]. Its main idea is to minimize repeated memory accesses to the same pixels.

During image filtering in the detector stage of SURF, scattered memory accesses at multiple filter sizes according to Figure 4 are needed for the calculation of the filter responses. However, memory footprints for neighboring points overlap. Figure 5 shows the combined footprint which results from applying 9×9 filter kernels to a group of 4×4 neighboring points. The darkness of a cell indicates how often the respective memory location is accessed. A *tile* is defined by the minimum rectangle enclosing the overlapping memory footprints for a group of points. The whole image is divided into such point groups, whose filter responses are now calculated in parallel. The *Flex-SURF+* module contains an array of small worker units called *Difference Elements (DE)*, whereby the size of the array corresponds to the arrangement of the point groups. Each *DE* is responsible for the calculation of the filter responses D_{xx}, D_{yy}, and D_{xy} for one particular point of the group. A central instance performs the memory accesses and efficiently reads the required tile data in a linear way. Each worker unit autonomously picks the relevant image data from the memory data stream. After completing the filter

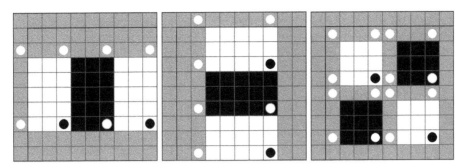

FIGURE 3: D_{xx}, D_{yy}, and D_{xy} filters of size 9×9.

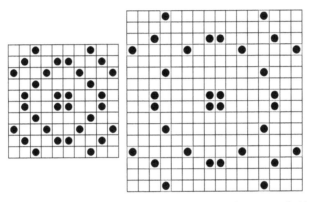

FIGURE 4: Joint memory footprint of D_{xx}, D_{yy}, and D_{xy} filter kernels of size 9×9 (left) and 15×15 (right).

response calculations, the worker units pass their results to a central unit which calculates determinants and Laplacians.

The main building blocks of *Flex-SURF+* are depicted in Figure 6. The *Memory Access Module (MAM)* contains the main controller logic which performs linear memory accesses over the system bus. After issuing burst read accesses to this bus, incoming pixel values are distributed to a configurable and arbitrarily large array of *Difference Elements (DEs)* over the *Image Data Bus (IDB)*. Simultaneously with the incoming *Image Data Enable* signal from the *MAM*, an *Enable Unit (EU)* generates enable signals, depending on the recent filter kernel size as illustrated in Figure 4. According to these enable signals, each *DE* picks the relevant pixel data from the *IDB* and calculates its filter responses.

In order to save area, multiple *DEs* may share one *EU*, together forming a *DE line*. Over the *Filter Response Chain (FRC)*, the filter responses are passed to the proximate *Determinant Calculation Pipeline (DCP)* which then calculates determinants and Laplacians. Finally, determinants and Laplacians are written back into system memory by the *MAM* which consecutively are used in the descriptor calculation step.

Unlike the work presented in [25] or [26], this whole system does not need any internal memory arrays and can therefore be implemented without using any valuable block RAM resources.

3.3. Array of Difference Elements. The efficiency of *Flex-SURF+* highly depends on the number of filter operations

which can be performed in parallel. To allow large arrays of *DEs*, it is essential to minimize the size of an individual *DE*.

One *DE* merely consists of two 26 bit adders, three 26 bit registers to hold intermediate results, and one 21 bit register for result propagation as depicted in Figure 7.

Each *DE* receives the image data stream, broadcasted via the *IDB*. According to the *EU's* enable signal, each *DE* picks relevant image data from the IDB and immediately accumulates this value to the corresponding D_{xx}, D_{yy} or D_{xy} filter value. As soon as all of the three filter responses are fully computed by a *DE*, they are passed to the *DCP*. To avoid large multiplexer structures, we decided to daisy-chain (*FRC*) the *DEs* for the result propagation towards the *DCP*. As the *DEs* provide filter responses one after another anyway, this propagation structure does not introduce any significant delay to the overall system.

3.4. Determinant Calculation Pipeline. The *DCP* can process incoming data at every clock cycle and sequentially receives the *DE's* filter responses. Filter values are additionally marked and recognized by a "valid" flag as they may arrive irregularly, for example, due to possible delays during memory access operations over the system bus when reading tile data. Determinants and Laplacians are calculated according to (3) and (4) and finally written back to system memory.

The *DCP* contains six 18 bit multipliers (e.g., 32 bit multiplications are broken down to four 18 bit multiplications), a small set of adders and some registers to hold intermediate results. The *DCPs* structure is shown in Figure 8, where

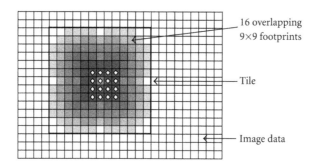

FIGURE 5: Overlapping footprints inside a *tile*.

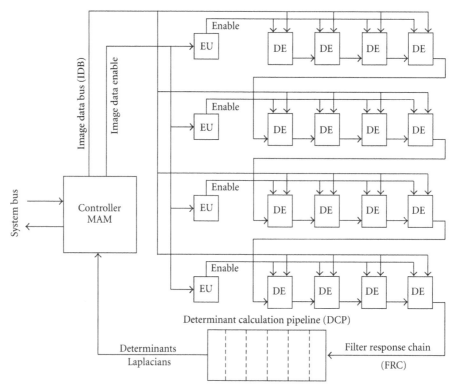

FIGURE 6: Overall structure of the *Flex-SURF+* module with 16 quadratically grouped *DEs* (4 *DE lines*, each containing 1 *EU* and 4 *DEs*).

inv_area is a precomputed constant required to normalize determinants according to the current filter size.

4. Object Recognition on a Single FPGA

The first system which makes use of the *Flex-SURF+* hardware module performs the task of object recognition. It searches for known objects within a live video stream, and labels them with their name in the output image. This system is completely integrated on a single FPGA chip. The following paragraphs give an overview on the overall system design, how object recognition is performed with help of the *Flex-SURF+* module, and the results which have been achieved in experiments.

4.1. System Overview. The entire hardware system for object recognition, covering all components to process the relevant image data, is depicted in Figure 9. It is integrated as a

System-on-Chip (SoC) which is implemented in a single medium-size FPGA (Xilinx Virtex-5 FX70T). Xilinx Platform Studio 11.5 was used for system synthesis.

The SoC consists of several custom IP soft cores, a hardwired PowerPC CPU core (400 MHz), and a DDR2-SDRAM controller. All these modules are connected via a CoreConnect bus system. It may be noted that this system is not constrained to the presence of a PowerPC processor, which may easily be replaced by another hard or soft core processor (as can be seen in Section 5). The custom IP cores are controlled by the main program running on the CPU and primarily handle image processing tasks.

The *VDEC* module fetches image data from a camera source and writes it into system RAM. It is parametrizable at operating time in terms of the desired resolution, the destination memory, and the operating modes "continuous stream" or "triggered single frame".

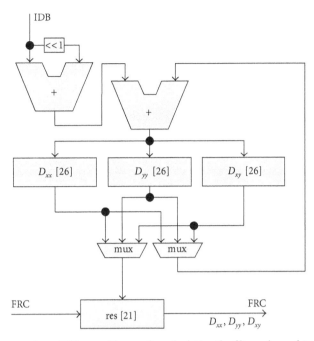

FIGURE 7: Structure of one *Difference Element* for calculating the filter values of D_{xx}, D_{yy}, and D_{xy}.

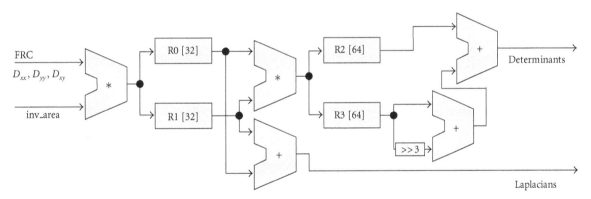

FIGURE 8: Structure of the *Determinant Calculation Pipeline* for calculating determinants and Laplacians according to (3) and (4).

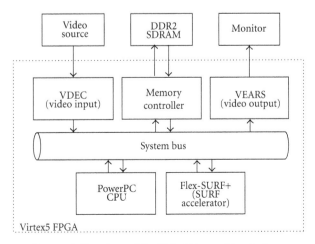

FIGURE 9: Structure of the Object Recognition System.

TABLE 1: Parameters of the first experiment.

Flex-SURF+ configuration	
DE lines	8
DEs per DE line	8
Database	
Image resolution	320×240
Number of images	16
Number of objects	9
Number of features	856
Live images	
Image resolution	320×240
Number of images	76
Number of object instances	73
Average live features	50

The *Flex-SURF+* module is used to accelerate the object recognition algorithm. It is clocked at the system bus clock rate of 100 MHz and was implemented at different configurations (varying number of *DEs*) in the Virtex-5 FX70T FPGA.

The *VEARS ("Visualization for Embedded Augmented Reality Systems")* module finally outputs augmented image data to a monitor. The live image data stream is read from memory and overlayed by information gained from the object recognition algorithm. Augmentation thereby is done by labeling all found objects in the video output stream.

4.2. Database Creation.
The object recognition system identifies objects by comparing live image descriptors with a database, which is created in advance by a PC tool. As input it takes a few images covering views of each object to be recognized. These images do not need to be specially prepared, and typically only one or very few snapshots depicting the object are sufficient.

Database creation plays a very important role in achieving good detection rates at high performance. Due to the limited resources in the live system, the database should be as small as possible, while still allowing a high recognition rate. This has been addressed by the following optimizations.

First, the database tool does not store all, but only a small number of "strong" descriptor vectors for each object. The "strength" of a feature is determined by the determinant $\det(H)$.

Second, the tool avoids to keep descriptors for features which may similarly be found on another object already stored in the database. Such descriptors may be liable for mismatches and detecting objects incorrectly. To achieve this goal, the tool continuously matches new descriptors against existing ones and, in case of similarity (low Euclidian distance), marks them and discards all of the corresponding descriptors at the end of database creation.

Keeping only few and strong descriptor vectors helps to reduce the computational complexity of the live system in two ways. First, fewer comparisons of live image features with database features have to be performed in the matching stage. Second, since the determinant value $\det(H)$ is already known after the detector stage, time-consuming calculations of descriptors for "weak" features can be omitted.

The database itself is stored in a binary format, favoring short loading times and reducing data overhead. An object entry consists of the assigned object name and a small set of unique descriptors.

4.3. Matching and Recognition in the Live System.
In the object recognition system, live images are continuously acquired from the video source. For each live image, the detector and descriptor stages are applied successively. Both stages may be applied either to the whole image or to one or more regions of interest (ROI). When ROIs are used in the object recognition system, they are set to the detected objects center positions of the preceding frame and cover a square area with a fixed edge length of 100 pixels. The advantage of using ROIs is the expected large speedup compared to full image space search, but it also entails that new objects, which may appear outside the ROI, would not be found until a full image space search is applied.

After the execution of the SURF algorithm, the resulting descriptors are matched against the database. For each database descriptor, the two live image descriptors with the lowest Euclidian distance are determined. The ratio of the first and the second best match is an indicator for the uniqueness of the best match. Thus, ambiguous matches are discarded to avoid false matches [11]. If the algorithm has attained a minimum number of unique matches for one specific database object (three in our implementation), the object is considered to be recognized.

4.4. Experiments and Results.
For the experiments, we chose 9 different objects to be recognized by our system. In a first step, we took between 1 and 3 grayscale pictures of each object at a resolution of 320×240 pixels. The final database, which was used in all of our experiments, incorporated 16 images of 9 objects, which are all depicted in Figure 10, and contains a total of 856 SURF feature descriptors.

To evaluate the live system, a total of 76 test images (grayscale, 320×240 pixels), each showing 0, 1, or 2 known objects, were taken at various distances and angles. We used diffuse daylight as we decided not to lighten the scene specifically. Among the 76 test images, 12 contain extremely distracting background, but none of the known objects (see Figure 11(c) for an example), and one image contains a known object in front of distracting background (see Figure 11(b)). The remaining images show 1 or 2 of the known objects (see Figure 11(a) for an example). For ROI evaluation, the test image set contains a series of 23 images with the cup horizontally sliding through these images. If visible, the test objects covered between 8% and 98% of the image area. In three images, test objects were concealed by approximately 50% while in the other images they were fully visible.

Experiment 1 uses parameters as summarized in Table 1. Experiments 2 through 5 were performed to evaluate the impact of various parameters on the detection rate and performance of the system. Unless stated otherwise, the experimental setup was the same as in the first experiment.

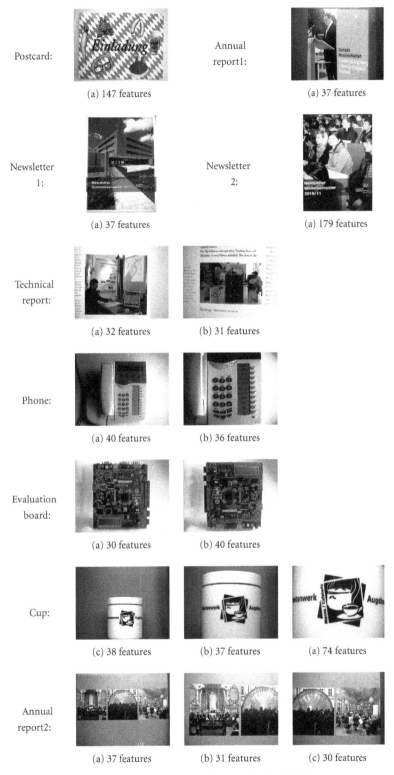

Postcard:

(a) 147 features

Annual report1:

(a) 37 features

Newsletter 1:

(a) 37 features

Newsletter 2:

(a) 179 features

Technical report:

(a) 32 features   (b) 31 features

Phone:

(a) 40 features   (b) 36 features

Evaluation board:

(a) 30 features   (b) 40 features

Cup:

(c) 38 features   (b) 37 features   (a) 74 features

Annual report2:

(a) 37 features   (b) 31 features   (c) 30 features

FIGURE 10: Reference images for creating the database.

In the first test run, the full image space was inspected by the detector and the descriptor stage (no ROI optimization). In all test images, 68 instances of known objects are found. Thus, 7 out of 73 object instances were not recognized, resulting in a sensitivity rate of 91%. The specificity was 100%, there were no false-positives in any of the 76 test images. Figure 12 shows the minimum, average and maximum execution times of the detector, descriptor, and matching stage. By the use of *Flex-SURF+*, the SURF detectors determinant calculation step requires just 70 ms per frame.

(a)　　　　　　　　　　(b)　　　　　　　　　　(c)

FIGURE 11: Test image examples.

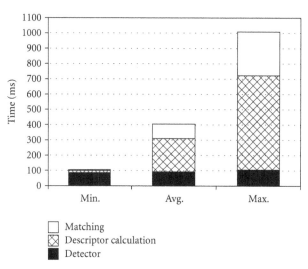

FIGURE 12: Time consumption of the object recognitions main tasks for 320 × 240 pixel images.

The minimum total execution time per frame was 120 ms. The maximum execution time was raised by an image comprising much distracting background, which demanded 1019 ms with 141 features found. On average, processing time took 418 ms with an average of 50 features found. Total execution time varies, as descriptor calculation and matching times are proportional to the number of features found in an image by the detector.

In the second test run we measured execution time for images with a resolution of 640 × 480 pixels in order to evaluate the impact of the image resolution on the execution time. Therefore we scaled the 76 test images up in order to maintain comparability to the previous results. Figure 13 shows the average resulting execution times. As expected, the feature detection task lasts four times longer as the image area also quadrupled. However, the durations of the descriptor and the matching stages varied to a smaller extent, and an amount of 138 features found in average contributes to the increasing general execution time.

In the third experiment, the use of ROIs was activated for the detector and descriptor stage in order to speed up the recognition system. This test covered the sliding cup image set (320 × 240 pixel images), and like in the test run on full image search, the cup was detected in 22 of 23 test images. This resulted in 2 full image searches as the ROI has not been set in the starting image and in the image

succeeding the one where the cup was not recognized. Within the remaining 21 images, a ROI was used and average and minimum execution times decreased significantly. Notably, the SURF detectors determinant calculation step was 5 times faster when using the ROI: instead of 70 ms it required only 13 ms per frame. The average execution times for all stages of the SURF algorithm are depicted in Figure 14.

In order to evaluate the performance of the matching stage, we varied the number of objects within the database in a fourth experiment. We performed the test run on databases which contained 1 object up to 9 objects. This variation had no observable influence on the detection rate. Figure 15 shows the resulting average execution times.

To explore the tradeoff between slice logic usage and speed of the *Flex-SURF+* module, we also varied the amount of implemented *DEs*. Experimental results such as detection rate remained all the same (see first test run), except calculation time for determinants. Table 2 gives an overview on the implemented configurations and time consumption.

5. Pose Estimation Using Two Intelligent FPGA Cameras

Our second system which utilizes the *FlexSURF+* module is an embedded platform for augmented reality systems. The

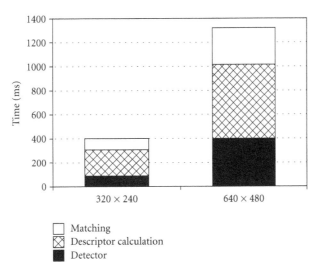

FIGURE 13: Average time consumption of the object recognitions main tasks for 640 × 480 pixel images.

TABLE 2: Different *Flex-SURF+* configurations.

Number of *DEs*	*DE lines*	*DEs* Per *DEline*	Virtex-5 Slices	Determinant calc. time (ms)
16	4	4	2243	134
32	4	8	4269	91
64	8	8	7577	70

system can recognize objects by natural features and determine their 3D pose, that is, their position and orientation. The platform contains a dual-core ARM microcontroller and is equipped with two FPGA-based cameras. The FPGAs in these cameras are smaller than in the system of the previous section and so the *Flex-SURF+* module's configuration is just half as big (4 × 8 *DEs*). The two cameras are connected to the dual-core ARM evaluation board via USB. Each FPGA of the cameras contains a system-on-chip with the *Flex-SURF+* module as a part of it. In this way the FPGAs are used to relieve the ARM platform from the time-consuming task of feature point detection.

An essential part of an AR system is an optical tracking component. Optical tracking is usually performed in two phases [28]. In the *initialization phase*, objects are detected and their 3D pose (6 degrees of freedom (DOF)) is calculated. The subsequent *tracking phase* keeps track of the objects from frame to frame. Each iteration of the tracking phase relies on the information from the initialization and from previous frames and can therefore be implemented efficiently (i.e., with interactive frame rates). However, the initialization phase cannot use any knowledge from previous frames and is considered to be very time-consuming in general (i.e., no interactive frame rates) [28]. The purpose of this work is to particularly accelerate the critical initialization phase as a basis for an efficient embedded real-time tracking system.

5.1. System Overview. The system consists of few hardware components which in combination are suited to be used in mobile devices, especially due to their low power consumption. An overview of the system's components is given in Figure 16.

First, the system captures image data with two cameras. They are each equipped with a grayscale image sensor (640 × 480 pixels), a Xilinx Spartan-3E-1600 FPGA, 64 MB of SDRAM, and a USB interface. Both camera FPGAs contain a *Flex-SURF+* module and perform the detector stage of the SURF algorithm for the respective image of the captured stereo pair. Hence, along with the captured image data, each FPGA camera module delivers a list of detected feature points, relieving the ARM CPUs from this task. The *Flex-SURF+* module is configured to contain 32 *DEs* (4 *DE lines* with 8 *DEs* each) and is clocked at the system bus clock rate of 50 MHz. An overview of the FPGA cameras SoC is depicted in Figure 17.

The SURF descriptor calculation stage, the subsequent feature matching and finally the 3D pose calculation stage are implemented in software, running on a *PandaBoard* evaluation platform. Its central component is a Texas Instruments OMAP4430 SoC, featuring two ARM Cortex-A9 CPU cores (1 GHz each). Furthermore, we use the available DDR2-SDRAM (1 GB), the SD card interface, and two USB interfaces, connecting the FPGA cameras to the board. For visualization we use a touch screen display with a resolution of 800 × 480 pixels which is directly connected to the board. As operating system we use Linux, which supports all involved peripherals.

5.2. Pose Calculation Algorithm. The algorithm starts with acquiring the image data from the cameras and then calculates the SURF algorithm. The most time-consuming part of

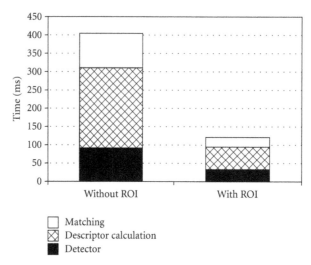

FIGURE 14: ROI-based average time consumption of the object recognition main tasks.

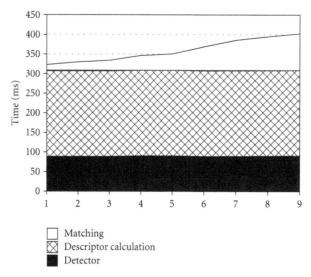

FIGURE 15: Average time consumption of the object recognitions main tasks for 320×240 pixel images at varying database sizes.

the SURF algorithm's feature detector is done on the FPGA of the camera, which is determinant calculation for the four filter stages at the highest image resolution. Subsequently the main system only needs to do the remaining part of SURF, which is basically the descriptor step. This is done in parallel on both ARM CPUs, each for one camera image.

After this, the recognition and pose calculation is done. The system uses a database of known objects assigned with a name, some meta data and a list of SURF descriptors, known to be on the surface of the object. For each descriptor, the 3D position in relation to the object-specific origin is also stored in this database. This 3D position is required for pose calculation after the matching step.

The software performs the following steps for each object stored in the database. In order to utilize the two ARM cores, the code is parallelized with OpenMP such that each CPU processes a part of the database.

(a) *Matching of the Database Object against the Live Images.* For each descriptor of the database object, the two descriptors of camera frame 1 with the lowest Euclidian distance are determined. As done in the object recognition system in Section 4.3, the ratio of the first and second best distance is used as an indicator for the uniqueness of the best match. For each unique matching pair, the index of the feature point in the database and a reference to the feature point in the live image are stored in a correspondence list, called the *db-cam1 list*. For camera 2, the same matching procedure is applied, but instead of comparing to all database features, only the ones from the results of camera 1 are used. The matching results of camera 2 are stored in a separate list, the *db-cam2 list*. The matching in this step is accelerated using an average nearest-neighbor algorithm based on randomized k-d trees as described in [29]. This algorithm allows the system to skip most of the feature comparisons. However, a tree structure

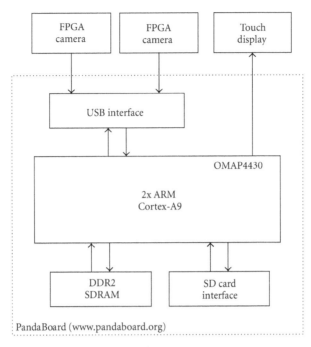

FIGURE 16: Structure of the pose estimation system.

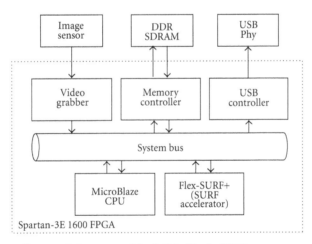

FIGURE 17: Structure of the SoC inside the FPGA cameras.

has to be built before matching can be done, but this is a very small overhead compared to the time cut down achieved by faster matching.

(b) Determination of Correspondences. In this step, the two lists, *db-cam1 list* and *db-cam2 list*, are merged. The algorithm searches for entries with identical database indices and stores them in a new list, the *db-cam1-cam2 list*.

(c) Reconstruction of 3D Points. For each element in the *db-cam1-cam2 list*, the two 2D elements of camera 1 and camera 2 are used to triangulate their respective 3D point in the world. Together with the 3D point from the database, a *db-world list* is created. Each of the pairs in this list is used as a support point for the final pose calculation. For the pose calculation, by theory, three such support points (which are

not coliniar) are enough to calculate the pose. But, there can be outliers in this list. So, just to be sure, only objects which got four or more support points are processed in the following step, the others are considered as not present in the camera image.

(d) Pose Calculation and Elimination of Outliers. As the set of support points, acquired in the previous step, may include outliers, the RANSAC algorithm is used as a coarse filter [30]. This algorithm basically tries different subsets (three random selected support points, in this case) and determines which of the tried subset's result would match the whole dataset best. With the cleaned set of support points the final pose is calculated with the method of least squares as described in [31]. The pose of the object in the world is returned as a 3×4 transformation matrix, which transforms the points in

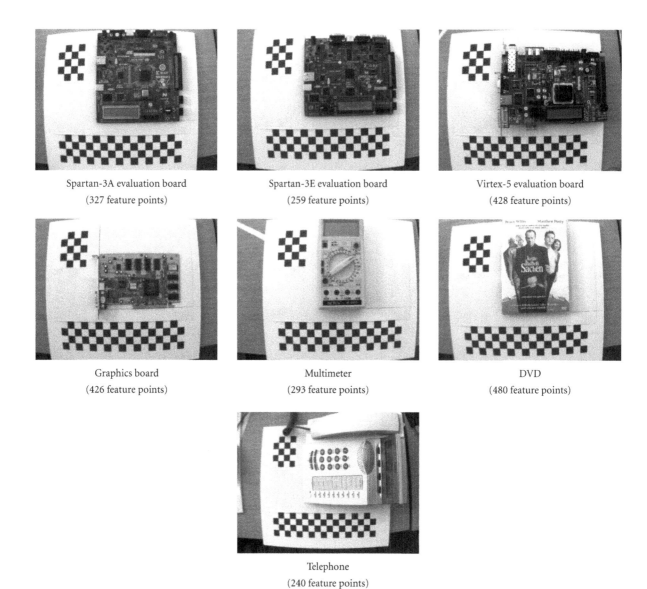

Spartan-3A evaluation board
(327 feature points)

Spartan-3E evaluation board
(259 feature points)

Virtex-5 evaluation board
(428 feature points)

Graphics board
(426 feature points)

Multimeter
(293 feature points)

DVD
(480 feature points)

Telephone
(240 feature points)

FIGURE 18: Samples of images used for the database creation. The chessboard defines the 3D pose of the object and at the same time the origin of the object-related coordinate system. It is required in database creation step to filter and transform the detected 3D features.

the database onto the points in the world as good as possible. The position of the object and its three rotation parameters can be extracted from the matrix easily.

5.3. Database Creation. The creation of the database is done with a tool which is able to record the SURF feature points of an object together with its 3D coordinates. Just like the live system, it uses two cameras watching the object. By matching the SURF feature points between the two camera pictures, the tool generates a list of corresponding 2D points and by triangulation calculates the related 3D points in world coordinates. Since not all of these calculated points belong to the new database object, they have to be filtered before they can be saved in the database.

The filtration is done automatically based on the 3D coordinate of each point. As shown in the example screenshots in Figure 18, a chessboard pattern is used for (and only for) database creation. The enclosing chessboard pattern

defines the exact position of the new object in the world. Since we know which size the object has, it is possible to filter the matched feature points automatically by means of their 3D position in the world. All feature points with 3D positions outside the bounding cuboid (also called *bounding box*) are discarded, and the remaining features are assigned to the object and saved in the database file. The 3D points have to be translated into the object-related coordinate system before storing to the database. Here, the chessboard pattern is needed again since it defines the origin of the object's coordinate system.

Also, it is possible to make an arbitrary number of stereo picture pairs per object in order to train different views of the object.

5.4. Experiments and Results. The database for the experiments was created with four image pairs per object, each with another light exposure direction. This is important, since

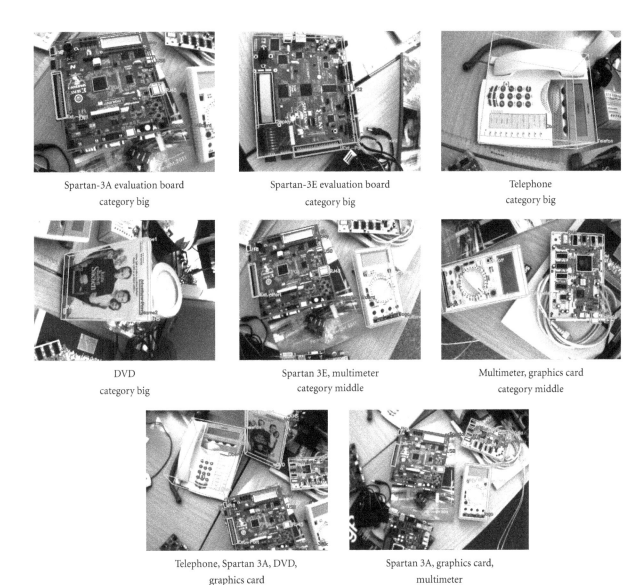

FIGURE 19: Screenshots of the test parcours: the pose of the estimated objects is drawn as bounding box into the images of the cameras. Additionally some smaller parts of the objects are marked as well.

the surfaces of our objects are not plain, so they look slightly different with other light exposure directions. The database consists of seven objects which are all shown on the example screenshots from the database creation in Figure 18.

To test the stability of the system, a parcours was created: a desk was filled with objects (trained and unknown) in random pose. Then the system was started and the cameras were moved slowly in random route over the desk. The route also covered different distances to the objects, so the objects appear in different sizes on the camera images. While the cameras were watching the objects, the system had to recognize the trained objects and calculate their pose autonomously. The results were recorded and evaluated afterwards. Example screenshots of the parcours are shown in Figure 19.

In the evaluation of the results, only objects which are fully visible were considered. An object is only considered

successfully detected if its pose, position, and rotation in 3D space were determined correctly. The results are checked visually through the augmented bounding box and the other displayed elements of the object in the camera image (for examples see Figure 19). The criterion for a correct pose was a maximum deviation of 10 pixels for all observable reference points. So if just one of the reference points deviated more than 10 pixels, the pose was considered as uncorrect. This criterion is considered to be sufficient for our envisioned AR applications.

The results of the evaluation are shown in Figure 20. The objects were assigned into different categories (*big, middle* and *small size*) according to their current visual appearance on the camera picture (measured by their covered relative area, wich is an indicator for the distance to the camera). In the category *big size*, the objects covered between 26% and 50% of the image. In this group, 97% of object poses

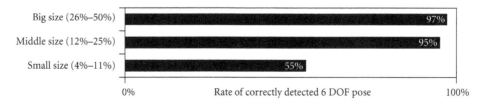

FIGURE 20: Detection rate of the pose of objects according to their distance (by covered area in image).

were determined correctly. This value means that the pose for most objects in this experiment is calculated correctly when the object distance to the camera is small enough. In category *middle size*, where objects covered 12% to 25% of the image, 95% were calculated correctly. This category contains objects which aren't directly in front of the camera, there is always space for a second object of same size left in the pictures. Also here, most of the objects were detected. In category *small size*, the correct pose calculation rate drops to 55%, but this is kind of expected behaviour here because each object covered only 4% to 11% of the image area. To reach a better result with the current system in this category, one could use cameras with higher image resolution, at the expense of higher hardware costs and longer computation times.

Altogether, there were 378 completely visible instances of known objects at 216 stereo image pairs. There were only 12 outliers at the pose estimation (correct object, but wrong pose) on fully visible objects. Most of the errors occurred at objects positioned close to the image border. And in all discovered cases, the outliers had a wrong rotation, but the position of the object center was near the expected one. There was only one case of false recognition, where a Spartan-3E board (see Figure 18) was detected at the position of the very similar Spartan-3A board (in addition to the correct one).

On average, 628 SURF feature points were calculated for each camera image. The utilization of the camera systems and the ARM CPU cores is quite the same. Using a pipeline concept enables the cameras to work in parallel to the main system on the next frame, so nearly all of the available processing power is used. The average computing time for each stereo image pair on the main system with the ARM CPUs was 1069 ms. Most of this time, around 70%, is spent to calculate the remaining part of the SURF algorithm. Around 20% is used to transfer data from the cameras to the main system and only 10% of the time is needed for matching and pose calculation with all database objects. The SoCs in the FPGAs of the cameras work in parallel with the ARM CPUs and need a constant time of 1014 ms per frame, including the time spent for the data transfer to the main system.

In further work, we plan to implement an additional tracking phase in our system, for example, by utilizing sparse optical flow algorithms as suggested in [28]. This way we expect to reach a performance that allows interactive frame rates.

6. Conclusion

We presented the *Flex-SURF+* hardware module which supports the feature detection stage of the SURF algorithm. It is highly customizable and allows a tradeoff between area and speed, depending on the application requirements. As application scenarios, we implemented two embedded systems for object recognition and pose estimation. The first system performs the task of object recognition in a single FPGA, with the *Flex-SURF+* module directly implemented in the system-on-chip within the FPGA. The second system is an embedded augmented reality platform which is equipped with two FPGA-based cameras. In this system, the *Flex-SURF+* modules relieve the ARM hardware from the time-consuming task of feature detection. Experimental results show that robust object recognition and pose estimation can be efficiently performed on mobile embedded hardware.

Acknowledgments

The authors would like to thank the following students, who were involved in the implementation of the systems: Andreas Becher, Markus Bihler, Albert Böswald, Thomas Britzelmeier, Christine Demharter, Stefan Durner, Andrei Ehrlich, Tobias Engelhard, Andreas Füger, Christian Hilgers, Frederik Hinze, Tobias Köglsberger, Werner Landsperger, Moritz Lessmann, Markus Litzel, Matthias Maiershofer, Markus von Mengden, Michael Morscher, Christoph Pöll, Matthias Pohl, Christopher Proske, Markus Rissmann, Matthias Ruhland, Elmar Scheier, Christoph Schwarz, and Christopher Simon. This work has been supported by the German Federal Ministry of Education and Research (BMBF), Grant no. 17N3709.

References

[1] H. M. Atiq, U. Farooq, R. Ibrahim, O. Khalid, and M. Amar, "Vehicle detection and shape recognition using optical sensors: a review," in *Proceedings of the 2nd International Conference on Machine Learning and Computing (ICMLC '10)*, pp. 223–227, February 2010.

[2] C. Hermes, J. Einhaus, M. Hahn, C. Wöhler, and F. Kummert, "Vehicle tracking and motion prediction in complex urban scenarios," in *Proceedings of the IEEE Intelligent Vehicles Symposium (IV '10)*, pp. 26–33, June 2010.

[3] D. M. Jang and M. Turk, "Car-Rec: a real time car recognition system," in *Proceedings of the IEEE Workshop on Applications of Computer Vision (WACV '11)*, pp. 599–605, January 2011.

[4] B. Höferlin and K. Zimmermann, "Towards reliable traffic sign recognition," in *Proceedings of the IEEE Intelligent Vehicles Symposium*, pp. 324–329, June 2009.

[5] J. F. Liu, Y. F. Su, M. K. Ko, and P. N. Yu, "Development of a vision-based driver assistance system with lane departure warning and forward collision warning functions," in *Proceedings of the Digital Image Computing: Techniques and Applications (DICTA '08)*, pp. 480–485, December 2008.

[6] S. J. Henderson and S. Feiner, "Evaluating the benefits of augmented reality for task localization in maintenance of an armored personnel carrier turret," in *Proceedings of the 8th IEEE International Symposium on Mixed and Augmented Reality (ISMAR '09)*, pp. 135–144, Orlando, Fla, USA, October 2009.

[7] B. Schwerdtfeger, R. Reif, W. A. Günthner et al., "Pick-by-vision: a first stress test," in *Proceedings of the 10th IEEE and ACM International Symposium on Mixed and Augmented Reality*, pp. 115–124, October 2009.

[8] G. Amato, F. Falchi, and P. Bolettieri, "Recognizing landmarks using automated classification techniques: an evaluation of various visual features," in *Proceedings of the 2nd International Conferences on Advances in Multimedia (MMEDIA '10)*, pp. 78–83, June 2010.

[9] H. Bay, A. Ess, T. Tuytelaars, and L. Van Gool, "Speeded-up robust features (SURF)," *Computer Vision and Image Understanding*, vol. 110, no. 3, pp. 346–359, 2008.

[10] C. Harris and M. Stevens, "A Combined corner and edge detector," in *Proceedings of the 4th Alvey Vision Conference*, pp. 147–151, Manchester, UK, 1988.

[11] D. G. Lowe, "Distinctive image features from scale-invariant keypoints," *International Journal of Computer Vision*, vol. 60, no. 2, pp. 91–110, 2004.

[12] X. Wu, Z. Shi, and Y. Zhong, "Detailed analysis and evaluation of keypoint extraction methods," in *Proceedings of the International Conference on Computer Application and System Modeling (ICCASM '10)*, vol. 2, pp. 562–566, October 2010.

[13] M. Schaeferling and G. Kiefer, "Flex-SURF: a flexible architecture for FPGA-based robust feature extraction for optical tracking systems," in *Proceedings of the International Conference on Reconfigurable Computing and FPGAs (ReConFig '10)*, pp. 458–463, December 2010.

[14] M. Schaeferling and G. Kiefer, "Object recognition on a chip: a complete SURF-based system on a single FPGA," in *Proceedings of the International Conference on Reconfigurable Computing and FPGAs (ReConFig '11)*, pp. 49–54, 2011.

[15] K. Murphy, A. Torralba, D. Eaton, and W. Freeman, "Object detection and localization using local and global features," in *Toward Category-Level Object Recognition*, vol. 4170, pp. 382–400, 2006.

[16] A. Collet, M. Martinez, and S. S. Srinivasa, "The MOPED framework: object recognition and pose estimation for manipulation," *The International Journal of Robotics Research*, vol. 30, no. 10, pp. 1284–1306, 2011.

[17] F. Ren, J. Huang, R. Jiang, and R. Klette, "General traffic sign recognition by feature matching," in *Proceedings of the 24th International Conference Image and Vision Computing New Zealand (IVCNZ '09)*, pp. 409–414, November 2009.

[18] D. Gossow, J. Pellenz, and D. Paulus, "Danger sign detection using color histograms and SURF matching," in *Proceedings of the IEEE International Workshop on Safety, Security and Rescue Robotics (SSRR '08)*, pp. 13–18, November 2008.

[19] B. Besbes, A. Apatean, A. Rogozan, and A. Bensrhair, "Combining SURF-based local and global features for road obstacle recognition in far infrared images," in *Proceedings of the 13th International IEEE Conference on Intelligent Transportation Systems (ITSC '10)*, pp. 1869–1874, September 2010.

[20] N. Cornells and L. V. Gool, "Fast scale invariant feature detection and matching on programmable graphics hardware," in *Proceedings of the IEEE Computer Society Conference on Computer Vision and Pattern Recognition Workshops (CVPR '08)*, pp. 1–8, Anchorage, Alaska, USA, June 2008.

[21] A. Schulz, F. Jung, S. Hartte et al., "CUDA SURF—a real-time implementation for SURF," http://www.d2.mpi-inf.mpg.de/surf.

[22] P. Azad, T. Asfour, and R. Dillmann, "Combining Harris interest points and the SIFT descriptor for fast scale-invariant object recognition," in *Proceedings of the IEEE/RSJ International Conference on Intelligent Robots and Systems (IROS '09)*, pp. 4275–4280, October 2009.

[23] W. C. Chen, Y. Xiong, J. Gao, N. Gelfand, and R. Grzeszczuk, "Efficient extraction of robust image features on mobile devices," in *Proceedings of the 6th IEEE and ACM International Symposium on Mixed and Augmented Reality (ISMAR '07)*, pp. 287–288, November 2007.

[24] J. Zhang, H. Sang, and X. Shen, "Overview of approaches for accelerating scale invariant feature detection algorithm," in *Proceedings of the International Conference on Electric Information and Control Engineering (ICEICE '11)*, pp. 585–589, April 2011.

[25] D. Bouris, A. Nikitakis, and I. Papaefstathiou, "Fast and efficient FPGA-based feature detection employing the SURF algorithm," in *Proceedings of the 18th IEEE International Symposium on Field-Programmable Custom Computing Machines (FCCM '10)*, pp. 3–10, May 2010.

[26] J. Šváb, T. Krajník, J. Faigl, and L. Přeučil, "FPGA based speeded up robust features," in *Proceedings of the IEEE International Conference on Technologies for Practical Robot Applications (TePRA '09)*, pp. 35–41, Woburn, Mass, USA, November 2009.

[27] C. Evans, "Notes on the OpenSURF Library," Tech. Rep. CSTR-09-001, University of Bristol, 2009.

[28] V. Lepetit and P. Fua, "Monocular model-based 3D tracking of rigid objects: a survey," *Foundations and Trends in Computer Graphics and Vision*, vol. 1, no. 1, 2005.

[29] M. Muja and D. G. Lowe, "Fast approximate nearest neighbors with automatic algorithm configuration," in *Proceedings of the 4th International Conference on Computer Vision Theory and Applications (VISAPP '09)*, pp. 331–340, February 2009.

[30] M. A. Fischler and R. C. Bolles, "Random sample consensus: a paradigm for model fitting with applications to image analysis and automated cartography," *Communications of the ACM*, vol. 24, no. 6, pp. 381–395, 1981.

[31] K. S. Arun, T. S. Huang, and S. D. Blostein, "Least-squares fitting of two 3-D point sets," *IEEE Transactions on Pattern Analysis and Machine Intelligence*, vol. 9, no. 5, pp. 698–700, 1987.

6

On the Feasibility and Limitations of Just-in-Time Instruction Set Extension for FPGA-Based Reconfigurable Processors

Mariusz Grad and Christian Plessl

Paderborn Center for Parallel Computing, University of Paderborn, 33098 Paderborn, Germany

Correspondence should be addressed to Mariusz Grad, mariusz.grad@uni-paderborn.de

Academic Editor: Viktor K. Prasanna

Reconfigurable instruction set processors provide the possibility of tailor the instruction set of a CPU to a particular application. While this customization process could be performed during runtime in order to adapt the CPU to the currently executed workload, this use case has been hardly investigated. In this paper, we study the feasibility of moving the customization process to runtime and evaluate the relation of the expected speedups and the associated overheads. To this end, we present a tool flow that is tailored to the requirements of this just-in-time ASIP specialization scenario. We evaluate our methods by targeting our previously introduced Woolcano reconfigurable ASIP architecture for a set of applications from the SPEC2006, SPEC2000, MiBench, and SciMark2 benchmark suites. Our results show that just-in-time ASIP specialization is promising for embedded computing applications, where average speedups of 5x can be achieved by spending 50 minutes for custom instruction identification and hardware generation. These overheads will be compensated if the applications execute for more than 2 hours. For the scientific computing benchmarks, the achievable speedup is only 1.2x, which requires significant execution times in the order of days to amortize the overheads.

1. Introduction

Instruction set extension (ISE) is a frequently used approach for tailoring a CPU architecture to a particular application or domain [1]. The result of this customization process is an application-specific instruction set processor (ASIP) that augments a base CPU with custom instructions to increase the performance and energy efficiency.

Once designed, the ASIP's instruction set is typically fixed and turned into a hardwired silicon implementation. Alternatively, a reconfigurable ASIP architecture can implement the custom instructions in reconfigurable logic. Such reconfigurable ASIPs have been proposed in academic research [2–6], and there exist a few commercially available CPU architectures that allow for customizing the instruction set, for example, the Xilinx Virtex 4/5FX FPGAs or the Stretch S5 processor [7]. But although the adaptation of the instruction set during runtime is technically feasible and provides a promising technology to build adaptive computer systems which optimize themselves according to

the needs of the actually executed workload [8], the idea of adapting the instruction set during runtime has been hardly explored.

A number of obstacles make the exploitation of just-in-time (JIT) ISE challenging: (1) there are only very few commercially available silicon implementations of reconfigurable ASIP architectures, (2) methods for automatically identifying custom instructions are algorithmically expensive and require profiling data that may not be available until runtime, and (3) synthesis and place-and-route tool flows for reconfigurable logic are known to be notoriously slow. While it is evident that even long runtimes of design tools will be amortized over time provided that an application-level speedup is achieved, it is so far an open question whether the total required execution time until a net speedup is achieved stays within practical bounds. The goal of this work is to gain insights into the question whether just-in-time processor customization is feasible and worthwhile under the assumption that we rely on commercially available FPGA devices and tools.

In our previous work we have presented initial results in each of these three areas. We have introduced the Woolcano reconfigurable instruction set architecture in Grad and Plessl [6] (obstacle 1). Woolcano is based on a Xilinx Virtex 4FX FPGA and augments the PowerPC core in the device with user-defined custom instructions (UDCI) that can be changed at runtime using partial reconfiguration. In Grad and Plessl [9] we presented a circuit library and data path generator that can generate custom instructions for this architecture. In recent work [10] we have presented new heuristics for reducing the runtime of methods for identifying and selecting custom instructions for JIT ISE (obstacle 2). Further, we have presented a first evaluation [11] of how the long runtimes of FPGA implementation tools, mentioned as (obstacle 3) above, limit the applicability of the approach.

This paper makes the following specific contributions over our previous work.

(i) In contrast to our previous work which treated the individual subproblems in JIT ISE in isolation, this paper presents them in a comprehensive way and covers the architecture, the design methods, and the corresponding tool flow along with a more detailed evaluation.

(ii) We provide an extended discussion and formal description of our candidate identification, estimation, selection, and pruning methods for a just-in-time context. Further we describe the algorithms which were developed for candidate estimation and selection in detail.

(iii) Finally, we present an extended experimental evaluation of the candidate identification and estimation methods. In particular, we focus on the candidate identification process and evaluate the suitability of three state-of-the-art ISE algorithms for our purposes by comparing their runtime, number of identified instruction candidates, and the impact of constraining the search space.

2. Related Work

This work is built on research in three areas: reconfigurable ASIP architectures, ISE algorithms, and just-in-time compilation, which have mostly been studied in separation in related works. Just-in-time ISE inherently needs a close integration of these topics; hence a main contribution of this work is the integration of these approaches into a consistent methodology and tool flow.

From the hardware perspective, this work does not target the static but reconfigurable ASIP architectures such as our Woolcano architecture [6] or comparable architectures like CHIMAERA [4], PRISC [3], or PRISM [12]. These architectures provide programmable functional units that can be dynamically reconfigured during the runtime in order to implement arbitrary custom instructions.

Research in the areas of ISE algorithms for ASIP architectures is extensive; a recent survey can be found in Galuzzi and Bertels [13]. However, the leading state-of-the-art algorithms

for this purpose have an exponential algorithmic complexity which is prohibitive when targeting large applications and when the runtime of the customization process is a concern as it is in the case for JIT ISE. This work leverages our preliminary work [10] in which new heuristics were studied for effective ISEs search space pruning. It was shown that these methods can reduce the runtime of ISE algorithms by two orders of magnitude.

The goal of this work is to translate software binaries on the fly into optimized binaries that use application-specific custom instructions. Binary translation is used, for example, to translate between different instruction sets in an efficient way and has been used, for example, in Digital's FX!32 product for translating X86 code to the Alpha ISA [14]. Binary translation has also been used for cases where the source and target ISAs are identical with the objective to create a binary with a higher degree of optimization [15, 16].

This work is conceptually similar to these approaches as it also does not translate between different instruction sets, but optimizes binaries to use specific user-defined instructions in a reconfigurable ASIP. This kind of binary translation has hardly been studied so far. One comparable research effort is the WARP project [17]. The WARP processor is a custom system on chip comprising a simple reconfigurable array, an ARM7 processor core, and additional cores for application profiling and place and route. This work differs from WARP in several ways. The main difference is that we target a reconfigurable ASIP with programmable processing units in the CPU's datapath, while WARP uses a bus-attached FPGA coprocessor that is more loosely coupled with the CPU. Hence, this work allows to offload operations at the instruction level where WARP needs to offload whole loops to the accelerators in order to cope with longer communication delays. Further, WARP operates at the machine-code level and reconstructs the program's higher-level structure with decompilation, while this work relies on higher-level information that is present in the virtual machine. Finally, WARP assumes a custom system on chip, while this work targets commercially available standard FPGAs.

Beck and Carro [18] present work on binary translation of Java programs for a custom reconfigurable ASIP architecture with coarse-grained reconfigurable datapath units. They show that for a set of small benchmarks an average speedup of 4.6x and power reduction of 10.9x can be achieved. The identification and synthesis of new instructions occur at runtime; however, the paper does not specify what methods are used for instruction identification and what overheads arise from instruction synthesis.

3. General ASIP Specialization Tool Flow and Just-in-Time Runtime System

Figure 1 illustrates the difference between a conventional static ASIP specialization process (ASIP-SP) and a runtime system with a just-in-time ASIP-SP support. The ASIP-SP is responsible for (a) generating *bistreams* for configuring the underlying reconfigurable ASIP hardware architecture with instruction extensions and (b) for modifying the source code

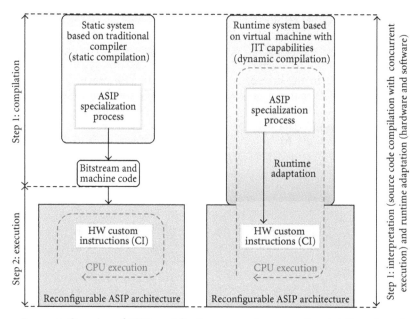

FIGURE 1: Overview of ASIP specialization process for conventional static and runtime systems.

to actually utilize the newly created instructions. So far, ASIP specialization has been applied almost exclusively in static systems, where steps (a) and (b) occur off line before the application is executed.

This work studies the feasibility of moving the ASIP specialization to runtime by integrating it into a virtual machine with just-in-time compilation capabilities. In such a system the ASIP specialization is performed concurrently with the execution of the application. As soon as (a) and (b) are available, the runtime adaptation phase occurs where ASIP architecture is reconfigured and the application binary is modified such that the newly available custom instructions are utilized. The main advantages of executing ASIP specialization as part of the runtime system are the following.

(i) The system can optimize its operation by reconfiguring the instruction set and by changing the code at runtime, which is fundamentally more powerful than static ASIP specialization.

(ii) The system can collect execution time, profiling, and machine level information in order to identify the code sections that are actually performance limiting at runtime; these sections are ideal candidates to be accelerated with custom instructions.

(iii) The virtual machine has the capability to execute various dynamic optimizations like hotspot detection, alias analysis, or branch prediction to further optimize the performance.

4. Our Tool Flow Implementation

For the purpose of evaluating the potential of just-in-time ASIP specialization, we have developed a prototypical tool flow that is presented in Figure 2. Our tool flow executes

ASIP specialization as part of a runtime system as introduced in the previous section. However, since Xilinx's proprietary FPGA design tools can be executed only on X86 CPUs, our current version of the tool flow runs the ASIP-SP on a host computer and not on the Woolcano ASIP architecture itself; see Section 10 for details considering the experimental setup.

The details of our implemented tool flow and the Woolcano hardware architecture are presented in Figure 2. The process comprises three main phases: *Candidate Search*, *Netlist Generation*, and *Instruction Implementation*.

During the first phase, Candidate Search, suitable candidates for custom instructions are identified in the application's bitcode with the help of ISE algorithms which search the data flow graphs for suitable instruction patterns.

The ISE algorithms are computationally intensive with runtimes ranging from seconds to days, which is a major concern for the just-in-time ASIP specialization. To avoid such scenarios, the candidate identification process is preceded by *basic block pruning* heuristics which prune the search space for candidate identification algorithms to the basic blocks from which the best performance improvements can be expected. It was shown by Grad and Plessl [10] that the runtime of the ISE algorithms can be reduced by *two orders of magnitude* by sacrificing 1/4 of the speedup. The ISE algorithm identifies a set of custom instruction candidates. Afterwards the *selection* process using the performance estimation data singles out only the best one.

The *estimation* data are computed by the PivPav tool [9], and they represent the performance difference for every candidate when executed either in software or in hardware. This is possible since PivPav has a database with a wide collection of the presynthesized hardware IP cores together with more than 90 different metrics; see Grad and Plessl [9] for details. The next two phases in the process cover the generation of hardware from a software candidate and are also implemented with the help of the PivPav tool.

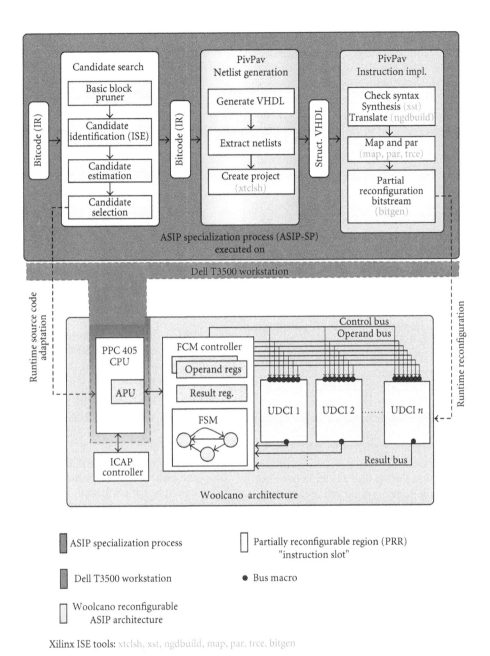

FIGURE 2: Overview of the developed tool flow and the targeted Woolcano hardware architecture. During experimental evaluation, instead of a PPC405 CPU, the ASIP specialization process was executed on a Dell T3500 workstation; see Section 10 for details.

The second phase, *Netlist Generation*, generates a VHDL code from the candidate's bitcode and prepares an FPGA CAD project for synthesizing the candidate. The *Generate VHDL* task is performed with PivPav's datapath generator. This generator iterates over the candidate's datapath and translates every instruction into a matching hardware IP core, wires these cores, and generates structural VHDL code for the custom instruction. Next, PivPav *extracts the netlist* for the IP cores from its circuit database. This is performed for every IP core instantiated during the VHDL generation and is used to speed up the *synthesis* and the *translation* processes during the FPGA CAD tool flow; that is, PivPav is used as a netlist cache. Finally, an FPGA CAD project for

Xilinx ISE is created, the parameters of the FPGA are set up, and the VHDL and the netlist files are added.

In the third phase, *Instruction Implementation*, the previously prepared project is processed with the Xilinx FPGA CAD tool flow. This results in an FPGA configuration bitstream for the given custom instruction candidate. This bitstream can be loaded to the Woolcano architecture using partial reconfiguration. These steps are also handled by PivPav.

5. Woolcano Hardware Architecture

The bottom part of Figure 2 shows the Woolcano dynamically reconfigurable ASIP architecture. The main components of the architecture are the PowerPC core, the internal configuration access port (ICAP) controller, the fabric co-processor module (FCM) controller, and the partial reconfiguration regions for implementing UDCI which we denote also as *instruction slots*. The FCM controller implements the interface between the CPU core and the UDCI. It forwards the inputs to the instruction slots via the operand bus and, after the custom instruction has finished computing, it transfers the output back to the CPU via the result bus. The control bus is used for sending control information, for example, activation or abort signals, to the UDCI.

Bus macros are placed at the interface between the instruction slot and the (a) operand, (b) control, and (c) result busses for enabling *dynamic partial reconfiguration* of the instruction slots. The instruction slots can be reconfigured via ICAP or the external configuration port of the FPGA.

The FCM controller was implemented as a *finite-state machine* (FSM) and is responsible for connection to the *auxiliary processor unit* (APU) interface of the *PowerPC 405* core. Its main function is to implement the APU protocol for transferring data and for dispatching instructions. During the UDCI execution the CPU is blocked and it is waiting for the UDCI results. The architectural constraints of the APU allow only for two input and one output operands to the UDCI. This restriction limits the amount of data a UDCI instruction can operate on, which in turn limits the achievable speedup. To circumvent this limitation, the FCM core implements internal operand registers for supplying the UDCI with additional operands.

The number of instruction slots as well as their input and output operands are compile-time configurable architecture parameters denoted as C_{max}, in_{max}, out_{max}, respectively. Since all inputs and outputs to the instruction slots must be fed through Xilinx bus macros, the size and geometric placement options of the bus macros limit the number of input operands and results.

6. Candidate Identification

The candidate identification process identifies subgraphs in the *intermediate representation* (IR) code, which are suitable for fusing into a new UDCI which can be implemented for the Woolcano architecture. Suitable candidates are rich in *instruction-level parallelism* (ILP) while satisfying the architectural constraints of the target architecture.

6.1. Formal Problem Definition. Formally, we can define the candidate identification process as follows. Given a data flow graph (DFG) $G = (V, E)$, the architectural constraints in_{max}, out_{max} and a set of infeasible instructions F, find all candidates (subgraphs) $C = (V', E') \subseteq G$ which satisfy the following conditions:

$$C_{in} \leq in_{max}, \qquad (1)$$

$$C_{out} \leq out_{max}, \qquad (2)$$

$$V' \cap F = \varnothing, \qquad (3)$$

$$\forall t \in C : \text{convex}(t). \qquad (4)$$

Here,

(i) the DFG is a *direct acyclic graph* (DAG) $G(V, E)$, with a set of *nodes* or *vertices* V that represent *IR operations* (instructions), *constants* and *values*, and an edge set E represented as binary relation on V which represents the data dependencies. The edge set E consists of ordered pairs of vertices where an edge $e_{ij} = (v_i, v_j)$ exists in E if the result of operation or the value defined by v_i is read by v_j.

(ii) $C = (V', E')$ is a subgraph of $G = (V, E)$ if $V' \subseteq V$ and $E' \subseteq E$.

(iii) C_{in} is the set of *input nodes* of C, where a node $v_i \notin C$ with $(v_i, v_j) \in E$ for some node $v_j \in C$ is called an input node.

(iv) C_{out} is the set of *output nodes* of C, where a node $v_0 \in C$ with $(v_0, v_k) \in E$ for some node $v_k \notin C$ is called an output node.

(v) in_{max}, out_{max} are constants that specify the input/ output operand constraints for UDCIs which apply to the instruction slot implementation of the Woolcano architecture.

(vi) $F \subseteq V$ is a subset of illegal graph nodes (IR instructions) which are not allowed to be included in an UDCI. This set includes for instance all memory access instructions like *loads* and *stores* (since a UDCI cannot access memory) and other instructions which are not suitable for a hardware implementation, for example, for performance reasons.

(vii) Convex means that there does not exist a path between two vertices in C which contains a node that does not belong to C. In other words candidate C is convex if $v_i \in C$, $i = 0, \ldots, k$ for all paths $\langle v_0, \ldots, v_k \rangle$ with $v_0 \in C$ and $v_k \in C$ where path is defined as follows. A *path* from a vertex u to a vertex v in a graph C is a sequence $\langle v_0, v_1, \ldots, v_k \rangle$ of vertices such that $v_0 = u$, $v_k = v$ and $(v_{i-1}, v_i) \in E$ for $i = 1, \ldots, k$. Convexity ensures that C can be executed atomically in the hardware. This property is required to make sure that an instruction can be executed as an atomic operation without exchanging intermediate results with the CPU.

Translating these formal definitions to practice means that the identification of UDCI candidates occurs at the level of *basic blocks* (BBs). BBs are suitable units for this purpose since they have a DAG structure as required by the ISE algorithms. In addition, it is feasible to enforce the convexity condition (cf. condition (4)) on them. When selecting IR code for a UDCI implementation, illegal instructions, such as control flow or memory operations, must be excluded (cf. condition (3)). Finally, the number of inputs and outputs of the candidate has to respect the architectural constraints (cf. conditions (1) and (2)). These architectural constraints are variable and are defined by the FCM controller and by the interface to the partially reconfigurable slots into which the UDCIs are loaded.

TABLE 1: Candidate identification ISE algorithms comparison.

Algorithm	# of inputs	# of outputs	Worst-case complexity	Overlapping candidates
MaxMiso	Invariant (∞)	Invariant (1)	$O(n)$	No
SingleCut	Variant	Variant	$O(\exp)$	Yes
Union	Variant	Variant	$O(\exp)$	No

6.2. Supported Instruction Set Identification Algorithms. For the identification process, we implemented three state-of-the-art ISE algorithms that are considered as the most suitable for runtime processor specialization: the *SingleCut* (SC) [19], the *Union* (UN) [20], and the *MaxMiso* (MM) [21] algorithm. The most relevant properties of these algorithms are presented in Table 1.

All identification algorithms do not try to find candidates in the entire application at once. Instead, they focus on the individual basic blocks of the application. Hence, in order to prune the search space, the ISE algorithm is executed selectively only for the most promising BBs (cf. Section 9). Each ISE algorithm analyzes the basic block to identify all feasible candidates. Further, some algorithms allow to constrain the number of inputs and outputs of candidates to match the architectural constraints of the targeted ASIP architecture. Finally, all algorithms fulfill the condition (3).

The advantage of the MM algorithm is its linear complexity $O(n)$. However, it finds only candidates which have a single output and does not allow to constrain number of inputs. Therefore, some of the generated candidates need to be discarded at additional costs later in the selection phase because they validate conditions and thus they cannot be implemented. In contrast, the SC and UN algorithms already allow for restricting the desired number of inputs and outputs for candidates during the identification phase. Finally, the SC algorithm may produce overlapping candidates. Hence, when using this algorithm an additional phase is needed in the selection process to eliminate the overlapping candidates.

7. Candidate Estimation

Since the number of UDCIs that can be implemented concurrently in the Woolcano architecture is limited, only the best candidates are selected for an implementation. The corresponding selection process which is described in the following section is based on the estimated performance of every candidate when executing in software on the CPU or in hardware as a UDCI. Based on these performance estimates the subsequent selection process can decide whether it is affordable and beneficial to implement a candidate as a hardware UDCI instruction.

7.1. Software Estimation. The Woolcano architecture consists of a PowerPC 405 CPU hard core which is used for software execution. In contrast to modern general-purpose CPUs, the PowerPC CPU has a relatively simple design. It has a scalar, in-order, five-stage pipeline, and most instructions

have a latency of a single cycle. This simple design makes the task of software estimation relatively easy since the execution of the instructions in the candidate is sequential. Hence, the presented bellow estimation method is not a novel idea, and it is based on research published in Gong et al. [22].

We estimate the performance of the execution with the expression shown in (5) which corresponds to the sum of latencies of all instructions found in the candidate multiplied by the CPU clock period. This estimation technique has an algorithmic complexity of $O(n)$ where n is the number of PowerPC instructions found in a candidate

$$T_{\text{sw}} = T_{\text{cpu}} \cdot L_{\text{sum}} \text{ [ns]},$$

$$L_{\text{sum}} = \sum_{i=0}^{n} L_i \text{ [ns]}. \tag{5}$$

Here,

- (i) T_{cpu} is the clock period of used PowerPC CPU.

- (ii) L_{sum} is the sum of latencies of all instructions found in a candidate, where n is the number of instructions and L_i is the latency of the ith instruction found in a candidate (the instruction latencies have been determined from the PowerPC manual [23]).

The use of the T_{cpu} in (5) ensures that the differences in clock periods between the PowerPC CPU and the UDCI hardware implementation are taken into account.

The presented method yields correct results only when the candidate's IR code is translated one to one into the matching PowerPC instructions. In the case of a mismatch between these two, the estimation results are inaccurate. The mismatch can happen due to a few reasons, that is, folding a few IR instructions into a single target instruction, or because of differences in the register sets. The PowerPC architecture has a fixed amount of registers (32 general-purpose registers) whereas the IR code uses an unlimited number of *virtual registers*. For larger code, which requires more registers than available, the backend of the compiler produces additional instructions which will move data from registers into temporary variables kept on the stack. These additional instructions are not covered in the software estimation process. For such cases it has been shown that the estimation inaccuracy can be as high as 29% [24].

7.2. Hardware Estimation. Since each instruction candidate can be translated to a wide variety of functionally equivalent datapaths, the task of hardware estimation is much more complicated than the task of software estimation. In the following, we choose to illustrate approach used in this work by means of an actual example. Listing 1 shows an excerpt from a raytracing algorithm. The corresponding IR code of one of the identified candidates is presented in Listing 2. This candidate is constructed from adders and multipliers and corresponds to the scalar product which is shown in Listing 1 on the 5th line.

When translated to hardware, the DFG **structure** of the candidate is preserved; that is, instead of complex high-level synthesis [25], a more restricted and thus simpler datapath

```
(1)    bool hitSphere (const ray &r, const sphere& s..)
(2)    {
(3)    ...
(4)    vecteur dist = s.pos - r.start;
(5)    float B = rdx * dx + rdy * dy + rdz * dz;
(6)    float D = B * B - dist * dist + s.size * s.size;
(7)    if (D < 0.0f) return false;
(8)    ...
(9)    }
```

LISTING 1: Part of the raytracing source code.

```
(1)    ...
(2)    %0 = mul float    %rdx,  %dx
(3)    %1 = mul float    %rdy,  %dy
(4)    %2 = add float    %0,    %1
(5)    %3 = mul float    %rdz,  %dz
(6)    %4 = add float    %2,    %3
(7)    ...
```

LISTING 2: IR of candidate found in 5th line of previous listing.

synthesis (DPS) process [1] is required which does not generate complex finite state machines in order to schedule and synchronize computational tasks. The first step in the hardware estimation for DPS involves translating each IR instruction (node) into a corresponding *hardware operator*, where operators may exist as purely *combinational* operators or as *sequential* operators. Sequential operators produce a valid result after one or—in the case of pipelined operators—several clock cycles. Also, functionally equivalent operators can have a large variety of different properties such as hardware area, speed, latency, and power consumption. Therefore, the hardware estimation tasks have to deal with three different types of datapath structures: combinational, sequential, and hybrid datapaths, where a mix of sequential and combinational operators exists. Examples for such datapaths for the discussed candidate are shown in Figure 3. The hardware estimation process used in this work for estimating the delay of a UDCI supports all of these scenarios and is formally defined as

$$C_{hw} = T_{udci} \cdot R_D \cdot P_{max} \, [\text{ns}], \tag{6}$$

$$T_{udci} = \max\{L\} \, [\text{ns}], \tag{7}$$

$$P_{max} = \max\{P\} \, [\#]. \tag{8}$$

Here,

(i) T_{udci} corresponds to the minimal allowable *clock period*, which is visualized as the tallest green box in Figure 3. For combinational datapaths, scenario (a), it is equivalent to the latency of critical path, whereas for the sequential datapaths, scenario (b), to the maximal latency of all operators (add[1] in this example). For hybrid datapaths, scenario (c), it corresponds to the highest latency of all sequential operators and combinational paths; in this case, to the sum of combinational mult[0] and sequential add[1] operator latencies.

(ii) R_D is an experimentally determined routing delay parameter which is used to decrease the T_{udci}. The routing delays are equivalent to the communication latencies between connected operators caused by the routing switch boxes and wires. The precise value of R_D is unknown until the physical placement of the operators is performed in the FPGA; however, experiments showed that R_D often corresponds to about half of all circuit latencies.

(iii) P_{max} is the maximum number of pipeline stages. It can be interpreted as the maximum number of all green rectangles covering a given DFG. For scenarios (a), (b), (c), and (d), P_{max} equals to 1, 3, 2, and 24, respectively.

(iv) L is a set of latencies generated in Algorithm 1, and its maximum for all operators defines the minimal allowable clock period; see (7). The graphical interpretation of L, as presented in Figure 3, corresponds to a list of the height of all green boxes. Thus, combinational datapaths, scenario (a), have the highest latencies, whereas the smallest latency can be found in highly pipelined sequential datapaths, scenario (d). The latency of each operator is obtained from the PivPav circuit library with the Latency() function found in the algorithm in the 4th line.

(v) P is a set of all pipeline stages generated by Algorithm 1. P is used in (8) to select the maximum number of stages in a given datapath. The number of pipeline stages for operator is retrieved with Pipeline() function and it is presented in square brackets in the operator name; thus, the mult [10]-reflects the 10 stages multiplier.

Algorithm 1 is used to compute the values of the L and P sets, which are associated with the height and the number of green boxes, respectively. In the first line of the algorithm, initialization statements are found. In the second line,

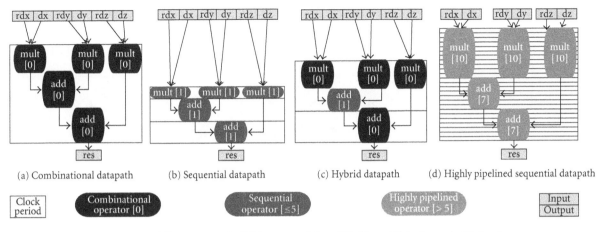

(a) Combinational datapath (b) Sequential datapath (c) Hybrid datapath (d) Highly pipelined sequential datapath

FIGURE 3: Different types of a DFG presented for a UDCI candidate shown in Listing 2.

(1) $L \leftarrow P \leftarrow \phi$
(2) **for** p in *critical_paths* **do**
(3)   **for** $n \in$ nodes(p) **do**
(4) $L_p \leftarrow L_p +$ Latency(n)
(5) $P_p \leftarrow P_p +$ Pipeline(n)
(6)   **if** Pipeline(n) $\neq 0$ **then**
(7) $L \leftarrow L \cup L_p$ and $L_p \leftarrow 0$
(8)   **end if**
(9)   **end for**
(10)   **if** Pipeline(n) $= 0$**then**
(11) $P_p \leftarrow P_p + 1$
(12)   **end if**
(13) $L \leftarrow L \cup L_p$ and $L_p \leftarrow 0$
(14) $P \leftarrow P \cup P_p$ and $P_p \leftarrow 0$
(15) **end for**

ALGORITHM 1: Hardware estimation.

the algorithm iterates and generates results for every *critical path*, which indicates that a path leads from the *input* to the *output* node. In next three lines, for each node in a given path, the latency and the number of pipeline stages are accumulated in L_p and P_p temporal variables, respectively. If the given node is sequential, the new green box is created and the current latency value L_p is moved to the L set (lines (6)–(8)). Lines (10)–(15) are executed when the algorithm reaches the last node in the given critical path. Thus, lines (10)–(12) add an additional pipeline stage if the last node is a combinational one, whereas lines (13)-(14) move the values of temporal variables to the resulting sets. Since the candidate's template does not overlap, each node of the candidate is visited only once, and therefore this estimation technique is of $O(n)$ complexity.

In order to illustrate the estimation process in detail, we show how C_{hw} is estimated for (b) sequential datapath and (d) highly pipelined sequential datapath representation of the candidate. The metrics of the used operators obtained from the PivPav circuit library are described below and are presented in Table 2. The upper and lower parts of the table

show the metrics of the operators used in scenarios (b) and (d), respectively. The estimation results found in Table 3 indicate that the sequential datapath is able to produce the first result almost twice as fast as the highly pipelined datapath (1.82x). However, processing many data (d) is able to fill the pipeline and work with 24 data at once, generating the results, accordingly to the formula $T_{udci} * R_D$, every 9.5 ns, whereas (b) generates a result only every 41.78 ns.

The T_{udci} and P_{max} factors in the equations depend on the characteristics of every used hardware operator; see *Latency()* and *Pipeline()* functions in Algorithm 1. Thus, the key to accurate hardware estimation is the quality of the characterization database that provides performance, latency, and area metrics for each operator. For some selected operators, for example, for floating point operators obtained from *IP Core Libraries*, data sheets that characterize each operator with the required performance metrics are available, for example, [26]. For most other operators—in particular those created on demand by HDL synthesis tools, such as integer, logic, or bit manipulation operators—no data sheets exist. Moreover, the characterization data in data sheets are not exhaustive and do not cover all FPGA families, models, and speed grades, which is problematic, since even within one device family the performance of operators can vary significantly. For example, the data sheet for Xilinx Coregen quotes the maximum speed of a floating-point multiplier as 192 MHz or 423 MHz, respectively, for two FPGA models from the Xilinx Virtex-6 family (Table 23 versus Table 25) [26]. This huge range makes it impractical to estimate accurate performance metrics for devices that are not even tabulated in the data sheets.

To meet the characterization data requirements for the hardware operators, we have developed the open-source PivPav tool [9], which we leverage also in this work to obtain accurate characterization metrics. PivPav generates a library of hardware operators, where each operator is specifically optimized for the targeted FPGA family. For each operator, the performance and many other metrics are automatically extracted from the implementation. These metrics are made available to the estimation process and other processes in the ASIP specialization tool flow via the PivPav API, which

TABLE 2: Excerpt from metrics requested by the candidate estimation process from PivPav circuit library for the XC4VFX100-FF1152-10 FPGA device.

HW Oper.	P_p	L_p	Max FRQ after PAR	FF	LUT	Slice	BUF	DSP
	#	ns	[MHz]	#	#	#	#	#
mul	1	24.81	40.3	66	76	46	103	0
add	1	32.15	31.1	66	377	250	103	5
mul	10	7.31	136.8	66	134	150	103	4
add	7	7.19	139.0	66	556	326	103	4

TABLE 3: Results of hardware estimation process for DFGs presented in Figures 3(b) and 3(d) implemented with two different sets of operators found in Table 2.

		Sequential datapath (Figure 3(b))	Highly pipelined sequential datapath (Figure 3(d))
L	[ns]	24.81 and 32.15	7.31 and 7.19
T_{udci}	[ns]	32.15	7.31
P	#	3 and 2	24 and 17
P_{max}	#	3	24
R_D	#	1.30	1.30
C_{hw}	[ns]	125.39	228.07

is illustrated in Figure 2. Since all the data are generated beforehand with the benchmarking facilities of the PivPav, there is no need to run the FPGA CAD tool flow in the estimation process.

It is worth noticing that the presented estimation method is not in itself a novel idea. There are many timing analysis approaches which perform equivalent steps to the one presented above [27]. Therefore, this subsection does not contribute to the hardware timing analysis field. The novelty in this estimation approach relies on the precise characterization data that were generated with PivPav tool. These data together with presented methods allow to precisely estimate the hardware performances for UDCI instructions.

8. Candidate Selection

Once the set of candidates has been determined and estimation data are available, the selection process makes the final decision about which candidates should be implemented in the hardware.

First, all the candidates that violate at least one of the constraints presented below are rejected:

$$C_{|in|} \le in_{max}, \qquad (9)$$

$$C_{|out|} \le out_{max}, \qquad (10)$$

$$\frac{C_{sw}}{C_{hw}} \le threshold. \qquad (11)$$

Here,

(i) $C_{|in|}$ and $C_{|out|}$ are equivalent to the constraints described in conditions (1) and (2), respectively. They correspond to architectural constraints for the number of input and output operands to the UDCI. They

are applied to the ISE algorithms that are not able to perform this step themselves, such as the MM algorithm.

(ii) C_{sw} and C_{hw} correspond to the software and hardware estimations, respectively. If threshold = 1.0, then there are no performance gains; when threshold >1.0 there is a performance gain since it takes more cycles to execute the candidate in software than in hardware. Finally, if threshold <1.0, the hardware implementation has a lower performance than the software.

After applying these conditions, the search space of the selection process is significantly reduced, since candidates that are either infeasible or would provide only low speedups are discarded. As a result, the runtime of the subsequent steps in the tool flow is considerably lower.

8.1. Candidate Selection. In general, selecting the optimal set of UDCI instructions under different architectural constraints is a demanding task. Related work has studied different selection approaches, such as greedy heuristics, simulated annealing, ILP, or evolutionary algorithms; see, for example, Meeuws et al. [28] or Pozzi et al. [19]. For the purpose of the ASIP specialization, we use the greedy candidate selection algorithm that is presented in Algorithm 2 and which has a computational complexity of $O(|C_{input}|)$. When using the SC algorithm which may produce overlapping candidates for ISE identification our algorithm rejects any candidates that overlap with any candidate that has been selected so far. The aim of this process is to select up to C_{max} candidates from the set of C_{input} candidates generated by the identification process that offers the greatest advantage in terms of some metric M; in this case the *application performance*:

$$C_{res} = \max\left(\forall C_i \in C_{input} : \sum M(C_i)\right). \qquad (12)$$

Here,

(i) C_{res} is the resulting set of best candidates, $|C_{res}|$ is a size of this set, and C_{max} is the architectural constraint representing the number of supported UDCI instructions.

(ii) M is a metric function defined as

$$M(C_i) = \frac{C_{sw}(C_i)}{C_{hw}(C_i)}. \qquad (13)$$

```
while |𝒞_res| ≤ 𝒞_max do
    c_i ← max{M(𝒞_i) | 𝒞_i ∈ 𝒞_input}
    if c_i does not overlap with 𝒞_res then
        𝒞_res ← 𝒞_res ∪ c_i
    end if
    𝒞_input ← 𝒞_input ∩ c_i.
end while
```

ALGORITHM 2: Best candidate selection.

8.2. Selection Metrics. The metric function is used as a policy in the greedy selection process and is responsible for selecting only the best candidates. While in (13), the *application performance* policy is used, and nothing prevents basing the decision preference on a different metric. It is worth mentioning that the PivPav tool could be used to provide a wealth of other metrics since the circuit library stores more than 90 different properties about every hardware operator. These properties could be used for instance to develop resource usage or power consumption policies. Consequently, they can be used to estimate the size of the final *bitstream* and partial reconfiguration time, the runtimes of netlist generation and instruction implementation, or many other metrics. Finally, all these policies could be merged together into a sophisticated ASIP specialization framework which would

(i) maximize the performances,

(ii) minimize the power consumption, and

(iii) constrain the resource area to the sizes of UDCI slot.

Such a combined metric can be defined as an *integer linear programming* model. While this method would allow a more precise selection of candidates based on more parameters, its algorithmic complexity is higher than $O(|C_{|input|}|)$, resulting in runtimes that are much longer, often by orders of magnitude. Since it is important to keep the runtimes of the ASIP-SP as low as possible, the tradeoff between the gains and the costs of the metric function is an interesting research topic in itself.

9. Pruning the Search Space

Pruning is the first process executed in the ASIP-SP outlined in Figure 2. Pruning uses a set of algorithms which act as *filters* to shrink the search space for the subsequent processes by rejecting or by passing certain BBs.

This decision is based on the data obtained from *program analysis* which provides information about loops, the sizes of BBs, and the contained instruction types. In addition, the ASIP-SP makes it possible to discard dead code by running the filters only for the code which was executed at least once.

The objective of the pruning process is described by the following term:

$$\max\left(\frac{\text{metric function}}{\text{runtime of candidate identification}}\right). \quad (14)$$

The pruning aims to maximize the ratio between a *metric function* to the time spent in the candidate identification process. The *metric function* is defined in (13) and is equivalent to the *application performance* gain. The denominator of the equation takes into the account only the *runtime of the candidate identification* since in comparison to this runtime the runtime of the *candidate estimation* and *selection* processes is insignificant.

For this work, we are using this *@50pS3L* filter heuristic, which has been shown in our previous work [10] to provide the best results for just-in-time systems. This filter has three sequential pruning stages which can be decoded from its name. The first filter stage (indicated by @) filters out *dead code*; that is, it discards all BBs that have not been executed at least once. This information is available during the ASIP-SP runtime without access to profiling data. The second filter stage (indicated by *50p*) selects BBs based on their size. Here, only BBs that have a size of at least 50% of the size of the largest BB in the application are selected. Preferring large over small BBs simplifies the task of identifying large candidates which are likely to provide more speedups. Finally, the last filter stage (indicated by *3L*) selects only BBs which are part of a loop and selects the 3 largest of these BBs. The rationale of this filter is that the BBs contained in a loop have a higher chance of being executed, and promoting candidates which are more frequently executed is one of the methods to increase the overall application speedup.

10. Experimental Setup

While this work targets the reconfigurable ASIPs, like our Woolcano architecture presented in Figure 2, due to practical limitations it is currently not feasible to execute the complete ASIP-SP on an embedded reconfigurable ASIP architecture. The specialization process heavily uses the LLVM compiler framework and the Xilinx ISE tools which require high-performance CPUs and desktop operating systems. These resources are not available in currently existing ASIP architectures. Hence, we used Linux and a Dell T3500 workstation (dual core Intel Xeon W3503 2.40 GHz, 4 M L3, 4.8 GT/s, 12 GB DDR3/1333 MHz RAM) as a host computer in place of the PowerPC 405 CPU of the Woolcano architecture to execute the ASIP-SP; see Figure 2.

The lack of the possibility to run the complete tool flow on the ASIP has a number of consequences for the experimental evaluation. Instead of running the ASIP-SP as a single process, we are forced to spilt this process into two steps. In the first step, the host computer is used to generate the partial bitstreams by executing the tasks corresponding to the upper half of Figure 2. In the second step, we switch to the Woolcano architecture where we use the generated bitstreams to reconfigure the UDCI slots and to measure the performance improvements.

It is also worth noticing that this two-step process has an impact on several reported measurements. First, all performance measurements reported in Table 5 and 6, in columns *Max ASIP-SP speedups* and *ASIP ratio*, are performed for Woolcano's PowerPC405 CPU and not for the host CPU.

TABLE 4: Characteristics of scientific and embedded applications. AVG-S represents the averages for scientific applications and AVG-E for the embedded applications. Ratio = AVG-S/AVG-E.

App	Sources		Compilation to IR				IR in BBs			Code coverage			Kernel size		
	files	loc	real	fun	blk	ins	max	avg	udci	live	dead	const	size	ins	freq
	#	#	[s]	#	#	#	#	#	[%]	[%]	[%]	[%]	[%]	#	[%]
164.gzip	20	8605	3.89	33	1006	6925	59	6.88	29.68	38.86	44.66	16.48	5.78	400	90.34
179.art	1	1270	1.06	21	376	2164	43	5.76	21.53	42.05	28.47	29.48	9.84	213	92.45
183.equake	1	1513	1.71	15	257	2670	132	10.39	23.0	75.39	8.91	15.69	15.32	409	92.9
188.ammp	31	13483	10.10	98	4244	26647	382	6.28	25.74	19.22	70.89	9.89	3.38	901	95.81
429.mcf	25	2685	0.97	18	284	1917	77	6.75	13.09	75.9	13.09	11.01	25.77	494	98.46
433.milc	89	15042	10.88	87	1538	14260	363	9.27	32.59	61.67	34.72	3.61	10.83	1545	93.99
444.namd	32	5315	22.77	84	5147	47534	291	9.24	37.82	31.71	62.81	5.48	7.33	3486	93.64
458.sjeng	23	13847	8.49	86	3373	20531	69	6.09	21.1	48.49	49.44	2.07	44.6	9157	100.0
470.lbm	6	1155	1.36	16	104	1988	405	19.12	57.55	55.23	24.9	19.87	32.75	651	97.57
473.astar	19	5829	3.68	45	757	6010	70	7.94	27.45	78.79	5.31	15.91	6.39	384	91.3
AVG_S	24.70	6874	6.49	50	1709	13065	189.1	8.77	28.95	52.73	34.32	12.95	16.20	1764	94.65
adpcm	6	448	0.29	6	43	233	39	7.21	33.48	60.66	29.18	10.16	41.97	128	91.79
fft	3	187	0.26	10	47	297	41	6.53	42.09	58.88	30.26	10.86	44.08	134	95.98
sor	3	74	0.13	4	19	99	22	7.06	34.34	46.51	50.39	3.1	24.81	32	97.52
whetstone	1	442	0.25	12	44	285	32	6.58	34.04	32.75	36.27	30.99	10.21	29	93.27
AVG_E	3.25	288	0.23	8	38.3	228.5	33.5	6.85	35.99	49.70	36.52	13.78	30.27	80.75	94.64
RATIO	7.60	23.89	28.22	6.29	44.67	57.18	5.64	1.28	0.80	1.06	0.94	0.94	0.54	21.85	1.00

TABLE 5: Specialization process executed for whole applications when targeting the Woolcano architecture without capacity constraints. The performance of the custom instructions has been determined with the PivPav tool. ISE algorithms: MM: MaxMiso, SC: SingleCut, UN: Union. SC and UN search is constrained to 4 inputs and 1 input.

App	Executionruntimes			ISE algorithm runtime			Candidates found			Max ASIP-SP Speedup		
	VM	Nat	Ratio	MM	SC	UN	MM	SC	UN	MM	SC	UN
	[s]	[s]	x	[ms]	[ms]	[ms]	#	#	#	x	x	x
164.gzip	23.71	18.47	1.28	40.6	549.0	11170.0	1621	44177	43682	1.172	1.213	1.213
179.art	69.92	74.70	0.94	12.3	55.1	3350.0	371	3534	3513	1.526	21.414	21.414
183.equake	7.97	6.79	1.17	13.5	457.9	4351.0	672	9690	9690	2.147	25.972	25.972
188.ammp	23.18	17.24	1.34	145.7	15840	—	7547	122441	—	3.449	20.826	—
429.mcf	23.94	24.06	1.00	11.1	68.7	200.5	571	3571	3562	1.112	1.112	1.112
433.milc	20.95	16.43	1.28	78.1	5065	—	3573	59450	—	1.301	21.546	—
444.namd	39.94	34.31	1.16	227.5	35854	—	11490	125970	—	1.609	24.846	—
458.sjeng	180.41	155.66	1.16	123.7	6244.1	235195.7	5540	83173	83035	1.118	1.137	1.137
470.lbm	5.68	5.36	1.06	8.6	2777.1	—	490	18216	—	2.554	**44.622**	—
473.astar	66.00	67.68	0.98	33.4	914.8	303796653	1408	37025	32368	1.159	1.19	1.19
AVG_S	46.17	42.07	1.14	69.45	6783	30405092	3328	50724	17585	1.71	16.39	5.20
adpcm	29.22	28.35	1.03	1.7	15.0	3869.4	83	819	819	1.243	1.309	1.293
fft	18.47	18.49	1.00	1.6	9.7	33.1	87	553	552	3.1	14.413	14.413
sor	15.83	15.85	1.00	0.7	4.3	14.6	35	384	375	14.418	14.422	14.418
whetstone	28.66	28.50	1.01	1.6	9.5	64.0	69	435	435	**18.012**	18.012	**18.012**
AVG_E	23.04	22.80	1.01	1.40	9.62	995.27	68.50	547.75	545.25	9.19	12.04	12.03
RATIO	2.00	1.85	1.13	49.61	705.05	30549.59	48.59	92.61	32.25	0.19	1.36	0.43

TABLE 6: The runtime overheads for the ASIP-SP.

App	Candidate Search: @50pS3L					ASIP ratio	Runtime overheads				Break-even
	real	pruner	blk	ins	can	ratio	const	map	par	sum	break-even time
	[ms]	effic	#	#	#	x	[m:s]	[m:s]	[m:s]	[m:s]	[d:h:m:s]
164.gzip	1.44	71.79	2	100	19	1.00	56:22	13:02	18:28	87:52	206:22:15:50
179.art	1.05	23.37	3	79	9	1.01	26:42	8:58	13:20	49:00	1:12:18:13
183.equake	2.25	8.33	2	244	11	1.00	32:38	7:56	16:12	56:46	259:02:28:33
188.ammp	3.27	52.29	1	382	92	1.41	272:58	102:12	142:49	517:59	0:14:56:39
429.mcf	1.05	28.2	1	77	5	1.00	14:50	4:06	7:48	26:44	213:20:05:55
433.milc	6.6	26.71	2	673	9	1.00	26:42	6:44	15:08	48:34	568:06:08:05
444.namd	7.68	57.43	3	776	129	1.03	382:45	117:24	178:04	678:13	6:16:00:48
458.sjeng	1.8	184.11	3	121	8	1.00	23:44	6:56	12:58	43:38	2403:01:35:57
470.lbm	10.62	2.43	3	961	179	2.53	531:07	181:51	308:24	1021:22	1:03:29:48
473.astar	2.25	38.2	3	184	33	1.00	97:54	29:46	46:59	174:39	5149:02:19:14
AVG_S	3.80	49.29	2.30	358	49	**1.20**	146:34	47:53	76:01	270:28	881:00:33:54
adpcm	0.84	5.59	2	61	8	1.08	23:44	6:00	10:34	40:18	0:04:34:10
fft	0.78	3.78	2	75	14	2.40	41:32	11:44	20:56	74:12	0:01:53:07
sor	0.24	2.21	1	22	2	1.00	5:56	4:48	10:12	20:56	0:00:24:19
whetstone	0.54	7.7	2	49	9	15.43	26:42	11:34	25:52	64:08	0:01:08:04
AVG_E	0.60	4.82	1.75	52	8	**4.98**	24:28	8:31	16:53	**49:53**	**0:01:59:55**
RATIO	6.33	10.23	1.31	6.95	5.99	0.24	5.99	5.62	4.50	5.42	10580

Further, in order to compute the *break-even* time reported in Table 6 we used the *runtime overheads* values from the same table which were measured on the host computer. Therefore, this value is computed as if Woolcano's PowerPC CPU had the processing power of the host machine. Finally, while the ASIP specialization tool flow is capable of performing UDCI reconfiguration during runtime, in practice, we had to switch from the first to the second step manually.

The hardware limitations of Woolcano, in particular the number of UDCI slots, in practice do not allow us to measure the performance improvements on a real system for all applications. To this end, for these applications we estimate the speedups with the help of the techniques presented in Section 7.

11. Applications for Experimental Evaluation

Table 4 shows the characteristics of used applications divided into two groups. The upper part of the table shows data for applications obtained from the SPEC2006 and SPEC2000 benchmark suites which represent scientific computing domain whereas the lower part represents applications from the embedded computing domain obtained from the SciMark2 and MiBench.

While the used benchmark suites count 98 different applications altogether, we could not run our evaluation on all of them due to cross-compilation errors. Hence, from the set of available applications, we selected the ones which are the most representative and allow us to get comprehensive insights into the JIT ASIP specialization methodology. While we have used slightly different application sets in our previous publications which evaluated specific parts of the tool flow, we have chosen an adapted common set of applications

for this work in order to get a consistent end-to-end evaluation of the whole tool flow.

11.1. Source Code Characterization and Compilation. The second and third columns of Table 4 contain the number of *source files* and *lines of code* and tell that scientific applications have on average 23.89x more code than the embedded applications. This difference influences the *compilation time* shown in the fourth column which for scientific applications is 28.22x longer on average, but still the average compilation time is only 6.5 s. The next three columns express the characteristics of the *bitcode* reflecting the total number of *functions*, *basic blocks*, and *intermediate instructions*, respectively. For the scientific applications the ratio between *ins* (13065) and the *LOC* (6874) is 1.9. This means that an average single high-level code line is expressed with almost two IR instructions and less than one (0.8) for embedded applications. Since scientific applications have 24 times more LOCs than embedded applications, this results in a 57x difference in the IR instructions.

The ISE algorithms operate on the BBs, and thus the *IR in BBs* column indicates the characteristics of these BBs in more detail. The *max* column indicates the BB with the highest number of IR instructions and *avg* is the average number of IR instructions in all BBs. These values in combination with the data presented in Figures 4, 5, and 6 allow to understand the *runtime* of the ISE and the *number of candidates*.

For embedded applications the largest BBs cover on average more than 14.7% of the application whereas the largest basic block for scientific applications covers only 1.4% of the total application. The difference between average-size BBs for embedded and scientific applications is 1.28x and results in a small average number of IR instructions of less than

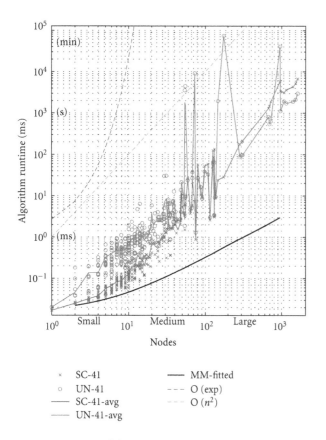

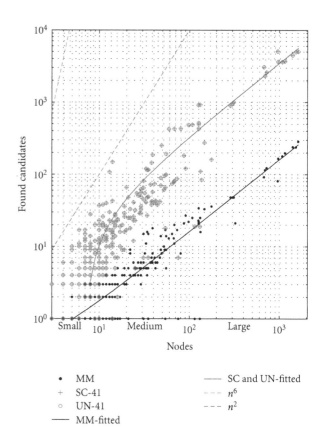

FIGURE 4: Runtimes of the ISE identification algorithm for different basic block sizes (nodes). The SC: SingleCut, UN: Union, MM: MaxMiso algorithms. The label "41" means that the SC and UN search has been constrained to 4 inputs and 1 output.

FIGURE 5: Number of found candidates by ISE algorithms for a large spectrum of BB nodes, where SC and UN are constrained to 4 inputs and 1 output.

10 for both cases. The small size of BBs in our applications needs to be attributed to the actual benchmark code, the compiler, and the properties of the intermediate representation. Our experiments have shown that the size of the BBs does not change significantly for different compiler optimizations, transformations, or with the size of application (LOC).

11.2. Feasible UDCI Instructions. The *udci* column lists the percentage of all IR instructions which are feasible for a hardware implementation. Feasible instructions include the arithmetic, logic, and cast instructions for all data types and make up to 1/3 of all instructions of the application. Considering the small average size of BBs this means that the size of an average-found candidate is only between 2 and 3 IR instructions. This fact emphasizes the need for a proper BB and candidate selection and stresses even more the importance of the proper pruning algorithms in order to avoid spending time with analyzing candidates that will likely not result in any speedup.

11.3. Code Coverage. The *Code Coverage* columns show the percentages of the size of *live*, *dead*, and *constant* code. These values were determined by executing each application for different input data sets and by recording the execution

frequency of each BB. For the SPEC benchmark suite applications, the standard *test, train,* and *ref* data sets were used, whereas for the embedded ones, due to the unavailability of standard data sets, each application was tested with at least three different custom-prepared input data sets. After execution, the change in execution frequency per block between the different runs was compared. If the frequency was equal to 0, the code was marked as *dead*. If the frequency was different from 0 but did not change for different inputs, the code was marked as *constant*, and if the frequency has changed, the block was marked as *live*. This frequency information was used to compute the *break-even points* in the following section. In addition, the *live* frequency information indicates that roughly only 50% of the application has a dynamic behavior in which the ISE algorithms are interested in searching for candidates.

11.4. Kernel Size. The last three columns contain data on the size of the kernel of the application. These data are derived from the frequency data. The kernel of an application is defined as the code that is responsible for more than 90% of the execution time. The size of the kernel is measured as the total number of IR instructions contained in the basic blocks which represent the kernel. For scientific applications, 16.20% of the code affects 94.65% of the total application execution time, and it corresponds to more than 1.7 k IR

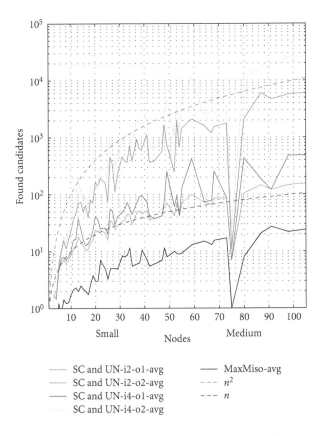

FIGURE 6: Number of found candidates by ISE algorithms for a medium spectrum of BB nodes, where SC and UN have variable constraints.

instructions. For embedded applications, the average relative kernel size is 30.27% and is expressed only with 80 IR instructions. These numbers indicate that it is relatively easier to increase the performances of the embedded applications than the scientific ones, since they require 22x smaller UDCI instructions.

11.5. Execution Runtimes. The *VM* column in Table 5 represents the application runtime when executed on the LLVM virtual machine. The runtime of the application depends heavily on the input data which, in the case of the scientific applications, were obtained from the *train* datasets of the SPEC benchmark suite. Due to the unavailability of standard data sets for the embedded applications, custom-made data sets were used. For both application classes, the input data allowed to exercise the most computationally intensive parts of the application for a few or several tens of seconds. The *Nat* column shows the *real* runtime of the application when statically compiled, that is, without the overhead caused by the runtime translation. The *Ratio* column shows the proportion of *Nat* and *VM* and represents the overhead involved with the interpretation during the runtime. For the small embedded applications, the overhead of the *VM* is insignificant (1%). For the large scientific applications, the average overhead caused by the VM equals on average 14%. However, it is important to notice that for some applications like *179.art* or

473.astar, the *VM* was significantly faster than the statically compiled code by 6% and 2%, respectively. This means that the *VM* optimized the code in a way which allowed to overcome the overhead involved in the optimization as well as the dynamic just-in-time compilation.

12. Experimental Evaluation of the Candidate Identification

In this section, we evaluate and compare the ISE algorithms which have been used for candidate identification as presented in Figure 2. Our evaluation covers the runtime characteristics of the algorithms as well as the number of identified candidates for different architectural constraints, the maximum gain in application performance, and the runtime of our benchmark algorithms when statically compiled to native code and when executing in a virtual machine. The discussion is based on data presented in Table 5 which was obtained for the benchmark applications introduced in the previous section.

12.1. ISE Algorithm Runtimes and Comparison. The average ISE algorithm runtimes are presented in the 5th to 7th columns of Table 5. As stated previously, the MM algorithm has a linear complexity and therefore is the fastest, resulting in a 0.22 s runtime for 444.namd, which is the largest application. Due to its larger algorithmic complexity, the runtime of the UN algorithm should generally exceed the runtime of SC but this is not the case for applications which include specific types of BBs. For example, it took 3837 ms to process such a specific BB consisting of 55 nodes in the adpcm application, which is 99.15% of the overall runtime of the UN algorithm. On contrast, the same BB was analyzed by the SC algorithm in a mere 4.7 ms.

Since both SC and UN have exponential complexity, their runtimes are a few orders of magnitude higher than for MM. In average, MM is 96.94x faster than the SC algorithm.

The identification times for BBs of similar sizes also vary significantly for the same algorithm since the number of candidates that need to be actually considered in a BB depends not only on the total size of the BB but also on the structure of the represented DFG, the number and location of infeasible instructions in the DFG, the architectural constraints, and other factors. For example, it took the SC algorithm 1707 ms to analyze a BB of 433.milc with 102 instructions, while the analysis of a slightly larger BB in 470.lbm with 120 instructions took only 76 ms, which is a 22.5x difference in runtime. This example illustrates that it is impossible to accurately estimate the runtime of the exponential ISE algorithms SC and UN in advance when basing the estimation solely on the size of the BB.

It is worth pointing out that for keeping the search space and thus the algorithm runtimes manageable, we had to apply rather tight architectural constraints for the custom instructions (4 inputs, 1 output) in our comparison of ISE algorithm in Table 5. When loosening these constraints, the execution times for the SC and UN algorithms rapidly grow from seconds to many hours.

The overall runtime characterization of the instruction identification algorithms is summarized in Figure 4 which plots the runtime of the different algorithms for varying BB sizes. Each data point represents an average which was computed by running the ISE algorithm 1000 times on each BB. The multitude of data points for a fixed BB size illustrates that the runtime of the same algorithm can vary over several orders of magnitude for BBs which have an equal size but differ in their structure as pointed out above. This effect is particularly strong for larger BBs where many variants of DAG structures exist.

For visualizing the overall behavior of the algorithms we have also added the average runtime for the SC and the UN algorithms for each BB size. It can be observed that the variability for the UN algorithm is larger than for the SC algorithm. Another interesting observation is that although the SC and UN algorithms have a worst-case algorithmic complexity of $O(\exp)$, on average their runtime is only polynomial $O(n^2)$, which can be seen by comparing the blue dotted lines with the red and green lines, respectively.

We are able to fit the runtime of the MM algorithm with a linear polynomial model which is represented with a black line which has an almost ideal characteristic (goodness of the fit: $R^2 = 0.9995$). This means that the runtime of the MM algorithm always depends linearly on the BB size $O(n)$. Unfortunately, the behavior of the other algorithms is not sufficiently regular to perform a meaningful curve fitting with similar quality.

In general, we can say that the MM is the fastest algorithm and outperforms the SC and UN algorithms easily in terms of runtime for small, medium, and large basic blocks. For small BBs of up to 10 instructions, the runtime difference is in the range of up to an order of magnitude; for medium inputs (10^2 instructions), up to two orders of magnitude and for the largest BBs (10^3 and more instructions), a difference of more than three orders of magnitude can be observed. While the runtime of the MM stays on the millisecond time scale even for the largest inputs, the SC and UN algorithms work on a scale of seconds or minutes.

It is important to note that runtime of the exponential algorithms tend to literally explode when these algorithms are constrained less tightly than 4 input 1 output (41), in particular when allowing a larger number of outputs. For instance, when applying an 8-input 2-output (82) constraint, common runtimes are in the order of 10^8 ms, which is three orders of magnitude higher than for the 41 constraint.

In terms of runtime, SC is approximately one order of magnitude faster than UN. However, the runtime for both algorithms grows similarly for increasing BB sizes with the exception of significant outliers for the UN algorithm, for peaks with a runtime difference of three orders of magnitude which can be observed for large BBs. A similar behavior was also found for architectural constraints other than 41.

The results presented here have been obtained using a special *benchmarking mode* of our tool flow where the instruction candidates are identified but not copied to a separate data structure for further processing. Additionally, the time needed to reject overlapping candidates for SC algorithm as well as the time needed for the MM algorithm

to validate condition (1) presented in Section 6 was not included. As a result, the runtimes of the candidate identification algorithms will be slightly longer in practice when they are applied as part of the complete tool flow.

12.2. Candidates Found by the ISE Algorithms. The number of candidates found by the ISE identification algorithms is presented in columns 8, 7, and 9 of Table 5. In addition, an overview of all identified candidates as a function of the BB size is shown in Figure 5, while Figure 6 presents a close up of the same data for medium-sized BBs. As illustrated by the *red* line in Figure 5, the SC and the UN algorithms generate an equal number of candidates, given that the same architectural constraints are used and that any overlapping UDCI candidates generated by the SC algorithm are removed.

In general, the total number of subgraphs that can be created from an arbitrary graph G is exponential $\exp(n)$ in the number of nodes of G. For ASIP specialization scenarios, that is, when architectural constraints are applied cf. conditions (1), (2), and (4) [29] has shown that the number of subgraphs is bounded by $n^{(C_{in}+C_{out}+1)}$. Thus, for the 4-input/1-output constraints applied in this study, the search space is equal to n^6, which is represented by the gray dotted line found in the upper-left corner of Figure 5. When applying the final constraint condition (3), the search space is significantly reduced from n^6 by at least a power of 4 to n^2, which is presented with the blue dotted line above all results.

The *black* line represents a linear fitting for the MM algorithm, whereas the *red* line shows a second-order polynomial curve fitting for the SC and UN algorithms. The goodness of these fits represented with R^2 parameter is equal to 0.9663 for MM and to 0.9564 for the SC and UN algorithms. Therefore, it is safe to assume that the number of candidates for the 4-input/1-output constraint is limited by a second-order polynomial.

Figure 6 shows that the longer runtimes of the SC and the UN algorithm also result in the identification of more candidates. The difference for small and medium BBs is up to one order of magnitude and increases for even larger BBs.

The data points (number of candidates) were obtained by running the ISE algorithms on the applications presented in Section 11. Thus, each data point is associated with a single BB, and closely located data points tell that there are many BBs of similar sizes.

It can be observed in Figure 6 that there are less data points with large BBs than medium or small BBs. This is a consequence of the distribution of basic block sizes; that is, most BBs found in these applications have sizes of up to 100 instructions. For such BBs, the number of feasible candidates reaches more than 10 when using the MM algorithm and more than 100 when using the SC and UN algorithms. Given that the average application has at least a few dozens (38 for embedded) or hundreds (1709 for scientific) of BBs this results in thousands of feasible candidates that are suitable for hardware implementation. In our experiments, we considered 3328 MM (50724 SC) candidates for the scientific and 68.5 MM (547.75 SC) candidates for the embedded applications. These high numbers are more than enough since an average ISA consists of around 80 core instructions for X86 platform and around 100 for PowerPC. If one assumes 10% modification to the ISA, it results in a task of selecting less than 10 UDCI instructions from a set of thousands of feasible candidates.

The number of found candidates depends strongly on the architectural constraints that are applied. Tighter constraints, that is, allowing a smaller number of inputs and outputs, lead to a smaller number of candidates for the SC and UN algorithm. This behavior can be seen in Figure 6 where the average number of candidates is plotted as a function of the BB size for various constraints. There are two groups of constraints: the 21,41 and 22,42, between which a rising gap of one order of magnitude is established. Applying the MM algorithm to BBs with a size of 100 instructions leads to more than 10 feasible candidates whereas applying SC or UN leads to more than 100 candidates for the first set of constraints and even two orders of magnitude more candidates (10^4) for the second set of constraints. This validates the second-order polynomial characteristic n^2 of the number of candidates for the SC or UN algorithms.

The similar behavior of the lines representing the average number of identified candidates is caused by the *less or equal* ($\leq$) relationships found in conditions (1) and (2). That is, the less constrained algorithms (like 41) include all candidates of more constrained ones like 21. The area between the *red* and *gray* line corresponds exactly to the number of additional candidates found in less constrained algorithms. Also, the graphs illustrate that the number of candidates depends much stronger on the number of allowable outputs than on the number of allowable inputs.

For BBs with sizes of approximately 75 instructions, we see an interesting decay from which all ISE algorithms suffer. This decay is found only in a concrete benchmark and is the result of a high concentration of illegal instructions in basic blocks of those sizes, for which only a few feasible candidates were found.

Finally, it can be seen that the MM algorithm has a linear characteristic $a \cdot n$ where $a \leq 1$. The SC and UN algorithms also show a linear characteristic with $a \geq 1$ for the case of the 21 and 41 constraints, whereas for the 22 and 42 constraints, the characteristic changes by a power (n^2).

12.3. Achievable Performance Gain. The *Max ASIP-SP Speedup* columns presented in Table 5 describe the upper limit of performance improvement that can be achieved with the Woolcano reconfigurable ASIP architecture and the presented ASIP-SP. These values show the hypothetical best-case potential in which all candidates found by three different ISE algorithms are implemented as custom instructions. In reality, the overheads caused by implementing all possible instructions and the limited hardware resources of the reconfigurable ASIP require pruning of the set of candidates that are evaluated and implemented to a tractable subset. Therefore, the speedup quoted in these columns should be treated only as an upper boundary on the achievable performance.

The ISE algorithms have a lot to offer, reaching a speedup of up to 44.62x for SC algorithm and 18.01x for MM and

UN algorithms. The average speedups achieved with MM, SC, and UN are 1.71, 16.39, and 5.20, respectively for the scientific applications and 9.19, 12.04, and 12.03 for the embedded applications. For all applications, the average speedups achieved with MM, SC, and UN are 3.85, 15.15, and 10.02, with the value of median 1.57, 16.22, and 7.85, respectively. These results clearly indicate that the SC algorithm is superior for static systems where identification runtimes are not a major concern.

For a JIT specialization process, one needs to balance the achievable speedup with the identification time. Comparing the ratios of average speedup to identification runtime for embedded applications results in the following ratios: 6.56 (MM), 1.25 (SC), and 0.01 (UN). These figures suggest that the MM algorithm is the most suitable for such systems. In addition, the considerable difference of 0.19 between average speedups for different application sets suggests that the MM algorithm could find better candidates in the smaller applications with more pronounced kernels and that these applications will benefit most from JIT-based systems.

It is important to remember that these results were obtained for the first time for the FPGA-based Woolcano architecture and not as presented in related work for a fixed CMOS ASIP architecture. This distinction is significant since the same hardware custom instructions will achieve significantly higher speedups when implemented in CMOS technology, often by more than one order of magnitude. But at the same time, a fixed architecture will sacrifice the flexibility and runtime customization capabilities of the Woolcano architecture.

13. Runtime Overhead of the ASIP Specialization Process

As elaborated in the previous section, the reconfigurable ASIP architecture is considerably faster than the underlying CPU alone for both benchmark domains. Thus, the overheads of just-in-time software compilation, optimization, and custom instruction generation can be amortized provided that the application will be executed long enough. In this section, we analyze the achievable performance gains by ASIP specialization, presented in Figure 2, and the runtime costs of the three different phases of that process. These figures are used to compute for how long the application needs to be executed until the hardware generation overheads are amortized, that is, when a net speedup is achieved.

13.1. Candidate Search. As described in Section 4, the *Candidate Search* phase is responsible for finding and selecting only the best custom instruction candidates from the software. As this task is frequently very time consuming, we are using our pruning mechanisms introduced in Section 9 to reduce the search space for instruction candidates. The number of selected candidates, after pruning, is indicated in the *can* column of Table 6.

The third column of Table 6 represents the *pruning efficiency* ratio which is defined as the quotient of two terms. The first term is the ratio of the average maximum ASIP speedup to the runtime of the identification algorithm when no pruning is used. The second term is the same ratio when using the *@50pS3L* pruning mechanism. The pruning efficiency can be used as a metric to describe the relative gain in the speedup-to-identification-time ratio with and without pruning.

The *blk* and *ins* columns represent the number of basic blocks and instructions which have been passed to the identification process. These numbers are significantly lower than the total number of blocks and instructions presented in the *6th* and *7th* columns of Table 4. That is, the pruning mechanism reduced the size of the bitcode that needs to be analyzed in the identification task by a factor of 36.49x and 4.4x for scientific and embedded applications, respectively.

The overall runtime of the data pruning, identification, estimation, and selection is aggregated in the *real* column. The total candidate search time is in the order of milliseconds and thus insignificant in comparison to the overheads involved in the hardware generation.

13.2. Performance Improvements. The column *ASIP ratio* represents the speedup of the augmented hardware architecture when all candidates selected by Candidate Search are offloaded from the software to custom instructions. In contrast to the maximum performance shown in the 11th column in Table 5 which assumes that *all* candidates are moved to hardware, the average speedup drops by 30% from 1.71x–1.20x for scientific applications and by 46% from 9.19x–4.98x for the embedded ones. Comparing the *fft* with the *470.lbm* applications illustrates the main difference between embedded and scientific applications. Both applications have a similar speedup of 2.40x versus 2.53x, respectively, but differ significantly in the number of candidates that need to be translated to hardware to achieve these speedups (14 versus 179 candidates). This correlates with the previously described observation that scientific applications have a significantly larger kernel size.

13.3. Netlist Generation. The tasks discussed in this section are represented by the second phase in Figure 2. The task *Generate VHDL* is performed with the PivPav datapath generator which produces the *structural VHDL* code. The datapath generator traverses the datapath graph of the candidate and matches every node with a VHDL component. This is a constant time operation requiring 0.2 s per candidate. The *extract netlist* task retrieves the netlist files for each hardware component used in the candidate's VHDL description from the PivPav database. This step allows reduction of the FPGA CAD tool flow runtimes, since the synthesis process needs to build only a final netlist for the top module. The next step is to *create the FPGA CAD project* which is performed by PivPav with the help of the *TCL* scripting language. After the project is created, it is configured with the FPGA parameters and the generated VHDL code as well as the extracted netlist files are added. On average this process took 2.5 s per candidate, making this the most time-consuming task of the netlist generation phase. The average total runtime for these three tasks is presented in the *C2V* column of Table 7 and amounts

TABLE 7: Constant overheads involved in the ASIP-SP. *C2V* corresponds to the *Netlist Generation* phase in Figure 2. Syn, Xst, Tra, and Bitgen are the FPGA CAD tool flow processes and correspond to the syntax check, synthesis, translate, and partial reconfiguration bitstream generation processes, respectively, which can be found in the third phase in Figure 2.

	C2V [s]	Syn [s]	Xst [s]	Tra [s]	Bitgen [s]	Sum [s]
Average	3.22	4.22	10.60	8.99	151.00	178.03
Stdev	0.10	0.10	0.23	1.22	2.43	

to 3.22 s. As the standard deviation is only 0.10, this time can be considered as constant.

13.4. Instruction Implementation. Once the project is created it can be used to generate the partial reconfiguration bitstream representing the FPGA implementation of the custom instruction. This step is performed with the FPGA CAD tool flow which includes several steps. First, the VHDL source code is checked for any *syntax* errors. The runtime of this task is presented in the second column of Table 7. On average it takes 4.22 s to perform this task for every candidate. Since the *stdev* is very low (0.10) we can assume that this is a constant time too.

Once the source code is checked successfully the *synthesis* process is launched. Since all the netlists for all hardware components are retrieved from a database there is no need to resynthesize them. The synthesis process thus has to generate a netlist just for the top-level module which on average took 10.60 s. The runtime of this task does not vary a lot since the VHDL source code for all candidates has a very similar structure and changes only with the number of hardware components. After this step all netlists and constraint files are consolidated into a single database with the *translate* task, which runs for 8.99 s on average.

In the next step, the most computationally intensive parts of the tool flow are executed. These are the *mapping* and the *place and route* tasks which are not constant time processes as the previous tasks, but their duration depends on the number of hardware components and the type of operation they perform. For instance, the implementation of the shift operator is trivial in contrast to a division. The spectrum of runtimes for the *mapping* process ranges from 40 s for small candidates up to 456 s for large and complex ones, whereas the *place and route* task takes 56 s–728 s. There is no strict correlation between the duration of these processes; the ratio of *place and route* and *mapping* runtimes vary from 1.4x for small candidates to 2.5x for large candidates. The last step in the hardware custom instruction generation process is the bitstream generation. Our measurements show that this is again a constant time process depending only on the characteristics of the chosen FPGA. Surprisingly, the runtime of this task is substantial. On average, 151 s per candidate are spent to generate the partial reconfiguration bitstream. This runtime is constant and does not depend on the characteristics of a candidate. In many cases, the bitstream creation consumed more time than all other tasks of the instruction synthesis process combined (including synthesis and place-and-route). The runtime is mainly caused by using the early access partial reconfiguration Xilinx 12.2 FPGA CAD tools (EAPR). In comparison, creating a full-system bitstream that includes not only the custom instruction candidate but also the whole rest of the FPGA design takes just 41 s on average when using the regular (non-EAPR) Xilinx FPGA CAD tools.

In Table 7, we summarize the runtime of the processes which cause constant overheads that are independent of the candidate characteristics. These are the *Candidate to VHDL translation (C2V)*, *Syntax Check (Syn)*, *Synthesis (Xst)*, *Translation (Tra)*, and *Partial Reconfiguration Bitstream Generation (Bitgen)*. The total runtime for these processes is 178.03 s and is inevitable when implementing even the most simple custom instruction. The *Bitgen* process accounts for 85% of the total runtime.

The overall runtime involved in the FPGA CAD Tool Flow execution is presented in the column *Runtime Overheads* in Table 6. The column *const* represents the runtime of constant processes shown in Table 7. The column *map* stands for the mapping process, the column *par* for the *place and route*, and the values in the column *sum* adds all three columns together. These columns aggregate the total runtime involved in the generation of all candidates for a given application. The candidate's partial reconfiguration times were not included in these runtimes since they consume just a fraction of a second [6]. On average it takes less than 50 minutes (49 : 53 min) to generate all candidates for the embedded applications but more than 4 : 30 hours (270 : 28 min) for the scientific applications. One can see that this large difference is closely related to the number of candidates and that *sum* column grows proportionally with the number of candidates. This behavior can be observed for example for the *444.namd* and the *470.lbm* applications, which consist of 179 and 129 candidates, respectively. The total runtime overhead for them is more than 11 hours (678 : 13 min) and 17 hours (1021 : 22 min), respectively and is caused primarily by the high constant time overheads (*const*).

This observation emphasizes the importance of the pruning algorithms, particularly for the large scientific applications. We can observe the difference for the embedded applications where a smaller number of candidates exists. On average, the *const* time drops for the scientific applications from 146 : 34 min to 24 : 28 min, that is, by a factor of 5.99x, which is exactly the difference in the number of candidates *(can)* between the scientific and the embedded applications.

13.5. Break-Even Times. In this section, we analyze the *break-even time* for each application; that is, the minimal time each application needs to execute before the overheads caused by the ASIP-SP is compensated.

A simplistic way of computing the break-even time would be to divide the total runtime overhead (*sum* in Table 6) by the time saved during one execution of the application, which can be computed using the *VM execution time* and the *Max ASIP Speedup* (speedup) (see Table 5). This computation assumes a scenario, where the size of the input data is fixed and the application is executed several times.

We have followed a more sophisticated approach of computing the break-even time, which assumes that more input data is processed instead of multiple execution of the same application. Hence, the additional runtime is spent only in the parts of the code which are *live* while code parts that are *const* or *dead* are not affected. To this end, we use the information about the execution frequency of basic blocks and the variability of this execution frequency for different benchmark sizes which we have collected during profiling; see Section 11.3. The resulting break-even times are presented in the last column of Table 6.

It is evident that there exists a major difference in the break-even times for the embedded and the scientific applications. While the break-even time of the embedded applications is in the order of minutes to a few hours, the scientific applications need to be executed for days to amortize the overhead caused by custom instruction implementation (always under the assumption that *all* candidates are implemented in hardware). The reason for these excessive times is the combination of rather long ASIP-SP runtimes (>4 : 30 h) and modest performance gains of 1.2x. As described above, the long runtimes are caused by implementing many candidates. One might expect that this large number of custom instructions should cover a sizable amount of the code and that significant speedups should be obtained, but evidently this is not the case. The reason for this is that the custom instructions are rather small, covering only 6.9 IR instructions on average. Although there are many custom instructions generated, they cover only a small part of the whole computationally intensive kernels of the scientific application, which has a size of 1764 IR instructions on average. Adding more instructions will not solve this issue since every candidate adds an additional FPGA CAD tool flow overhead.

In contrast, the break-even point for embedded applications is reached more easily. On average, the break-even time is five orders of magnitude lower for these applications. In contrast to the scientific applications, the custom instructions for embedded application can cover a significant part of the computationally intensive kernel. This results in reasonable performance gains with modest runtime overheads. For an average-embedded application, a 5x speedup can be achieved, resulting in a runtime overhead of less than 50 minutes and a break-even time of less than 2 hours.

The difference between scientific and embedded applications is not caused by a significant difference in the number of IR instructions in the selected candidates. Scientific applications have on average 7.31 instructions per candidate, while embedded applications have on average 6.5 instructions per candidate.

Since we cannot decrease the size of the computational kernel, we should strive for finding larger candidates in order to cover a larger fraction of the kernel. Unfortunately, this turns out to be difficult because the reason that the candidates are small is that the BBs *(blk)* in which they are identified are also small. The average basic block has only 7.64 (5.94) IR instructions for a scientific (embedded) application (see Table 5).

The pruning mechanism we are using is directing the search for custom instruction to the largest basic blocks;

hence, the average basic block that passes the pruning stage has 155.65 instructions for a scientific and 29.71 for embedded application (see Table 6). However, even these larger blocks include a sizable number of the hardware-infeasible instructions, such as accesses to global variables or memory, which cannot be included in a hardware custom instruction. As a result, there are only 7.31 instructions per candidate in a scientific application which causes high break-even times for them.

This observation illustrates that there are practical limitations for the ASIP-SP when using code that has been compiled from imperative languages.

14. Reduction of Runtime Overheads

In this section, we propose two approaches for reducing the total runtime overheads and in turn also the break-even times: partial reconfiguration bitstream caching and acceleration of the CAD tool flow.

14.1. Partial Reconfiguration Bitstream Caching. As in many areas of computer science, caching can be applied also in the context of our work. Much like virtual machines cache the binary code that was generated on the fly for further use, we can cache the generated partial bitstreams for each custom instruction. To this end, each candidate needs to have a unique identifier that is used as a key for reading and writing the cache. We can, for example, compute a signature of the LLVM bitcode that describes the candidate for this purpose. The cached bitstreams can be stored for example in an on-disk database.

14.2. Acceleration of the CAD Tool Flow. A complementary method for reducing the runtime overheads is to accelerate the FPGA CAD tool flow. There are several options to achieve this goal. One possibility is to use a faster computer that provides faster CPUs and faster and larger memory or to run the FPGA tool concurrently. Alternatively, it may be possible to use a smaller FPGA device, since the *constant* processes of the tool flow depend strongly on the capacity of the FPGA device. We have used a rather large *Virtex-4 FX100* device, therefore switching to a smaller device would definitely reduce the runtime of the tool flow. Another option would be to use a memory file system for storing the files created by the tool flow. As the FPGA CAD tool flow is known to be I/O intensive, this should speed up the tool flow. Finally, we could change our architecture to a more coarse-grained architecture with simplified computing elements and limited or fixed routing. It has been shown that it is possible to develop customized tools for such architectures which work significantly faster [30].

14.3. Extrapolation. In Table 8 we calculate the average *breaking-even time* for the embedded applications when applying these ideas. When the cache is disabled and we do not assume any performance gain from the tool flow, the first value is equal to the *AVG_E* row and the last column in Table 6. One can note also that these values do not scale

TABLE 8: The average *breaking-even time* for the embedded applications using a *partial reconfiguration bitstream* cache and a faster FPGA CAD tool flow.

Cache hit [%]	Faster FPGA CAD tool flow [%]			
	0	30	60	90
	[h:m:s]	[h:m:s]	[h:m:s]	[h:m:s]
0	01:59:55	01:24:48	00:48:27	00:12:07
10	01:47:44	01:15:25	00:43:06	00:10:46
20	01:32:59	01:05:05	00:37:11	00:09:18
30	**01:28:09**	**01:01:42**	**00:35:15**	**00:08:49**
40	01:13:08	00:51:11	00:29:15	00:07:19
50	01:01:00	00:42:42	00:24:24	00:06:06
60	00:48:50	00:34:10	00:19:32	00:04:53
70	00:35:12	00:24:38	00:14:05	00:03:31
80	00:29:19	00:20:31	00:11:43	00:02:56
90	00:14:07	00:09:53	00:05:39	00:01:24

linearly because we consider the frequency information for basic blocks.

For this evaluation, we varied the assumed cache hit rate to be between 0%–90%. That is, for simulating a cache with a 20% hit rate, we have populated the cache with 20% of the required bitstreams for a particular application, whereas the selection whose bitstreams are stored in the cache is random. Whenever there is a *hit* in the cache for a given candidate, the whole runtime associated with the generation of the candidate is subtracted from the total runtime; see *sum* column in Table 6. The values in the *Faster FPGA CAD tool flow* columns are decreasing linearly with the assumed speedup.

If we assume that the FPGA CAD tool flow can be accelerated by 30% and that we have 30% cache hits, the average break-even time drops almost by half (1.94x), from *1:59:55 h* to *1:01:42 h*. This means that the whole runtime of the ASIP-SP could be compensated in a bit more than one hour and for the rest of the time the adapted architecture would provide a performance gain by an average factor of 5x. These assumptions are modest values since the *cache hit* rate depends only on the size of the cache, and our Dell T3500 workstation could be easily replaced by a faster one.

15. Conclusion and Future Work

In this work, we have studied the just-in-time ASIP-SP for an FPGA-based reconfigurable architecture. The most significant parts of this process, including the candidate identification, estimation, selection, and pruning mechanisms were not only described with precise formalisms but were also experimentally evaluated. In particular, we discussed and compared characteristics of three state-of-the-art instruction set extension algorithms in order to study the candidate identification mechanism in detail. This study included not only algorithm runtimes, number of found UDCI candidates, their properties, and impact of algorithm constraints on the search space, but more importantly the achievable maximum performance gains for various embedded computing and scientific benchmark applications.

The study of the ASIP process was performed both separately for every element but more importantly also for the entire ASIP process, where the feasibility and limitations were investigated. The study has shown that for embedded applications an average speedup of 5x can be achieved with a runtime overhead of less than 50 minutes. This overhead can be compensated if the application executes for two hours or for one hour when assuming a 30% cache hit rate and a faster FPGA CAD tool flow. Our study further showed that the larger and more complex software kernels of scientific applications, represented by the SPEC benchmarks, do not map well to custom hardware instructions targeting the Woolcano architecture and lead to excessive times until the break-even point is reached. The reason for this limitation can be found in the properties of the intermediate code generated by LLVM when compiling C code, in particular, rather small basic block sizes with an insufficient amount of instruction level parallelism. Similar results are expected for other imperative languages. Simultaneously, this work has explored the potential of our Woolcano reconfigurable architecture, the ISE algorithms, and pruning mechanism for them as well as the PivPav estimation and datapath synthesis tools.

References

[1] P. Ienne and R. Leupers, *Customizable Embedded Processors: Design Technologies and Applications*, Morgan Kaufmann, San Francisco, Calif, USA, 2006.

[2] M. J. Wirthlin and B. L. Hutchings, "Dynamic instruction set computer," in *Proceedings of the 3rd IEEE Symposium on FPGAs for Custom Computing Machines, (FCCM '95)*, pp. 99–107, IEEE Computer Society, April 1995.

[3] R. Razdan and M. D. Smith, "A high-performance microarchitecture with hardware-programmable functional units," in *Proceedings of the 27th International Symposium on Microarchitecture, (MICRO '94)*, pp. 172–180, ACM, New York, NY, USA, November 1994.

[4] Z. A. Ye, A. Moshovos, S. Hauck, and P. Banerjee, "Chimaera: a high-performance architecture with a tightly-coupled reconfigurable functional unit," in *Proceedings of the 27th Annual International Symposium on Computer Architecture, (ISCA '00)*, pp. 225–235, ACM, June 2000.

[5] P. M. Athanas and H. F. Silverman, "Processor reconfiguration through instruction-set metamorphosis," *Computer*, vol. 26, no. 3, pp. 11–18, 1993.

[6] M. Grad and C. Plessl, "Woolcano: an architecture and tool flow for dynamic instruction set extension on Xilinx Virtex-4 FX," in *Proceedings of the 9th International Conference on Engineering of Reconfigurable Systems and Algorithms (ERSA '09)*, pp. 319–322, CSREA Press, Monte Carlo Resort, Nev, USA, July 2009.

[7] J. M. Arnold, "S5: the architecture and development flow of a software configurable processor," in *Proceedings of the International Conference on Field Programmable Technology, (ICFPT '05)*, pp. 121–128, IEEE Computer Society, Kent Ridge Guild House, Singapore, December 2005.

[8] S. Borkar, "Design challenges of technology scaling," *IEEE Micro*, vol. 19, no. 4, pp. 23–29, 1999.

[9] M. Grad and C. Plessl, "An open source circuit library with benchmarking facilities," in *Proceedings of the 10th International Conference on Engineering of Reconfigurable Systems and Algorithms (ERSA, '10)*, T. P. Plaks, D. Andrews, R. F. DeMara et al., Eds., pp. 144–150, CSREA Press, Las Vegas, Nev, USA, July 2010.

[10] M. Grad and C. Plessl, "Pruning the design space for just-in-time processor customization," in *Proceedings of the International Conference on ReConFigurable Computing and FPGAs (ReConFig '10)*, pp. 67–72, IEEE Computer Society, Cancun, Mexico, December 2010.

[11] M. Grad and C. Plessl, "Just-in-time instruction set extension—feasibility and limitations for an FPGA-based reconfigurable ASIP architecture," in *Proceedings of the 18th Reconfigurable Architectures Workshop, (RAW '11)*, pp. 278–285, IEEE Computer Society, May 2011.

[12] M. Wazlowski, L. Agarwal, T. Lee et al., "PRISM-II compiler and architecture," in *Proceedings of the IEEE Symposium on Field-Programmable Custom Computing Machines, (FCCM '93)*, pp. 9–16, IEEE Computer Society, April 1993.

[13] C. Galuzzi and K. Bertels, "The instruction-set extension problem: a survey," in *Proceedings of the International Conference on Architecture of Computing Systems, (ARCS '08)*, Lecture Notes in Computer Science, no. 4943, pp. 209–220, Springer/Kluwer Academic, Dresden, Germany, February 2008.

[14] R. J. Hookway and M. A. Herdeg, "DIGITAL FX!32: combining emulation and binary translation," *Digital Technical Journal*, vol. 9, no. 1, pp. 3–12, 1997.

[15] V. Bala, E. Duesterwald, and S. Banerjia, "Transparent dynamic optimization," Tech. Rep. number HPL-1999-78, HP Laboratories Cambridge, 1999.

[16] K. Ebcioglu and E. R. Altman, "DAISY: dynamic compilation for 100% architectural compatibility," in *Proceedings of the 24th Annual International Symposium on Computer Architecture*, pp. 26–37, New York, NY, USA, June 1997.

[17] F. Vahid, G. Stitt, and R. Lysecky, "Warp processing: dynamic translation of binaries to FPGA circuits," *Computer*, vol. 41, no. 7, pp. 40–46, 2008.

[18] A. C. S. Beck and L. Carro, "Dynamic reconfiguration with binary translation: breaking the ILP barrier with software compatibility," in *Proceedings of the 42nd Design Automation Conference, (DAC '05)*, pp. 732–737, New York, NY, USA, June 2005.

[19] L. Pozzi, K. Atasu, and P. Ienne, "Exact and approximate algorithms for the extension of embedded processor instruction sets," *IEEE Transactions on Computer-Aided Design of Integrated Circuits and Systems*, vol. 25, no. 7, pp. 1209–1229, 2006.

[20] P. Yu and T. Mitra, "Scalable custom instructions identification for instruction-set extensible processors," in *Proceedings of the International Conference on Compilers, Architecture, and Synthesis for Embedded Systems, (CASES '04)*, pp. 69–78, Washington, DC, USA, September 2004.

[21] C. A. William, W. Fornaciari, L. Pozzi, and M. Sami, "A DAG-based design approach for reconfigurable VLIW processors," in *Proceedings of the Design, Automation and Test in Europe Conference, (DATE '99)*, pp. 778–779, ACM, Munich, Germany, January 1999.

[22] J. Gong, D. D. Gajski, and S. Narayan, "Software estimation from executable specifications," *Journal of Computer Software Engineering*, vol. 2, pp. 239–258, 1994.

[23] *The PowerPC 405TM Core*, IBM, 1998.

[24] A. Ray, T. Srikanthan, and W. Jigang, "Practical techniques for performance estimation of processors," in *Proceedings of the International Workshop on System-on-Chip for Real-Time Applications, (IWSOC '05)*, pp. 308–311, IEEE Computer Society, Washington, DC, USA, 2005.

[25] B. So, P. C. Diniz, and M. W. Hall, "Using estimates from behavioral synthesis tools in compiler-directed design space exploration," in *Proceedings of the 40th Design Automation Conference*, pp. 514–519, New York, NY, USA, June 2003.

[26] *Floating-Point Operator v5.0*, Xilinx.

[27] N. Maheshwari and S. S. Sapatnekar, *Timing Analysis and Optimization of Sequential Circuits*, Springer/Kluwer Academic Publishers, Norwell, Mass, USA, 1999.

[28] R. Meeuws, Y. Yankova, K. Bertels, G. Gaydadjiev, and S. Vassiliadis, "A quantitative prediction model for hardware/software partitioning," in *Proceedings of the International Conference on Field Programmable Logic and Applications, (FPL '07)*, pp. 735–739, Amsterdam, The Netherlands, August 2007.

[29] P. Bonzini and L. Pozzi, "Polynomial-time subgraph enumeration for automated instruction set extension," in *Proceedings of the Design, Automation and Test in Europe Conference and Exhibition*, pp. 1331–1336, Nice, France, April 2007.

[30] E. Bergeron, M. Feeley, and J. P. David, "Hardware JIT compilation for off-the-shelf dynamically reconfigurable FPGAs," in *Proceedings of the Joint European Conferences on Theory and Practice of Software 17th International Conference on Compiler Construction (CC/ETAPS'08)*, pp. 178–192, Springer-Verlag, Berlin, Heidelberg, 2008.

7

A Hardware-Accelerated ECDLP with High-Performance Modular Multiplication

Lyndon Judge, Suvarna Mane, and Patrick Schaumont

Bradley Department of Electrical and Computer Engineering, Center for Embedded Systems for Critical Applications (CESCA),
Virginia Tech, Blacksburg, VA 24061, USA

Correspondence should be addressed to Lyndon Judge, lvjudge1@vt.edu

Academic Editor: René Cumplido

Elliptic curve cryptography (ECC) has become a popular public key cryptography standard. The security of ECC is due to the difficulty of solving the elliptic curve discrete logarithm problem (ECDLP). In this paper, we demonstrate a successful attack on ECC over prime field using the Pollard rho algorithm implemented on a hardware-software cointegrated platform. We propose a high-performance architecture for multiplication over prime field using specialized DSP blocks in the FPGA. We characterize this architecture by exploring the design space to determine the optimal integer basis for polynomial representation and we demonstrate an efficient mapping of this design to multiple standard prime field elliptic curves. We use the resulting modular multiplier to demonstrate low-latency multiplications for curves secp112r1 and P-192. We apply our modular multiplier to implement a complete attack on secp112r1 using a Nallatech FSB-Compute platform with Virtex-5 FPGA. The measured performance of the resulting design is 114 cycles per Pollard rho step at 100 MHz, which gives 878 K iterations per second per ECC core. We extend this design to a multicore ECDLP implementation that achieves 14.05 M iterations per second with 16 parallel point addition cores.

1. Introduction

Elliptic curve cryptosystems (ECC), independently introduced by Miller [1] and Koblitz [2], have now found significant place in the academic literature, practical applications, and security standards. Their popularity is mainly because their shorter key sizes offer high levels of security relative to other public key cryptosystems, such as RSA. The security of ECC relies on the difficulty of elliptic curve discrete logarithmic problem (ECDLP) [3]. By definition, ECDLP is to find an integer n for two points P and Q on an elliptic curve E defined over a finite field $\mathbb{F}_q$ such that

$$Q = [n]P. \qquad (1)$$

Here, $[n]$ denotes the scalar multiplication with n.

The Pollard rho method [4] is the strongest known attack against ECC today. This method solves ECDLP by generating points on the curve iteratively using a pseudorandom iteration function $f : \langle S \rangle \rightarrow \langle S \rangle$ such that $X_{i+1} = f(X_i)$.

Since the elliptic curve is defined over a finite field, $\langle S \rangle$ is finite and the walk will eventually encounter the same point twice resulting in a collision. When a collision occurs, the ECDLP is solved (for well-chosen form of X_c; see Section 3). Several optimizations to the Pollard rho method have been proposed to allow independent parallel walks [5], better iteration functions [6, 7], and more efficient collision detection [8].

There have been several different approaches to implement Pollard rho algorithm on software and hardware platforms. Most of the solutions are implemented on software platforms using general purpose workstations, such as clusters of PlayStation3 [9], Cell CPUs [10], and GPUs [11, 12]. These software approaches are inherently limited by the sequential nature of software on the target platform.

Programmable hardware platforms are an attractive alternative to the above because they efficiently support parallelization. However, most of the FPGA-based solutions that have been proposed do not deal well with the control complexity of ECDLP. Instead, they focus on the efficient implementation of datapath operations and ignore the system integration aspect of the solution.

There has been little work in the area of supporting or accelerating a full Pollard rho algorithm on a hardware-software platform. Our solution, therefore, goes one step further as we demonstrate the parallelized Pollard rho algorithm on FPGA along with its integration to a software driver. We start from a reference software implementation, and demonstrate an efficient, parallel implementation of the prime field arithmetic for primes of the form $(2^n - m)/k$. We also present a novel high-performance architecture for modular multiplication that can be applied to a variety of standard prime field elliptic curves specified by the National Institute of Standards and Technology (NIST) [13] and Standards for Efficient Cryptography Group (SECG) [14].

Most existing ECDLP solutions for hardware platforms target curves over binary fields because the arithmetic is more hardware friendly. However, our work shows that implementation of prime field arithmetic on hardware can be as feasible as binary field arithmetic.

We use a computing platform by Nallatech, which consists of a quad-core Xeon core (E7310, 1.6 GHz) with a tightly coupled Virtex-5 (xq5vsx240t) FPGA. The hardware runs at 100MHz and uses 5229 slices per ECC core.

2. Related Work

The software solution proposed by Bernstein on Cell CPUs is the fastest existing software solution to the ECDLP for secp112r1 curve [15]. It uses the negation map and noninteger polynomial-basis arithmetic to report speedup over a similar solution by Bos et al. [9]. Both of these software solutions use prime field arithmetic in an affine coordinate system, and they exploit the SIMD architecture and rich instruction set of the Cell CPU. Another software solution by Bos [10] describes the implementation of parallel Pollard rho algorithm on synergistic processor units of cell broadband engine architecture to approach the ECC2K-130 Certicom challenge. High-performance ECDLP solutions for GPUs platforms have also been proposed in [12].

Fan et al. propose the use of a normal-basis, binary field multiplication to implement a high-speed attack on ECC2K-130 [16] using Spartan-3 FPGAs. Fan's solution outperforms attacks on the same curve using GPUs [12] and Cell CPUs [10], demonstrating the suitability of FPGA platforms for solving large ECDLPs in binary fields. Another binary field solution, for the COPACOBANA [17] FPGA cluster, targets a 160-bit curve [18]. Güneysu et al. propose an architecture to solve ECDLP over prime fields using FPGAs and analyze its estimated performance for different ECC curves ranging from 64-to 160-bit fields [19].

Among hardware-based solutions, Meurice de Dormale et al. propose an FPGA solution to attack the ECC Certicom challenge for $GF(2^{113})$ [20]. Though it discusses the hardware-software integration aspect of the solution, the authors did not confirm if their system was operational. The authors of [19] discuss some aspects of system-level

integration for their prime-field ECDLP system. A three-layer hybrid distributed system is described by Majkowski et al. to solve ECDLP over binary field [21]. It uses the general purpose computers with FPGAs and integrates them with a main server at the top level.

The outline of the paper is as follows. In the next section, we discuss the background of the parallel Pollard rho algorithm. We present our high-performance architecture for modular multiplication and demonstrate its applicability to primes of the form $(2^n - m)/k$ in Section 4. In Section 5, we discuss the additional modular arithmetic units and we describe the complete hardware-software integrated system architecture in Section 6. Section 7 shows implementation results, including measured performance for secp112r1 ECDLP, and we conclude the paper in Section 8.

3. Pollard Rho Algorithm

Let p be a prime and $\mathbb{F}_p = GF(p)$. Given the elliptic curve E over $\mathbb{F}_p$ of order $l = |E(\mathbb{F}_p)|$, let $S \in E(\mathbb{F}_p)$ be a point of order l. Solving the ECDLP requires finding an integer n given two points $P, Q \in \langle S \rangle$ such that $Q = nP$.

The Pollard rho algorithm [4] uses a pseudorandom iteration function $f : \langle S \rangle \rightarrow \langle S \rangle$ to solve the ECDLP. It conducts a pseudorandom walk by starting from a random seed point on the curve, $X_0 = a_0 P + b_0 Q$ for random $a_0, b_0 \in \mathbb{Z}$, and generating subsequent points using the iteration function $X_{i+1} = f(X_i)$. Since the elliptic curve is defined over a finite field, the iteration function will eventually produce the same point twice, resulting in a cycle.

The name of the algorithm, rho, expresses the Greek letter ρ, which shows a walk ending in a cycle. Cycles can be efficiently detected using Floyd's cycle-finding method or Brent's cycle-finding algorithm [8]. The collision point, which gives the solution to the ECDLP, is located at the starting point of the cycle. Therefore, the underlying idea of this algorithm is to search for two distinct points on the curve such that $f(X_i) = f(X_j)$. Due to the birthday paradox, assuming a random iteration function, the expected number of iterations to find collision is $\sqrt{(\pi \cdot |\langle X \rangle|)/2}$ [4].

The effectiveness of Pollard's rho method depends on the randomness of the iteration function. As such, studies have been conducted to evaluate the strength of various proposed iteration functions [6, 7, 22]. Teske proposes an additive iteration function:

$$f(X_i) = X_i + R_i(X_i), \qquad (2)$$

where R_i is an index function $\langle S \rangle \rightarrow \{0, 1, \ldots, r - 1\}$ and each element $R_j = a_j P + b_j Q$, for random values $a_j, b_j \in \mathbb{Z}$ [7]. Based on analysis by Teske [6, 7] and Bos et al. [22], the additive iteration function is more similar to a truly random walk than Pollard's original function and other proposed variants. Furthermore, an additive walk with $r \geq 16$ is very close to a true randomness and achieves speedup of 1.25X over Pollard's iteration function [6]. Thus, we perform an additive walk and choose $r = 16$.

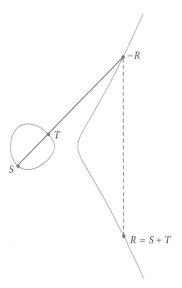

FIGURE 1: Geometric representation of elliptic curve point addition.

Using the additive walk, a collision occurs when two points are found such that

$$X_i + R_i = X_j + R_j. \tag{3}$$

Based on the definition of the index function R_i, the collision points can be rewritten as

$$c_i P + d_i Q = c_j P + d_j Q, \tag{4}$$

where $c_i = \sum_{k=0}^{i} a_k$ and $d_i = \sum_{k=0}^{i} b_k$. The solution can then be obtained as

$$n = \left[\frac{c_i - c_j}{d_j - d_i} \right] \mathrm{mod} l. \tag{5}$$

3.1. Point Addition. Each iteration of the Pollard's rho algorithm requires a point addition of the current point, X_i, with a precomputed combination of P and Q, $R_i(X_i)$. Addition of two distinct points for an elliptic curve over a finite field $GF(p)$, $S + T = R$ is defined geometrically as shown in Figure 1. To compute the addition, a line is drawn through the two points S and T. The line intersects exactly one other point of the elliptic curve. The intersection point is $-R$, which can be reflected across the x-axis to find R.

Algebraically, adding two points $S = (x_S, y_S)$ and $T = (x_T, y_T)$ gives the sum $R = (x_R, y_R)$, where

$$x_R = \lambda^2 - (x_S + x_T),$$

$$y_R = \lambda(x_S - x_R) - y_S, \tag{6}$$

$$\lambda = \frac{y_S - y_T}{x_S - x_T}.$$

Each point addition requires 2 multiplications modulo p, 1 modular squaring, 5 modular subtractions, 1 modular addition, and 1 modular inversion. The sequence of arithmetic operations for a point addition is shown in Table 1.

TABLE 1: Arithmetic operations for point addition: $S + T = R$.

Operation	Function performed
Modular subtraction	$t1 = y_S - y_T$
Modular subtraction	$t2 = x_S - x_T$
Modular inversion	$t2 = t2^{-1}$
Modular multiplication	$t4 = t2 \cdot t1 : \lambda$
Modular squaring	$t1 = t4 \cdot t4$
Modular addition	$t3 = x_S + x_T$
Modular subtraction	$t1 = t1 - t3 : x_R$
Modular subtraction	$t2 = x_R - t1$
Modular multiplication	$t3 = t2 \cdot t4$
Modular subtraction	$t3 = t3 - y_S : y_R$

By Fermat's Little Theorem, $z^{-1} = z^{p-2}$ for $z \in GF(p)$. Thus, computing modular inversion requires modular exponentiation, making inversion the most computationally expensive operation of the point addition. Optimization at the system level can reduce the cost of inversion through the use of Montgomery's trick [23]. Montgomery's trick makes it possible to share the cost of an inversion among M computations by performing inversions on vectors of M points simultaneously. Since the computational cost of inversion is two orders of magnitude more than other arithmetic operations, this results in significant savings over computation of M individual modular inversions. We apply Montgomery's trick by implementing a vectorized point addition datapath that computes M random walks on a single ECC core and shares the inversion cost across all walks.

Despite optimizations, inversion remains an expensive operation. Since exponentiation is achieved using multiplication, the cost of inversion is directly tied to the cost of modular multiplication. Therefore, design of an efficient modular multiplier is an important aspect of the system to maximize overall performance.

3.2. Comparison of Field Arithmetic in $GF(p)$ and $GF(2^m)$. Standards for elliptic curve cryptography have been defined for curves over both binary and prime fields [13, 14]. Binary fields can be represented with a polynomial basis or normal basis. In general, hardware implementations favor polynomial basis because it allows simplified reduction through the use of an irreducible polynomial of the form $x^{m-1} + \cdots + x^2 + x^1 + x^0$. Prior work has confirmed the idea that binary field curves are better suited for hardware platforms. A comparison of ECDLP engines by [20] shows a significant speedup for binary field ECDLP over prime field ECDLP implemented on FPGA platform. The performance discrepancy between ECDLPs for binary field and prime field curves is due to differences in the required arithmetic operations for each field and the use of search optimization techniques for selected curves.

The Pollard rho method is the best known attack on ECC for curves defined over both binary and prime fields, but the cost of the attack varies based on the properties of the finite field arithmetic. Elliptic curves over prime fields require conventional integer arithmetic operations followed by costly reduction modulo p. However, the properties of curves over GF(2^m) allow optimizations that can reduce the cost of point addition. Additions and subtractions in the binary finite field are reduced to XOR operations with no carry. Furthermore, the cost of modular reduction is reduced to parallel XOR gates for binary fields. For comparison, reduction modulo p requires sequential additions of carry bits and has a cycle cost approximately equal to that of multiplication. Although attacks on curves over GF(2^m) can be considerably faster than attacks on curves over GF(p), NIST security standards recommend approximately equivalent field sizes for both binary and prime field curves at a given security level [13].

3.3. Parallelization.

Van Oorschot and Wiener [5] described a parallelization technique that enables parallel walks on a single curve of Pollard rho algorithm to speed up the computation of ECDLP. The idea is to define a subset of $\langle S \rangle$ as distinguished points (DPs), points which have a distinguishing characteristic. Each parallel walk starts from a distinct random seed point of the form $X_0 = a_0 P + b_0 Q$ and continues a Pollard rho walk until it encounters a point that satisfies the distinguishing property. Due to properties of the index function of the additive iteration function, a collision between two parallel walks at any point causes the walks to be identical from that point forward. Therefore, checking only DPs for collisions reduces communication and search overhead, while ensuring that any collision between walks is detected. Once a collision is detected, the server must derive the secret key using the collision point and the distinct seed points of the colliding walk. Therefore, whenever a DP is found, it is transmitted to the server along with the random seed point that generated the walk. The parallel Pollard rho method allows distribution of the random walks among multiple processing clients and sharing all DPs found with a central server that performs a collision search. This technique results in a linear speedup as the number of clients increases.

The expected number of DPs required to find a collision is a fraction of the expected path length. This depends on the density of DPs in a point set $\langle S \rangle$, which in turn depends on the chosen distinguishing property. Consider a distinguishing property defined as a point with d-bits fixed in its y-coordinate. This results in a probability of 2^{-d} that a given point is a DP and $|\langle S \rangle|/2^d$ total DPs on the curve. Each walk will require 2^d steps on average to find a DP. Based on the birthday paradox, the number DPs required to find a collision is

$$\phi \geq \frac{\sqrt{(\pi \cdot |\langle S \rangle|)/2}}{2^d}. \tag{7}$$

Since each DP is generated from a walk with a unique random seed point, the number of parallel walks required to solve the ECDLP is also ϕ.

4. Modular Multiplication

We have designed a novel architecture for modular multiplication in a prime field. Typically, hardware solutions use binary field arithmetic, primarily due to the assumption that binary field avoids the costly carry propagation of prime field arithmetic. However, we demonstrate that prime field arithmetic can be efficiently implemented in hardware.

We target the 112-bit secp112r1 elliptic curve in GF($(2^{128} - 3)/76439$), but demonstrate that the proposed architecture can be generalized to perform multiplication modulo any prime of the form $(2^n - m)/k$.

We perform prime field arithmetic using a redundant 128-bit polynomial representation in an affine coordinate system, as proposed by Bernstein et al. in [15] and Bos et al. in [9]. We represent the integers in secp112r1 redundantly in the ring $R = \mathbb{Z}/q\mathbb{Z}$, where $q = p * 76439$. This allows us to perform reduction modulo $2^{128} - 3$, rather than modulo $(2^{128} - 3)/76439$. We perform all arithmetic over the 128-bit field using following method.

Reduction for the unbalanced coefficient $q = 2^{128} - 3$ is a constant multiplication and an addition. Assuming $A = A_1 \cdot 2^{128} + A_0$, then $A \mod q = A_0 + 3 \cdot A_1$. Integers represented redundantly mod q can be converted into a canonical form in GF(p) by multiplying with $a = 76439$. Let $a \mid q$ and $p = q/a$. Then, $v \mod p \equiv v \cdot a \mod q$. Therefore, we start with a unique representation in GF(p), perform arithmetic in R, and canonicalize the results in R to a unique representation by multiplying with $a = 76439$. Similar redundant representation can be used to simplify reduction for any prime $p = (2^n - m)/k$ where $k \neq 0$ by performing arithmetic modulo $q = 2^n - m$ and canonicalizing results by multiplication with k.

4.1. Modular Multiplication Algorithm.

Bernstein et al. [15] use noninteger basis for polynomial representation of data to achieve an efficient software implementation. We choose integer basis representation to make the partial product computation uniform across all coefficients, which also makes the design scalable over larger fields. Each l-bit operand is represented as $\sum_{i=0}^{n_a-1} x_i \cdot 2^{i \cdot l_a}$, where $n_a = l/l_a$, l is the length of the operand, and l_a is the integer basis. For secp112r1 curve, $l = 128$ and we discuss optimization of quantity l_a in a subsequent section.

Our approach to modular multiplication is based on the design proposed by Güneysu and Paar in [25]. We use schoolbook multiplication to compute the product $R = F \cdot G$, for $F, G \in$ GF(q). Schoolbook multiplication requires computation of n_a^2 partial products in $O(n^2)$ time, where $R = \sum_{i=0}^{2n_a} 2^{i \cdot n_a} \sum_{j=0}^{i} F_j \cdot G_{i-j}$. We parallelize computation of the partial products to perform n_a multiplications in parallel by multiplying one field of one operand, G, with all fields from the other operand, F. As proposed by Güneysu and Paar in [25], placing G in a shift register and F in a rotating register ensures that each multiplier produces aligned results, that can be directly accumulated. Our design adds an important optimization of the reduction step. We integrate reduction modulo q into the multiplication by multiplying the most significant field of F by m when rotating it to the least significant field. In order to accommodate the multiplication by m of each field of F, we represent each field of F with $l_a + \log_2 m$ bits.

Each partial product is an $l_a + \log_2 m \times l_a$-bit multiplication and produces a $2l_a + \log_2 m$-bit result. After accumulation,

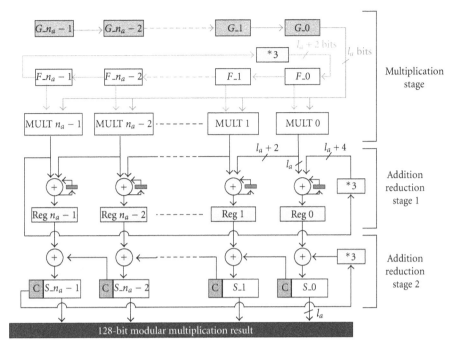

FIGURE 2: Modular multiplication architecture.

each field of the result can be up to $2l_a + \log_2 m + \log_2 n_a$ bits. We reduce each field to l_a bits using two parallel carry chains. The first carry chain is integrated into partial product accumulation and accumulates the lower l_a-bits of partial product i with the upper bits of partial product $i - 1$. The second carry chain adds the upper bits of each accumulated partial product in column i to the lower bits of the next accumulated partial product in column $i + 1$. In both carry chains, reduction modulo q is achieve by multiplying the upper bits of the most significant field, $i = n_a - 1$, by m before adding them to the least significant field, $i = 0$. The final l-bit result is obtained by concatenating the l_a-bit reduced outputs. The parallel carry chains allow us to overlap the multiplication and reduction stages of the the algorithm to achieve significantly lower latency relative to prior work [25].

4.2. Hardware Architecture.

Figure 2 depicts our hardware architecture to implement modular multiplication for secp112r1 elliptic curve with general field size parameters $l = 128$; l_a, n_a. This architecture targets a Xilinx Virtex 5 FPGA platform and makes use of dedicated DSP blocks for high-performance arithmetic. Each DSP block includes a 25×18-bit multiplier and the FPGA fabric includes dedicated routing paths for high-speed connections between DSP blocks [26]. The DSP blocks allow each $l_a + 2 \times l_a$-bit partial product multiplication and accumulation to be computed in a single clock cycle. The modular multiplication takes two 128-bit inputs, F and G, divided into $n_a l_a$-bit fields and produces a 128-bit output of the product reduced modulo $2^{128} - 3$. There are n_a DSP48 multipliers employed to compute partial products of l_a-bit coefficients. Since the n_a^2 partial products are required, it takes n_a multiplication cycles to complete the full unreducedmultiplication result.

Reduction modulo $q = 2^{128} - 3$ adds to the cycle cost of a modular multiplication. By multiplying the shifting operand F_{l_a-1} with 3, we perform the reduction in parallel with the multiplication. For the 128-bit data field with $l_a = 16$ and $n_a = 8$, it takes eight cycles of multiplication and 12 iterations of reduction. This results in a total cycle cost of 20 cycles per modular multiplication. However, our algorithm reduces this cost by overlapping reduction with partial product multiplication and accumulation using the previously described parallel carry adder chains. Thus, the cost has been reduced to 14 cycles, a significant improvement in latency over the architecture proposed by Güneysu and Paar in [25], which takes 70 clock cycles for 256-bit modular multiplication.

4.3. Optimizations.

To achieve optimal performance, we evaluate the impact of the integer basis for the polynomial representation on the latency of our design. The performance of the modular multiplier is heavily influenced by the value selected for l_a, which determines the length of each field in the operands and the number of partial products to be computed. Our architecture relies on fast computation of partial products using the available DSP blocks on the FPGA; so performance is also impacted by the suitability of the selected field size to efficiently use these resources.

Modification of our architecture to support different field lengths for polynomial representation is straightforward requiring only that the number of multiplier-adder columns be changed. The number of multiplier-adder columns is given by n_a, which is related to the field length l_a. Increasing the field length requires fewer columns in the architecture and reduces the number of partial products computed. The results of this exploration will be discussed in Section 7.2.

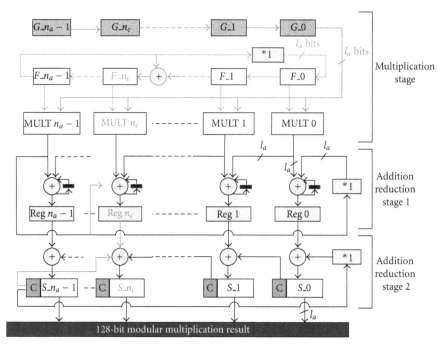

FIGURE 3: Modular multiplication architecture: extension to NIST P-192 curve.

4.4. Extension to Other Curves. Our modular multiplier is a generalized architecture that can be easily adapted to any overellipticcurve over GF(p), where p has the form $(2^n - m)/k$. We demonstrate this by adapting the architecture for NIST standard P-192 curve, which uses the prime $p = 2^{192} - 2^{64} - 1$. The multiplier architecture is shown in Figure 3. The multiplication for this 192-bit NIST curve is similar to that of secp112r1 curve, but the 192-bit curve needs additional multiplication-adder columns. Additionally, P-192 uses $m = 2^{64} - 1$, rather than $m = 3$ for secp112r1, which requires the following reduction operation. With polynomial field size l_a, we define n_c as the field containing 2^{64}, which is $n_c = 64/l_a$. For $A = A_{n_a-1} \cdot 2^{192} + A_{n_c} \cdot 2^{64} + A_0$, the reduction modulo p is $A \bmod p = (A_{n_c} + A_{n_a} - 1) \cdot 2^{64} + (A_0 + A_{n_a-1})$.

We modify the modular multiplier architecture as follows to make it compatible with P-192 curve.

(i) Multiplication factor 3 is replaced by 1 in the rotation path of multiplication stage as well as in the addition reduction feedback path. This reduces the number of bits in each field of operand F to l_a-bits and the length of partial product outputs to $2l_a$-bits.

(ii) In the rotation path, operand field F_{n_a-1} is fed back to two F_{n_c} and F_0. An adder is introduced before F_{n_c} for this purpose. Thus, $F_{n_c} = F_{n_c-1} + F_{n_a-1}$.

(iii) In addition reduction stage 1, carry bits of highest accumulator output (Reg $n_a - 1$) are fed back to both Reg n_c and Reg 0. Similarly in addition reduction stage 2, carry bits of S_{n_a-1} are folded and added back to both S_{n_c} and S_0.

The adapted architecture has a latency of 17 clock cycles at 193 MHz for $l_a = 16$ and has area of 364 Virtex 5 FPGA slices and 12 DSP cores. This is comparable to the multiplier performance for curve secp112r1 (given in Section 7.2) and demonstrates the flexibility of our design to accelerate modular multiplier for general standard prime field elliptic curve.

5. Additional Modular Arithmetic Units for ECDLP

The field operation of a point addition in GF(p) corresponds to a Pollard rho step that consists of four subtractions, one addition, four modular multiplications, and one inversion. This requires design of modular adder/subtractor and modular inversion units. Subsequent sections explain the architecture of these arithmetic modules in detail.

5.1. Addition/Subtraction. We use an integer basis polynomial representation to perform addition and subtraction modulo q using high-speed DSP blocks in the FPGA. We choose a field size of 32, which allows the use of four parallel DSP adder/subtractors to compute the sum of the two 128-bit operands. Our design requires one cycle for the addition/subtraction and one additional cycle for reduction modulo q.

5.2. Inversion. From Fermat's little theorem, it follows that the modular inverse of $z \in \mathbb{F}_q$ can be obtained by computing z^{p-2}. Therefore, computation of the modular inverse requires exponentiation to the $p - 2$ power, which is achieved through successive square and multiply operations. For secp112r1 curve, we start with z and compute $z^{((2^{128}-3)/76439)-2}$. We perform exponentiation using a variant of the left to right binary method, also known as square and multiply method

```
Input: z ∈ 𝔽_q, e[t : 0]
Output: z^e mod q
    r ← 1
    for i = t → 0 do
        r ← r · r mod q
        if e[i] = 1 then
            r ← r · z mod q
    return r
```

ALGORITHM 1: Square and multiply modular exponentiation [24].

[24]. This method scans a bitwise representation of the exponent left to right considering one bit at a time. A squaring is performed for each bit in the exponent, and an additional multiplication by the input operand is performed whenever the current bit is 1. The basic algorithm is shown as Algorithm 1. Due to dependencies between each operation, parallelization of the algorithm is not possible; it needs 112 squarings and 59 multiplications to compute an inversion for secp112r1 curve in 128-bit arithmetic. We improve these figures by applying the following techniques to optimize the inversion operation.

5.2.1. Windowing Optimization.
We apply the sliding window method [24] to reduce the number of squarings and multiplications required for inversion. The windowing method is an optimization of the square and multiply algorithm that considers multiple bits of the exponent simultaneously. Computing z^{p-2} with window size k requires precomputation of z^2 and the first $2^{k-1} - 1$ odd powers of z. This method considers up to k bits of the exponent in each iteration and performs a multiplication with one of the precomputed powers of z based on the value of those bits. The sliding window method for modular exponentiation is shown as Algorithm 2.

We achieve optimal performance for a window size of four, which allows inversion with only 108 squarings and 29 modular multiplications. This results in a total of 137 multiplication operations, rather than 171 operations without windowing, a speedup of 1.25.

5.2.2. Vector Inversion.
To further reduce the cost of an inversion, we use Montgomery's trick [23], which allows multiple modular inverses to be computed together for significant latency savings. Montgomery's trick is based on the observation that given $(z_1 \cdot z_2 \cdots \cdot z_M)^{-1}$, the individual inverses $z_1^{-1}, z_2^{-1}, \ldots, z_M^{-1}$ can be easily computed. This allows computation of M modular inverses using $3(M-1)$ multiplications and one inversion. Although the cost of a single inversion is two orders of magnitude higher than multiplication, this approach allows the cost of inversion to be shared across M operations so the marginal cost of an inversion becomes comparable to other arithmetic operations for large vector size M. The algorithm for vector inversion using Montgomery's trick is shown as Algorithm 3.

```
Input: z ∈ 𝔽_q, e[t : 0], k ≥ 1
Output: z^e mod q
    // Precomputation
    p_0 ← z, s ← z · z mod q
    for i = 1 → 2^{k-1} - 1 do
        p_i ← p_{i-1} · s
    // Inversion
    r ← 1
    i ← t
    while i ≥ 0 do
        if e_i = 0 then
            r ← r · r mod q
            i ← i - 1
        else
            Find longest string e[i : l] where e[l] = 1
            and i - l + 1 ≤ k
            r ← r · p_{e[i:l]} mod q
            for j = 0 → (i - l + 1) do
                r ← r · r mod q
            i ← i - l - 1
    return r
```

ALGORITHM 2: Sliding window modular exponentiation [24].

```
Input: z_1, z_2, … z_M ∈ 𝔽_q
Output: z_1^{-1}, z_2^{-1}, … z_M^{-1} ∈ 𝔽_q
    // Preprocessing
    x_1 ← z_1
    for i = 2 → M do
        x_i ← x_{i-1} · z_i mod q
    // Inversion
    y_M ← x_M^{-1}
    // Postprocessing
    for i = M - 1 → 1 do
        y_i ← y_{i+1} · z_{i+1} mod q
        z_{i+1} ← y_{i+1} · x_i mod q
    z_1 ← y_1
    return z_1^{-1}, z_2^{-1}, … z_M^{-1}
```

ALGORITHM 3: Vector inversion using Montgomery's trick [23].

We apply this method by implementing a vectorized inversion module that applies Algorithm 3 for any vector size M. To take advantage of vectorized inversion, we design a vectorized point addition datapath that performs random walks on a vector of points simultaneously. We choose vector size $M = 32$, which yields speedup of $19\times$ over 32 individual inversions, and leave optimization of this quantity for future work.

5.3. Squaring.
An inversion involves a total of 137 modular multiplications out of which 75% are squaring operations. Having a dedicated squaring unit allows specific optimizations to take advantage of the properties of squaring and reduces the time required to compute an inversion. Consequently, a dedicated module optimized for squaring provides significant acceleration of the point addition operation.

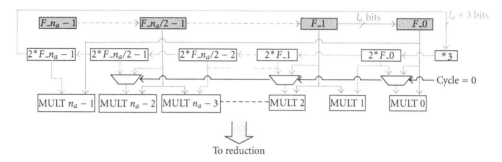

FIGURE 4: Dedicated squaring architecture.

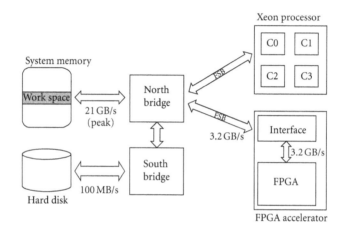

FIGURE 5: Nallatech system.

Squaring is a special case of the general multiplication of two 128-bit operands F and G. During squaring $F = G$, all off-diagonal partial products, represented as $F_i \cdot F_j$ for $i \neq j$, are computed twice by the conventional schoolbook multiplication method used by our modular multiplier. To reduce computational cost of squaring, we avoid computing any partial product more than once by altering the operand control structure of our multiplier design as shown in Figure 4.

We represent the operand F using the same integer basis for polynomial representation previously described for our modular multiplier. We copy F into a shift register and a rotating register, each with $n_a l_a$-bit fields for polynomial representation, to achieve aligned accumulation of partial products. As shown in Figure 4, the first cycle of multiplication computes the partial products on the diagonal, that is, $F_i * F_j$ where $i = j$. All remaining partial products are off-diagonal. Since off-diagonal partial products are computed twice in schoolbook multiplication, we multiply each field of the rotating register by 2 before computing these partial products. The multiplication by 2 is implemented as a bit shift left at negligible cost. This reduces the number of partial product multiplications from n^2 to $n(n + 1)/2$. The reduction stage for the square module is identical to that of multiplication.

6. ECDLP System Architecture

Our complete ECDLP system is implemented on a Nallatech cointegrated hardware software platform. Figure 5 depicts the architecture of the Nallatech system. It consists of one quad-core Xeon processor E7310 and three Virtex-5 FPGAs (1 xc5vlx110, 2 xc5vsx240t). A fast North Bridge integrates high-speed components, including a Xeon, FPGA, and main memory. A slower South Bridge integrates peripherals into the system, including the hard disk. Both the Xeon and the FPGA can directly access system memory using a Front Side Bus (FSB). The FPGA performs the computationally expensive Pollard rho iterations, while the Xeon processor manages the central database of distinguished points and executes collision search. The communication between software and hardware is carried out only for the exchange of seed points and distinguished points, which minimizes the communication overhead.

6.1. Software Driver. The Xeon processor executes a software driver (in C) and manages software interface to FSB. The software driver mainly handles the communication interface with FPGA; seed point (SP) generation; storage and sorting of DPs. As shown in Figure 5, two-way communication between the Xeon and the FPGA takes place over the FSB.

When the program execution starts, the software calls APIs to configure FPGA card, to initialize the FSB link, and

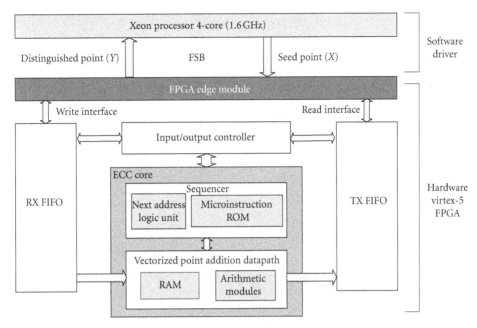

FIGURE 6: System architecture.

to allocate the workspace memory. It then generates random SPs on the curve E and starts an attack by sending them to the FPGA over FSB. Every point has x- and y-coordinates of 128-bit length each.

The hardware finds a DP for each SP received and sends it to the software along with its corresponding SP. When the software receives SP-DP pair from the FPGA, it performs a collision search among all the received DPs. Once a collision is detected, it computes the secret scalar and reports the solution to the ECDLP. As the software takes care of the central database of DPs, a collision search is conducted in parallel with hardware computations.

6.2. Hardware Accelerator. On the hardware side, as shown in Figure 6, the FPGA edge core provides an interface between the FSB and the ECC core. The edge core consists of control logic and two 256-bit wide FIFOs. The RX FIFO buffers the incoming SPs received over FSB and the TX FIFO stores the DPs found for transmission to the Xeon.

The ECC core performs a random walk by computing the point addition operation iteratively until it finds a DP and stores that in the TX FIFO. We have defined DP as a point with 16 zeros in fixed positions such that $y[123 : 116] = 0$ and $y[59 : 52] = 0$. The probability of a point being distinguished is almost exactly 2^{-16}.

The distinguishing property of points allows to send only few points back to the Xeon, which reduces the communication overhead and minimizes the storage requirement in the hardware. The required bandwidth of communication bus is around 8 K bits/sec, which is well within the range of FSB. In the following are the details of key components in the design.

6.2.1. IO Controller. The IO controller manages the read/write interfaces of TX-RX FIFOs and controls the ECC

core operation. It loads the SPs from the RX FIFO to each ECC core and initiates a Pollard rho walk. When a DP is found, the IO controller halts the ECC core operation until a new SP is loaded from the RX FIFO. The computed DPs are buffered in the TX FIFO and then transferred to the Xeon along with corresponding SPs.

6.2.2. ECC Core. The ECC core consists of a microinstruction sequencer and the vectorized point addition (PA) datapath. The core operates on vectors of M-elements to perform M-independent random walks simultaneously. Each walk continues until it finds a DP or crosses the iteration limit, which is currently set to 2^{20}.

6.2.3. Vectorized Datapath. The datapath consists of modular arithmetic operators and memory. Each of these modules is designed to support vectorized point additions. A block diagram of the vectorized datapath is shown in Figure 7. As shown, each of the arithmetic modules interfaces directly to memory in order to load operands and store results. The modular add/sub, modular multiply, and distinguished point check modules are nonvectorized components and operate on inputs from one vector at a time. In order to complete each arithmetic operation over the vectorized walks, computation is serialized and repeated M times for each of these operations. Conversely, the inversion module receives inputs from all M vectors simultaneously and computes the inverse of all inputs together using the previously described vector inversion algorithm.

Based on the sequence of arithmetic operations required for point addition shown in Table 1, we need eight registers ($t1$, $t2$, $t3$, $t4$, Px, Py, Qx, and Qy) to hold the intermediate results for a each point addition. For vector size of M, we use M-entry register files to store these intermediate results.

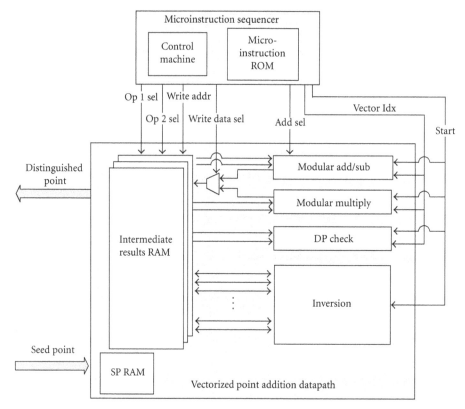

FIGURE 7: Vectorized point addition datapath with microinstruction sequencer.

Each of the memories is 128 bits wide and has a depth equal to the vector size M. The memory address corresponds to the vector index for each stored data value. We map these register files to the distributed RAMs available in the Xilinx Virtex 5 FPGA. We use an additional 256-bit M-entry memory to store the original seed points for each parallel walk. When a distinguished point is found, that point, along with the original seed point stored in the SP RAM, is send to the IO controller for transmission to the software driver.

6.2.4. Microinstruction Sequencer. We implement a microinstruction sequencer that operates alongside the vectorized point addition datapath to provide control signals necessary to compute vectorized point addition. This allows control of the execution flow of the low-level arithmetic operations for a point addition without modification of the datapath. As shown in Figure 6, the sequencer consists of a microinstruction ROM, which stores instructions to implement point addition, and a next address logic unit (NALU), which determines instruction execution order based on outputs from the datapath. The interconnections between the point addition datapath and microinstruction sequencer are shown in Figure 7.

The vectorized point addition datapath requires a number of control signals to implement each arithmetic operation. A microcoded controller allows us to encode these various control signals into compact form, while maintaining maximum flexibility to modify design parameters including vector size and number of parallel ECC cores.

It provides an efficient mechanism to separate our system's control and datapath. Since we use a very specific datapath to perform the particular sequence of operations for point addition, we include only microinstructions needed for the point addition. These correspond directly to the operations shown in Table 1. Common instructions required for general purpose microprocessors, such as *jump, check flag* and are not implemented for our design.

Our microinstruction format is shown in Figure 8. Each microinstruction includes three main segments, arithmetic operation selection, controlled by microinstruction bits 4–0, operand selection, controlled by bits 10–5, and register file write command, controlled by bits 20–11. Decoded control signals from each instruction are connected to datapath inputs as shown in Figure 7.

The next address logic unit (NALU) controls execution order of the microinstructions contained in the ROM. The NALU also handles vectorization of the point addition datapath by repeating each addition, subtraction, multiplication, and distinguished point check operation M times for vector size M. This ensures that the same microinstruction is applied sequentially to each element in the vector. Since the modular arithmetic operations have different latencies, the NALU relies on ready signals generated by datapath components to detect the completion of each instruction. This maximizes flexibility of the microinstruction sequencer and allows the NALU to be independent of the datapath implementation.

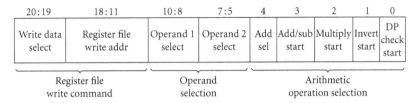

FIGURE 8: Microcoded instruction format.

In a given cycle, the NALU reads a microinstruction i and issues the corresponding control signals to point addition datapath. These control signals include a start pulse, operand selection, register file write, destination register select, and vector index. Unlike the other control signals, vector index is generated by a finite-state machine within the NALU, rather than decoded directly from microinstruction i. To execute nonvectorized operations, that is all arithmetic operations other than inversion, the vector index is reset and control signals are applied to the datapath. The vector control finite-state machine increments the vector index when the datapath operation completes and asserts the control signals for the next vector element. This continues until the operation is completed for all M vector elements. Then, the vector index resets and the NALU reads the next microinstruction from the ROM.

For an inversion operation, the NALU asserts control signals to load operands and store results from all vector elements. This allows loading of M inputs into the inversion module and writing M results into the corresponding register files. In this way, we efficiently implement vector inversion using Montgomery's trick within the point addition datapath. An inversion is performed only once per M vectors, whereas the other instructions are repeated M times.

6.2.5. Parallel Pollard Rho Walks. We have extended our design to support parallel Pollard rho walks by implementing multiple ECC cores on the FPGA. Each ECC core receives a separate set of SPs and performs a vectorized walk. We have extended the IO controller to support multiple ECC cores so that control signals from all cores are monitored. When a DP is found, the walk by the corresponding ECC core is halted while the IO controller retrieves the DP and loads a new SP. Since each ECC core contains its own microinstruction sequencer module, the multiple cores are not restricted to SIMD execution. When one core is in the process of sending DPs or receiving SPs, the other cores continue execution, avoiding costly latency associated with SIMD configuration.

Our design is scalable to support any number of parallel cores. The IO controller can be configured to support any number of cores. The total number of ECC cores in our design is only limited to the capacity of the FPGA. Our Nallatech computing platform includes two Xilinx Virtex 5 FPGA accelerators and both can be used simultaneously to implement ECC cores to maximize parallelization of Pollard rho walks to solve the ECDLP. Each core performs an independent walk and there is no additional overhead in the point addition iterations due to using multiple cores. Therefore, implementing multiple ECC cores produces a linear increase in performance.

7. Implementation Results

We have implemented our proposed system on the described Nallatech platform in both single- and multicore variants. For demonstration purposes, the seed points that we generate are carefully chosen to be of order 2^{50} [15], which means we would need only 2^{25} steps to solve the ECDLP. This allows us to demonstrate collisions, proving that our solution works.

7.1. Overall Performance. The whole system runs at 100 MHz and uses 5229 slices which is 13% area of the Virtex-5 device xq5vsx240t with a single ECC core. It takes 1.14 microseconds per Pollard rho step and can perform up to 878,000 iterations per second per ECC core.

Our design can easily be extended to include multiple ECC cores performing parallel walks. Each additional ECC core produces as linear increase in performance with negligible control overhead. With 16 ECC cores working in parallel, our system would achieve 14,050,000 iterations per second for secp112r1 ECDLP.

7.2. Evaluation of Modular Multiplier. We have modified the modular multiplier architecture shown in Figure 2 to vary the field length for the polynomial representation, l_a, from 8 bits to 64 bits. Our results are given in Table 2. As shown, increasing the length of the field of the polynomial representation reduces the number of cycles required for the modular multiplication. However, using larger fields also degrades the maximum clock speed of the design. The 64-bit field size requires the fewest cycles per modular multiplication, but achieves worse overall performance due to the low maximum clock frequency.

We also evaluate the impact of the modular multiplier design on overall point addition performance. These results are also shown in Table 2. Modular multiplication is the dominant operation in each point addition, with approximately 85% of iteration cycle count used for multiplication. Thus, we show that decreasing the cycle count of the modular multiplication operation has significant impact on the overall performance of our design. Our results show that best overall performance is achieved for field length of 16-bits when the full system runs at 180 MHz. However, since maximum clock frequency of our complete design is 100 MHz, we select field length of 32 bits, which gives 1.3X increase in performance relative to 16 bit field size.

Güneysu and Paar's architecture described in [25] targets 256-bit prime arithmetic over two fixed NIST primes. Our solution shows an improvement in terms of latency for

TABLE 2: Modular multiplier performance.

Field length l_a	Computation time (cycles)	Max. clock frequency (MHz)	Area (slices, DSPs)	Latency per iteration (μs)	System performance (PA/s)	ECC core area (slices, DSPs)
8	21	181	263, 18	1.24 (237 cycles)	808 K	5199, 114
16	14	181	217, 10	0.790 (151 cycles)	1.27 M	4862, 66
32	7	104	253, 20	1.09 (114 cycles)	913 K	5229, 130
64	3	68	370, 36	1.17 (80 cycles)	854 K	5776, 214

TABLE 3: Comparison with software ECDLP implementations.

Platform	Latency per iteration (ns)	Performance (PA/s)
Cell processor at 3.192 GHz, secp112r1 curve [15]	113 (362 cycles)	8.81 M
Cell processor, at 3.192 GHz, secp112r1 curve [9]	142 (453 cycles)	7.04 M
Cell processor, at 3.192 GHz, ECC2K-130 binary field [10]	233 (745 cycles)	4.28 M
Our system, secp112r1	1140 (114 cycles)	878 K: single core 14.05 M: 16 cores

TABLE 4: Comparison with Hardware ECDLP implementations (per core).

Platform	Target curve	Performance (PA/s)	Area (Slices)	(BRAMs)	(DSPs)
Spartan-3 [16]	Binary (130 bit)	111 M	26,731	20	0
Spartan-3 [20]	Binary (113 bit)	20 M	13,900	18	0
Spartan-3 [18]	Prime (160 bit)	46.80 K	3,230	15	0
Spartan-3 [18]	Prime (128 bit)	57.80 K	2,520	16	0
Spartan-3 [19]	Prime (160 bit)	50.12 K	2,660	Not given	0
Virtex-5, our system	Prime (112 bit)	878 K	5,229	9	130

the important ECC arithmetic operations. Assuming the cycle cost for 256-bit arithmetic as twice of that for 128-bit arithmetic (worst-case scenario), our architecture has cycle cost of 14 for a modular multiplication and 228 for the point addition. This is 5X and 3.5X times lower latency for a modular multiplication and point addition operation respectively, than those of the design in [25].

7.3. Comparison with Prior Work. Due to inherent differences between elliptic curves defined over binary and prime fields, performance comparison among various ECDLP implementations is not straightforward. Performance figures are also influenced by a variety of other factors, including target platform, curve size, and coordinate system. To minimize the impact of the target platform and coordinate system, we compare performance of different ECDLP implementations based on the total number of point addition operations performed per second.

Table 3 compares our solution with other software implementations. It shows that a multicore implementation of our design using 16 ECC cores achieves 1.6X improvement over the fastest existing software attack on secp112r1 curve.

Comparison with prior hardware ECDLP implementations is shown in Table 4. Our design achieves high-performance relative to other prime field solutions. When adjusting for curve size, we demonstrate significant speedup over prior designs by [18, 19].

We also show comparison with existing binary field solutions. However, it is difficult to make a fair comparison due to significant differences between binary and prime field arithmetic. In particular, properties of binary field arithmetic and reduction are well-suited for hardware designs, which allows them to achieve much higher performance.

The solution proposed in [16] reports 111 M point addition iterations per second. The authors of [16] claim their system is capable of solving ECC2K-130 within a year using five COPACOBANA machines. Similarly, the solution reported in [20] achieves 20 M iterations per second. We assume that the difference of performance figures exists due to factors including binary field arithmetic, different curve sizes, and use of pipelined architectures.

8. Conclusion

We successfully demonstrate a complete multicore ECC cryptanalytic machine to solve ECDLP on a hardware-software cointegrated platform. We also implement a novel architecture on hardware to perform modular multiplication over prime field and this is the most efficient implementation reported at present for prime field multiplication. We then present a generalized modular multiplication architecture for primes of the form $(2^n - m)/k$ and demonstrate its application to NIST standard P-192 curve. This work also demonstrates the use of microinstruction-based sequencing logic to support a vectorized point addition datapath with variable vector sizes. We compare our performance results with the previous implementations and show that a multicore implementation of our solution has competitive performance relative to existing hardware and software solutions.

Acknowledgments

An earlier version of this paper appeared as "*An Integrated prime-field ECDLP hardware accelerator with high-performance modular arithmetic units*" in the Proceedings of the 2011 International Conference on Reconfigurable Computing and FPGAs (RECONFIG) [27]. This research was supported in part by the National Science Foundation Grant no. 0644070.

References

[1] V. Miller, "Use of elliptic curves in cryptography," in *Advances in Cryptology CRYPTO 85 Proceedings*, H. Williams, Ed., vol. 218 of *Lecture Notes in Computer Science*, pp. 417–426, Springer, Berlin, Germany, 1986.

[2] N. Koblitz, "Elliptic curve cryptosystems," *Mathematics of Computation*, vol. 48, no. 177, pp. 203–209, 1987.

[3] I. Blake, G. Seroussi, N. Smart, and J. W. S. Cassels, *Advances in Elliptic Curve Cryptography*, London Mathematical Society Lecture Note Series, Cambridge University Press, New York, NY, USA, 2005.

[4] J. M. Pollard, "Monte carlo methods of index computation (mod p)," *Mathematics of Computation*, vol. 32, no. 143, pp. 918–924, 1978.

[5] P. C. Van Oorschot and M. J. Wiener, "Parallel collision search with cryptanalytic applications," *Journal of Cryptology*, vol. 12, no. 1, pp. 1–28, 1999.

[6] E. Teske, "On random walks for Pollard's rho method," *Mathematics of Computation*, vol. 70, no. 234, pp. 809–825, 2001.

[7] E. Teske, "Speeding up Pollard's rho method for computing discrete logarithms," in *Algorithmic Number Theory*, J. Buhler, Ed., vol. 1423 of *Lecture Notes in Computer Science*, pp. 541–554, Springer, Berlin, Germany, 1998.

[8] R. P. Brent, "An improved Monte Carlo factorization algorithm," *BIT Numerical Mathematics*, vol. 20, pp. 176–184, 1980.

[9] J. W. Bos, M. E. Kaihara, T. Kleinjung, A. K. Lenstra, and P. L. Montgomery, "On the security of 1024-bit RSA and 160-bit elliptic curve cryptography," Report 2009/389, IACR Cryptology ePrint Archive, 2009, http://eprint.iacr.org/2009/389.

[10] J. Bos, T. Kleinjung, R. Niederhagen, and P. Schwabe, "ECC2K-130 on cell CPUs," in *Progress in Cryptology—AFRICACRYPT 2010*, D. Bernstein and T. Lange, Eds., vol. 6055 of *Lecture Notes in Computer Science*, pp. 225–242, Springer, Berlin, Germany, 2010.

[11] D. V. Bailey, L. Batina, D. J. Bernstein et al., "Breaking ECC2K-130," Report 2009/541, IACR Cryptology ePrint Archive, 2009, http://eprint.iacr.org/2009/541.

[12] D. Bernstein, H.-C. Chen, C.-M. Cheng et al., "ECC2K-130 on Nvidia GPUs," in *Progress in Cryptology—INDOCRYPT 2010*, G. Gong and K. Gupta, Eds., vol. 6498 of *Lecture Notes in Computer Science*, pp. 328–346, Springer, Berlin, Germany, 2010.

[13] *FIPS 186-3: Digital Signature Standard (DSS)*, National Institute of Standards and Technology (NIST), June 2009, http://csrc.nist.gov/publications/fips/fips186-3/fips_186-3.pdf.

[14] *SEC 2: Recommended Elliptic Curve Domain Parameters*, Standards for Efficient Cryptography Group (SECG), January 2010, http://www.secg.org/download/aid-784/sec2-v2.pdf.

[15] D. Bernstein, T. Lange, and P. Schwabe, "On the correct use of the negation map in the Pollard rho method," in *Public Key Cryptography—PKC 2011*, D. Catalano, N. Fazio, R. Gennaro, and A. Nicolosi, Eds., vol. 6571 of *Lecture Notes in Computer Science*, pp. 128–146, Springer, Berlin, Germany, 2011.

[16] J. Fan, D. V. Bailey, L. Batina, T. Güneysu, C. Paar, and I. Verbauwhede, "Breaking elliptic curve cryptosystems using reconfigurable hardware," in *Proceedings of the 20th International Conference on Field Programmable Logic and Applications (FPL '10)*, pp. 133–138, IEEE Computer Society, September 2010.

[17] S. Kumar, C. Paar, J. Pelzl, G. Pfeiffer, and M. Schimmler, "Breaking ciphers with COPACOBANA a cost-optimized parallel code breaker," in *Cryptographic Hardware and Embedded Systems—CHES 2006*, L. Goubin and M. Matsui, Eds., vol. 4249 of *Lecture Notes in Computer Science*, pp. 101–118, Springer, Berlin, Germany, 2006.

[18] T. Gueneysu, C. Paar, and J. Pelzl, "Attacking elliptic curve cryptosystems with special-purpose hardware," in *Proceedings of the 15th ACM/SIGDA International Symposium on Field-Programmable Gate Arrays (FPGA '07)*, pp. 207–215, ACM, New York, NY, USA, February 2007.

[19] T. Güneysu, C. Paar, and J. Pelzl, "Special-purpose hardware for solving the elliptic curve discrete logarithm problem," *ACM Transactions on Reconfigurable Technology and Systems*, vol. 1, no. 2, pp. 8:1–8:21, 2008.

[20] G. Meurice de Dormale, P. Bulens, and J.-J. Quisquater, "Collision search for elliptic curve discrete logarithm over $GF(2^m)$ with FPGA," in *Cryptographic Hardware and Embedded Systems—CHES 2007*, P. Paillier and I. Verbauwhede, Eds., vol. 4727 of *Lecture Notes in Computer Science*, pp. 378–393, Springer, Berlin, Germany, 2007.

[21] P. Majkowski, T. Wojciechowski, M. Wojtyński, M. Rawski, and Z. Kotulski, "Heterogenic distributed system for cryptanalysis of elliptic curve based cryptosystems," in *Proceedings of the 19th International Conference on Systems Engineering (ICSEng '08)*, pp. 300–305, August 2008.

[22] J. W. Bos, M. E. Kaihara, T. Kleinjung, A. K. Lenstra, and P. L. Montgomery, "Solving a 112-bit prime elliptic curve discrete logarithm problem on game consoles using sloppy reduction," *International Journal of Applied Cryptography*, vol. 2, no. 3, pp. 212–228, 2012.

[23] P. L. Montgomery, "Speeding the Pollard and elliptic curve methods of factorization," *Mathematics of Computation*, vol. 48, no. 177, pp. 243–264, 1987.

[24] D. R. Hankerson, S. A. Vanstone, and A. J. Menezes, *Guide to Elliptic Curve Cryptography*, Springer, New York, NY, USA, 2004.

[25] T. Güneysu and C. Paar, "Ultra high performance ECC over NIST primes on commercial FPGAs," in *Cryptographic Hardware and Embedded Systems—CHES 2008*, E. Oswald and P.

Rohatgi, Eds., vol. 5154 of *Lecture Notes in Computer Science*, pp. 62–78, Springer, Berlin, Germany, 2008.

[26] *Virtex-5 FPGA XtremeDSP Design Considerations*, Xilinx, Inc., January 2010, http://www.xilinx.com/support/documentation/user guides/ug193.pdf.

[27] S. Mane, L. Judge, and P. Schaumont, "An integrated prime-field ECDLP hardware accelerator with high-performance modular arithmetic units," in *Proceedings of the International Conference on Reconfigurable Computing and FPGAs (ReConFig '11)*, P. M. Athanas, J. Becker, and R. Cumplido, Eds., pp. 198–203, IEEE Computer Society, December 2011.

8

Exploring Many-Core Design Templates for FPGAs and ASICs

Ilia Lebedev,[1] Christopher Fletcher,[1] Shaoyi Cheng,[2] James Martin,[2] Austin Doupnik,[2] Daniel Burke,[2] Mingjie Lin,[2] and John Wawrzynek[2]

[1] *CSAIL, Massachusetts Institute of Technology, Cambridge, MA 02139, USA*
[2] *Department of EECS, University of California at Berkeley, CA 94704, USA*

Correspondence should be addressed to Ilia Lebedev, ilebedev@csail.mit.edu

Academic Editor: Claudia Feregrino

We present a highly productive approach to hardware design based on a many-core microarchitectural template used to implement compute-bound applications expressed in a high-level data-parallel language such as OpenCL. The template is customized on a per-application basis via a range of high-level parameters such as the interconnect topology or processing element architecture. The key benefits of this approach are that it (i) allows programmers to express parallelism through an API defined in a high-level programming language, (ii) supports coarse-grained multithreading and fine-grained threading while permitting bit-level resource control, and (iii) reduces the effort required to repurpose the system for different algorithms or different applications. We compare template-driven design to both full-custom and programmable approaches by studying implementations of a compute-bound data-parallel Bayesian graph inference algorithm across several candidate platforms. Specifically, we examine a range of template-based implementations on both FPGA and ASIC platforms and compare each against full custom designs. Throughout this study, we use a general-purpose graphics processing unit (GPGPU) implementation as a performance and area baseline. We show that our approach, similar in productivity to programmable approaches such as GPGPU applications, yields implementations with performance approaching that of full-custom designs on both FPGA and ASIC platforms.

1. Introduction

Direct hardware implementations, using platforms such as FPGAs and ASICs, possess a huge potential for exploiting application-specific parallelism and performing efficient computation. As a result, the overall performance of custom hardware-based implementations is often higher than that of software-based ones [1, 2]. To attain bare metal performance, however, programmers must employ hardware design principles such as clock management, state machines, pipelining, and device specific memory management—all concepts well outside the expertise of application-oriented software developers.

These observations raise a natural question: *does there exist a more productive abstraction for high-performance hardware design?* Based on modern programming disciplines, one viable approach would (1) allow programmers to express parallelism through some API defined in a high-level programming language, (2) support coarse-grain multithreading

and fine-grain threading while permitting bit-level resource control, and (3) reduce the effort required to repurpose the implemented hardware platform for different algorithms or different applications. This paper proposes an abstraction that constrains the design to a *microarchitectural template*, accompanied by an API, that meets these programmer requirements.

Intuitively, constraining the design to a template would likely result in performance degradation compared to fully-customized solutions. Consider the high-level chart plotting designer effort versus performance, shown in Figure 1. We argue that the shaded region in the figure is attainable by template-based designs and warrants a systematic exploration. To that end, this work attempts to quantify the performance/area tradeoff, with respect to designer effort, across template-based, hand-optimized, and programmable approaches on both FPGA and ASIC platforms. From our analysis, we show how a disciplined approach with architectural constraints, without resorting to manual hardware design,

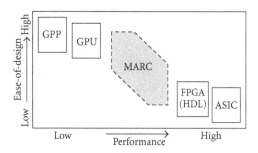

FIGURE 1: Landscape of modern computing platforms. Ease of application design and implementation versus performance (GPP stands for *general purpose processor*).

may reduce design time and effort while maintaining acceptable performance.

In this paper; we study microarchitectural templates in the context of a compute-intensive data-parallel Bayesian inference application. Our thesis, therefore, is that we can efficiently map our application to hardware while being constrained to a *many-core* template and parallel programming API. We call this project MARC, for *Many-core Approach to Reconfigurable Computing*, although template-based architectures can be applied outside the many-core paradigm.

We think of a *template* as an architectural model with a set of parameters to be chosen based on characteristics of the target application. Our understanding of which aspects of the architecture to parameterize continues to evolve as we investigate different application mappings. However, obvious parameters in the many-core context are the number of processing cores, core arithmetic-width, core pipeline depth, richness and topology of an interconnection network, and customization of cores—from addition of specialized instructions to fixed function datapaths as well as details of the cache and local store hierarchies. In this study we explore a part of this space and compare the performance/area between MARC and hand-optimized designs in the context of a baseline GPGPU implementation.

The rest of the paper is organized as follows: Section 2 introduces the Bayesian network inference application, the case study examined in this paper. Section 3 describes the execution model used by OpenCL, the high-level language used to describe our MARC and GPGPU implementations. The application mapping for the GPGPU platform is detailed in Section 4. We discuss the hand-optimized and MARC implementations in Section 5. Section 6 covers hardware mappings for both the hand-optimized and MARC designs as well as a comparison between FPGA and ASIC technology. Finally, in Section 7, we compare the performance/area between the MARC hand-optimized and GPGPU implementations.

1.1. Related Work. Numerous projects and products have offered ways to ease FPGA programming by giving developers a familiar C-style language in place of HDLs [3]. Early research efforts including [4–6] formed the basis for recent commercial offerings: Catapult C from Mentor Graphics, ImpulseC, Synfora Pico from Synopsys, and AutoESL from

Xilinx, among others. Each of these solutions requires developers to understand hardware-specific concepts and to program using a model that differs greatly from standard C—in a sense, using an HDL with a C syntax. Unlike these approaches, the goal of MARC is to expose software programming models applicable to design of efficient hardware.

There has been a long history of mapping conventional CPU architectures to FPGAs. Traditionally, soft processors have been used either as a controller for a dedicated computing engine, or as an emulation or prototyping plat-form for design verification. These efforts have primarily employed a single or small number of processor cores. A few FPGA systems with a large number of cores have been implemented, such as the RAMP project [7]. However, the primary design and use of these machines have been as emulation platforms for custom silicon designs.

There have been many efforts both commercially and academically on customization of parameterized processor cores on an application-specific basis. The most widely used is Xtensa from Tensilica, where custom instructions are added to a conventional processor architecture. We take processor customization a step further by allowing the instruction processors to be replaced with an application-specific datapath that can be generated automatically via our C-to-gates tool for added efficiency and performance. We leverage standard techniques from C-to-gates compilation to accomplish the generation of these custom datapaths.

More recently, there have been several other efforts in integrating the C-to-gates flow with parallel programming models, [8, 9]. These projects share with MARC the goal of exploiting progress in parallel programming languages and automatically mapping to hardware.

2. Application: Bayesian Network Inference

This work's target application is a system that learns Bayesian network structure from observation data. Bayesian networks (BNs) and graphical models have numerous applications in bioinformatics, finance, signal processing, and computer vision. Recently they have been applied to problems in systems biology and personalized medicine, providing tools for processing everincreasing amounts of data provided by high-throughput biological experiments. BNs' probabilistic nature allows them to model uncertainty in real life systems as well as the noise that is inherent in many sources of data. Unlike Markov Random Fields and undirected graphs, BNs can easily learn sparse and causal structures that are interpretable by scientists [10–12].

We chose to compare MARC in the context of Bayesian inference for two primary reasons. First, Bayesian inference is a computationally intensive application believed to be particularly well suited for FPGA acceleration as illustrated by [13]. Second, our group, in collaboration with Stanford University, has expended significant effort over the previous two years developing several generations of a hand-optimized FPGA implementation tailored for Bayesian inference [13, 14]. Therefore, we have not only a concrete reference design but also well-corroborated performance results for fair comparisons with hand-optimized FPGA implementations.

2.1. Statistics Perspective. BNs are statistical models that capture conditional independence between variables via the local Markov property: *that a node is conditionally independent of its nondescendants, given its parents.* Bayesian inference is the process by which a BN's graph structure is learned from the quantitative observation, or *evidence*, that the BN seeks to model. Once a BN's structure (a set of nodes $\{V_1, \ldots, V_{\mathcal{N}}\}$) is determined, and the conditional dependence of each node V_i on its parent set Π_i is tabulated, the joint distribution over the nodes can be expressed as

$$P(V_1, \ldots, V_{\mathcal{N}}) = \prod_{i=1}^{\mathcal{N}} P(V_i \mid \Pi_i). \tag{1}$$

Despite significant recent progress in algorithm development, computational inference of a BN's graph structure from evidence is still NP-hard [15] and remains infeasible except for cases with only a small number of variables [16].

The algorithm surveyed in this paper is the union of two BN inference kernels, the order and graph samplers (jointly called the "order-graph sampler"). An *order* is given by a topological sort of a graph's nodes, where each node is placed after its parents. Each order can include or be *compatible* with many different graphs. The order sampler takes a BN's observation data and produces a set of "high-scoring" BN orders (orders that best explain the evidence). The graph sampler takes this set of high-scoring orders and produces a single highest-scoring graph for each order. The observation data is generated in a preprocessing steps and consists of $\mathcal{N}$ (*for each node*) sets of $\mathcal{P}$ local-score/parent-set pairs (which we will refer to as "data" for short). A local score describes the likelihood that a given parent set is a node's true parent set, given an order. A postprocessing step is performed after the order-graph sampler to normalize scores and otherwise clean up the result before it is presented to the user.

In this work, we only study the order and graph sampler steps for two reasons. First, the order-graph sampler is responsible for most of the algorithm's computational complexity. Second, the pre- and postprocessing phases are currently performed on a GPP (general purpose processor) platform regardless of the platform chosen to implement the order-graph sampler.

Following [14, 16, 17], the order-graph sampler uses Markov chain Monte Carlo (MCMC) sampling to perform an iterative random walk in the space of BN orders. First, the algorithm picks a random initial order. The application then iterates as follows (1) the current order is modified by swapping two nodes to form a "proposed order," which is (2) scored, and (3) either accepted or rejected according to the Metropolis-Hastings rule. The scoring process, itself, (1) breaks the proposed order into $\mathcal{N}$ disjoint "local orders," and (2) iterates over each node's parent sets, accumulating each local score whose parent set is *compatible* with the node's local order. For a network of $\mathcal{N}$ nodes, the proposed order's score can be efficiently calculated by [18]

$$\text{Score}\left(\mathcal{O}_p \mid \mathcal{D}\right) = \prod_{i=1}^{\mathcal{N}} \sum_{\Pi_i \in \Pi_{\mathcal{P}}} \text{LocalScore}\left(V_i, \Pi_i; \mathcal{D}, \mathcal{O}_p\right), \tag{2}$$

where $\mathcal{D}$ is the set of raw observations that are used by the preprocessor to generate local scores, and $\mathcal{O}_p$ is the proposed order. This iterative operation continues until the score has converged.

To decrease time to convergence, $\mathcal{C}$ orders (together called a *chain*) can be dispatched over a temperature ladder and exchanged per iteration in a technique known as parallel tempering. Additionally, $\mathcal{R}$ independent chains (called multiple *restarts*) can be dispatched to increase confidence that the optimum score is a global optimum.

2.2. Compute Perspective. The order-graph sampler is a compute intensive set of nested loops, shown in Algorithm 1, while the *score()* function arithmetic is shown in Algorithm 2. To put the number of loop iterations into perspec-tive, typical parameter values for $\{\mathcal{I}, \mathcal{R} * \mathcal{C}, \mathcal{N}\}$ are $\{10000, 512, 32 \text{ or } 37\}$, where $\mathcal{I}$ is the number of MCMC iterations. Furthermore, $\mathcal{P} = \sum_{i=0}^{4} \binom{\mathcal{N}-1}{i}$, which equates to 36457 and 66712 ($\mathcal{N} = 32$ and $\mathcal{N} = 37$, resp.) for the design points that we study (see Section 7).

We classify the reformulated loop nest as compute intensive for two reasons. First, a relatively small amount of input (a local order) is needed for the *score()* function to compute per-node results over the $\mathcal{R} * \mathcal{C}$ orders. Second, $\mathcal{D}[n]$ (shown in Algorithm 1) depends on $\mathcal{N}$ and not $\mathcal{R} * \mathcal{C}$. Since $\mathcal{N} \approx 37$ and $\mathcal{R} * \mathcal{C} = 512$ (i.e., $\mathcal{R} * \mathcal{C} \gg \mathcal{N}$), in practice there is a large amount of compute time between when n in $\mathcal{D}[n]$ changes.

3. The OpenCL Execution Model

To enable highly productive hardware design, we employ a high-level language and execution model well suited for the paradigm of applications we are interested in studying: data-parallel, compute-bound algorithms. Due to its popularity, flexibility, and good match with our goals, we employ OpenCL (Open Computing Language) as the programming model used to describe applications.

OpenCL [19] is a programming and execution model for heterogeneous systems containing GPPs, GPGPUs, FPGAs [20], and other accelerators designed to explicitly capture data and task parallelism in an application. The OpenCL model distinguishes control thread(s) (to be executed on a GPP host) from kernel threads (data parallel loops to be executed on a GPGPU, or similar, device). The user specifies how the kernels map to an n-dimensional dataset, given a set of arguments (such as constants or pointers to device or host memory). The runtime then distributes the resulting workload across available compute resources on the device. Communication between control and kernel threads is provided by shared memory and OpenCL system calls such as barriers and bulk memory copy operations.

A key property of OpenCL is its memory model. Each kernel has access to three disjoint memory regions: private, local, and global. Global memory is shared by all kernel threads, local memory is shared by threads belonging to the same group, while private memory is owned by one kernel thread. This alleviates the need for a compiler to perform

```
    for {r, c} in R × C  do
        initialize(O[r][c])
    end for
    for i in I do
5:      for {r, c} in R × C  do
            O_p[r][c] ← swap(O[r][c])
            Variable initialization:
            O_p[r][c] · S_o, O_p[r][c] · S_g ← 0
            O_p[r][c] · G ← []
10:     end for
        for n in N do
            for {r, c} in R × C  do
                (s_o, s_g, g) = score(D[n], O_p[r][c][n])
                O_p[r][c] · S_o ← O_p[r][c] · S_o + s_o
15:             O_p[r][c] · S_g ← O_p[r, c] · S_g + s_g
                O_p[r][c] · G · append(g)
            end for
        end for
        for r in R do
            Metropolis-hastings:
20:         for c in C do
                if (1/T_c) × (O_p[r][c] · S_o - O[r][c] · S_o) >
                log(rand(0, 1))  then
                    O[r, c] · S_o ← O_p[r][c] · S_o
                    save({O_p[r][c] · S_g, O_p[r, c] · G})
                end if
25:         end for
            Parallel tempering:
            for c in C do
                d ← O[r][c] · S_o - O[r][c + 1] · S_o
                if log(rand(0, 1)) < d × (1/T_c - 1/T_{c+1})  then
30:                 exchange(O[r][c], O[r][c + 1])
                end if
            end for
        end for
    end for
```

ALGORITHM 1: The reformulated order-graph sampler loop nest. {S_o, S_g} and G are the current {order, graph} scores and graph associated with an order. *initialize()* generates a random order, *swap()* exchanges nodes in an order, and *save()* saves a result for the postprocessing step.

costly memory access analysis to recognize dependencies before the application can be parallelized. Instead, the user specifies how the application is partitioned into data-parallel kernels. With underlying SIMD principles, OpenCL is well suited for data-parallel problems and maps well to the parallel thread dispatch architecture found in GPGPUs.

4. Baseline GPGPU Implementation

To implement the order-graph sampler on the GPGPU, the application is first divided to different parts according to their characteristics. The scoring portion of the algorithm, which exhibits abundant data parallelism, is partitioned into a kernel and executed on the GPGPU, while the less parallelizable score accumulation is executed on a GPP. This ensures that the kernel executed on the GPGPU is maximally parallel and exhibits no interthread communication—an approach we experimentally determined to be optimal. Under this scheme, the latency of the control thread and score accumulation phases of the application, running on a GPP, are dominated by the latency of the scoring function running on the GPGPU. Moreover, the *score()* kernel (detailed in the following section) has a relatively low bandwidth requirement, allowing us to offload accumulation to the GPP, lowering total latency. The GPP-GPGPU implementation is algorithmically identical to the hardware implementations, aside from minor differences in the precision of the $log1p(\exp(d))$ operation, and yields identical results up to the random sequence used for Monte Carlo integration.

4.1. Optimization of Scoring Kernel. We followed four main strategies in optimizing the scoring unit kernel: (1) minimizing data transfer overhead between the control thread and the scoring function, (2) aligning data in device memory, (3)

$$
\begin{aligned}
&s_o, s_g \leftarrow -\infty \\
&g \leftarrow \text{NULL} \\
&\textbf{for } p \text{ in } \mathcal{P} \textbf{ do} \\
&\quad \textbf{if } compatible(\mathcal{D}[p] \cdot ps, \mathcal{O}_l) \textbf{ then} \\
5:&\quad\quad \textit{Order sampler:} \\
&\quad\quad d \leftarrow \mathcal{D}[p] \cdot ls - s_o \\
&\quad\quad \textbf{If } d \geq \text{HIGH\_THRESHOLD} \textbf{ then} \\
&\quad\quad\quad s_o \leftarrow \mathcal{D}[p] \cdot ls \\
&\quad\quad \textbf{else if } d > \text{LOW\_THRESHOLD} \textbf{ then} \\
10:&\quad\quad\quad s_o \leftarrow s_o + log(1 + exp(d)) \\
&\quad\quad \textbf{end if} \\
&\quad\quad \textit{Graph sampler:} \\
&\quad\quad \textbf{if } \mathcal{D}[p] \cdot ls > s_g \textbf{ then} \\
&\quad\quad\quad s_g \leftarrow \mathcal{D}[p] \cdot ls \\
15:&\quad\quad\quad g \leftarrow \mathcal{D}[p] \cdot ps \\
&\quad\quad \textbf{end if} \\
&\quad \textbf{end if} \\
&\textbf{end for} \\
&\textbf{Return:}(s_o, s_g, g)
\end{aligned}
$$

ALGORITHM 2: The $score(\mathcal{D}, \mathcal{O}_l)$ function takes the data $\mathcal{D}$ (made of parent set (ps) and local score (ls) pairs) and a local order ($\mathcal{O}_l$) as input. The scoring function produces an order score (s_o), graph score (s_g), and graph fragment (g).

allocating kernel threads to compute units on the GPGPU, and (4) minimizing latency of a single kernel thread.

First, we minimize data transfers between the GPP and GPGPU by only communicating changing portions of the data set throughout the computation. At application startup, we statically allocate memory for all arrays used on the GPGPU, statically set these arrays' pointers as kernel arguments, and copy all parent sets and local scores into off-chip GPGPU memory to avoid copying static data each iteration. Each iteration, the GPP copies $\mathcal{R} * \mathcal{C}$ proposed orders to the GPGPU and collects $\mathcal{R} * \mathcal{C} * \mathcal{N}$ proposed order/graph scores, as well as $\mathcal{R} * \mathcal{C}$ graphs from the GPGPU. Each order and graph is an $\mathcal{N} \times \mathcal{N}$ matrix, represented as $\mathcal{N}$ 64 bit integers, while partial order and graph scores are each 32 bit integers (additional range is introduced when the partial scores are accumulated). The resulting bandwidth requirement per iteration is $8 * \mathcal{R} * \mathcal{C} * \mathcal{N}$ bytes from the GPP to the GPGPU and $16 * \mathcal{R} * \mathcal{C} * \mathcal{N}$ bytes from the GPGPU back to the GPP. In the BNs surveyed in this paper, this bandwidth requirement ranges from 128 to 256 KB (GPP to GPGPU) and from 256 to 512 KB (GPGPU to GPP). Given these relatively small quantities and the GPGPU platform's relatively high transfer bandwidth over PCIe, the transfer latency approaches a minimal value. We use this to our advantage and offload score accumulation to the GPP, trading significant accumulation latency for a small increase in GPP-GPGPU transfer latency. This modification gives us an added advantage via avoiding intra-kernel communication altogether (which is costly on the GPGPU because it does not offer hardware support for producer-consumer parallelism).

Second, we align and organize data in memory to maximize access locality for each kernel thread. GPGPU memories are seldom cached, while DRAM accesses are several words wide—comparable to GPP cache lines. We therefore coalesce memory accesses to reduce the memory access range of a single kernel and of multiple kernels executing on a given compute unit. No thread accesses (local scores and parent sets) are shared across multiple nodes, so we organize local scores and parent sets by $[\mathcal{N}][\mathcal{P}]$. When organizing data related to the $\mathcal{R} * \mathcal{C}$ orders (the proposed orders, graph/order scores, and graphs), we choose to maximally compact data for restarts, then chains, and finally nodes ($[\mathcal{N}][\mathcal{C}][\mathcal{R}]$). This order is based on the observation that a typical application instance will work with a large number of restarts relative to chains. When possible, we align data in memory—rounding both $\mathcal{R}$, $\mathcal{C}$ and $\mathcal{P}$ to next powers of two to avoid false sharing in wide word memory operations and to improve alignment of data in memory.

Third, allocating kernel threads to device memory is straightforward given the way we organize data in device memory; we allocate multiple threads with localized memory access patterns. Given our memory layout, we first try dispatching multiple restarts onto the same compute unit. If more threads are needed than restarts available, we dispatch multiple chains as well. We continue increasing the number of threads per compute unit in this way until we reach an optimum—the point where overhead due to multithreading overtakes the benefit of additional threads. Many of the strategies guiding our optimization effort are outlined in [21].

Finally, we minimize the scoring operation latency over a single kernel instance. We allow the compiler to predicate conditional to avoid thread divergence. Outside the inner loop, we explicitly precompute offsets to access the $[\mathcal{N}][\mathcal{P}]$ and $[\mathcal{N}][\mathcal{C}][\mathcal{R}]$ arrays to avoid redundant computation. We experimentally determined that loop unrolling the $score()$ loop has minimal impact on kernel performance, so we allow the compiler to unroll freely. We also evaluated a direct implementation of the $log1p(exp(d))$ operation versus the use of a lookup table in shared memory (which mirrors the hand-optimized design's approach). Due to the low utilization of the floating point units by this algorithm, the direct implementation tends to perform better than a lookup table given the precision required by the algorithm.

4.2. Benchmarking the GPGPU Implementation. To obtain GPGPU measurements, We mapped the data parallel component to the GPGPU via OpenCL, and optimized the resulting kernel as detailed in Section 4.1. We measured the relative latency of each phase of the algorithm by introducing a number of GPP and GPGPU timers throughout the iteration loop. We then computed the latency of each phase of computation (scoring, accumulation, MCMC, etc.) and normalized to the measured latency of a single iteration with no profiling syscalls. To measure the iteration time, we ran the application for 1000 iterations with no profiling code in the loop and then measured the total time elapsed using the system clock. We then computed the aggregate iteration latency.

5. Architecture on Hardware Platforms

As with the GPGPU implementation, when the Bayesian inference algorithm is mapped to hardware platforms (FPGA/ASIC), it is partitioned into two communicating entities: a data-parallel scoring unit (a collection of Algorithmic-cores or A-cores) and a control unit (the Control-core, or C-core). The A-cores are responsible for all iterations of the *score()* function from Algorithm 1 while the C-core implements the serial control logic around the *score()* calls. This scheme is applied to both the hand-optimized design and the automatically generated MARC design, though each of them has different interconnect networks, memory subsystems, and methodologies for creating the cores.

5.1. Hand-Optimized Design. The hand-optimized design mapping integrates the jobs of the C-core and A-cores on the same die and uses a front-end GPP for system initialization and result collection. At the start of a run, network data and a set of $\mathcal{R} * \mathcal{C}$ initial orders are copied to a DRAM accessible by the A-cores, and the C-core is given a "Start" signal. At the start of each iteration, the C-core forms $\mathcal{R} * \mathcal{C}$ proposed orders, partitions each by node, and dispatches the resulting $\mathcal{N} * \mathcal{R} * \mathcal{C}$ local orders as threads to the A-cores. As each iteration completes, the C-core streams results back to the front-end GPP while proceeding with the next MCMC iteration.

The hand-optimized design is partitioned into four clock domains. First, we clock A-cores at the highest frequency possible (between 250 and 300 MHz) as these have a direct impact on system performance. Second, we clock the logic and interconnect around each A-core at a relatively low frequency (25–50 MHz) as the application is compute bound in the cores. Third, we set the memory subsystem to the frequency specified by the memory (~200 MHz, using a DRAM DIMM in our case). Finally, the C-core logic is clocked at 100 MHz, which we found to be ideal for timing closure and tool

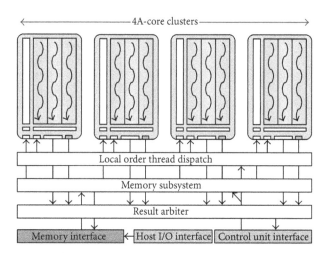

FIGURE 2: The hand-optimized scoring unit (with 4 A-core clusters).

run time given a performance requirement (the latency of the C-core is negligible compared to the A-cores).

5.1.1. Scoring Unit. The scoring unit (shown in Figure 2) consists of a collection of clustered A-cores, a point-to-point interface with the control unit, and an interface to off-chip memory.

A scoring unit cluster caches some or all of a node's data, taking a stream of local orders as input and outputs order/graph scores as well as partial graphs. A cluster is made up of {A-cores, RAM} pairs, where each RAM *streams* data to its A-core. When a cluster receives a local order, it (a) pages in data from DRAM as needed by the local orders, strip-mines that data evenly across the RAMs and (b) dispatches the local order to each core. Following Algorithm 1, $\mathcal{R} * \mathcal{C}$ local orders can be assigned to a cluster per DRAM request. Once data is paged in, each A-core runs $\mathcal{P}_f/U_c$ iterations of the *score()* inner loop (from Algorithm 2), where $\mathcal{P}_f$ is the subset of $\mathcal{P}$ that was paged into the cluster, and U_c is the number of A-cores in the cluster.

A-core clusters are designed to maximize local order throughput. A-cores are replicated to the highest extent possible to maximize read bandwidth achievable by the RAMs. Each A-core is fine-grained multithreaded across multiple iterations of the *score()* function and uses predicated execution to avoid thread divergence in case of non-compatible (!*compatible()*) parent sets. To avoid structural hazards in the scoring pipeline, all scoring arithmetic is built directly into the hardware.

Mapping a single node's scoring operation onto multiple A-cores requires increased complexity in accumulating partial node scores at the end of the *score()* loop. To maximally hide this delay, we first interleave cross-thread accumulation with the next local order's main scoring operation (shown in Figure 3). Next, we chain A-cores together using a dedicated interconnect, allowing cross-core partial results to be interleaved into the next local order in the same way as threads. Per core, this accumulation scheme adds T cycles

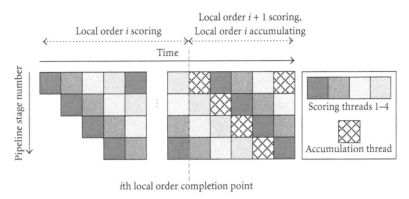

FIGURE 3: Thread accumulation over a 4-thread/stage core for two adjacent local orders.

of accumulation overhead to the scoring process, for a T-thread datapath and a single additional cycle for cross-core accumulation. To simplify the accumulation logic, we linearly reduce all threads across an A-core and then accumulate linearly across A-cores. The tradeoff here is that the last local order's accumulation is not hidden by another local order being scored and takes $T^2 + T * U_c$ cycles to finish, where U_c is the number of A-cores in the cluster.

Given sufficient hardware resources, more advanced A-core clusters can be built to further increase system throughput. First, the number of A-cores per RAM can be increased to the number of read ports each RAM has. Second, since a given node's data ($\mathcal{D}[n]$) does not change over the $\mathcal{R} * \mathcal{C}$ local orders, A-core chains can be replicated entirely. In this case, we say that the cluster has been split into two or more *lanes*, where A-cores from each lane are responsible for a different local order. In this setup, the cluster's control strip-mines local orders across lanes to initiate scoring. While scoring, corresponding A-cores (the first A-core in each of several lanes, e.g.) across the lanes (called *tiles*) read and process the same data from the same RAM data stream. An example of an advanced A-core cluster is shown in Figure 4.

The following analytic model can be used to estimate the parallel completion time to score $\mathcal{O}_l$ local orders over the $\mathcal{P}_f$ subset of the data (for a single cluster):

$$\text{Cycles}_{\text{DRAM}} + \frac{\mathcal{O}_l}{U_l} * \left(\frac{\mathcal{P}_f}{U_c} + (T+1) \right) + (T^2 + T * U_c),$$

$$(3)$$

where $\text{Cycles}_{\text{DRAM}}$ is the number of cycles (normalized to the core clock) required to initialize the cluster from DRAM, U_c is the number of A-cores per lane (doubles when two SRAM ports are used, etc.), U_l is the number of lanes per cluster, and T is the number of hardware threads per A-core.

5.1.2. Memory Subsystem.

The scoring unit controls DRAM requests when an A-core cluster requires a different subset of the data. Regardless of problem parameters, data is always laid out contiguously in memory. As DRAM data is streamed to a finite number of RAMs, there must be enough RAM write bandwidth to consume the DRAM stream. In cases where the RAM write capability does not align to the DRAM read capacity, dedicated alignment circuitry built into the scoring unit dynamically realigns the data stream.

5.1.3. Control Unit.

We implemented the MCMC control unit directly in hardware, according to Figure 5. The MCMC state machine, node swapping logic, parallel tempering logic, and Metropolis-Hasting logic is mapped as hardware state machines. Furthermore, a DSP block is used for multiplicative factors, while $log(rand(0,1))$ is implemented as a table lookup. The random generators for row/column swaps, as well as Metropolis-Hastings and parallel tempering, are built using free-running LFSRs.

At the start of each iteration, the control unit performs node swaps for each of the $\mathcal{R} * \mathcal{C}$ orders and schedules the proposed orders onto available compute units. To minimize control unit time when $\mathcal{R} * \mathcal{C}$ is small, orders are stored in row order in RAM, making the swap operation a single cycle row swap, followed by an $\mathcal{N}$ cycle column swap. Although the control unit theoretically has cycle accurate visibility of the entire system and can therefore derive optimal schedules, we found that using a trivial greedy scheduling policy (first come first serve) negligibly degrades performance with the benefit of significantly reducing hardware complexity. To minimize A-core cluster memory requirements, all $\mathcal{R} * \mathcal{C}$ local orders are scheduled to compute units in bulk over a single node.

When each iteration is underway, partial scores received from the scoring unit are accumulated as soon as they are received, using a dedicated A-core attached to a buffer that stores partial results. In practice, each A-core cluster can only store data for a part of a given node at a time. This means that the A-core, processing partial results, must perform both the slower *score()* operation and the simpler cross-node "+" accumulations. We determined that a single core dedicated to this purpose can rate match the results coming back from the compute-bound compute units.

At the end of each iteration, Metropolis-Hastings checks proceed in $[\mathcal{R}][\mathcal{C}]$ order. This allows the parallel tempering exchange operation for restart r to be interleaved with the Metropolis-Hastings check for restart $r + 1$.

5.2. The MARC Architecture

5.2.1. Many-Core Template.

The overall architecture of a MARC system, as illustrated in Figure 6, resembles a scalable, many-core-style processor architecture, comprising one

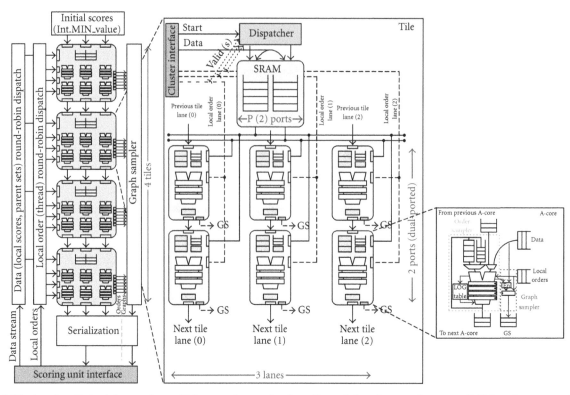

FIGURE 4: The hand-optimized A-core cluster. This example contains four tiles and three lanes and uses two RAM read ports per tile. "GS" stands for graph sampler.

Control Processor (C-core) and multiple Algorithmic Processing Cores (A-cores). Both the C-cores and the A-core can be implemented as conventional pipelined RISC processors. However, unlike embedded processors commonly found in modern SOCs, the processing cores in MARC are completely parameterized with variable bit width, reconfigurable multithreading, and even aggregate/fused instructions. Furthermore, A-cores can alternatively be synthesized as fully customized datapaths. For example, in order to hide global memory access latency, improve processing node utilization, and increase the overall system throughput, a MARC system can perform fine-grained multithreading through shift register insertion and automatic retiming. Finally, while each processing core possesses a dedicated local memory accessible only to itself, a MARC system has a global memory space implemented as distributed memories accessible by all processing cores through the interconnect network. Communication between a MARC system and its host can be realized by reading and writing global memory.

5.2.2. Execution Model and Software Infrastructure. Our MARC system builds upon both LLVM, a production-grade open-source compiler infrastructure [22] and OpenCL.

Figure 7 presents a high-level schematic of a typical MARC machine. A user application runs on a host according to the models native to the host platform—a high-performance PC in our study. Execution of a MARC program occurs in two parts: kernels that run on one or more A-cores of the MARC devices and a control program that runs on the C-core. The control program defines the context for the kernels and manages their execution. During the execution, the MARC application spawns kernel threads to run on the A-cores, each of which runs a single stream of instructions as SPMD units (each processing core maintains its own program counter).

5.2.3. Application-Specific Processing Core. One strength of MARC is its capability to integrate fully customized application-specific processing cores/datapaths so that the kernels in an application can be more efficiently executed. To this end, a high-level synthesis flow depicted by Figure 8 was developed to generate customized datapaths for a target application.

The original kernel source code in C/C++ is first compiled through llvm-gcc to generate the intermediate representation (IR) in the form of a single static assignment graph (SSA), which forms a control flow graph where instructions are grouped into basic blocks. Within each basic block, the instruction parallelism can be extracted easily as all false dependencies have been removed in the SSA representation. Between basic blocks, the control dependencies can then be transformed to data dependencies through branch predication. In our implementation, only memory operations are predicated since they are the only instructions that can generate stalls in the pipeline. By converting the control dependencies to data dependencies, the boundaries between basic blocks can be eliminated. This results in a single data flow graph with each node corresponding to a single instruction

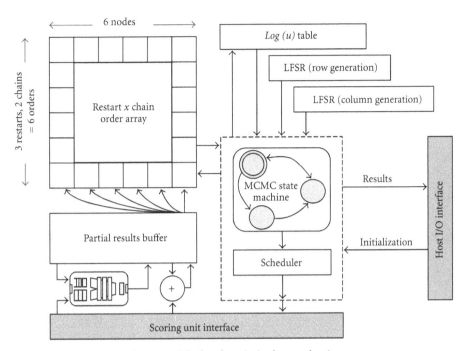

FIGURE 5: The hand-optimized control unit.

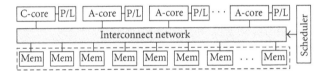

FIGURE 6: Diagram of key components in a MARC machine.

in the IR. Creating hardware from this graph involves a one-to-one mapping between each instruction and various predetermined hardware primitives. To utilize loop level parallelism, our high-level synthesis tool also computes the minimal interval at which a new iteration of the loop can be initiated and subsequently generates a controller to pipeline loop iterations. Finally, the customized cores have the original function arguments converted into inputs. In addition, a simple set of control signals is created to initialize a C-core and to signal the completion of the execution. For memory accesses within the original code, each nonaliasing memory pointer used by the C function is mapped to a memory interface capable of accommodating variable memory access latency. The integration of the customized cores into a MARC machine involves mapping the input of the cores to memory addresses accessible by the control core, as well as the addition of a memory handshake mechanism allowing cores to access global and local memories. For the results reported in this paper, the multithreaded customized cores are created by manually inserting shift registers into the single-threaded, automatically generated core.

5.2.4. Host-MARC Interface. Gigabit Ethernet is used to implement the communication link between the host and the MARC device. We leveraged the GateLib [23] project

from Berkeley to implement the host interface, allowing the physical transport to be easily replaced by a faster medium in the future.

5.2.5. Memory Organization. Following OpenCL, A-core threads have access to three distinct memory regions: private, local, and global. Global memory permits read and write access to all threads within any executing kernels on any processing core (ideally, reads and writes to global memory may be cached depending on the capabilities of the device, however in our current MARC machine implementation, caching is not supported). Local memory is a section of the address space shared by the threads within a computing core. This memory region can be used to allocate variables that are shared by all threads spawned from the same computing kernel. Finally, private memory is a memory region that is dedicated to a single thread. Variables defined in one thread's private memory are not visible to another thread, even when they belong to the same executing kernel.

Physically, the private and local memory regions in a MARC system are implemented using on-chip memories. Part of the global memory region also resides on-chip, but we allow external memory (i.e., through the DRAM controller) to extend the global memory region, resulting in a larger memory space.

5.2.6. Kernel Scheduler. To achieve high throughput, kernels must be scheduled to avoid memory access conflicts. The MARC system allows for a globally aware kernel scheduler, which can orchestrate the execution of kernels and control access to shared resources. The global scheduler is controlled via a set of memory-mapped registers, which are implementation specific. This approach allows for a range of

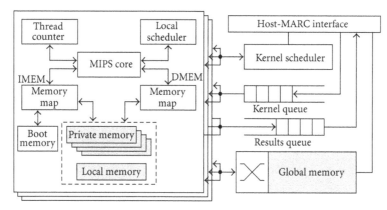

FIGURE 7: Schematic of a MARC machine's implementation.

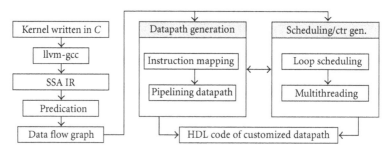

FIGURE 8: CAD flow of synthesizing application-specific processing cores.

schedulers, from simple round-robin or priority schedules to complex problem-specific scheduling algorithms.

The MARC machine optimized for Bayesian inference uses the global scheduler to dispatch threads at a coarse grain (ganging up thread starts). The use of the global scheduler is therefore rather limited as the problem does not greatly benefit from a globally aware approach to scheduling.

5.2.7. System Interconnect. One of the key advantages of reconfigurable computing is the ability to exploit application-specific communication patterns in the hardware system. MARC allows the network to be selected from a library of various topologies, such as mesh, H-tree, crossbar, or torus. Application-specific communication patterns can thus be exploited by providing low-latency links along common routes.

The MARC machine explores two topologies: a pipelined crossbar and a ring, as shown in Figure 9. The pipelined crossbar contains no assumptions about the communication pattern of the target application—it is a nonblocking network that provides uniform latency to all locations in the global memory address space. Due to the large number of endpoints on the network, the crossbar is limited to 120 MHz with 8 cycles of latency.

The ring interconnect only implements nearestneighbor links, thereby providing very low-latency access to some locations in global memory, while requiring multiple hops for other accesses. Nearest neighbor communication is important in the Bayesian inference accumulation phase and helps reduce overall latency. Moreover, this network topology is significantly more compact and can be clocked at a much

higher frequency—approaching 300 MHz in our implementations. The various versions of our MARC machine, therefore, made use of the ring network because of the advantages it has shown for this application.

5.2.8. Mapping Bayesian Inference onto the MARC Machine. The order-graph sampler comprises a C-core for the serial control logic and A-cores to implement the *score*() calls. Per iteration, the C-core performs the node swap operation, broadcasts the proposed order, and applies the Metropolis-Hastings check. These operations consume a negligible amount of time relative to the scoring process.

Scoring is composed of (1) the parent set compatibility check and (2) an accumulation across all compatible parent sets. Step 1 must be made over every parent set; its performance is limited by how many parent sets can be simultaneously accessed. We store parent sets in on-chip RAMs that serve as A-core private memory and are therefore limited by the number of A-cores and attainable A-core throughput. Step 2 must be first carried out independently by each A-core thread, then across A-core threads, and finally across the A-cores themselves. We serialize cross-thread and cross-core accumulations. Each accumulation is implemented with a global memory access.

The larger order-graph sampler benchmark we chose (see Section 7) consists of up to 37 nodes, where each of the nodes has 66712 parent sets. We divide these 66712 elements into 36 chunks and dedicate 36 A-cores to work on this data set. After completion of the data processing for one node, data from the next node is paged in, and we restart the A-cores.

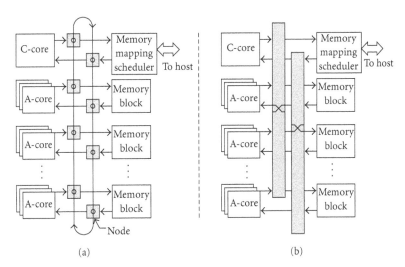

FIGURE 9: System diagram of a MARC system. (a) Ring network. (b) Pipelined crossbar.

6. Hardware Prototyping

For this research, both the hand-optimized design and MARC machines are implemented targeting a Virtex-5 (XCV5LX155T-2) of a BEEcube BEE3 module for FPGA prototyping. We also evaluate how each design performs when mapped through a standard ASIC design flow targeting a TSMC 65 ns CMOS process. A design point summary, that we will develop over the rest of the paper, is given in Table 1.

The local memory or "RAMs", used in each design point, were implemented using block RAMs (BRAMs) on an FPGA and generated as SRAM (using foundry-specific memory generators) on an ASIC. All of our design points benefit from as much local memory read bandwidth as possible. We-increased read bandwidth on the FPGA implementation by using both ports of each BRAM block and exposing each BRAM as two smaller single-port memories. For the ASIC platform, the foundry-specific IP generator gives us the capability to create small single-ported memories suitable for our use.

In addition to simple memories, our designs used FIFOs, arbiters, and similar hardware structures to manage flow control and control state. On an FPGA, most of these blocks were available on the Virtex-5 through Xilinx Coregen while the rest were taken from the GateLib library. On an ASIC, all of these blocks were synthesized from GateLib Verilog or generated using foundry tools.

To obtain all FPGA measurements, we designed in Verilog RTL and mapped the resulting system using Synplify Pro (Synopsys) and the Xilinx ISE flow for placement and routing (PAR). To obtain ASIC measurements, we used a standard cell-bawed Synopsis CAD flow including Design Compiler and IC Compiler.

No manual placement or hierarchical design was used for our studies. We verified the resulting system post-PAR by verifying (a) timing closure, and (b) functionality of the flat-tened netlist. The tools were configured to automatically re-time the circuit to assist timing closure, at the expense of hard-ware resources. It is worth noting that the automatic retiming did not work as well with the MARC multithreaded

cores because of a feedback path in the core datapath. Therefore, manual retiming was required for performance improvement with the MARC multithreaded design points.

6.1. Hand-Optimized Configurations. On the FPGA platform, the best performing configurations were attained when using 48 cores per FPGA running at a 250 MHz core clock and 36 cores at 300 MHz (the former outperforming the latter by a factor of 1.1 on average). Both of these points were used between 65% and 75% of available device LUTs and exactly 95% of device BRAMs. We found that implementing 48 cores at 300 MHz was not practical due to routing limitations and use of the 48 core version at 250 MHz for the rest of the paper.

For the ASIC implementation, because performance is a strong function of the core clock's frequency, we optimize the core clock as much as possible. By supplying the Verilog RTL tp the Synopsys Design Compiler with no prior optimization, the cores can be clocked at 500 MHz. Optimizing the core clock requires shortening the critical path, which is in the datapath. By increasing the number of threads from 4 to 8 and performing manual retiming for the multithreaded datapath, the core clock achieves 1 GHz.

6.2. MARC Configurations. The MARC implementation comprises one C-core and 36 A-cores. While the C-core in all MARC machines is a fully bypassed 4-stage RISC processor, MARC implementations differ in their implementation of the A-cores. For example, fine-grained multithreaded RISC cores, automatically generated application-specific datapaths, and multithreaded versions of the generated cores are all employed to explore different tradeoffs in design effort and performance. To maintain high throughput, the better performing A-cores normally execute multiple concurrent threads to saturate the long cycles in the application dataflow graph.

6.2.1. Memory System. As in other computing platforms, memory accesses significantly impact the overall performance of a MARC system. In the current MARC implemen-

TABLE 1: A-core counts, for all design points, and a naming convention for all MARC configurations used in the study. If only one core count is listed, it is the same for both 32 and 37 node ($32n$ and $37n$) problems (see Section 7). All A-core counts are given for area normalized designs, as discussed in Section 7.

Alias	Description	Number of cores ($32n$, $37n$)
Hand design FPGA	—	48
Hand design ASIC	—	2624, 2923
MARC-Ropt-F	RISC A-core with optimized network on FPGA	36
MARC-C1-F	Customized A-core on FPGA	36
MARC-C2-F	Customized A-core (2-way MT) on FPGA	36
MARC-C4-F	Customized A-core (4-way MT) on FPGA	36
MARC-Ropt-A	RISC A-core with optimized network on ASIC	1269, 1158
MARC-C1-A	Customized A-core on ASIC	1782, 1571
MARC-C2-A	Customized A-core (2-way MT) on ASIC	1768, 1561
MARC-C4-A	Customized A-core (4-way MT) on ASIC	1715, 1519
GPGPU	—	512

tation, private or local memory accesses take exactly one cycle, while global memory accesses typically involve longer latencies that are network dependent. We believe that given different applications, such discrepancies between local and global memory access latencies provide ample opportunities for memory optimization and performance improvements. For example, the MARC machine in this work has been optimized for local memory accesses, reflecting the needs of the Bayesian inference algorithm.

6.2.2. Clock Speed and Area on FPGA and ASIC. For better throughput, we have implemented single-threaded, two-way multithreaded, and four-way multithreaded application-specific A-cores for MARC devices. When individually instantiated on the Virtex-5 FPGA, these cores are clocked at 163 MHz, 234 MHz, and 226 MHz, respectively. There is a decrease in clock frequency when the number of threads is changed from two to four. This is due to the increased routing delay to connect LUT-FF pairs further apart in a larger physical area. When the completely assembled MARC machines traverse the hardware generation flow, the cores' clock frequency decreases further to 144 MHz, 207 MHz, and 206 MHz, respectively due to added FPGA resource utilization. The same A-cores are used for the ASIC implementation, where they operate at 526 MHz, 724 MHz, and 746 MHz, respectively. Due to a higher degree of freedom in ASIC place and route, we do not see the performance dip observed when the two-threaded FPGA implementation is changed to four-threaded. However, it is apparent that despite the decrease in levels of logic in the critical path, it is difficult to squeeze out more performance by simple register insertion and retiming.

With respect to area, the overhead of multithreading is more pronounced on an FPGA relative to an ASIC. For the 37 node benchmark, the MARC machines with single, two-way, and four-way multithreaded customized A-cores utilize 47%, 65%, and 80% of the flip-flops on Virtex-5. Since they operate on the same amount of data, 85% of BRAMs are used for each of the three design points. Meanwhile, on an ASIC we only observe an area increase from 6.2 mm² in the single-threaded case to 6.4 mm² for the four-way multithreaded

design. This is because the ASIC implementation exposes the actual chip area, where the increase in number of registers is dwarfed by the large SRAM area.

7. Performance and Area Comparisons

We compare the performance of the hand-optimized design and the MARC machines on FPGA as well as ASIC platforms. For both the hand-optimized and the MARC implementations on an ASIC, we normalize our area to the FPGA's die area. FPGA die area was obtained by X-ray imaging the packaged dies and estimating the die area from the resulting photographs. For the remainder of the paper, all devices whose die areas and process nodes are relevant are given in Table 2.

For the FPGA designs, we packed the device to its limits without performance degradation. Effectively, the designs are consuming the entire area of the FPGA. We then performed a similar evaluation for the ASIC platform by attempting to occupy the same area as an FPGA. This is achieved by running the design for a small number of cores and then scaling up. This technique is valid as the core clock is not distributed across the network, and the network clock can be slow (50–100 MHz) without adversely affecting performance.

The specific Bayesian network instances we chose consist of 32 and 37 nodes, with dataset of 36457 and 66712 elements, respectively. The run times on each hardware platform are shown in Tables 4 and 5, for the 32 and 37 node-problem, respectively. The execution time for each platform is also normalized to the fastest implementation—hand-optimized design on ASIC—to show the relative performance of every design point.

7.1. Benchmark Comparison. The large gap between the amount of data involved in the two problems gives each distinct characteristics, especially when mapped to an ASIC platform. Because data for the 32 node problem can fit on an ASIC for both MARC and the hand-optimized design, the problem is purely compute bound. The hand-optimized solution benefits from the custom pipelined accumulation

TABLE 2: Device die areas and process nodes.

Device	Die area (mm^2)	Process (nm)
Virtex-5 LX155T FPGA	270	65
Nvidia GeForce GTX 580	520	40

TABLE 3: Scaled GPGPU design for 65 nm process.

Problem	Per-iteration time 40 nm (μs)	Scaled per-iteration time 65 nm (μs)
32-Node	21.0	174
37-Node	37.8	312

and smaller and faster cores, resulting in its 2.5x performance advantage over the best MARC implementation. The 37 node problem, on the other hand, could not afford to have the entire dataset in the on-chip SRAMs. The required paging of data into the on-chip RAMs becomes the performance bottleneck. Having exactly the same DRAM controller as the MARC machines, the hand-optimized design only shows a small performance advantage over MARC, which can be attributed to its clever paging scheme. For the FPGA platform, both the 32 and 37 node problems involve paging of data, but as the run time is much longer, data transfer only accounts for a very small fraction of the execution time (i.e., both problems are compute bound).

7.2. MARC versus Hand-Optimized Design. For compute-bound problems, it is clear that MARC using RISC instruction processors to implement A-cores achieves less than 2% of the performance exhibited by the hand-optimized implementation, even with optimized interconnect topology (a ring network versus a pipelined crossbar). Customizing the A-cores, however, yields a significant gain in performance, moving MARC to within a factor of 4 of the performance of the hand-optimized implementation. Further optimizing the A-cores through multithreading pushes the performance even higher. The best performing MARC implementation is within a factor of 2.5 of the hand-optimized design and corresponds to two-way multithreaded A-cores. Like the FPGA platform, further increase to four threads offers diminishing returns and is outweighed by the increase in area, and therefore the area-normalized performance actually decreases.

7.3. Cross-Analysis against GPGPU. We also benchmark the various hardware implementations of the order-graph sampler against the GPGPU reference solution, running on Nvidia's GeForce GTX 580.

As the GTX 580 chip has a much larger area than Virtex-5 FPGA and is also on 40 nm process rather than 65 nm, we scaled its execution time according to the following equations, following Table 2:

$$\text{Scaled Area}_{\text{GPU}} = \text{Area}_{\text{GPU}} * S^2 = 520 * \left(\frac{65}{40}\right)^2 = 1373, \tag{4}$$

$$T_{\text{scaled}} = \frac{\text{Scaled Area}_{\text{GPU}}}{\text{Area}_{\text{FPGA}}} * S * T = 8.264 * T. \tag{5}$$

To make sure the comparison is fair, the technology scaling [24] takes into account the absolute area difference between the GPU and FPGA, as well as the area and delay scaling (i.e., S, the technology scaling factor) due to different processes. Our first assumption is that the performance scales linearly

with area, which is a good approximation due to our Bayesian network problem and device sizes. Second, we assume zero wire slack across both process generations for all designs. The original and scaled execution times are displayed in Table 3.

It can be seen from Tables 4 and 5 that MARC on FPGA can achieve the same performance as the GPGPU when application-specific A-cores are used. With multithreading, the best MARC implementation on FPGA can achieve more than a 40% performance advantage over the GPGPU. Hand-optimized designs, with more customization at the core and network level, push this advantage even further to 3.3x. The reason for this speedup is that each iteration of the inner loop of the *score*() function takes 1 cycle for A-cores on MARC and the hand-optimized design, but 15 to 20 cycles on GPGPU cores. It is apparent that the benefit from exploiting loop level parallelism at the A-cores outweighs the clock frequency advantage that the GPGPU has over the FPGA.

When an ASIC is used as the implementation platform, the speedup is affected by the paging of data as explained in Section 7.1. For the 32 node problem where paging of data is not required, the best MARC implementation and the hand-optimized design achieve 156x and 412x performance improvement over the GPGPU, respectively. For the 37 node problem, which requires paging, we observe a 69x and 84x performance advantage from the best MARC variant and hand-optimized implementation, respectively. Using only a single dual channel DRAM controller, we have about 51.2 Gb/sec of memory bandwidth for paging. However the GPGPU's memory bandwidth is 1538.2 Gb/sec—30x that of our ASIC implementations. As a result, the GPGPU solution remains compute bound while our ASIC implementations are getting constrained by the memory bandwidth. Thus, the performance gap between the 32 and 37 node problems is because of the memory-bound nature of our ASIC implementations.

It is also interesting that the MARC implementation with RISC A-cores on ASIC is about 6 times faster for the 32 node problem and 8 times faster for 37 node problem, compared to the GPGPU. With both MARC RISC A-cores and GPGPU cores, the kernel is executed as sequence of instructions rather than by a custom datapath. In addition, the clock frequency gap between MARC on ASIC and the GPGPU is small. We claim that the performance gap is due to the application-specific nature of the MARC design—MARC is able to place more cores per unit area (see Table 1) while still satisfying the requirements of local caching. In addition, the network structure in MARC machines is also optimized to the Bayesian inference accumulation step. The combined effect results in a significantly better use of chip area for this application.

TABLE 4: 32-Node. Performance comparison between MARC, hand-optimized, and GPGPU.

Configuration	Per iteration Time (μs)	Relative Perf.
GPGPU scaled reference	174	0.0024
MARC-Ropt-F	2550	0.0002
MARC-C1-F	172	0.0025
MARC-C2-F	124	0.0034
MARC-C4-F	136	0.0031
Hand design FPGA	51.4	0.0082
MARC-Ropt-A	27.6	0.0152
MARC-C1-A	1.47	0.2863
MARC-C2-A	1.11	0.3808
MARC-C4-A	1.17	0.3608
Hand design ASIC	0.422	1.0000

TABLE 5: 37-Node. Performance comparison between MARC, Hand-optimized, and GPGPU.

Configuration	Per iteration Time (μs)	Relative Perf.
GPGPU scaled reference	312	0.0119
MARC-Ropt-F	5130	0.0007
MARC-C1-F	310	0.0120
MARC-C2-F	221	0.0169
MARC-C4-F	235	0.0158
Hand design FPGA	110	0.0339
MARC-Ropt-A	38.1	0.0978
MARC-C1-A	5.02	0.7429
MARC-C2-A	4.53	0.8231
MARC-C4-A	4.61	0.8083
Hand design ASIC	3.73	1.0000

8. Conclusion

MARC offers a methodology to design FPGA and ASIC-based high-performance reconfigurable computing systems. It does this by combining a many-core architectural template, high-level imperative programming model [19], and modern compiler technology [22] to efficiently target both ASICs and FPGAs for general-purpose, computationally intensive data-parallel applications.

The primary objective of this paper is to understand whether a many-core architecture is a suitable abstraction layer (or execution model) for designing ASIC and FPGA-based computing machines from an OpenCL specification. We are motivated by recently reemerging interest and efforts in parallel programming for newly engineered and upcoming many-core platforms, and feel that if we can successfully build an efficient many-core abstraction for ASICs and FPGAs, we can apply the advances in parallel programming to high-level automatic synthesis of computing systems. Ofcourse, constraining an execution template reduces degrees of freedom for customizing an implementation using application-specific detail. However, we work under the hypothesis that much of the potential loss in efficiency can be recovered through customization of a microarchitectural template designed for a class of applications using application-specific information. The study in this paper represents our initial effort to quantify the loss in efficiency incurred for a significant gain in design productivity for one particular application.

We have demonstrated via the use of a many-core microarchitectural template for OpenCL that it is at least sometimes possible to achieve competitive performance relative to a highly optimized solution and to do so with considerable reduction in development effort (days versus months). This approach also achieves significant performance advantage over a GPGPU approach—a natural platform for mapping this class of applications. In this study, the most significant performance benefit came from customization of the processor cores to better fit the application kernel—an operation within reach of modern high-level synthesis flows.

Despite these results, the effectiveness of MARC in the general case remains to be investigated. We are currently limited by our ability to generate many high-quality hand-optimized custom solutions in a variety of domains to validate and benchmark template-based implementations. Nonetheless, we plan to continue this study, exploring more application domains, extending the many-core template tailored for OpenCL and exploring template microarchitectures for other paradigms. We are optimistic that a MARC-like approach will open new frontiers for rapid prototyping of high-performance computing systems.

Acknowledgments

The authors wish to acknowledge the contributions of the students, faculty, and sponsors of the Berkeley Wireless Research Center and the TSMC University Shuttle Program. This work was funded by the NIH, Grant no. 1R01CA130826-01 and the Department of Energy, Award no. DE-SC0003624.

References

[1] M. Lin, I. Lebedev, and J. Wawrzynek, "Highthroughput Bayesian computing machine with reconfigurable hardware," in *Proceedings of the 18th annual ACM/SIGDA International Symposium on Field Programmable Gate Arrays (FPGA '10)*, pp. 73–82, ACM, Monterey, California, USA, 2010.

[2] M. Lin, I. Lebedev, and J. Wawrzynek, "OpenRCL: from sea-of-gates to sea-of-cores," in *Proceedings of the 20th IEEE International Conference on Field Programmable Logic and Applications*, Milano, Italy, 2010.

[3] Wikipedia, "C-to-hdl," November 2009, http://en.wikipedia.org/wiki/C_to_HDL/.

[4] M. Gokhale and J. Stone, "Napa c: compiling for a hybrid risc/fpga architecture," in *Proceedings of the IEEE Symposium on FPGAs for Custom Computing Machines (FCCM '98)*, Napa, Calif, USA, 1998.

[5] T. J. Callahan, J. R. Hauser, and J. Wawrzynek, "Garp architecture and C compiler," *Computer*, vol. 33, no. 4, pp. 62–69, 2000.

[6] M. Budiu, G. Venkataramani, T. Chelcea, and S. C. Goldstein, "Spatial computation," in *Proceedings of the 11th International Conference on Architectural Support for Programming Languages and Operating Systems (ASPLOS-XI '04)*, pp. 14–26, New York, NY, USA, October 2004.

[7] J. Wawrzynek, D. Patterson, M. Oskin et al., "RAMP: research accelerator for multiple processors," *IEEE Micro*, vol. 27, no. 2, pp. 46–57, 2007.

[8] A. Papakonstantinou, K. Gururaj, J. A. Stratton, D. Chen, J. Cong, and M. W. Hwu, "Fcuda: enabling efficient compilation of cuda kernels onto fpgas," in *Proceedings of the 7th IEEE Symposium on Application Specific Processors (SASP '09)*, San Francisco, Calif, USA, 2009.

[9] M. Owaida, N. Bellas, K. Daloukas, and C. D. Antonopoulos, "Synthesis of platform architectures from opencl programs," in *Proceedings of the 19th IEEE Annual International Symposium on Field-Programmable Custom Computing Machines (FCCM '11)*, Salt Lake City, Utah, USA, 2011.

[10] J. Friedman, T. Hastie, and R. Tibshirani, "Sparse inverse covariance estimation with the graphical lasso," *Biostatistics*, vol. 9, no. 3, pp. 432–441, 2008.

[11] D. Heckerman, D. Geiger, and D. M. Chickering, "Learning Bayesian networks: the combination of knowledge and statistical data," *Machine Learning*, vol. 20, no. 3, pp. 197–243, 1995.

[12] J. Pearl, *Probabilistic Reasoning in Intelligent Systems: Networks of Plausible Inference*, Morgan Kaufmann, San Francisco, Calif, USA, 1988.

[13] C. Fletcher, I. Lebedev, N. Asadi, D. Burke, and J. Wawrzynek, "Bridging the GPGPU-FPGA efficiency gap," in *Proceedings of the 19th ACM/SIGDA International Symposium on Field Programmable Gate Arrays (FPGA '11)*, pp. 119–122, New York, NY, USA, 2011.

[14] N. Bani Asadi, C. W. Fletcher, G. Gibeling et al., "Paralearn: a massively parallel, scalable system for learning interaction networks on fpgas," in *Proceedings of the 24th ACM International Conference on Supercomputing*, pp. 83–94, ACM, Ibaraki, Japan, 2010.

[15] D. M. Chickering, "Learning Bayesian Networks is NP-Complete," in *Learning from Data: Artificial Intelligence and Statistics V*, pp. 121–130, Springer, New York, NY, USA, 1996.

[16] B. Ellis and W. H. Wong, "Learning causal Bayesian network structures from experimental data," *Journal of the American Statistical Association*, vol. 103, no. 482, pp. 778–789, 2008.

[17] M. Teyssier and D. Koller, "Ordering-based search: a simple and effective algorithm for learning Bayesian networks," in *Proceedings of the 21st Conference on Uncertainty in AI (UAI '5)*, pp. 584–590, Edinburgh, UK, July 2005.

[18] N. Friedman and D. Koller, "Being Bayesian about network structure," in *Proceedings of the 16th Conference on Uncertainty in Artificial Intelligence*, pp. 201–210, Morgan Kaufmann, San Francisco, Calif, USA, 2000.

[19] Khronos OpenCL Working Group, The OpenCL Specification, version 1.0.29, December 2008, http://khronos.org/registry/cl/specs/opencl-1.0.29.pdf.

[20] M. Lin, I. Lebedev, and J. Wawrzynek, "OpenRCL: low-power high-performance computing with reconfigurable devices," in *Proceedings of the 18th International Symposium on Field Programmable Gate Array*, 2010.

[21] NVIDIA OpenCL Best Practices Guide, 2009, http://www.nvidia.com/content/cudazone/CUDABrowser/downloads/papers/NVIDIA_OpenCL_BestPracticesGuide.pdf.

[22] C. Lattner and V. Adve, "LLVM: a compilation framework for lifelong program analysis & transformation," in *Proceedings of the International Symposium on Code Generation and Optimization (CGO '04)*, pp. 75–86, Palo Alto, Calif, USA, March 2004.

[23] G. Gibeling et al., "Gatelib: a library for hardware and software research," Tech. Rep., 2010.

[24] J. Rabaey, A. Chandrakasan, and B. Nikolic, *Digital Integrated Circuits*, chapter 5, Prentice Hall, New York, NY, USA, 2nd edition, 2003.

9

Modeling and Implementation of a Power Estimation Methodology for SystemC

Matthias Kuehnle,[1] Andre Wagner,[1] Alisson V. Brito,[2] and Juergen Becker[1]

[1] *Institute for Information Processing Technology, KIT, 7602 Karlsruhe, Germany*
[2] *Department of Informatics, Federal University of Paraiba (UFPB), 58051-900 João Pessoa, PB, Brazil*

Correspondence should be addressed to Alisson V. Brito, alissonbrito@dce.ufpb.br

Academic Editor: Massimo Conti

This work describes a methodology to model power consumption of logic modules. A detailed mathematical model is presented and incorporated in a tool for translation of models written in VHDL to SystemC. The functionality for implicit power monitoring and estimation is inserted at module translation. The translation further implements an approach to wrap RTL to TLM interfaces so that the translated module can be connected to a system-level simulator. The power analysis is based on a statistical model of the underlying HW structure and an analysis of input data. The flexibility of the C++ syntax is exploited, to integrate the power evaluation technique. The accuracy and speed-up of the approach are illustrated and compared to a conventional power analysis flow using PPR simulation, based on Xilinx technology.

1. Introduction

The need for more abstract system on chip development techniques is evident due to rising system complexity. Consequently, accurate system evaluation in less time will increase the productivity. According to the Semiconductor roadmap, especially the consideration of energy consumption is becoming more important and is also a limiting factor for many applications [1, 2]. Modeling strategies are driven by system and software engineers on the one hand and hardware engineers on the other hand. The first group develops RTL models written in hardware description languages (HDLs) since they are the basis for synthesis tools. The second group uses transaction level models (TLMS), most commonly written in SystemC [3] since these models enable fast system simulation. SystemC is a library based on the object-oriented programming language C++. A TLM specification extends SystemC to separate communication from computation. TLM improves modeling and simulation speed. The simulation speed depends on the level of abstraction [4]. Also, modeling at different abstraction levels is possible. This increases the flexibility of SystemC.

A remaining problem is the trade-off between accuracy and simulation speed and with that, the link and synchronization between the two layers. Translation tools are solving this problem to some extent. They inherit some limitations in the translation of syntax constructs that do not have direct counterparts. The presented tool extends this feature list. The main goal of this work, however, is the integration of a power analysis methodology into the translation process. The power estimation methodology estimates switching activities in DSP units such as adders or multipliers according to actual input data. The approach is based on a statistical methodology. It implements the measurement functionality implicitly into the SystemC model by defining overloaded operators, in the sense of object-oriented programming. These can be differently characterized based on technology parameters. The operators can be automatically integrated at system translation. DSP units are considered, since a power analysis of such systems shows that the major part of the dynamic power dissipation is consumed in the data-processing part of the architecture. In addition, the power dissipation is highly data dependent. Therefore a fast but reasonably accurate estimation of the dynamic power dissipation of such data-driven kernels is of high interest and the analysis using representative input data is essential. From the hardware point of view, the additional flexibility inherent in reconfigurable architecture and easy-to-use implementation flows make reconfigurable computing, especially FPGA architectures, attractive for power-aware computing solutions. Since CPUs are not sufficiently energy efficient (power consumption up to 200 W) and, on the other hand, ASICS are unaffordable for a low market volume, reconfigurable computing is considered an alternative especially for data-driven applications. Their benefit has been shown, for example, in [5, 6].

The described situation in the system development landscape motivates the development of a strategy for abstract, hence faster data-dependent power analysis for LUT-(lookup-table-) based systems in this work. The results were presented in [7] and are compared here to a standard power estimation flow. Beside it a detailed mathematical modeling strategy for power consumption estimation is presented. To ease and accelerate the development cycle, the power estimation method is embedded in a translation tool, so that the process of power estimation is transparent for the user and can be validated.

The remainder of this work is structured as follows. Section 2 summarizes related work. Section 6 embeds the strategy in an overall tool flow. Section 3 discusses the strategy to evaluate power dissipation for LUT-based hardware based on a statistical model to estimate toggle rates. This is related to a hardware mapping analysis of representing macroblocks (adders and multipliers) for data processing. Section 7 describes the implementation of the technology into the VHDL to SystemC converter. Section discusses the results. Section 9 concludes and gives an outline on future extensions.

2. Related Works

Code translation tools can help guaranteeing the consistency of translated and original models across languages and speeding up development time, since tool-supported translation takes seconds instead of hours to days for manual translation. In the system development cycle, top-down approaches [8–10] are used in HLS (high-level synthesis) tools; bottom-up approaches [11, 12] are used for IP reuse and module abstraction to achieve faster simulation models. In many hardware engineering problems, optimization is necessary on RTL Level. However, readability and efficiency of the translated code are two major problems of the HLS code translators. Because of that a bottom-up strategy is followed in this work. The authors in [13] further illustrates the effects of IP reuse on design time, hence motivates the bottom up approach.

The presented methodology differs from the existing solutions since it targets, beside correct code translation, the automatic integration of further functionality: bus interface wrapping and a power estimation methodology. The power estimation methodology estimates switching activities in DSP units such as adders and multipliers according to actual input data. The approach is based on probability theory. With that it differs from approaches that need to run a conventional time-consuming power estimation flow (e.g., XPA from Xilinx) or other estimators that are based on synthesis results without considering input data (e.g., XPE from Xilinx).

The approach presented in [14] is also implemented for SystemC. It enables the usage of different power models. In comparison with this work, it uses a strategy based on logging the execution of special modules and signals extended from regular SystemC ones, instead of a probability model, as presented here. In [15] a SystemC class library is proposed to the calculate the energy consumption of hardware described with SystemC TLM, and the power model was based on experimental results performed in laboratory, while approach of the presented work is based on the translation of modules from VHDL to SystemC RTL and on probability models. Further works concern the extension of the approach also to TLM.

The work [16] presents an architectural level framework for power analysis, based on parameterized power models of common structures of microprocessors, but does not consider any probability model, as presented in this work. In [17] a methodology is presented for simulation and verification of low-power systems using SystemC. It is based on disabling modules during execution to simulate the power switch-off used by the technique of power gating. The technique for disabling SystemC modules at simulation time is detailed in [18]. At the same time, these related works are not specific to reconfigurable architectures, in contrast to our work, which considers specific characteristics of FPGAs.

3. Power Evaluation Strategy

This project uses an activity-based power estimation and calculation based on the switching frequency of the inputs, outputs, and the internal signals of the individual sub-modules. The proposed power estimation and calculation is tailored for signal processing units where the major part of the power consumption is produced by multiply-accumulate instructions, which is computed in hardware by ripple carry adders and field multipliers based on ripple carry adders. To guarantee that the synthesized hardware for computing MAC is realized on the given adder and multiplier structures, a hardware model on register transfer level of the processing unit is needed. Both implementation and calculation are optimized for area consumption on FPGAs with little slice count. The accuracy of the estimation is based on two areas.

First there is the realization on hardware which is done by the synthesis tools for a specific LUT-based FPGA. Later in this section synthesis results for given FPGAs are examined for getting the fan-out parameters which are needed for a exact calculation of the power dissipation of each element. Further general rules for optimal synthesis of ripple carry adders and field multipliers are formulated.

Secondly, input data is analyzed for predicting the switching frequency on the expected synthesized hardware structure. This means that the probability distribution of the input data has to be computed. The probability distribution of the output data is derived from that. The input data should be taken from the original implementation. This means, for example, in case of an audio decoder, a corresponding audio stream should be used. For better comprehension an complete workflow for power estimation is shown.

The first step to be done is the analysis of the input data. For example, the input data is uniformly distributed on the complete accepted range with the boundaries 0 and u, where u is a natural number. This assumption is suitable if the distribution of the input data is unknown. By the way this concept was first formulated by Gauss and is known as the Gaussian indifference principle.

Next the binary coding of the numbers between 0 and u is analyzed. The value of the MSB is distributed as followed:

(i) in the range between 0 and $u/2$, the value of the MSB is 0,

(ii) in the range between $u/2$ and u, the value of the MSB is 1.

With the condition of the uniform distribution, all numbers in range are selected with the same frequency. This means, for the probability that the MSB bit is set to 1,

$$p(\text{MSB}) = \frac{u/2}{u} = \frac{1}{2}. \tag{1}$$

The analysis of the next less significant bit is made the same way. The value of the (MSB-1) bit is the follows:

(i) in the range between 0 and $u/4$, value of (MSB-1) is 0,

(ii) in the range between $u/4$ and $u/2$, value of (MSB-1) is 1,

(iii) in the range between $u/2$ and $3u/4$, value of (MSB-1) is 0,

(iv) in the range between $3u/4$ and u, value of (MSB-1) is 1,

The calculation of the probability that (MSB-1) bit is set to 1:

$$p(\text{MSB} - 1) = \frac{2 * (u/4)}{u} = \frac{1}{2}. \tag{2}$$

Based on the calculations for the MSB and the (MSB-1) bit, a prediction can be made.

For every step you make from MSB towards LSB, the number of intervals in which the bit is set to 1 is doubled but the length of the intervals is halved. In consequence this means that the accumulated length of the intervals in which the bit is set to 1 is equal for all bits. Because of this fact the probability that a bit on the input is set to 1 is calculated for all bits:

$$p = \frac{1}{2}. \tag{3}$$

After the computation of the probabilities on the input vector, the probabilities for the output vectors of the ripple

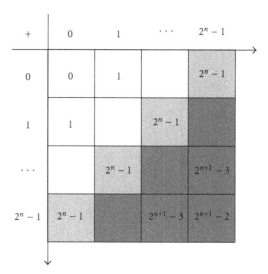

FIGURE 1: Carry generation in the adder.

carry adder and the field multiplier can be calculated. First the probability of the occurrence of carry bits of the ripple carry adder is determined.

For the possibility that a carry-on location n is generated, all input vectors of the adder between 0 and $2^n - 1$ are relevant. Figure 1 shows the addition of two summands in this range.

Each cell in this figure corresponds to the sum of the row and column number. To calculate the the probability that the carry is set, it is suitable to count the number of cell in which a carry is generated and divide this count by the total number of cells. This figure has 2^{2n} entries of which $2^{2n-1} - 2^{n-1}$ generate the carry. The division leads to

$$p_{c,n} = \frac{2^{2n-1} - 2^{n-1}}{2^{2n}} = \frac{1}{2} - 2^{n-1}. \tag{4}$$

Additionally the following statement can be made: because the generation nth carry is only possible if the upper bound of the accepted input values is 2^n, all the probabilities for all carry bits on locations higher than $ld(u)$ can be set to zero.

After calculating the probability of the carry bits, the probability of the sum bits of the adder can follow. The boolean equation of the sum on location n is

$$s_n = \left(i1_n \wedge in2_n \vee \overline{i1_n} \wedge \overline{i2_n} \right) \wedge c_n$$
$$\vee \left(\overline{i1_n} \wedge in2_n \vee i1_n \wedge \overline{i2_n} \right) \wedge \overline{c_n}. \tag{5}$$

Transferring this equation to the probability domain leads to

$$p_{s,n} = \left(p_{i1,n} * p_{i2,n} + \overline{p_{i1,n}} * \overline{p_{i2,n}} \right) * p_{c,n}$$
$$+ \left(\overline{p_{i1,n}} * p_{i2,n} + p_{i1,n} * \overline{p_{i2,n}} \right) * \overline{p_{c,n}}. \tag{6}$$

Setting $p_{i1,n} = 0.5$, $p_{i2,n} = 0.5$ (uniform distribution) and $p_{c,n}$ equals

$$p_{b,n} = 0.5. \tag{7}$$

Like the statement for carry bits with location near the MSB, a likewise statement can be made for the sum bits: because the generation nth sum bit is only possible if the upper bound of the accepted input values is 2^n, all the probabilities for all carry bits on locations higher than $ld(u)$ can be set to zero. Similar to these calculations, likewise calculations for other probability are possible. The following paragraph describes the approach for calculating the probability of sum and carry bits with calculated nonequal probabilities for each bit of the adder input. The given input probabilities are named $p_{i1,n}$ and $p_{i2,n}$. In this project a 32-bit adder was analyzed so the valid indices are in the range from 0 to 31. With this new assumption, the proceeding is as follows.

First the boolean equation of the carry bit is annotated:

$$\overline{cn} = \left(i1_n \wedge \overline{i2_n} \vee \overline{i1_n} \wedge i2_n\right) \wedge c_{n-1} \vee \overline{i1_n} \vee \overline{i2_n}. \quad (8)$$

Based on this equation, a transformation to probability domain is made:

$$\overline{p_{c,n}} = \left(p_{i1,n} * \overline{p_{i2,n}} + \overline{p_{i1,n}} * p_{i2,n}\right) * p_{c,n-1} + \overline{p_{i1,n}} * \overline{p_{i2,n}}. \quad (9)$$

With the extra knowledge that the carry bit in the least significant adder is never set (this means $p_{c,n}$ is zero), all the carry probabilities can be calculated in a recursive manner. With the formula for calculating the $p_{s,n}$ probabilities the examination of the ripple carry adder with nonequal distributed input vectors is completed.

Based on these observations a derivation for the calculation of the signal probabilities of the field multiplier is possible.

The idea is to connect the calculations for the ripple carry adder with individual input probabilities. According to Figure 2, the input probability p_{i1n} of one adder is the same value like the $ps(n+1)$ probability of the previous level. With the extra assumption of uniform distributed input vectors of the adder and the knowledge that a AND-gate is equal to a multiplication of its input probabilities, the $p_{i2,n}$ probability equals the multiplication of the probabilities of the inputs of the multiplier; that is, $0.5 * 0.5 = 0.25$. If the distribution is restricted to the range 0 to u, all $p_{i2,n}$ with a index and level higher than $ld(u)$ have to be set to zero.

Also these calculations can be performed on other input probability distributions. After the calculation of the probabilities of occurrence, the transition to the switch frequency is made. The normalized statistical switching frequency is given by

$$f_{norm,stat} = p(1-p). \quad (10)$$

That definition of the frequency is equal to the probability of the occurrence of a positive transition of the signal. By means of this frequency definition, the dynamic power dissipation of CMOS circuits is described as follows:

$$P_{dyn,stat} = C * U^2 * f_{norm,stat} * f_{base} * \text{fanout}, \quad (11)$$

where f_{base} defines the bit rate on the observed signal. The parameter C for the input capacity and the supply voltage

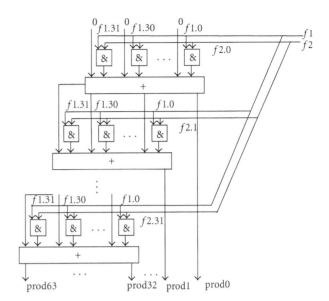

FIGURE 2: Structure of a field multiplier.

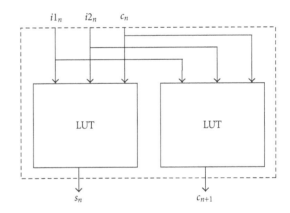

FIGURE 3: Optimized elementary cell for three-to-four-input LUT.

U can be extracted from the data sheet while the fanout parameter which describes the number of inputs to be driven is dependent on the circuit synthesis on the FPGA. For getting the fanout parameters of the individual signals, the synthesis result of Xilinx ISE is analyzed. The following pictures show the elementary cells of the adder for different FPGAs.

Figure 3 shows the synthesis result of the basic cell of a ripple carry adder for a LUT-FPGA with three to four inputs and one output, Figure 4 shows the synthesis result of the basic cell of a ripple carry adder for a LUT-FPGA with five to six inputs and one output, Figure 5 shows the synthesis result of the basic cell of a field multiplier for a LUT-FPGA with four to five inputs, and Figure 6 shows the synthesis result for a LUT-FPGA with six to seven inputs.

Out of the synthesis result, it is obvious that the maximal size of a elementary cell is limited by the LUT fanin which calculates the carry for the next elementary cell. The elementary cell synthesized for the adder equals a radix-floor $((n-1)/2)$ adder which is shown in Figure 7.

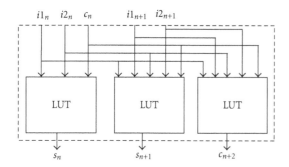

FIGURE 4: Optimized elementary cell for five-to-six-input LUT.

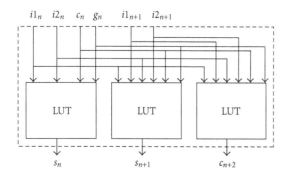

FIGURE 5: Optimized elementary cell for four-to-five-input LUT.

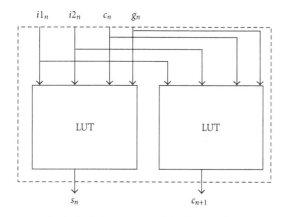

FIGURE 6: Optimized elementary cell for six-to-seven-input LUT.

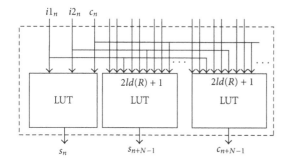

FIGURE 7: The high radix adder mapped to LUTs.

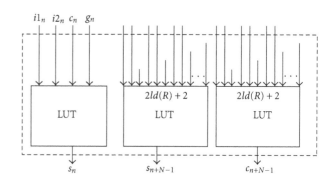

FIGURE 8: The high-radix adder with gate mapped to LUTs.

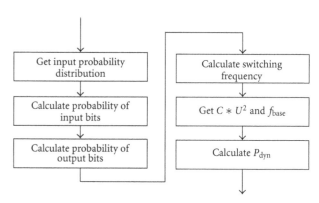

FIGURE 9: Setup of a new power estimation.

Similar to the high-radix adder elementary cell, the elementary cell of the multiplier consists of a high-radix adder and set of AND-Gates which are controlling the optional addition of summand no. 2 (shown in Figure 8).

With help of this circuit diagrams, it is possible to get the fan-out parameters for the power dissipation formula. The overall workflow can be seen in Figure 9 and is described as follows.

4. Improving Probability Analysis by Carry-Computation

Another possibility for the quality of the probabilities of signal occurrence is the replacement of signal by transfer of a specifically calculated value. It raises the question of which carry bit achieved through the replacement of an exact signal calculation has the best effect. The first consideration is the simplified assumption that all bits are equally distributed, then, for the probability of occurrence for each carry bit of the formula:

$$p^N(c, n) = \frac{1}{2} - \frac{1}{2^{n+1}}. \tag{12}$$

In case that the n_1th bit is calculated exactly for the signal, the maximum difference applies to

$$\text{Diff}_{c,n_1} = \sum_{n=0}^{N-n_1} \left| p_{c,n}^N - /p_{c,n}^N \right|,$$

$$\text{Diff}_{c,n_1} = \sum_{n=0}^{N-n_1} 1 - 2 * p_{c,n}^N,$$

$$\text{Diff}_{c,n_1} = \sum_{n=0}^{N-n_1} \frac{1}{2}^n,$$

$$\text{Diff}_{c,n_1} = \frac{1}{2} - \frac{1}{2}^{N-n_1}.$$

$$(13)$$

This maximum deviation occurs with the probability of $p_{cn}^N a$. Hence, for the probable deviation,

$$p_{\text{Diff}_{c,n_1}} = \text{Diff}_{c,n_1} * p_{c,n_1}^N,$$

$$p_{\text{Diff}_{c,n_1}} = \left(\frac{1}{2} - \frac{1}{2^{n+1}} \right) * \left(\frac{1}{2} - \frac{1}{2}^{N-n_1} \right). \qquad (14)$$

To get the maximum deviation probability, the first derivative of $p_{c\text{diff},n_1}$ should be used:

$$p'_{\text{Diff}_{c,n_1}} = \ln(2) * \frac{1}{2}^{n_1} \left[\frac{1}{2} - \frac{1}{2}^{N-n_1} \right] - \ln(2)$$
$$* \frac{1}{2}^{N-n_1} \left[\frac{1}{2} - \frac{1}{2}^{n_1+1} \right] \neq 0. \qquad (15)$$

It can be seen from the equation that it must apply for a zero:

$$N - n_1 \overset{!}{=} n_1 + 1,$$

$$n_1 = \frac{N-1}{2}. \qquad (16)$$

With an additional graphic, it can be seen that it is found at the point where only the maximum of the function is located. Now it is possible to find the point in the equation that determines the maximum:

$$\max\left(p_{\text{Diff}_{c,(N-1)/2}}; \text{Diff}_{c,(N-1)/2} * p_{c,(N-1)/2}^N \right) \leq 0.25. \qquad (17)$$

At this point it becomes clear why the exact calculation of the carry is not worthwhile: the probability of occurrence of a input signal bit is already, by assumption, 0.5 and can be determined without calculation; the calculation of a carry must be made in each run of the adder and helps only to avoid errors in average of 0.25. The distribution of the most probable estimation error for different length adders is presented in Figure 10. The calculation of a carry bit, however, is costly. The n_1th carry is calculated as follows:

$$\text{Carry}_{n_1} = ([\text{Summand } 1 \bmod (1 \ll i)]$$
$$+ [\text{Summand } 2 \bmod (1 \ll i)]) \div (1 \ll i), \qquad (18)$$

the total of

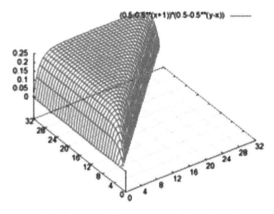

FIGURE 10: Distribution of the most probable estimation error for n-bit adder.

(i) 3 identical left-shift operations

(ii) 1 division

(iii) 2 modulo (division with remainder).

5. Interface: Power Loss Estimation

In order to generate as little code overhead, a basic C data type was created for unsigned integers `unsigned int` for the equivalent class `sc_int_power`, which is equipped with the same operator overloads like the original data type. These include all the arithmetic operators that are required for signal processing (addition, subtraction, multiplication, division), the assignment operator, and the operator for streaming output with `cout`. In addition, a cast operator for `unsigned int` casting in a safe situation in which only the numeric value of the `sc_int_power` object must be such as that with an array indexing. The real power estimation takes place only in the multiplication and addition operators, because these functions are the main focus of this work. The functions occurring in this energy consumption model are stored by the class static member `power`.

To take advantage of the presented class `sc_int_power` in a SystemC project, it should be compared to a standard implementation requiring the following additional code fragments:

(1) include the header file `power.h`;

(2) call the static function `set_calc` to indicate the accuracy of calculations;

(3) call the static function `set_mu` set parameters for the estimation;

(4) call the static function `set_lut` to adjust the power estimation of the target FPGA.

Anything else due to the replication of the functionality of `unsigned int` in `sc_int_power` must be ignored. It is also possible to define a simple design already in the VHDL source code with pragmas, such as the type `integer` in the types `sc_int_power` by the modified V2SC during translation. Instead of the function calls in an equivalent

SystemC project boundary bonds are defined by the above pragmas as follows:

(1) `set powerestimation_lut number;`

(2) `set powerestimation_mu number;`

(3) `set powerestimation_calc 0 or CALC_ALL;`

(4) `powerestimation on`: all of the following integers in `sc_int_power` translated;

(5) `powerestimation off`: all of the following integers in `int` translated.

These pragmas are recognized when translated from VHDL to SystemC and automatically converted into the corresponding SystemC functions. By this procedure, additional user settings are generated into the source code.

5.1. The Class prob_bit. The class `prob_bit` implements the functions to estimate the amount of time for the inputs, outputs, and internal signals of a 32-bit adder to be high and the estimation of the switching frequency. To fill the individual estimated, six arrays are implemented:

(1) `input` contains the estimation of bit = "1" for input bits;

(2) `input_rising_edges` contain the estimation for the switching frequency of the input;

(3) `output` contain the estimation of bit = "1" for the sum bit;

(4) `output_rising_edges` contain the estimation for the switching frequency of the sum bits;

(5) `signal` contains the estimation of bit = "1" for the carry bit;

(6) `signal_rising_edges` contains the estimation for the switching frequency of the carry bit.

To store a new estimate for bit = "1" in each field, the functions `add_input_prob`, `add_output_prob` and `add_signal_prob` provided that again over the functions `get_input_prob`, `get_output_prob`, and `get_signal_prob` can be retrieved. To simplify these getter and setter methods, the class has the static methods `in1`, `in2`, `carry` and `out`, which return the corresponding array index in the fields. For example, an estimate probability of bit = "1" for the 3rd bit of the adder `adder1` is set to 0.5 with the following call:

`adder1.add_input_prob(prob_bit::in2(3),0.5).`

The estimated switching frequencies on the power dissipation of the adder can have the class of functions `input_weight_function`, `signal_weight_function`, and `output_weight_function`, corresponding fan-ins for the individual inputs, outputs, and signal. By multiplying the switching frequencies associated with the switching frequency, we have the following relationship:

$$P_v = C_{\text{LUT}} * V^2 * (f * \text{fanin}). \tag{19}$$

Thus, all weighted switching frequencies must be multiplied only by the same factor in order to infer the loss of

performance. The actual value for each weighting function depends on the specific type of LUT-optimized design.

The weighting factors provided with the switching frequencies can be accessed through the functions `get_input_power`, `get_output_power`, and `get_signal_power`. The parameters of these functions can also have the static function `in1`, `in2` be `carry` and `out` to select the desired bits.

These functions only refer to individual bits of each type. A new group of functions was defined to access the accumulated probabilities of occurrence of bit = "1" and the weighted switching frequencies. The functions are named following the same pattern as the getter and setter methods:

(1) `get_weighted_input_sum` accumulates all the probabilities of occurrence of the inputs;

(2) `get_weighted_input_power_sum` accumulates all the switching frequency of the inputs;

(3) `get_weighted_signal_sum` accumulates all the probabilities of occurrence of the signals;

(4) `get_weighted_signal_power_sum` accumulates all the switching frequency of the signals;

(5) `get_weighted_output_sum` accumulates all the probabilities of occurrence of the outputs;

(6) `get_weighted_output_power_sum` accumulates all the switching frequency of the outputs.

It is also possible to accumulate over the functions `get_weighted_all_sum` and `get_weighted_all_power_sum` all weighted probabilities of occurrence or all the weighted switching frequencies. For further support of statistics on different `prob_bit` objects, two other functions were created for each port and signal to return the probability of occurrence and the switching frequency, as follows

(1) `print_input_all_prob` returns the probability of occurrence of all inputs;

(2) `print_input_all_power` outputs the switching frequency of all inputs;

(3) `print_signal_all_prob` returns the probability of occurrence of all signals;

(4) `print_signal_all_power` outputs the switching frequency of all signals;

(5) `print_output_all_prob` returns the probability of occurrence of all outputs;

(6) `print_output_all_power` returns the frequency switching of all outputs.

The class uses a custom constructor with three parameters for the transfer of the number of input and output signals, which also allows the formation of any combinational logic result.

5.2. The Class exact_bit. The class `exact_bit` implements functions for the accurate determination of probability of occurrence and switching frequency of 32-bit adders and is analogue of the class `prob_bit` which estimates these parameters. In order to not duplicate code and to keep the naming of the methods most consistently, the class exact_bit inherits from the parent class prob_bit and can largely use the methods of the parent class. The difference from the parent class makes itself felt in the determination of the exact switching frequency. During the estimation in the class prob_bit, an estimation of the switching frequency can be made directly from occurrence probability, this is not an exact determination because positive edges can be made only in the context of the last state of the adder. For this reason, the class attribute last_state holds a pointer to an associated exact_bit object that stores the last state of the input and output signals. With this additional information, it is now the exact determination of the number of positive edges occurred and therefore the exact determination of the switching frequency possible.

The determination of the accumulated amount of time in which one remains on high bit (equivalent to the probability of occurrence) is also possible without the context of the last condition; therefore the implementation of the class prob_bit is used. All other functions such as statistical functions to accumulate or print functions can also be used without modification, as there are the fields' input, input_rising_edges for the stored values to access from the direct calculation.

5.3. Addition Class.

The class addition provides the methods for estimation and exact determination of the probabilities of occurrence and switching frequencies of individual bits in a prepared 32-bit ripple-carry adder, which are used in the class sc_int_power. Addition has the functions power_add_approx2, power_add_approx2_complex, and power_add_exact2, where the first two estimate the switching frequency and the last ones accurately determine the switching frequency of the individual inputs, broadcast, and outputs.

The two estimators power_add_approx2 and power_add_approx2_complex differ in the specification of the probability of occurrence of the input bits. For the case when the adders are used as a single unit, it can be assumed as a multiplier, according to the principle of indifference when all input vectors are equally distributed within an interval. The function power_add_approx2 can be used to get the average of the input vectors and a statistic value that the prob_bit object returns. There is the case when the adder is part of a multiplier, the perception of the equal distribution is no longer made, and the function power_add_approx2_complex is used. This function takes an input statistic in the form of a prob_bit counter object and returns the output statistics again in a prob_bit object.

The function for accurate calculation of the switching frequency power_add_exact2 was implemented, two terms for the associated switching frequencies, whilst the output statistics are in an exact_bit object are used as parameters. The exact determination of the required associated switching frequency is associated to exact_bit object with the latest state of the adder stored by the class in the private attribute last_state.

5.4. Multiplication Class.

The class Multiplication provides methods for accurate determination and estimation of the probability of occurrence and the switching frequency in a 32-bit multiplier, which are required in the parent class sc_int_power. The class has the functions power_multiply_approx2 for the estimated and the power_multiply_exact2 for accurately determined switching frequency. The parameters of both functions are analogous to the methods of the class Addition. The estimator gives the mean value for the factors, while the function is used to the exact determination of the two factors to be multiplied. Because of the considered carry of the multiplier, the class Addition takes into account the wiring structure and take intermediate AND gates completely.

5.5. Random Generator for gcc.

First, to test the estimation of the classes Addition and Multiplication, the built-in random generator of C was used with the function rand from stdlib library. In the first test the estimations had similar variations (about 10%) to the exact values calculated as in the subsequent tests with the Mersenne-Twister random number generation. Due to the fact that the C standard requires no algorithm for random number generation, the author does not know which algorithm is used in the current implementation by gcc.

5.6. Random Generator LFSR.

In a second test the classes Addition and Multiplication were used for a linear feedback shift register. In the present implementation, the first 32 CRC polynomials were stored; that is, it can pseudo-randomize sequences to generate numbers in intervals up to 2^{32}. Tests, however, showed that the generated pseudo-random numbers are distributed very unevenly, most obviously in direct comparison with the C-random number generator or the Mersenne-Twister. Due this statistical property, this random number generator was considered unsuitable and was not included in further tests.

5.7. Mersenne-Twister Random Number Generator.

The GNU suite delivers a Mersenne-Twister random number generator. This type of random generator works on an extremely long interval of $2^{19937-1}$ and its most important feature is the uniform distribution of all output bits. Due to these excellent statistical properties, the Mersenne-Twister random number generator has been selected as a reference for testing the power loss estimation. In a comparison to integrated random in C, the Mersenne-Twister cuts marginally better due to the fact that in the random number generator rand of C, the least significant bits are not equally distributed.

5.8. Random NDIST Based on gcc.

To test the implementation of the power estimation with normally distributed random variables, the C-function NDIST was used, which approximates to function rand, but with uniformly distributed random numbers. With the aid of the central limit theorem, which states that the mean of a sufficiently large number of independent random variables, each with finite mean and variance, will be approximately normally

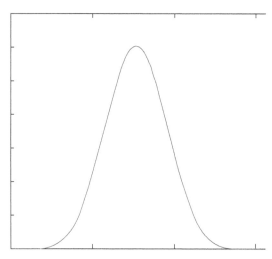

FIGURE 11: Normal distribution.

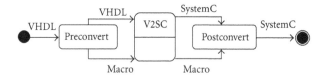

FIGURE 12: Combination of wrapper and V2SC.

TABLE 1: V2SC features.

Feature	Included
If	Yes
While	Yes
For	Yes
Function	Yes
Procedure	Yes
Packet	Yes
Record	Partly
Array	Partly

TABLE 2: V2SC + wrapper extras.

Feature	Included
Alias	Yes
Cast functions	Yes
Generate	Yes
Port map	Yes
Records	Yes
Arrays	Yes
Configuration	No
File IO	No

distributed, six different random numbers are added and displayed as a normally distributed random number. The actual number of six random numbers to be accumulated was determined experimentally. The chart of Figure 11 shows the theoretical distribution of the generated numbers in this six-accumulated random variable.

5.9. Generating a Large Random Number Set. The problematics when comparing different implementations of the estimation with the classes `Addition` and `Multiplication` in comparison with the VHDL implementation are to regenerate the random numbers used in each run. For this reason a common set of uniform distribution of $2 * 1000$ random numbers 0–1024 was generated and from this set all the relevant statistical characteristics of was calculated the probability of occurrence of individual bits. But the numbers from 0 to 1, which are the basis for determining the switching frequency, change. In addition to this, statistical characteristics were raised to what extension they can differ from the requirement to assess the validity of the estimation result.

6. Module Translation and Integration

An integrated system simulation can be accomplished in homogeneous or heterogeneous environments. The adoption of homogeneous system simulations has several advantages: (i) it achieves faster simulation since synchronization tasks between different simulation kernels can be omitted; (ii) the usage of SystemC instead of for example, VHDL and the possibility to simulate models on higher abstraction

levels further increment the simulation speed and additionally; (iii) since SystemC models are inevitable for system simulations and RTL models are necessary for synthesis flows, a module translation helps in keeping synchronism among the different module implementations and reduces error sources. On the other hand, this strategy requires a module translator. The VHDL to SystemC translator (V2SC) that was used in this work as basis has been developed by [19].

It was designed for SystemC 1.0 and basically supports constructs that can be directly translated from VHDL to SystemC. In this work, the translator has been extended to be compatible with the actual SystemC version 2.2 and to translate synthesisable VHDL constructs. Table 1 presents the features provided by V2SC and Table 2 shows a selection of extensions included as a contribution of this work. Further convertible VHDL syntax elements are listed in [20]. The converter has been verified against a set of VHDL modules, among them a IMDCT (for calculating the inverse modified discrete cosine transform) module including an AHB master and a APB slave interface with a complexity of >5000 lines of code, a FFT module (for calculating the fast Fourier transform) with about 250 lines of code, and a GCD module (for calculating the greatest common divisor) with about 100 lines of code.

The extensions are implemented with the compiler building tools flex and bison in the same way as the original converter. Furthermore the macroprocessor m4 and the text manipulation tool sed were used. The whole extension is build as a wrapper around V2SC (Figure 12) and is divided in two parts. A preconvert filter simplifies syntax elements by converting them to V2SC compatible constructs, or the filter masks constructs such that they can pass the V2SC

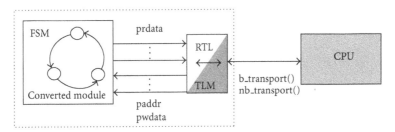

FIGURE 13: Interface conversion for generating a heterogeneous accuracy simulation model.

TABLE 3: Simulation speed comparison.

SystemC	SystemC with `int`	SystemC with `sc_int_power` (approx.)	SystemC with `sc_int_power` (exact)
Addition	1	0.5	0.03
Multiplication	1	0.5	0.001

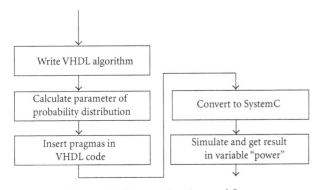

FIGURE 14: Power estimation workflow.

without modification, if the V2CS cannot handle them. The masked blocks are converted by the postconverter to SystemC constructs.

The converted IPs own a pin accurate RTL interface whereas the system simulator provides TLM interfaces. To decrease the design time, a protocol conversion has been integrated in the translation tool. The modified V2SC enables connecting VHDL RTL IPs to a SystemC TLM system by implementing a library that contains design patterns for pin accurate to TLM functional units according to the interface specifications. Appropriate modules are exemplary implemented for AMBA, AHB, and APB. The resulting translated modules can be directly connected to a AMBA-TLM 2.0 base system (see Figure 13).

7. Implementation of Power Estimation Features

The extension contains beside the compatibility pack, as described in Section 6, a tool for the automated integration of the previously discussed power estimation and calculation. This section explains a strategy, with which the conventional flow may be omitted if a certain decrease of accuracy can be accepted. Generally, the extension of functional parts with monitoring capabilities is an efficient way for automated system analysis. Since accurate power analysis flows are one

the most time-consuming steps in the development process, their integration in a SystemC environment, with the techniques discussed in Section 3, are expected to speed up the evaluation process. Conventional accurate power analysis tools need mainly two kinds of input information. On the one hand a model of the placed and routed design allows to calculate capacitive loads of each net by evaluating fan-out numbers and the characteristics of the primitives (LUTs for FPGA technology) and with that the energy consumption per net per activity. On the other hand dynamic activities are collected during post-place and route simulation in value Change Dumps (VCD). Especially the accurate simulation with enabled signal tracing is a very time-consuming step.

The power evaluation extension of the modified V2SC can be enabled by the flag -powerestimation of preconvert. After setting this flag, preconvert converts the VHDL-type integer in the new-user-defined type `sc_int_power` and not to the standard SystemC-type `int`. `sc_int_power` is a new type which is constructed in this project to do all power estimation and calculation. It acts a replacement for `int` and its behaviour is similar to it. To get this functionality, all common arithmetic operators $(+,-,*,/)$ are overloaded while the addition and the multiplication operator definitions contain the power estimation and calculating algorithms. Additionally all arithmetic operators are overloaded for mixed-type operation with `int`. Another feature is the overloaded cast operator of `int`, which is especially for indexing arrays. With a view to the use of `sc_int_power` as a complete SystemC data type, the streaming operator ≪, the test of equality ==, the test of inequality !=, the assignment operator =, and the function `sc_trace` are overloaded. Thus in this manner defined type can be used as a template class in `sc_signal<>`, for example. To get a high prediction quality of the power estimation, the algorithms have to be parameterised. This is done by the static class methods `set_mu` (defines the average value of the input vectors) and the `set_lut` (for optimizing the design to architecture). The static class method `set_calc` defines a switch between estimation (value is zero) and calculation (value is equal `CALC_ALL` constant). The result of the calculation respectively estimation can be retrieved

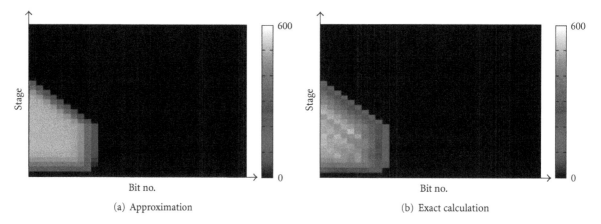

(a) Approximation   (b) Exact calculation

FIGURE 15: Toggle distribution estimation.

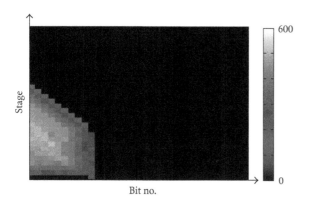

FIGURE 16: Reference from XPA tool.

from the static variable power. For improvement of the manageability of the power analyser tool the parametrisation of the algorithms is also possible in VHDL code by special comments called pragmas. These pragmas consist of the prefix "powerestimation" followed by the parametrisation function (i.e., set_calc, set_mu or set_lut) and the value to set. The following example shows the proceeding.

The original VHDL code:

(1) signal a,b,c: integer;

(2) --powerestimation set_lut 5

(3) --powerestimation set_calc 0

(4) --powerestimation set_mu 10.0

(5)

(6) c<=a+b.

Is translated in SystemC code:

(1) #include "power.h"

(2) ..

(3) sc_int_power a,b,c;

(4) c=a+b;

(5) //the powerestimation result

(6) //is stored in sc_int_power::power

(7) return 0;

The whole workflow is like that presented following that Figure 14.

8. Results

8.1. Accuracy of Toggle Estimation. The accuracy of the power estimation algorithms in sc_int_power to the also implemented exact calculation is about 13% for a average of more than 100 single additions or multiplications. Figure 15 shows the estimated toggle counts on the left and the exact calculated toggle count on the right of the partial sums (summands no. 1 of each stage) for a data set of 1000 two factors namely summands which are equally distributed in the range between 0 and 1024.

In comparison to the Xilinx XPower tool (see Figure 16), an almost similar accuracy was reached. On the following picture is the count of toggles for the partial sum bits visualized.

8.2. Speed Improvement. The integration of the proposed power estimation slows the calculation in contrast to the calculations on the standard type int about the factor two, but the also implemented exact power calculation slows the additions and multiplications about the factor 32, namely, 1024 (see Table 3). But the estimation is only slightly worse than the exact determination of the power dissipation; however the estimation is about the factor 16, namely, 512 faster. In sum this means that the proposed estimation is a good tradeoff between accuracy and simulation speed.

9. Conclusion and Future Work

This work proposes a methodology for switching activity estimation, taking into account the underlying hardware structure. The methodology has been exercised for MAC units. Different FPGAs have been used to show the portability of the method to other technologies. The loss of accuracy of 13% in the case of the MAC unit compared to post-place and route simulation results comes along with a simulation speed up of a factor up to 1024. The transparent implementation of that methodology into a VHDL to SystemC converter further accelerates and eases the development process. The general approach of the methodology can be also applied to other regular computation structures. With the implementation of further computational units (e.g., dividers or other adder architectures) and the support for other FPGA architectures, an analysis of complex data paths and a faster evaluation of design alternatives are envisioned.

References

[1] N. Dhanwada, I. C. Lin, and V. Narayanan, "A power estimation methodology for SystemC transaction level models," in *Proceedings of the 3rd IEEE/ACM/IFIP International Conference on Hardware/Software Codesign and Systems Synthesis (CODES+ISSS '05)*, pp. 142–147, September 2005.

[2] N. Dhanwada, R. A. Bergamaschi, W. W. Dungan et al., "Transaction-level modeling for architectural and power analysis of PowerPC and CoreConnect-based systems," *Design Automation for Embedded Systems*, vol. 10, no. 2-3, pp. 105–125, 2005.

[3] M. Lang, "System C for Embedded System Design," Seminar, 2006, http://dl.acm.org/citation.cfm?id=339657.

[4] S. Boukhechem and E. B. Bourennane, "TLM platform based on systemC for STARSoC design space exploration," in *Proceedings of the NASA/ESA Conference on Adaptive Hardware and Systems (AHS '08)*, pp. 354–361, June 2008.

[5] S. Hauck and A. Dehon, *Reconfigurable Computing the Theory and Practice of FPA-Based Computing*, Elsevier, 2008.

[6] N. Voros, A. Rosti, and M. Hübner, *XDynamic System Reconfiguration in Heterogeneous Platforms*, Elsevier, 2009.

[7] M. Kuehnle, A. Wagner, and J. Becker, "A statistical power estimation methodology embedded in a SystemC code translator," in *Proceedings of the 24th Symposium on Integrated Circuits and Systems Design (SBCCI '11)*, pp. 79–84, IEEE Computer Society, 2011.

[8] Forte, "Cynthesizer," 2011, http://www.forteds.com/products/cynthesizer.asp.

[9] M. Graphics, "Catapultc," 2011, http://www.mentor.com/esl/catapult/overview.

[10] Cadence, "C-to-silicon compiler," 2011, http://www.cadence.com/products/ sd/silicon compiler/pages/default.aspx.

[11] N. Bombieri, "Hif suite 2.0: hdl translating and manipulation tools," 2009, http://hifsuite.edalab.it/.

[12] University of Cincinnati, "Savant," 2011, http://www.clifton-labs.com/savant/.

[13] M. e. a. Bocchi, "A system level IP integration methodology for fast SOC design," in *Proceedings International Symposium on System-on-Chip*, pp. 127–130, 2003.

[14] G. B. Vece and M. Conti, "Power estimation in embedded systems within a SystemC-based design context: the PKtool environment," in *Proceedings of the 7th Workshop on Intelligent Solutions in Embedded Systems (WISES '09)*, pp. 179–184, June 2009.

[15] M. Giammarini, M. Conti, and S. Orcioni, "System-level energy estimation with Powersim," in *Proceedings of the 18th IEEE International Conference on Electronics, Circuits and Systems (ICECS '11)*, pp. 723–726, December 2011.

[16] D. Brooks, V. Tiwari, and M. Martonosi, "Wattch: a framework for architectural-level power analysis and optimizations," *ACM SIGARCH Computer Architecture News*, vol. 28, no. 2, pp. 83–94, 2000, http://portal.acm.org/citation.cfm?id=339657.

[17] G. S. Silveira, A. V. Brito, and E. U. K. Melcher, "Functional verification of power gate design in systemc RTL," in *Proceedings of the 22nd Symposium on Integrated Circuits and Systems Design (SBCCI '09)*, I. S. Silva, R. P. Ribas, and C. Plett, Eds., ACM, September 2009.

[18] A. V. Brito, M. Kühnle, M. Hübner, J. Becker, and E. U. K. Melcher, "Modelling and simulation of dynamic and partially reconfigurable systems using System C," in *Proceedings of the IEEE Computer Society Annual Symposium on VLSI (ISVLSI '07)*, pp. 35–40, 2007.

[19] U. Tuebingen, 2001, http://www-ti.informatik.uni-tuebingen.de/systemc/.

[20] A. Wagner, *Diplomarbeit Randbedingungen der HW-Modellierung auf RTL-und Systemebene*, 2011.

10

Analysis of Fast Radix-10 Digit Recurrence Algorithms for Fixed-Point and Floating-Point Dividers on FPGAs

Malte Baesler and Sven-Ole Voigt

Institute for Reliable Computing, Hamburg University of Technology, Schwarzenbergstraße 95, 21073 Hamburg, Germany

Correspondence should be addressed to Malte Baesler; malte.baesler@tu-harburg.de

Academic Editor: René Cumplido

Decimal floating point operations are important for applications that cannot tolerate errors from conversions between binary and decimal formats, for instance, commercial, financial, and insurance applications. In this paper we present five different radix-10 digit recurrence dividers for FPGA architectures. The first one implements a simple restoring shift-and-subtract algorithm, whereas each of the other four implementations performs a nonrestoring digit recurrence algorithm with signed-digit redundant quotient calculation and carry-save representation of the residuals. More precisely, the quotient digit selection function of the second divider is implemented fully by means of a ROM, the quotient digit selection function of the third and fourth dividers are based on carry-propagate adders, and the fifth divider decomposes each digit into three components and requires neither a ROM nor a multiplexer. Furthermore, the fixed-point divider is extended to support IEEE 754-2008 compliant decimal floating-point division for decimal64 data format. Finally, the algorithms have been synthesized on a Xilinx Virtex-5 FPGA, and implementation results are given.

1. Introduction

Many applications, particularly commercial and financial applications, require decimal floating-point operations to avoid errors from conversions between binary and decimal formats. This paper presents five different decimal fixed-point dividers and analyzes their performances and resource requirements on FPGA platforms. All five architectures apply a radix-10 digit recurrence algorithm but differ in the quotient digit selection (QDS) function.

The first fixed-point divider (type1) implements a simple shift-and-subtract algorithm. It is characterized by an unsigned and nonredundant quotient digit calculation. Nine divisor multiples are precomputed, and in each iteration step nine carry-propagate subtractions are performed on the residual. Finally, the smallest, nonnegative difference is selected by a large fan-in multiplexer. This type1 implementation is characterized by a high area use.

The second divider (type2) uses a signed-digit quotient calculation with a redundancy of $\rho = 8/9$ and operands scaling to get a normalized divisor in the range of $0.4 \leq$ divisor < 1.0. The quotient digit selection (QDS) function

can be implemented fully by a ROM because it depends only on the two most significant digits (MSDs) of the residual as well as the divisor. The residual uses a redundant carry-save representation but, because of performance issues, the two MSDs are implemented by a nonredundant radix-2 representation.

The quotient digit selection (QDS) functions of the third and fourth divider (type3.a and type3.b) are based on comparators for the two most significand digits. The comparators consist of short binary carry-propagate adders (CPA), which can be implemented very efficiently in the FPGA's slice structure. The corresponding comparative values depend on the divisor's value and are precomputed and stored in a small ROM. The redundancy is $\rho = 8/9$; thus, 17 binary CPAs are required. Similar to the type2 divider, the type3.a and type3.b dividers use prescaling of the divisor $0.4 \leq$ divisor < 1.0, a redundant carry-save representation of the residual, and a nonredundant radix-2 representation of the two MSDs. The dividers type3.a and type3.b differ only in the implementation of large fan-in multiplexers in the digit recurrence step. The type3.a divider implements multiplexers that minimize the LUT usage but have long latencies, whereas the type3.b divider implements a faster dedicated multiplexer that exploits the FPGA's internal carry chains.

The quotient digit selection function of the last divider (type4) requires neither a ROM nor a multiplexer. It is characterized by divisor scaling ($0.4 \leq$ divisor < 0.8) and a signed-digit redundant quotient calculation with a redundancy of $\rho = 8/9$. The quotient digit is decomposed into three components having values $\{-5, 0, 5\}$, $\{-2, 0, 2\}$, and $\{-1, 0, 1\}$. The components are computed one by one, whereby the digit selection function is constant; that is, the selection constants do not depend on the divisor's value. Similar to the type2, type3.a, and type3.b dividers, the type4 divider uses a carry-save representation for the residual with a nonredundant radix-2 representation of the two MSDs.

The fixed-point division algorithms are implemented and analyzed on a Virtex-5 FPGA. Finally, the type2 divider, which shows the best tradeoff in area and delay, is extended to a floating-point divider that is fully IEEE 754-2008 compliant for decimal64 data format, including gradual underflow handling and all required rounding modes.

The architectures of the type1, type2, and type4 dividers have already been published in [1]. However, this paper gives a more detailed description of the previous research and introduces two new dividers, which fill the design gap between the type1 and type2 dividers because they are based on two extreme examples of algorithms: the type1 divider implements a restoring quotient digit selection (QDS) function that requires nine decimal carry-propagate adders (CPAs) of full precision, whereas the nonrestoring QDS function of the type2 divider is implemented fully by means of a ROM with limited precision. In comparison, the new dividers implement nonrestoring QDS functions that are based on fast *binary* CPAs with *limited precision*.

The outline of this paper is given as follows: Section 2 motivates the use of decimal floating-point arithmetic and its advantage compared to binary floating-point arithmetic. The underlying decimal floating-point standard IEEE 754-2008 is introduced in Section 3. The digit recurrence division algorithms as well as the five different architectures of fixed-point dividers are presented in Section 4. These fixed-point dividers are extended to a decimal floating-point divider in Section 5. Postplace and route results are presented in Section 6, and finally in Section 7 the main contributions of this paper are summarized.

2. Decimal Arithmetic

Since its approval in 1985, the *binary* floating-point standard IEEE 754-1985 [2] is the most widely used implementation of floating-point arithmetic and the dominant floating-point standard for all computers. In contrast to binary arithmetic, decimal units are more complex, require more area, and are more expensive, and the simple binary coded decimal (BCD) data format has a storage overhead of approximately 20%. Thus, at that time of approval the use of binary in preference to decimal floating-point arithmetic was justified by the better efficiency.

Most people in the world think in decimal arithmetic. These decimal numbers must be converted to binary numbers when using a computer. However, some common finite numbers can only be *approximated* by binary floating-point numbers. The decimal number 0.1, for example, has a periodical continued fraction $0.1_{10} = 0.000\overline{1100}_2$. It cannot be represented exactly in a binary floating-point arithmetic with finite precision, and the conversion causes rounding errors.

As a consequence, binary floating-point arithmetic cannot be used for any calculations which do not tolerate conversion errors between decimal and binary numbers. These are, for instance, financial and business applications that even require decimal arithmetic by law [3]. Therefore, commercial application often use nonstandardized software to perform decimal floating-point arithmetic. However, these software implementations are usually from 100 to 1000 times slower than equivalent binary floating-point operations in hardware [3].

Because of the increasing importance, specifications for decimal floating-point arithmetic have been added to the IEEE 754-2008 standard for floating-point arithmetic [4] that has been approved in 2008 and offers a more profound specification than the former radix-independent floating-point arithmetic IEEE 854-1987 [5]. Therefore, new efficient algorithms have to be investigated, and providing hardware support for decimal arithmetic is becoming more and more a topic of interest.

IBM has responded to this market demand and integrates decimal floating-point arithmetic in recent processor architectures such as z9 [6], z10 [7], Power6 [8], and Power7 [9]. The Power6 is the first microprocessor that implements IEEE 754-2008 decimal floating-point format fully in hardware, while the earlier released z9 already supports decimal floating-point operations but implements them mainly in millicode. Nevertheless, the Power6 decimal floating-point unit is as small as possible and is optimized to low cost. It reuses registers from the binary floating-point unit, and the computing unit mainly consists of a wide decimal adder. Thus, its performance is rather low. Other floating-point operations such as multiplication and division are based on this adder and are performed sequentially. The decimal floating-point units of z10 and Power7 are designed similarly to those of the Power6 [7, 9].

3. IEEE 754-2008

The floating-point standard IEEE 754-2008 [4] has revised and merged the IEEE 754-1985 standard for binary floating-point arithmetic [2] and IEEE 854-1987 standard for radix-independent floating-point arithmetic [5]. As a consequence, the choice of radices has been focused on two formats: binary and decimal. In this paper we consider only the decimal data format. A decimal number is defined by the triple consisting of the sign (s), significand (c), and exponent (q):

$$x = (-1)^s \cdot c \cdot 10^q, \qquad (1)$$

with $s \in \{0, 1\}$, $c \in [0, 10^p - 1] \cap \mathbb{N}$, and $q \in [q_{min}, q_{max}] \cap \mathbb{Z}$. IEEE 754-2008 uses two different designators for the exponent (q and e) as well as for the significand (c and m). The exponent e is applied when the significand is regarded as an

1 bit	$w + 5$ bits	$t = J \cdot 10$ bits
S (sign)	G (combination field)	T (trailing significand field)

FIGURE 1: Decimal interchange formats [4].

TABLE 1: Interchange format parameters [4].

Parameter	dec32	dec64	dec128
k : storage width (bits)	32	64	128
p: precision (digits)	7	16	34
q_{min}: min. exponent	−101	−398	−6176
q_{max}: max. exponent	90	369	6111
Bias = $E - q$	101	398	6176
s: sign bit	1	1	1
$w + 5$: combination field (bits)	11	13	17
t: trailing significand field (bits)	20	50	110

integer digit and fraction field, denoted by m. The exponent q is applied when the significand is regarded as an integer, denoted by c. The relation is given through

$$e = q + p - 1, \qquad m = c \cdot b^{-p+1}. \qquad (2)$$

In this paper we exclusively use the integer representation c with the exponent q.

Unlike binary floating-point format, the decimal floating-point number is not necessarily normalized. This leads to a redundancy, and a decimal number might have multiple representations. The set of representations is called the floating-point number's *cohort*. For example, the numbers $123 \cdot 10^0$, $1230 \cdot 10^{-1}$, and $12300 \cdot 10^{-2}$ are all members of the same cohort. More precisely, if a number has $n \leq p$ significant digits, the number of representations is $p - n + 1$.

IEEE 754-2008 defines three decimal interchange formats (*decimal32*, *decimal64*, and *decimal128*) of fixed width 32, and 128 bits. As depicted in Figure 1, a floating-point number is encoded by three fields: the *sign bit s*, the *combination field G*, and the *trailing significand field*. The combination field encodes whether the number is finite, infinite, or not a number (NaN). Furthermore, in case of finite numbers the combination field comprises the biased exponent ($E = q +$ bias) and the most significant digit (MSD) of the significand. The remaining $3 \cdot J$ digits are encoded in the trailing significand field of width $t = J \cdot 10$. The trailing significand can either be implemented as a binary integer or as a densely packed decimal (DPD) number [4]. Binary encoding makes software implementations easier, whereas DPD encoding is favored by hardware implementations, as it is the case in this paper.

The encoding parameters for the three fixed-width interchange formats are summarized in Table 1. This paper focuses on the data format *decimal64* with DPD coded significand. DPD encodes three decimal digits (four bits each) into a declet (10 bits) and vice versa [4]. It results in an storage overhead of only 0.343% per digit.

IEEE 754-2008 defines five rounding modes. These are two modes to the nearest (*round ties to even* and *round*

ties to away) and three directed rounding modes (*round toward positive*, *round toward negative*, and *round toward zero*) [4]. As floating-point operations are obtained by first performing the exact operation in the set of real numbers and then mapping the exact result onto a floating-point number, rounding is required whenever all significant digits cannot be placed in a single word of length p. Moreover, inexact, underflow, or overflow exceptions are signaled when necessary.

4. Decimal Fixed-Point Division

Oberman and Flynn [10] distinguish five different classes of division algorithms: digit recurrence, functional iteration, very high radix, table look-up, and variable latency, whereby many practical algorithms are combinations of multiple classes. Compared to binary arithmetic, decimal division is more complex. Currently, there are only a few publications concerning radix-10 division.

Wang and Schulte [11] describe a decimal divider based on the Newton-Raphson approximation of the reciprocal. The latency of a decimal Newton-Raphson approximation directly depends on the latency of the decimal multiplier. A pipelined multiplier has the advantage that more than one division operation can be processed in parallel; otherwise the efficiency is poor. However, the algorithm lacks remainder calculation, and the rounding is more complex. The first FPGA-based decimal Newton-Raphson dividers are presented in [12]. The dividers as well as the underlying multipliers are sequential; hence, these dividers have a high latency.

Digit recurrence division is the most widely implemented class of division algorithms. It is an iterative algorithm with linear convergence; that is, a fixed number of quotient digits is retired every iteration step. Compared to radix-2 arithmetic, radix-10 digit recurrence division is more complex because, on the one hand, decimal logic is less efficient by itself and, on the other hand, the range of the quotient digit selection (QDS) function comprises a larger digit set. Therefore, the performance of the digit recurrence divider depends on the choice of the QDS function and the implementation of decimal logic.

Nikmehr et al. [13] select quotient digits by comparing the truncated residual with limited precision multiples of the divisor. Lang and Nannarelli [14] replace the divisor's multiples by comparative values obtained by a look-up table and decompose the quotient digit into a radix-2 digit and a radix-5 digit in such a way that only five and two times the divisor are required. Vázquez et al. [15] take a different approach: the selection constants in the QDS function are obtained of truncated multiples of the divisor, avoiding look-up tables. Therefore, the multiples are computed on-the-fly. Moreover, the digit recurrence iteration implements a slow carry-propagate adder, but an estimation of the residual is computed to make the determination of the quotient digits independent of this carry-propagate adder. The decimal divider of the Power6 microprocessor [16] uses extensive prescaling to bound the divisor to be greater than or equal to 1.0 but lower than 1.1112 in order to simplify the digit selection function. However, this prescaling is very costly, it requires a 2-digit multiply, and it needs overall six cycles on each operand. Furthermore, the digit selection function still requires a look-up table.

The first decimal fixed-point divider designed for FPGAs applies digit recurrence algorithm and is proposed by Ercegovac and McIlhenny [17, 18]. However, it has a poor cycle time, because it does not fit well on the slice structure of FPGAs but would probably fit well into ASIC designs with dedicated routing.

4.1. Digit Recurrence Division. In the following, we use different decimal number representations. A decimal number B is called BCD-$\beta_0\beta_1\beta_2\beta_3$ coded when B can be expressed by

$$B = \sum_{i=0}^{p-1} B_i \cdot 10^i$$

$$\text{with } B_i = \sum_{k=0}^{3} B_{ik} \cdot \beta_k, B_{ik} \in \{0, 1\}. \tag{3}$$

A number representation is called redundant if one or more digits have multiple representations.

Moreover, we consider a division $z = x/d$ in which the decimal dividend x and the decimal divisor d are positive and normalized fractional numbers of precision p, that is, $0.1 \leq x, d < 1$. The quotient z and the remainder rem are calculated as follows:

$$x = z \cdot d + \text{rem}, \quad \text{rem} \leq d \cdot \text{ulp}, \quad \text{ulp} = 10^{-p}. \tag{4}$$

Then the radix-10 digit recurrence is implemented by

$$w[j+1] = 10w[j] - z_{j+1} \cdot d, \quad j = 0, 1, \ldots, p \tag{5}$$

with the initial residual $w[0] = x/10$ and with the quotient digit calculated by the selection function

$$z_{j+1} = \text{SEL}(10w[j], d)$$

$$\text{with } z = z_1.z_2z_3 \cdots z_p = \sum_{j=0}^{p-1} z_{j+1} \cdot 10^{-j}. \tag{6}$$

Digit recurrence division is subdivided into the classes of restoring and nonrestoring algorithms, that differ in the quotient digit selection (QDS) function and the dynamical range of the residual. A restoring divider selects the next positive quotient digit $0 \leq z_{j+1} \leq 9$ such that the next partial residual is as small as possible but still positive. The IBM z900 architecture, for instance, implements such a decimal restoring divider [19]. By contrast, the QDS function of a decimal nonrestoring divider uses a digit set that is positive as well as negative $-a \leq z_{j+1} \leq a$, and the partial residual $w[j+1]$ might also be negative.

One advantage of restoring division is the enhanced performance since estimates of limited precision ($\widehat{w[j]} \approx w[j]$ and $\hat{d} \approx d$) might be used in the QDS function

SEL ($10\widehat{w[j]}, \hat{d}$). This performance gain is achieved by using a redundant digit set, $-a \leq z_j \leq a$, which defines a redundancy factor

$$\rho = \frac{a}{10 - 1} = \frac{a}{9}. \tag{7}$$

Then, in each iteration step the quotient digit z_{j+1} should be selected such that the next residual $w[j+1]$ is bounded by

$$-\rho d \leq w[j+1] \leq \rho d, \tag{8}$$

which is called the convergence condition [20].

This paper presents five different decimal fixed-point dividers that are described in the following. The first divider (type1) is a restoring divider whereas the four others (type2, type3.a, type3.b, and type4) are nonrestoring dividers.

4.2. Type1 QDS Function. The QDS function of the type1 algorithm is very simple. Nine multiples of the divisor ($1d, \ldots, 9d$) are subtracted in parallel from the residual by carry-propagate adders (CPAs), and the smallest positive result is selected. The CPAs exploit the FPGA's internal fast carry logic, as described in [21].

The nine multiples are precomputed and are composed of the multiples $1d$, $2d$, $5d$, $10d$ and their negatives (10's complement), which require at most one additional CPA per multiple. The multiples $2d$ and $5d$ can be easily computed by digit recoding and constant shift operations

$$(X)_{\text{BCD-5421}} \ll 1 \equiv (X \cdot 2)_{\text{BCD-8421}}, \tag{9}$$

$$(X)_{\text{BCD-8421}} \ll 3 \equiv (X \cdot 5)_{\text{BCD-5421}}, \tag{10}$$

where (9) is read as follows. A BCD-5421 coded number X left-shifted by one bit is equivalent to the corresponding BCD-8421-coded number multiplied by two. In a similar fashion we obtain a multiplication by five using (10).

The implementation of the type1 digit recurrence divider is characterized by a high area use, due to the utilization of nine parallel CPAs. The corresponding algorithm of the type1 digit recurrence is shown in Algorithm 1.

4.3. Type2 QDS Function. The approach of the type2 division algorithm is based on the implementation of the QDS function fully by a ROM. This ROM is addressed by estimates of the residual and divisor. The use of estimates is feasible because a signed digit set together with a redundancy greater than 1/2 is used. The estimates $\widehat{10w[j]}$ and $\hat{d}$ are obtained by truncation; that is, only a limited number of MSDs of the residual $10w[j]$ and divisor d are regarded. Furthermore, the residual is implemented in BCD-4221 carry-save representation such that the maximum error introduced by an estimation with precision t (one integer digit and $t - 1$ fractional digits) is bounded by $\epsilon = 2 \cdot 10^{-t+1}$. Negative residuals are represented by their 10's complement.

The divisor is subdivided into subranges $[d_i, d_{i+1})$ of equal width $d_{i+1} - d_i = 10^{-\delta}$. For each subrange i, the QDS function $z_{j+1} = \text{SEL}_{\text{ROM}}(\widehat{10w[j]}, \hat{d})$ is defined by selection constants $m_k(i)$:

$$z_{j+1} = k \iff m_k(i) \leq \widehat{10w[j]} < m_{k+1}(i). \tag{11}$$

$$
\begin{aligned}
\text{(1) Compute } \delta_1 &= 10w\,[j] - d \\
&\;\;\vdots \\
\delta_9 &= 10w\,[j] - 9d
\end{aligned}
$$

(2) if $\delta_1 < 0$ then
$\quad z_{j+1} = 0$ and $w\,[j+1] = 10 \cdot w\,[j]$
else if $\delta_2 < 0$ then
$\quad z_{j+1} = 1$ and $w\,[j+1] = \delta_1$
$\quad\vdots$
else if $\delta_9 < 0$ then
$\quad z_{j+1} = 8$ and $w\,[j+1] = \delta_8$
else
$\quad z_{j+1} = 9$ and $w\,[j+1] = \delta_9$

ALGORITHM 1: Pseudocode for type1 digit recurrence division.

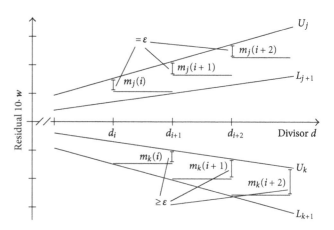

FIGURE 2: P-D diagram for the type2 QDS function.

These selection constants are bounded by selection intervals $m_k(i) \in [L_k, U_{k-1}]$, with the containment condition [20]

$$L_k(d_i) = (k - \rho)\, d_i, \qquad (12a)$$

$$U_k(d_i) = (k + \rho)\, d_i. \qquad (12b)$$

Furthermore, the continuity condition states that every value $10w[j]$ must belong at least to one selection interval [20]. Considering the maximum error due to truncation, the continuity condition can be expressed by

$$U_{k-1}(d_i) - L_k(d_{i+1}) \geq \epsilon = 2 \cdot 10^{-t+1}. \qquad (13)$$

If we suppose the subrange width to be constant ($d_{i+1} - d_i = 10^{-\delta}$) and consider that the minimum overlapping occurs for minimum $d_{\min}$ and maximum $k_{\max}$, then we obtain the term

$$
\begin{aligned}
x := &\;(k_{\max} - 1 + \rho)\, d_{\min} \\
&- (k_{\max} - \rho)\,(d_{\min} + 10^{-\delta}) \geq 2 \cdot 10^{-t+1}.
\end{aligned}
\qquad (14)
$$

We choose $\rho = 8/9$ ($k_{\max} = 8$) and $d_{\min} = 0.4$ that leads to $\delta = 2$ and $t = 2$. Thus, for the divisors's estimation $\hat{d}$ is required an accuracy of two fractional digits, and for the residual's estimation $\widehat{10w}$ is required an accuracy of one integer and one fractional digit. Furthermore, the divisor must be pre-scaled such that $0.4 \leq d < 1.0$.

The P-D diagram is a visualization technique for designing a quotient digit selection function and for computing the decision boundaries $m_k(i)$. It plots the shifted residual versus the divisor. The P-D diagram for the type2 quotient digit selection function with the selection constants $m_k(i)$ is shown in Figure 2.

The two MSDs of the dividend and residual address the ROM in order to obtain the signed quotient digit, which comprises 5 bits. In order to reduce the ROM's size, the two MSDs of the divisor and the residual are implemented by using a nonredundant radix-2 representation. This leads to an address that is composed of 15 bits: seven bits from the

(1) compute $L_k(\hat{d}_i)$ and $U_k(\hat{d}_i)$ for each $\hat{d}_i \in$
$\quad \{0.40, 0.41, \ldots, 0.99\}$ and $k \in \{-8, \ldots, +8\}$ according
$\quad$ to (12a) and (12b)
(2) for all $10 \cdot \hat{w}_n \in \{-8.8, -8.7, \ldots, +8.8\}$ with $|\hat{w}| \leq$
$\quad \rho \cdot \hat{d}_{\max} = 0.88$ compute the quotient digits z as
$\quad$ follows:
$\qquad$ if $10 \cdot \hat{w}_n \geq U_7 - \epsilon = U_7 - 0.2$ then $z = 8$
$\qquad$ else if $10 \cdot \hat{w}_n \geq U_6 - 0.2$ then $z = 7$
$\qquad\vdots$
$\qquad$ else if $10 \cdot \hat{w}_n \geq U_0 - 0.2$ then $z = 1$
$\qquad$ else if $10 \cdot \hat{w}_n \geq L_0$ then $z = 0$
$\qquad\vdots$
$\qquad$ else if $10 \cdot \hat{w}_n \geq L_{-8}$ then $z = -8$

ALGORITHM 2: Algorithm for the calculation of the type2 ROM entries.

unsigned radix-2 representation of the divisor's two MSDs and eight bits from the signed radix-2 representation of the residual's two MSDs. Hence, the size of the ROM is $2^{15} \times 5$ bits. Unfortunately, the use of radix-2 representation complicates the multiplication by 10, which is required according to (5). Therefore, an additional binary adder is needed:

$$10 \cdot w\,[j] = 8 \cdot w\,[j] + 2 \cdot w\,[j] = w\,[j] \ll 3 + w\,[j] \ll 1. \qquad (15)$$

The corresponding algorithm for the calculation of the ROM entries can be derived from the P-D diagram and is depicted in Algorithm 2. It should be noted that the radix-2 representations of $\hat{d}$ and $\hat{w}$ are truncations of d and w; that is, $\hat{d} \leq d$ and $\hat{w} \leq w$.

Once the quotient digit z_{j+1} has been determined, the multiple $z_{j+1} \cdot d$ is subtracted from the current residual to compute the next residual, as stated in (5). The subtracter is a fast redundant BCD-4221 carry-save adder (CSA), as described in [21], except for the two MSDs in wich we apply

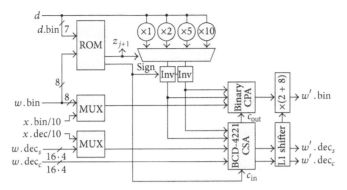

FIGURE 3: Block diagram of type2 digit recurrence.

(1) Select $z_{j+1} = \text{SEL}_{\text{ROM}}(\widehat{10w[j]}, \hat{d})$
(2) Compute $(w_s[j+1] + w_c[j+1]) =$
    $10(w_s[j] + w_c[j]) - z_{j+1} \cdot d$

ALGORITHM 3: Pseudocode for the type2 digit recurrence.

radix-2 CPAs. Thus, the multiple $z_{j+1} \cdot d$ is composed of two summands:

$$z_{j+1} \cdot d = d_{j+1}^1 + d_{j+1}^2, \qquad (16)$$

where $d^{1,2} \in \{0, \pm 1d, \pm 2d, \pm 5d, \pm 10d\}$ are precomputed. The multiplies $2d$ and $5d$ can be easily and fast computed by digit recoding and constant shift operation as shown in (9) and (10). The 10's and 2's complements are applied for $d^{1,2} < 0$. For both, radix-2 and BCD-4221 radix-10 representation, the complements can be computed by inverting each bit and adding one. In summary, the subtraction uses a $(3:1)$ radix-2 CPA for the two MSDs and a redundant radix-10 $(4:2)$ CSA for the remaining digits. The digit recurrence algorithm of the type2 divider is summarized in Algorithm 3, and its block diagram is depicted in Figure 3.

4.4. Type3 QDS Function. The frequency limiting component of the type2 divider is the digit recurrence step, which comprises the ROM (BRAM) to calculate the next quotient digit. This BRAM is slower compared to common FPGA logic. Hence, it appears to be beneficial to remove the slow BRAM from the critical path and use fast FPGA logic instead. To analyze this impact of the BRAM delays, we implement two dividers (type3.a and type3.b), which can also be realized without BRAM in the critical path.

Lang and Nannarelli [14] propose a divider that implements a quotient digit selection function based on CPAs and sign detection. These CPAs subtract fixed values from the current residual with limited precision. These fixed values depend on the estimates of the divisor and are precomputed and stored in a ROM. Furthermore, the quotient digit is divided into two parts, which further simplifies the quotient digit selection function and reduces the critical path. Unfortunately, this divider cannot be implemented efficiently

on FPGAs because the required carry-save adder with small error estimation shows a poor performance on the FPGA's slice structure. Nevertheless, to investigate the impact of BRAM delays in the type2 divider, we implement another two dividers (type3.a and type3.b) that have no BRAM in the critical path but a CPA-based quotient digit selection function instead.

The type3 dividers are modifications of the type2 divider. The common architectural features are

(i) the multiples of the divisor are compos of two components: $z_{j+1} \cdot d = d_{j+1}^1 + d_{j+1}^2$, where $d^{1,2} \in \{0, \pm 1d, \pm 2d, \pm 5d, \pm 10d\}$,

(ii) the fast redundant BCD-4221 carry-save adders for the digit recurrence step as stated in (5),

(iii) the radix-2 implementation of the two MSDs, and

(iv) the 10's and 2's complements for $d^{1,2} < 0$.

Furthermore, since the architectures of the type2 and type3 dividers are similar, with the exception of the quotient digit selection function, most of the dividers' characteristics are also identical, including the

(i) the P-D diagram,

(ii) the redundancy factor $\rho = 8/9$, $k_{\max} = 8$,

(iii) the need of prescaling the divisor $0.4 \le d < 1.0$,

(iv) the accuracy of the divisor's estimation $\delta = 2$, and

(v) the accuracy of the residual's estimation $t = 2$.

Contrary to the type2 divider, the QDS functions of the type3 dividers are implemented by 16 carry-propagate adders with sign detection. These adders subtract fixed selection constants from the estimation of the current residual. The selection constants are dependent on the current divisor and are stored in a ROM, which is then no more part of the critical path. The selection constants are computed according to Algorithm 4. The common digit recurrence algorithm of the type3.a and type3.b dividers is shown in Algorithm 5, and the corresponding block diagram is depicted in Figure 4.

The sign signals of the binary carry-propagate adders are used to determine the corresponding quotient digit and to select the multiples of the divisor in the digit recurrence

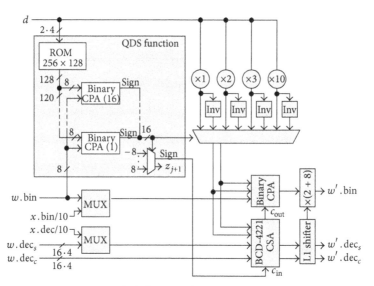

FIGURE 4: Block diagram of type3 digit recurrence.

(1) compute $L_k(\widehat{d_i})$ and $U_k(\widehat{d_i})$ for each $\widehat{d_i} \in$
$\{0.40, 0.41, \ldots, 0.99\}$ and $k \in \{-8, \ldots, +8\}$ according
to (12a) and (12b)
(2) compute the selection constants $m_k(\widehat{d_i})$:
$$m_8\left(\widehat{d_i}\right) = U_7\left(\widehat{d_i}\right) - \epsilon = U_7\left(\widehat{d_i}\right) - 0.2$$
$$m_7\left(\widehat{d_i}\right) = U_6\left(\widehat{d_i}\right) - 0.2$$
$$\vdots$$
$$m_1\left(\widehat{d_i}\right) = U_0\left(\widehat{d_i}\right) - 0.2$$
$$m_0\left(\widehat{d_i}\right) = L_0\left(\widehat{d_i}\right)$$
$$\vdots$$
$$m_{-7}\left(\widehat{d_i}\right) = L_{-7}\left(\widehat{d_i}\right)$$

ALGORITHM 4: Algorithm for the calculation of the type3 selection constants.

(1) if $m_8\left(\widehat{d_i}\right) - \widehat{10w\,[j]} < 0$ then $z_{j+1} = 8$
    else if $m_7\left(\widehat{d_i}\right) - \widehat{10w\,[j]} < 0$ then $z_{j+1} = 7$
    $\vdots$
    else if $m_{-7}\left(\widehat{d_i}\right) - \widehat{10w\,[j]} < 0$ then $z_{j+1} = -7$
    else $z_{j+1} = -8$
(2) Compute $(w_s[j+1] + w_c[j+1]) =$
    $\qquad 10\left(w_s\,[j] + w_c\,[j]\right) - z_{j+1} \cdot d$

ALGORITHM 5: Pseudocode for the type3 digit recurrence.

iteration step. The advantage of the type3 QDS function is its short critical path, which comprises only one 8-bit binary carry-propagate adder. However, this short critical path is bought at a high price because the complexity is moved to the selection of the divisors multiples. Hence,

large fan-in multiplexers with poor latencies are required. In order to minimize the impact of these multiplexers, we designed a new dedicated (17 : 1) multiplexer that exploits the FPGA's fast carry chains and has a delay of only one LUT instance. In the following we name the divider with improved fast multiplexers type3.b and with traditional multiplexers type3.a. The new dedicated (17 : 1) multiplexer uses the 16-sign bits as select lines and is coded as follows:

if sel $= \,'1111.1111.1111.1111'$ then $y = x\,(16)$

if sel $= \,'0111.1111.1111.1111'$ then $y = x\,(15)$

$$\vdots \qquad\qquad (17)$$

if sel $= \,'0000.0000.0000.0001'$ then $y = x\,(1)$

if sel $= \,'0000.0000.0000.0000'$ then $y = x\,(0)$,

with $\text{sel}(-1) := 1$ and $\text{sel}(16) := 0$. In other words, bit $x(i)$ is selected when $\text{sel}(i) = 0$ and $\text{sel}(i-1) = 1$. The selection of two input signals is implemented in one (5 : 1) LUT, and all signals are combined by a long OR gate that is implemented exploiting the FPGA's fast carry chain. Therefore, one (17 : 1) multiplexer requires nine LUTs, and the type3.b divider with fast multiplexers uses much more LUTs than the type3.a divider (see Section 6). The block diagram of such a (17 : 1) multiplexer is depicted in Figure 5.

4.5. Type4 QDS Function. The type4 divider applies a new algorithm as proposed by us in a previous paper [22]. It is based on the decomposition of the signed quotient digit into three components having values $\{-5, 0, 5\}$, $\{-2, 0, 2\}$, and $\{-1, 0, 1\}$ as well as a fast constant digit selection function. In this implementation, neither a ROM for the QDS function nor a multiplexer to select the multiple $z_j \cdot d$ in the digit recurrence iteration step is required. The divider is intended to utilize less resources than other implementations. As

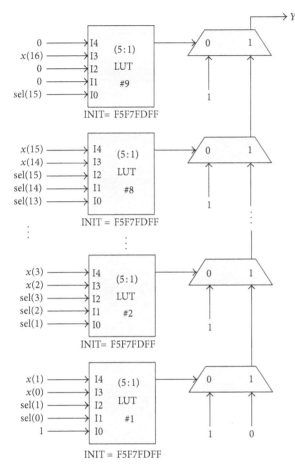

FIGURE 5: Fast multiplexer.

the type2, type3.a, and type3.b dividers, the type4 divider uses signed-digit redundant quotient calculation, carry-save representation of the residual, fast BCD-4221 CSAs for the digit recurrence, and a radix-2 implementation of the MSDs.

Quotient digits are decomposed into three components $z_{j+1} = 5 \cdot z_{j+1}^3 + 2 \cdot z_{j+1}^2 + z_{j+1}^1$, and each component z^i is computed by a distinct selection function. These components can hold three values $z^i \in \{-1, 0, 1\}$ so that only two comparators per component are required to distinguish between these values. Since $-8 \le z_{j+1} \le 8$, we get a redundancy factor of $\rho = 8/9$. Furthermore, the selection functions become very simple due to prescaling of the divisor $(0.4 \le d < 0.8)$; that is, they are constant functions SEL^i that do not depend on the divisor anymore:

$$z_{j+1}^3 = \text{SEL}^3 \left(10\widehat{w[j]} \right), \tag{18a}$$

$$z_{j+1}^2 = \text{SEL}^2 \left(\widehat{v^1[j]} \right), \tag{18b}$$

$$z_{j+1}^1 = \text{SEL}^1 \left(\widehat{v^2[j]} \right). \tag{18c}$$

The recurrence is then defined as follows:

$$v^1[j] = 10w[j] - z_{j+1}^3 \cdot 5d, \tag{19a}$$

$$v^2[j] = v^1[j] - z_{j+1}^2 \cdot 2d, \tag{19b}$$

$$w[j+1] = v^2[j] - z_{j+1}^1 \cdot d. \tag{19c}$$

The multiples $2d$ and $5d$ can be easily and fast computed according to (9) and (10). Each selection function requires two comparators implemented as carry-save adders that subtract constant values from the residuals' estimations ($\widehat{w[j]}$, $\widehat{v^1[j]}$, and $\widehat{v^2[j]}$). As we will show in the following, these estimations require only the two most significant digits (MSDs) of the corresponding exact values.

First, the selection intervals $[L_k^i, U_k^i]$ for $z_{j+1}^i = k$ with $k \in \{-1, 0, 1\}$ and $i \in \{1, 2, 3\}$ have to be determined, where L_k^i is the smallest and U_k^i is the greatest value of the selection constant $m_k(i)$ such that the next residual is still bounded. Applying the convergence condition (8), the digit recurrence (19a), (19b), and (19c), and the redundancy factor $\rho = 8/9$, we obtain

$$|w[j]| \le \rho d = \frac{8}{9}d, \tag{20a}$$

$$|v^2[j]| \le (\rho + 1)d = \frac{17}{9}d, \tag{20b}$$

$$|v^1[j]| \le (\rho + 1 + 2)d = \frac{35}{9}d. \tag{20c}$$

From the recurrence $v^1[j] = 10w[j] - z_{j+1}^3 \cdot 5d$, $v^1[j] \le (35/9)d$, $z_{j+1}^3 \in \{-1, 0, 1\}$, and replacing $10w[j]$ by the upper limit U_k^3, we get

$$U_k^3 = (5k + \rho + 3)d = \left(5k + \frac{35}{9}\right)d. \tag{21a}$$

Similarly, we obtain the upper limits U_k^2 and U_k^1 from the recurrence (19b) and (19c), respectively,

$$U_k^2 = (2k + \rho + 1)d = \left(2k + \frac{17}{9}\right)d, \tag{21b}$$

$$U_k^1 = (k + \rho)d = \left(k + \frac{8}{9}d\right). \tag{21c}$$

Likewise, the lower limits L_k^i can be computed

$$L_k^3 = (5k - \rho - 3)d = \left(5k - \frac{35}{9}\right)d, \tag{22a}$$

$$L_k^2 = (2k - \rho - 1)d = \left(2k - \frac{17}{9}\right)d, \tag{22b}$$

$$L_k^1 = (k - \rho)d = \left(k - \frac{8}{9}d\right). \tag{22c}$$

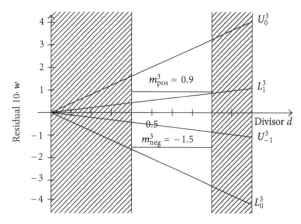

FIGURE 6: P-D diagram for the type4 QDS function.

TABLE 2: Constants for type4 quotient digit selection function.

	m_{pos}^i	m_{neg}^i	$U_0^i(0.4) - m_{\text{pos}}^i$	$U_{-1}^i(0.8) - m_{\text{neg}}^i$
z^3	0.9	−1.5	0.656	0.611
z^2	0.1	−0.7	0.656	0.611
z^1	0.1	−0.3	0.255	0.211

Due to the redundancy factor $\rho = 8/9 > 1/2$ we have overlapping regions $[L_{k+1}^i, U_k^i]$, where more than one quotient digit component z_{j+1}^i may be selected. The decision boundary of a selection function should lie inside this overlapping regions. Figure 6 shows the P-D diagram for z^3. The figures for z^2 and z^1 look similar. As z^3 can hold three different values, the selection function requires two decision boundaries. Generally, it is implemented by a staircase function (see Figure 2), but for the bounded divisor $d \in [0.4, 0.8]$ it is independent of the divisor and is reduced to a constant function (see Figure 6). Fortunately, the selection functions for z^2 and z^1 are also independent of the divisor and can also be implemented by constant functions in a similar fashion.

We now determine the required number of fractional digits for the estimates $\widehat{10w}$, $\widehat{v^1}$, and $\widehat{v^2}$. Moreover, we choose suitable selection constants m_{pos}^i and m_{neg}^i. These constants depend on the maximum error due to the estimates and on the minimum overlapping width, which is given by $U_0^i(0.4) - L_1^i(0.8)$ as well as $U_{-1}^i(0.8) - L_0^i(0.4)$. Since we use BCD-4221 carry-save redundant digit representation, for a precision of t digits (one integer digit and $t - 1$ fractional digits), we have a maximum error of $\epsilon = 2 \cdot 10^{-(t-1)}$. Moreover, the estimations $\widehat{w}$ are computed by truncations ($w - \widehat{w} \le \epsilon$). This means, for given positive and negative selection constants $m_{\text{pos}}^i > 0$ and $m_{\text{neg}}^i < 0$, the following expressions must be true:

$$U_0^i(0.4) - m_{\text{pos}}^i \ge \epsilon, \qquad L_1^i(0.8) \le m_{\text{pos}}^i, \qquad (23)$$

$$L_0^i(0.4) \le m_{\text{neq}}^i, \qquad U_{-1}^i(0.8) - m_{\text{neg}}^i \ge \epsilon. \qquad (24)$$

If we choose the selection constants as listed in Table 2, all conditions are fulfilled for a precision of $t = 2$ digits, and each selection function is reduced to two simple 2-digit comparators.

As soon as one component z^i of the quotient digit is computed, the corresponding multiple of the divisor must be subtracted from the partial residual. Each component z^i can hold three different values $z^i \in \{-1, 0, +1\}$ that are multiplied with the corresponding weighted divisor $n \cdot d$ with $n \in \{5, 2, 1\}$. In other words, $n \cdot d$ is either passed, negated,

or reset. Passing and resetting the multiple of the divisor is performed at no extra cost. Negation is accomplished by bit inversion and adding +1 through the carry inputs of the carry-save adders in (19a), (19b), and (19c). In summary, this is a very fast operation and requires only two LUTs per digit.

Similar to type2 and type3 division, we implement the two MSDs of the type4 residual by using a nonredundant radix-2 representation, which requires less LUTs and results in faster quotient digit selection function. The pseudocode for the digit recurrence iteration is shown in Algorithm 6, and the corresponding block diagram is depicted in Figure 7.

4.6. Proposed Decimal Fixed-Point Divider. For each type of division algorithms presented in the preceding sections we have implemented a corresponding fixed-point divider, which is described in the following. For all fixed-point dividers we expect the input operands to be normalized.

The block diagram of the type1 divider is depicted in Figure 8. First, the divisor multiples $\{2d, \ldots, 9d\}$ are precomputed. In the following cycles $p = 16$ quotient digits ($16 + 1$ if the first digit is zero) are computed one by one, followed by an additional rounding digit. The quotient (Z) and the quotient +1 (ZP1) are computed on-the-fly by using two registers that are updated every cycle. The algorithm has the advantage that no additional slow decimal CPA is required to compute the incremented quotient. It is described more precisely in Section 5. The normalization of the result is also performed on-the-fly by locking the conversion when $16 + 1$ quotient digits for the significand and the rounding digit have been computed; that is, in the worst case, when the first quotient digit is zero, $16 + 1 + 1 = 18$ cycles are required. Furthermore, the sticky bit is calculated, which is required for rounding. It is set to one whenever the final remainder is unequal to zero.

The architectures of the type2, type3.a, type3.b, and type4 are similar in their structure but differ in their digit recurrence algorithm and scaling. The common block diagram is shown in Figure 9. First, the dividend and the divisor are re-scaled

$$d \in [0.1, 1.0)$$

$$\Longrightarrow d' \in \begin{cases} [0.4, 1.0) & \text{for type2, type3.a/b} \\ [0.4, 0.8) & \text{for type4} \end{cases} \qquad (25)$$

and five as well as two times the divisor are precomputed according to (9) and (10). Then, the operands are recoded because the digit recurrence iteration uses a redundant digit representation with BCD-4221 carry-save adders.

The digit recurrence retires in each iteration one signed quotient digit z_k. The on-the-fly-conversion algorithm converts this signed-digit representation to the BCD-8421-coded

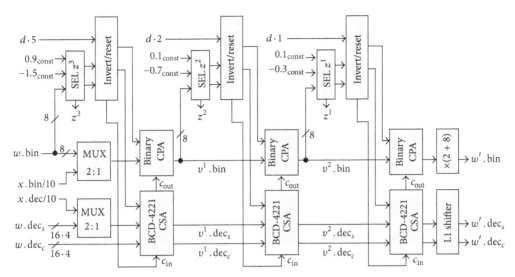

FIGURE 7: Block diagram of type4 digit recurrence.

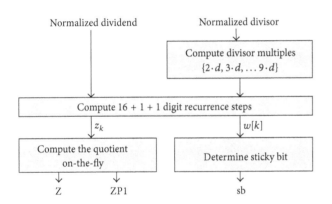

FIGURE 8: Block diagram of the normalized type1 division.

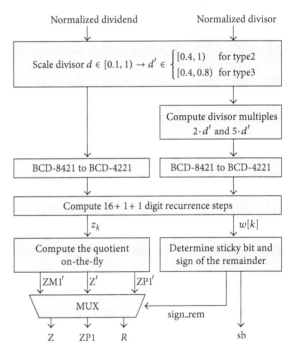

FIGURE 9: Block diagram of the normalized type2, type3.a, type3.b, and type4 divisions.

ALGORITHM 6: Pseudo code for the type 4 digit recurrence.

(1) select
$$z_{j+1}^3 = \begin{cases} 1 & \text{if } 0.9 \le \widehat{10w}\,[j] \\ 0 & \text{if } -1.5 \le \widehat{10w}\,[j] < 0.9 \\ -1 & \text{if } \widehat{10w}\,[j] < -1.5 \end{cases}$$
and compute
$$(v_s^1\,[j] + v_c^1\,[j]) = 10\,(w_s\,[j] + w_c\,[j]) - z_{j+1}^3 \cdot 5d$$
(2) select
$$z_{j+1}^3 = \begin{cases} 1 & \text{if } 0.1 \le \widehat{v^1}\,[j] \\ 0 & \text{if } -0.7 \le \widehat{v^1}\,[j] < 0.1 \\ -1 & \text{if } \widehat{v^1}\,[j] < -0.7 \end{cases}$$
and compute
$$(v_s^2\,[j] + v_c^2\,[j]) = (v_s^1\,[j] + v_c^1\,[j]) - z_{j+1}^2 \cdot 2d$$
(3) select
$$z_{j+1}^1 = \begin{cases} 1 & \text{if } 0.1 \le \widehat{v^2}\,[j] \\ 0 & \text{if } -0.3 \le \widehat{v^2}\,[j] < 0.1 \\ -1 & \text{if } \widehat{v^2}\,[j] < -0.3 \end{cases}$$
and compute $(w_s\,[j+1] + w_c\,[j+1]) =$
$$(v_s^2\,[j] + v_c^2\,[j]) - z_{j+1}^1 d$$

result [20] and computes the quotient (Z), the quotient +1 (ZP1), and quotient −1 (ZM1). This conversion is accomplished every iteration step and does not need a slow CPA. The incremented and decremented quotients are required for rounding. Moreover, the quotient is also normalized on-the-fly by locking the conversion when 16 + 1 quotient digits (including the rounding digit) have been computed. The algorithm is described explicitly in Section 5 because it is accomplished together with the gradual underflow handling of the floating-point divider.

if $(\overline{qNaN_X} \wedge \overline{sNaN_X}) \wedge (qNaN_D \vee sNaN_D)$ then
   $C'_X = C_D, \quad C'_D = 0\dots01$
   $q'_X = q_D, \quad q'_D = 0 + \text{bias} = 398$
else if $(qNaN_X \vee sNaN_X)$ then
   $C'_X = C_X, \quad C'_D = 0\dots01$
   $q'_X = q_X, \quad q'_D = 0 + \text{bias} = 398$
else   // no changes
   $C'_X = C_X, \quad C'_D = C_D$
   $q'_X = q_X, \quad q'_D = q_D$

ALGORITHM 7: Algorithm of NaN handling.

Furthermore, the sticky bit is calculated, which is required for rounding. It is set to one whenever the final remainder is unequal to zero. Moreover, when the final remainder is negative, the quotient of the type2, type3.a, type3.b, and type4 dividers has to be adjusted by subtracting one LSD. This subtraction does not need another slow CPA because the quotient −1 (ZM1) has already been computed on-the-fly. The calculations of both, the sticky and sign bit, require the reduction of the redundant remainder by a CPA. This CPA might be subdivided into multiple smaller CPAs to keep the latency low.

5. IEEE 754-2008 Floating-Point Division

The IEEE 754-2008 compliant decimal floating-point divider is an extension of the normalized fixed-point divider. The divider presented in this paper supports the interchange format IEEE 754-2008 *decimal64* with DPD encoding, but it can be easily adapted to any other precision and exponent range.

The block diagram of the divider is depicted in Figure 10. The DFP division begins with decoding of the dividend X and divisor D and the extraction of their signs, significands, and exponents. In the following, the significands of the operands X (c_X) and D (c_D) are regarded as integers. Therefore, the corresponding exponents are q_X and q_D.

According to [4], if one of the operands is a signaling NaN (sNAN) or quiet NaN (qNAN), then the result is also a quiet NaN with the payload of the original NaN. Hence, in order to preserve the payload while using an unmodified divider, the NaN handling unit sets the NaN holding operand as the dividend and resets the divisor to $1.0 \cdot 10^0$, as depicted in Algorithm 7.

The fixed-point dividers presented in Section 4 require normalized operands. Therefore, the number of leading zeros for both operands is counted, and the significands are normalized by barrel shifters. Due to performance issues, the leading zeros counter exploit the FPGA's fast carry chains, as proposed in [23].

The exponent of a floating-point division is first estimated by the normalized quotient in fractional representation (QNF) and is updated iteratively in each digit recurrence step. Since most of the decimal floating-point numbers specified by IEEE 754-2008 have multiple representations of the same

value, the result of a division might also have more than one correct representations that differ in the exponent. However, to obtain a unique and reproducible result in the case of such an ambiguity, IEEE 754-2008 defines the exponent of the result, which is called preferred exponent (QP).

Both exponents, QNF and QP, are positive integers and are determined as follows:

$$\Delta q := (q_X - q_D),$$
$$\Delta LZ := (LZ_X - LZ_D), \tag{26}$$
$$QNF = \Delta q - \Delta LZ + \text{offset1},$$
$$QP = \Delta q + \text{offset1}. \tag{27}$$

The *offset1* is a bias and assures the quotients to be positive since unsigned integer calculation is used in this paper. The bias is composed of

$$
\begin{aligned}
\text{offset1} &= 783 \\
&= 398 \; // \; \text{IEEE754-2008 bias} \\
&+ 369 \; // \; q_{\max} \\
&+ 15 \; // \; \text{conversion fractional to integer} \\
&+ 1 \; // \; \text{normalization of the result.}
\end{aligned}
\tag{28}
$$

The normalized fixed-point division unit then computes $p = 16$ significand digits and one additional rounding digit. Additionally, the divider encompasses the on-the-fly conversion unit that also detects and handles gradual underflow with zero delay overhead. One signed quotient digit z_j is retired in each cycle, and the on-the-fly-conversion algorithm converts this signed-digit representation into the BCD-8421-coded partial result [20]. The conversion is accomplished every iteration step and does not need a slow CPA (see Algorithm 8). The partial quotient is stored in a register Z'. Moreover, two additional registers $ZM1'$ and $ZP1'$ are provided. $ZM1'$ is the partial quotient decremented by one least significant digit (LSD), and $ZP1'$ is the partial quotient incremented by one LSD. $ZM1'$ is selected when the final residual in the last iteration is negative, and $ZP1'$ is required by the following rounding operation. Furthermore, the exponent for the normalized significand in integer representation (QNI) is calculated (see (29)), and gradual underflow handling is performed at no extra cost (see Algorithm 8). The exponent QNI is computed by decrementing the exponent of the normalized significand in fractional representation (QNF) in each iteration step by one. The recurrence iteration terminates earlier in case of gradual underflow. The gradual underflow signal (GUF) is asserted *high* when QNI = $q_{\min}$, and the calculated integer quotient is less than 10^p:

$$
QNI = \begin{cases}
q_{\min} & \text{if GUF} = 1 \\
QNF - (p-1) & \text{if } z_1 > 0 \\
QNF - p & \text{if } z_1 = 0.
\end{cases}
\tag{29}
$$

The extended quotient (composed of the calculated quotient and the rounding digit) must be decremented by one if the

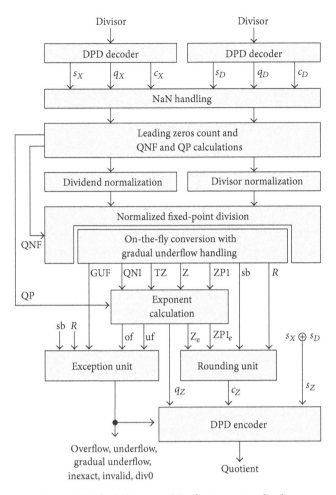

FIGURE 10: Block diagram of the floating-point divider.

$$QNI' = QNF + 1$$
$$Z' = ZM1' = ZP1' = 0$$
$$TZ' = 0, j = 0$$
while $(Z' < 10^p)$ and $(QNI' \geq q_{\min})$ {

$$Z' = \begin{cases} 10 \cdot Z' + z_{j+1} & \text{if } z_{j+1} \geq 0 \\ 10 \cdot ZM1' + (z_{j+1} + 10) & \text{if } z_{j+1} < 0 \end{cases}$$

$$ZM1' = \begin{matrix} 10 \cdot Z' + (z_{j+1} - 1) & \text{if } z_{j+1} > 0 \\ 10 \cdot ZM1' + (z_{j+1} + 9) & \text{if } z_{j+1} \leq 0 \end{matrix}$$

$$ZP1' = \begin{cases} 10 \cdot Z' + (z_{j+1} + 1) & \text{if } z_{j+1} \geq -1 \\ 10 \cdot ZM1' + (z_{j+1} + 11) & \text{if } z_{j+1} < -1 \end{cases}$$

$$TZ' = \begin{cases} TZ' + 1 & \text{if } z_{j+1} = 0 \\ 0 & \text{else} \end{cases}$$

$$QNI' = QNI' - 1$$
$$j = j + 1$$
}
$$QNI = QNI' + 1 \text{ // remove the impact of the rounding digit}$$

$$R' = \begin{cases} z_{j+1} - 1 & \text{if remainder} < 0 \\ z_{j+1} & \text{else} \end{cases}$$

$$ZM1'' = \lfloor ZM1' \cdot 10^{-1} \rfloor$$
$$Z'' = \lfloor Z' \cdot 10^{-1} \rfloor$$
$$ZP'' = \lfloor ZP1' \cdot 10^{-1} \rfloor$$

$$(Z, ZP1, R) = \begin{cases} (ZM1'', Z'', R' + 10) & \text{if } R' < 0 \\ (Z'', ZP1'', R') & \text{else} \end{cases}$$

$$sb = \begin{cases} 0 & \text{if remainder} = 0 \\ 1 & \text{else} \end{cases}$$

$$GUF = \begin{cases} 1 & \text{if } QNI = q_{\min} \text{ and } Z' < 10^p \\ & \text{and } (sb = 1 \text{ or } R \neq 0) \\ 0 & \text{else} \end{cases}$$

if GUF = 1 then underflow!

$$TZ = \begin{cases} 0 & \text{if } sb = 1 \\ TZ' & \text{else} \end{cases}$$

ALGORITHM 8: On-the-fly conversion with gradual underflow handling.

final remainder is less than zero. The sticky bit (sb) is used for rounding and is asserted *high* whenever the remainder is unequal to zero.

Moreover, the number of trailing zeros (TZ) is computed on-the-fly. This number indicates by how many digits the computed quotient might be shifted to the right without loosing accuracy. The number of trailing zeros has to be counted only for Z' because if $ZM1'$ is selected, the residual will be unequal to zero and TZ = 0 anyway. The number of trailing zeros is used for the selection between the preferred exponent (QP) and the normalized exponent for integer representation (QNI), as described in the following paragraph.

The exponent calculation unit selects either QP or QNI. The preferred exponent should be selected whenever possible. This is only feasible when QNI < QP ≤ QNI + TZ; that is, there is a sufficient number of trailing zeros to shift the significand to the right. Furthermore, the final exponent must satisfy the minimum and maximum exponent range. The algorithm of the exponent calculation is illustrated in Algorithm 9, where the value

$$\text{offset2} = 783 - \text{bias} = 783 - 398 = 385 \tag{30}$$

is used to add the IEEE 754-2008 bias and to remove *offset1* again (which was introduced in (27)).

Rounding is required when the number of significant digits of the quotient exceeds the length p of a decimal word. The divider presented in this paper provides the five rounding modes as requested by [4]. Rounding either selects the integer quotient Z_e or the incremented quotient $ZP1_e = Z_e + 1$. As proven by Theorem A.1 in the appendix, rounding overflow cannot occur in DFP division. Rounding overflow would occur, if $Z_e + 1$ overflows due to rounding. The selection of the quotient depends on the rounding mode, the rounding digit (R), the sticky bit (sb), and the least significant digit (LSD) of the quotient. The calculation of the round up detection is summarized in Table 3.

Finally, the result is encoded again, and the exception unit might assert six exception signals. These are division by zero, invalid operation, result is infinite, inexact, overflow, and underflow. Division by zero is asserted when the divisor equals zero but the dividend is unequal to zero. The operation is called invalid when both operands are zero, both operands are infinity, or any of the operands is either a signaling or a quiet NaN. The inexact flag is asserted when the

TABLE 3: Round-up detection.

Rounding mode	Round-up detection
Round Ties To Even	$(R > 5) + (R \equiv 5) \cdot \text{sb}$ $\quad\quad +(R \equiv 5) \cdot \overline{\text{sb}} \cdot \text{LSD}(0)$
Round Ties To Away	$(R \geq 5)$
Round Toward Positive	$\overline{\text{sign}} \cdot ((R > 0) + \text{sb})$
Round Toward Negative	$\text{sign} \cdot ((R > 0) + \text{sb})$
Round Toward Zero	0

Legend: "+": logical OR, "·": logical AND.

$$\text{offset2} = 783 - 398 = 385$$
if $(\text{QP} \leq \text{QNI})$ or $(\text{QNI} + \text{TZ} < \text{QP})$
$\quad\quad\quad\quad$ or $(\text{QP} > q_{max})$ then
$\quad$ (a) $\text{QNI} > q_{max} \Rightarrow$ overflow!
$\quad$ (b) $q_{min} \leq \text{QNI} \leq q_{max} \Rightarrow$
$\quad\quad\quad\quad q_Z = \text{QNI} - \text{offset2}$
$\quad\quad\quad\quad Z_e = Z$
$\quad\quad\quad\quad \text{ZP1}'_e = \text{ZP1}$
$\quad$ (c) $\text{QNI} < q_{min} \Rightarrow$ underflow!
else
$\quad$ (a) $q_{min} \leq \text{QP} \leq q_{max} \Rightarrow$
$\quad\quad\quad\quad q_Z = \text{QP} - \text{offset2}$
$\quad\quad\quad\quad Z_e = Z \gg (\text{QP} - \text{QNI})$
$\quad\quad\quad\quad \text{ZP1}_e = \text{ZP1} \gg (\text{QP} - \text{QNI})$
$\quad$ (b) $\text{QNI} < q_{min} \Rightarrow$ underflow!

ALGORITHM 9: Exponent calculation.

rounding digit or the sticky bit is unequal to zero. Overflow and underflow are computed as described in the exponent calculation unit and are listed in Algorithms 8 and 9. The infinity exception is asserted when the result is greater than the largest number, that is, when either overflow or division by zero exception is asserted, or when the dividend is infinity while the divisor is a finite number.

6. Implementation Results

All dividers are modeled using VHDL and are implemented for Xilinx Virtex-5 devices with speed grade −2 using Xilinx ISE 10.1. The postplace and route results of the fixed-point dividers are listed in Table 4.

All five types of fixed-point dividers require 19 cycles to perform a division. This includes 17 cycles to determine the quotient digits and the rounding digit, one additional cycle to normalize the result (when the first quotient digit is zero), and one cycle latency to perform on-the-fly conversion and sticky bit determination. As expected, the type1 divider uses the most resources in terms of look-up tables (LUTs) and flip-flops (FFs). The type2, type3.a, and type3.b divider consumes less LUTs but require, further five (type2) or two (type3.a and type3.b) BRAMs. However, comparing the delay of the three dividers leads to an unexpected result. Contrary to decimal divider implementations in ASIC designs, on FPGA platforms the shift-and-subtract algorithm is the fastest. The

reason is that the signal propagation on the FPGA's internal fast carry chains is faster than interconnections between slices over the FPGA's general routing matrix. The type1 divider exploits this fast carry chains, whereas type2, type3.a, type3.b, and type4 dividers only use the normal, slow slice interconnection resources. In ASIC implementations, for instance, the longest paths of the type4 divider would be much shorter than the longest path of the type1 divider, but on FPGA architectures the situation is the opposite.

One of the fastest decimal fixed-point divider on ASICs is the design of Lang and Nannarelli [14]. They minimize the critical path in the digit recurrence by using a fast quotient digit selection function based on binary carry-propagate adders that subtract fixed values from the estimation of the current residual. These fixed values are dependent on estimations of the divisor and are precomputed and stored in a ROM. Therefore, the latency of the ROM does not contribute to the critical path of the digit recurrence. The implementation of such a divider on FPGAs would have a poor performance because the required carry-save adder with small error estimation cannot be implemented efficiently on the FPGA's slice structure. However, the concept of removing the ROM from the critical path is applied to the type3.a and type3.b dividers, and the corresponding postplace and route results are shown in Table 4. These results point out that the type3.a utilizes a similar amount of LUTs as the type2 divider but the cycle time is much higher. The reason for this increased cycle time can be explained by the raised complexity of the multiplexers for the selection of the divisor's multiples in the digit recurrence step. These multiplexers show a poor performance in terms of propagation delay because they are implemented as a tree with slow slice interconnections. On the contrary, the type3.b divider applies dedicated fast multiplexers, which have a propagation delay of only one LUT instance and eight fast carry chains. This dedicated fast multiplexer speeds up the divider and reduces the maximum cycle time by one nanosecond. Unfortunately, the number of used LUTs is increased dramatically by approximately 1000 LUTs.

The comparison of the type2, type3.a, type3.b, and type4 dividers in terms of speed and area (number of occupied LUTs and FFs combined) shows that the type2 algorithm is the fastest and requires the least number of slices. Hence, there is no benefit in removing the ROM's latency from the critical path because the complexity is moved to the selection of the divisor's multiples. The type1 divider is only 5% faster than the type2 divider, but the speed is bought at a high price because the number of occupied slices is 75% higher. Therefore, the type2 divider shows a good tradeoff in terms of area and latency and is used for the floating-point divider presented in this paper. In the following paragraph we compare the type2 implementation with other published fixed-point dividers.

Four other FPGA-based dividers are presented by Ercegovac and McIlhenny [17, 18], Deschamp and Sutter [24], Zhang et al. [25], and Véstias and Neto [12]. These implementations are compared to our type2 divider in the following. The divider presented in [17, 18] is based on a digit recurrence algorithm that only requires limited-precision multipliers,

TABLE 4: Results for normalized decimal fixed-point dividers, $p = 16 + 1$.

	Type1	Type2	Type3.a	Type3.b	Type4
Number of LUTs	3595	1704	1749	2751	1846
Number of FFs	1234	1126	1262	1262	1031
Number of LUTs and FFs combined	3868	2210	2304	3240	2203
Number of 36 k BRAM	0	5	2	2	0
Number of LUTs normalized to the type2 divider	2.11	1.00	1.03	1.61	1.08
Number of FFs normalized to the type2 divider	1.10	1.00	1.12	1.12	0.92
Number of LUTs and FFs combined normalized to the type2 divider	1.75	1,00	1.04	1.47	1.00
Cycle time (ns)	8.1	8.5	10.1	9.1	12.1
Overall latency (ns) (19 × cycle time)	154	162	192	173	230
Max. frequency (MHz)	123	118	99	110	83
Max. frequency normalized to the type2 divider	1.05	1.00	0.84	0.93	0.70

TABLE 5: Performance comparison of fixed-point dividers.

	Occupied area	Cycle time (ns)	Latency (ns)
Ercegovac and McIlhenny [17] ($p = 14$, Virtex-5)	1263 (6 : 2) LUTs	13.1	197
Type2 divider, equalized to $p = 14$	1692 (6 : 2) LUTs	8.5	136
Deschamps and Sutter [24] ($p = 16$, Virtex-4)			
(i) Nonrestoring algorithm	2974 (4 : 1) LUTs	21.4	386
(ii) SRT-like algorithm	3799 (4 : 1) LUTs	16.6	300
Zhang et al. [25] ($p = 16$, Virtex-II Pro)	3976 slices	20.0	420
Véstias and Neto [12] ($p = 16$, Virtex-4, Newton-Raphson)			
(i) Type A3 (0 DSPs, 118 cycles)	2756 (4 : 1) LUTs	3.4	394
(ii) Type A4 (0 DSPs, 90 cycles)	3768 (4 : 1) LUTs	3.4	306
(iii) Type A5 (7 DSPs, 112 cycles)	2091 (4 : 1) LUTs	3.4	380
(iv) Type A6 (10 DSPs, 86 cycles)	2718 (4 : 1) LUTs	3.4	292
Type2 divider, equalized to $p = 16$	1704 (6 : 2) LUTs	8.5	153

adders, and LUTs. Furthermore, a compensation term is computed in the digit recurrence that compensates the error caused by this limited precision. The design is optimized for Virtex-5 FPGAs and has a good area characteristic (a 14-digit divider requires 1263 LUTs) but suffers from a high cycle time of 13.1 ns, which is more than 50% higher compared to the type1 or type2 design proposed in this paper. The reason for that high cycle time is (similar to the type4 divider) the long critical paths across many LUTs that cannot exploit the FPGA's fast carry chains. Therefore, the design would probably fit better on ASICs with dedicated routing. The dividers implemented in [24] apply two different digit recurrence algorithms with a redundancy of $\rho = 1$. The quotient digit selection function is very complex because it requires three MSDs of the divisor and four MSDs of the residual. The cycle times are high but it must be taken into account that these designs are optimized for Virtex-4 FPGAs. Nevertheless, the number of used LUTs is very high. The divider presented in [25] applies a radix-100 digit recurrence algorithm with comprehensive prescaling of the dividend and divisor. It is optimized for Virtex-II Pro devices; hence, it is hard to compare it with the dividers presented in this paper. However, the critical path includes a decimal carry-save adder tree, two carry-propagate adder stages, and three multiplexer stages. It can therefore be assumed that this

algorithm would also have a poor performance on Virtex-5 devices, although two quotient digits are retired in each iteration step. Véstias and Neto [12] propose four different decimal dividers optimized for different speed and area tradeoffs. Contrary to the circuits presented in this paper, the dividers apply the Newton-Raphson algorithm. The used multiplier is sequential; therefore, many cycles per division are required. However, each divider has a higher delay and a greater LUT usage compared to our type2 implementation.

Table 5 lists the results of the dividers presented in [17, 24, 25] together with the results of the type2 divider. However, for a fair performance comparison the precision of the type2 divider is equalized to match the number of calculated quotient digits of the corresponding divider. Furthermore it should be noted that the dividers presented in [12, 17, 24, 25] do not provide rounding support.

For the floating-point implementation, the fixed-point divider of type2 is used because type1 and type3.b consume too many resources, and type3.a and type4 are too slow. However, five additional BRAMs are required, but these are available in sufficient quantities on Virtex-5 devices. The corresponding postplace and route results for two configurations with different numbers of serialization stages are listed in Table 6. A comparison with other implementations is

TABLE 6: Postplace and route result of the floating-point divider based on type2.

	Config. 1	Config. 2
Number of cycles per float division	23	21
Number of LUTs	3231	3205
Number of FFs	1630	1377
Number of LUTs and FFs combined	3571	3566
Cycle time (ns)	8.5	9.1
Overall latency (ns)	195.5	191
Max. frequency (MHz)	118	110

TABLE 7: Postplace and route result of a 64-bit binary floating-point divider (Core Gen).

	Cycles per division			
	1	10	20	55
No. of LUTs	3161	592	425	394
No. of FFs	196	518	469	542
No. of LUTs and FFs comb.	3232	917	675	675
Cycle time (ns)	153.7	20.8	8.9	6.8
Overall latency (ns)	153.7	208	178	374
Max. frequency (MHz)	6.5	48	112	147

complicated because there are no other FPGA-based implementations of decimal floating-point dividers published yet. Therefore, we can only compare the decimal divider with binary dividers implemented on the same FPGA. In Table 7 postplace and route results of binary floating-point dividers for the double data format on a Virtex-5 provided by the Xilinx Core Generator [26] are listed. The dividers also provide exception signals *overflow*, *underflow*, *invalid operation*, and *divide-by-zero*. Unfortunately, the binary floating-point divider does not support gradual underflow because this feature increases the complexity. The divider with one cycle per division is an unpipelined and fully parallel design, and the divider that requires 55 cycles per division is a fully sequential design. The binary floating-point divider with 20 cycles per division is best suited for a comparison with the decimal floating-point divider because it requires a comparable number of cycles for one operation. Obviously, decimal arithmetic has a great overhead regarding the total number of used LUTs, but the cycle time and latency are similar. This resource overhead can be explained, on the one hand, by the inefficient representation of decimal values on binary logic and, on the other hand by the more complex specification of the decimal standard IEEE 754-2008. For instance, decimal floating-point division requires additional encoders, decoders, and a normalization stage.

7. Conclusion

In this paper we have presented five different radix-10 digit recurrence division algorithms. The type1 divider implements the simple shift-and-subtract algorithm. The type2 divider is based on a nonrestoring algorithm with ROM-based quotient digit selection function. The type3.a and type3.b dividers are both similar to type2 but use fast binary carry-propagate adders in the quotient digit selection function. However, the type3.a divider uses LUT-based multiplexers whereas the type3.b uses fast carry chain-based multiplexers. The type4 divider applies a new algorithm with constant digit selection functions. This type4 divider requires neither a ROM nor multiplexers to select multiples of the divisor.

We have shown that the subtract-and-shift algorithm with the worst latency in ASIC architectures is the fastest design on FPGAs, but uses the most FPGA resources in terms of LUTs. A good tradeoff between latency and area is the architecture type2 with a redundant carry-save representation of the residual, a radix-2 representation of the two MSDs, and a quotient digit selection function implemented in ROM. Furthermore, we have extended thisfixed-point to a fully IEEE 754-2008 compliant decimal floating-point divider for decimal64 data format, and, finally, we have shown implementation results of all dividers.

Appendix

Proofs

Theorem A.1 (rounding overflow). *Let us consider a decimal floating-point division* $Q = X/D$ *with the signs* s_i, *the significands* c_i, *the exponents* q_i, *and the precision* p

$$\left(-1^{s_Q} \cdot c_Q \cdot 10^{q_Q}\right) = \frac{\left(-1^{s_X} \cdot c_X \cdot 10^{q_X}\right)}{\left(-1^{s_D} \cdot c_D \cdot 10^{q_D}\right)}. \quad (A.1)$$

Then, rounding overflow, that is, an overflow that arises due to adding +1 to the least significant digit of the final result, cannot occur.

Proof. Assume to the contrary that there are a floating-point dividend X, a floating-point divisor D, and a proper rounding mode, where the decimal floating-point division produces a rounding overflow. Without loss of generality we consider in the following only positive operands ($s_X = s_D = 0$), normalized significands ($c_X, c_D \geq 10^{p-1}$), and the exponents to be zero ($q_X = q_D = 0$). In the case of rounding overflow, the p digits of the quotient must be all nines, and the remainder must be unequal to zero, that is,

$$\underbrace{c_X}_{p \text{ digits}} = c_Q \cdot c_D + \text{rem} = \underbrace{9.9\cdots9}_{p \text{ digits}} \cdot \underbrace{c_D}_{p \text{ digits}} + \underbrace{\text{rem}}_{p \text{ digits}}, \quad (A.2)$$

$$\text{with } 0 < \text{rem} < c_D \cdot 10^{-p+1}. \quad (A.3)$$

Condition (A.2) is fulfilled for

$$c_D = 10^{p-1}, \qquad c_X = \underbrace{9.9\cdots9}_{p \text{ digits}}, \quad (A.4)$$

but this violates condition (A.3) because the remainder is zero (rem = 0); that is, the result is exact, no round-up is applied, and hence no rounding overflow occurs.

Otherwise, if the divisor is greater than 10^{p-1} it follows that

$$\underbrace{c_X}_{p\ \text{digits}} = (9.9\cdots9) \cdot c_D + \text{rem}$$

$$= \left(10 - 10^{-p+1}\right) \cdot c_D + \text{rem}$$

$$= 10 \cdot c_D + \underbrace{\left(-10^{-p+1} \cdot c_D + \text{rem}\right)}_{<0} \qquad (\text{A.5})$$

$$= \underbrace{10 \cdot c_D + \mu}_{\geqslant p+1\ \text{digits}}$$

with $-10 < \mu < 0$. The left term of the equation has, by definition, a precision of p digits while the right term of the equation has a precision of more than p digits. This contradiction, finally, proves that no rounding overflow can occur. $\qquad\square$

References

[1] M. Baesler, S. Voigt, and T. Teufel, "FPGA implementations of radix-10 digit recurrence fixed-point and floating-point dividers," in *Proceedings of the International Conference on Reconfigurable Computing and FPGAs (ReConFig '11)*, pp. 13–19, IEEE Computer Society, Los Alamitos, CA, USA, December 2011.

[2] IEEE Task P754. *ANSI/IEEE 754-1985, Standard for Binary Floating- Point Arithmetic*. New York, NY, USA, August 1985.

[3] M. F. Cowlishaw, "Decimal floating-point: algorism for computers," in *Proceedings of the 16th IEEE Symposium on Computer Arithmetic (ARITH '03)*, pp. 104–111, IEEE Computer Society, Washington, DC, USA, June 2003.

[4] IEEE Task P754. *IEEE 754-2008, Standard for Floating-Point Arithmetic*. New York, NY, USA, August 2008.

[5] ANSI/IEEE. *ANSI/IEEE Std 854-1987: An American National Standard: IEEE Standard for Radix-Independent Floating-Point Arithmetic*. New York, NY, USA, October 1987.

[6] A. Y. Duale, M. H. Decker, H. G. Zipperer, M. Aharoni, and T. J. Bohizic, "Decimal floating-point in z9: an implementation and testing perspective," *IBM Journal of Research and Development*, vol. 51, no. 1-2, pp. 217–227, 2007.

[7] C. F. Webb, "IBM z10: the next-generation mainframe microprocessor," *IEEE Micro*, vol. 28, no. 2, pp. 19–29, 2008.

[8] L. Eisen, J. W. Ward, H. W. Tast et al., "IBM POWER6 accelerators: VMX and DFU," *IBM Journal of Research and Development*, vol. 51, no. 6, pp. 663–683, 2007.

[9] R. Kalla, B. Sinharoy, W. J. Starke, and M. Floyd, "Power7: IBM's next-generation server processor," *IEEE Micro*, vol. 30, no. 2, pp. 7–15, 2010.

[10] S. F. Oberman and M. J. Flynn, "Division algorithms and implementations," *IEEE Transactions on Computers*, vol. 46, no. 8, pp. 833–854, 1997.

[11] L. K. Wang and M. J. Schulte, "A decimal floating-point divider using newton-raphson iteration," *Journal of VLSI Signal Processing Systems*, vol. 49, no. 1, pp. 3–18, 2007.

[12] M. Véstias and H. Neto, "Revisiting the newton-raphson iterative method for decimal divisionpages," in *Proceedings of the International Conference on Field Programmable Logic and Applications (FPL '11)*, pp. 138–143, IEEE Computer Society Press, September 2011.

[13] H. Nikmehr, B. Phillips, and C. C. Lim, "Fast decimal floating-point division," *IEEE Transactions on Very Large Scale Integration (VLSI) Systems*, vol. 14, no. 9, pp. 951–961, 2006.

[14] T. Lang and A. Nannarelli, "A radix-10 digit-recurrence division unit: algorithm and architecture," *IEEE Transactions on Computers*, vol. 56, no. 6, pp. 727–739, 2007.

[15] A. Vázquez, E. Antelo, and P. Montuschi, "A radix-10 SRT divider based on alternative BCD codings," in *Proceedings of the 25th IEEE International Conference on Computer Design (ICCD '07)*, pp. 280–287, IEEE Computer Society Press, Los Alamitos, CA, USA, October 2007.

[16] E. Schwarz and S. Carlough, "Power6 decimal dividepages," in *Proceedings of the 18th IEEE International Conference on Application-Specific Systems Architectures and Processors (ASAP '07)*, pp. 128–133, IEEE Computer Society, July 2007.

[17] M. D. Ercegovac and R. McIlhenny, "Design and FPGA implementation of radix-10 algorithm for division with limited precision primitives," in *Proceedings of the 42nd Asilomar Conference on Signals, Systems and Computers (ASILOMAR '08)*, pp. 762–766, IEEE Computer Society, Pacific Grove, Calif, USA, October 2008.

[18] M. D. Ercegovac and R. McIlhenny, "Design and FPGA implementation of radix-10 combined division/square root algorithm with limited precision primitives," in *Proceedings of the 44th Asilomar Conference on Signals, Systems and Computers (Asilomar '10)*, pp. 87–91, IEEE Computer Society, Pacific Grove, Calif, USA, November 2010.

[19] F. Y. Busaba, C. A. Krygowski, W. H. Li, E. M. Schwarz, and S. R. Carlough, "The IBM z900 decimal arithmetic unit," in *Proceedings of the 35th Asilomar Conference on Signals, Systems and Computers*, vol. 2, pp. 1335–1339, IEEE Computer Society, November 2001.

[20] M. Ercegovac and T. Lang, *Division and Square Root: Digit-Recurrence Algorithms and Implementations*, Kluwer Academic Publishers, Norwell, Mass, USA, 1994.

[21] M. Baesler, S. O. Voigt, and T. Teufel, "A decimal floating-point accurate scalar product unit with a parallel fixed-point multiplier on a Virtex-5 FPGA," *International Journal of Reconfigurable Computing*, vol. 2010, Article ID 357839, 13 pages, 2010.

[22] M. Baesler, S. O. Voigt, and T. Teufel, "A radix-10 digit recurrence division unit with a constant digit selection function," in *Proceedings of the 28th IEEE International Conference on Computer Design (ICCD '10)*, pp. 241–246, IEEE Computer Society, Los Alamitos, CA, USA, October 2010.

[23] M. Baesler, S. O. Voigt, and T. Teufel, "An IEEE 754-2008 decimal parallel and pipelined FPGA floating-point multiplier," in *Proceedings of the 20th International Conference on Field Programmable Logic and Applications (FPL '10)*, pp. 489–495, IEEE Computer Society, Washington, DC, USA, September 2010.

[24] J. P. Deschamps and G. Sutter, "Decimal division: algorithms and FPGA implementations," in *Proceedings of the 6th Southern Programmable Logic Conference (SPL '10)*, pp. 67–72, IEEE Computer Society, March 2010.

[25] Y. Zhang, D. Chen, L. Chen et al., "Design and implementation of a readix-100 decimal division," in *Proceedings of IEEE Symposium on Circuit and System (ISCAS '09)*, Taibei, Taiwan, May 2009.

[26] Xilinx. Xilinx LogiCORE Floating-Point Operator v4.0, April 2008.

11

A Memory Hierarchy Model Based on Data Reuse for Full-Search Motion Estimation on High-Definition Digital Videos

Alba Sandyra Bezerra Lopes,[1] Ivan Saraiva Silva,[2] and Luciano Volcan Agostini[3]

[1] Federal Institute of Education, Science and Technology of Rio Grande do Norte, Campus João Câmara,
    59550-000 João Câmara, RN, Brazil
[2] Department of Computer Science and Statistics, Campus Ministro Petronio Portela, Federal University of Piauí,
    64049-550 Teresina, PI, Brazil
[3] Group of Architectures and Integrated Circuits-GACI, Federal University of Pelotas Pelotas, RS, Brazil

Correspondence should be addressed to Alba Sandyra Bezerra Lopes, alba.lopes@ifrn.edu.br

Academic Editor: Alisson Brito

The motion estimation is the most complex module in a video encoder requiring a high processing throughput and high memory bandwidth, mainly when the focus is high-definition videos. The throughput problem can be solved increasing the parallelism in the internal operations. The external memory bandwidth may be reduced using a memory hierarchy. This work presents a memory hierarchy model for a full-search motion estimation core. The proposed memory hierarchy model is based on a data reuse scheme considering the full search algorithm features. The proposed memory hierarchy expressively reduces the external memory bandwidth required for the motion estimation process, and it provides a very high data throughput for the ME core. This throughput is necessary to achieve real time when processing high-definition videos. When considering the worst bandwidth scenario, this memory hierarchy is able to reduce the external memory bandwidth in 578 times. A case study for the proposed hierarchy, using 32×32 search window and 8×8 block size, was implemented and prototyped on a Virtex 4 FPGA. The results show that it is possible to reach 38 frames per second when processing full HD frames (1920×1080 pixels) using nearly 299 Mbytes per second of external memory bandwidth.

1. Introduction

Nowadays, several electronic devices support high-definition digital videos. Applications like internet and digital television broadcasting are also massively supporting this kind of media. In this scenario, the video coding becomes an essential area to make possible the storage and principally the transmission of these videos, mainly when the focus is in high definition.

The most recent and advanced video coding standard is the H.264/AVC (advanced video coding) [1]. This standard includes high complexity on its modules, aiming to achieve high compression rates. This high complexity makes difficult to achieve real time (e.g. 30 frames per second) though software implementations, especially when high definition videos, like 1920×1080 pixels, are considered.

A digital video is a sequence of still images, called frames, typically sampled at a rate of 30 frames per second. In a video sequence, there is a considerable amount of redundant elements, like background scenes or objects that do not have any motion from a frame to another, that are not really essential for the construction of new images. These elements are usually called redundant information [2]. There are three types of redundancy: spatial redundancy (similarity in homogeneous texture areas), temporal redundancy (similarity between sequential frames) and entropic redundancy (redundancy in the bit stream representation). Those redundancies can be removed in order to achieve high compression rates.

The motion estimation (ME) is the most computationally intensive module of a video encoder. This module explores the temporal redundancy to reduce the amount of data needed to represent the video sequence.

A feature of the H.264/AVC and other video coding standards is the use of asymmetric compression algorithms. In this case, the encoder and the decoder have different

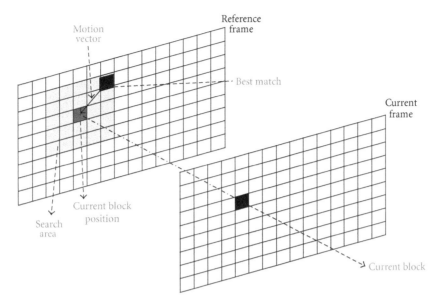

FIGURE 1: Motion estimation process.

definitions and the decoder, which is used in the higher number of devices, is less complex and cheaper than the encoder. The H.264/AVC standard introduces several new features when compared with others video compression standards. But the implementation of many of these new features is not mandatory [1]. Although the motion estimation is the most complex module in a digital video codec, it is presented only in the encoder side.

The motion estimation requires, besides the high processing throughput, also a very high bandwidth of external memory to realize its operations in real time when considering full HD videos (frames with 1920×1080 pixels) [3]. The throughput can be solved increasing the parallelism in the internal operations. The external memory bandwidth may be reduced using a memory hierarchy. Besides, the increase of the parallelism implies increasing the bandwidth. If more calculations must be performed at the same time, more data must be available to perform these operations.

The motion estimation presents the highest demand for external memory bandwidth, and it shares the external memory interconnection subsystem with others encoder modules like the motion compensation, the intraframe prediction and the deblocking filter. In this context, it is important to explore methods and architectural solutions which minimize the number of external memory accesses. An efficient memory hierarchy is the key point to respect the demands of a video encoder, mainly when high-definition videos are being processed.

This paper presents a memory hierarchy model for a full-search motion estimation core. The proposed memory hierarchy model is based on a data reuse scheme, and it aims to minimize the memory bandwidth and to maximize the data throughput delivered to the motion estimation core. The paper is structured as follows. Section 2 introduces the motion estimation process. Section 3 presents the data reuse exploration scheme. Section 4 presents the proposed memory hierarchy model. Section 5 presents some results

and discussions. Section 6 presents the implemented core using the proposed memory hierarchy which was used as a case study. Section 7 presents comparisons with some related works. Finally, Section 8 presents conclusions and future works.

2. Motion Estimation

The ME process (illustrated on Figure 1) uses at least two frames: one current frame and one or more reference frames. The current frame is the frame that is being encoded. The reference frame is a previously encoded frame in the video sequence.

The current frame is divided into nonoverlapped blocks. For each block, a search window is defined in the reference frame. A search process is performed to find the better match for each block in its respective search window. To determinate the better match, a similarity criteria like Sum of absolute differences (SAD) [4] are used. A motion vector is generated for each block to represent where the better match was found. In the H.264/AVC, multiple reference frames can be used. In this case, the same search is done for all available reference frames and the candidate block that presents the better value of similarity among all reference frames is selected.

There are several search algorithms that define how the search process is done inside a search window. The full search (FS) is an algorithm that generates optimal results in accuracy, with a high cost in complexity [5]. Fast algorithms, like diamond search (DS), provide a great complexity reduction with acceptable lossless in accuracy [5].

Besides to provide the best possible motion vector, another important feature in FS algorithm is that it has a regular pattern with no data dependencies.

The FS algorithm looks for the best match in all possible candidate blocks in the search window, from the superior left border until the inferior right border, shifting pixel by pixel in the search window. For each candidate block, a similarity calculation must be done to measure how similar is the candidate block to the current block. Once the similarity value is computed for all candidate blocks, the best match is the most similar candidate block (for instance, the lowest sum of absolute differences if SAD is used as similarity value). The FS process increases its complexity proportionally to the increase of search window range [6]. For a 32×32 search window and a 16×16 block size, there are 289 candidate blocks. A similarity calculation should be performed for each one of these blocks candidates. If a 64×64 is used, the number of candidate blocks increases to 1089.

Despite the complexity, in the FS motion estimation (FSME), there is no data dependency during the process of similarity calculation. So it is possible to design hardware architectures that provide the necessary resources in order to achieve high performance rates. It is possible to use systolic arrays [7] or tree structures to solve computational problems providing enough processing elements to compute the similarity between samples from the current block and the candidate block in parallel. However, the design of high performance motion estimation hardware is not an easy task. The parallelism exploitation increases the chip area proportionally to the parallelism level. The memory bandwidth also increases with the number of parallel similarity computation. Some criteria must be observed in order to achieve a good tradeoff between some parameters like. the degree of parallelism, the chip area, the memory bandwidth, and the power consumption.

On other hand, software solutions based on current general-purpose processors are not able to encode1080 HD digital video in real time (at a rate of 30 frames per second) when all H.264/AVC coding features are used. Then, the use of dedicated hardware architectures is mandatory to provide the required performance.

3. Data Reuse in Full-Search Motion Estimation

On FSME, data reuse refers to the use of each pixel of the search window (one or more n-bits words) to the similarity calculation of all candidate blocks that share the pixel without additional fetches in memory. A sample can be shared by neighboring candidate blocks of a same search window or by neighboring search windows in a reference frame. The number of candidate blocks that share a single sample depends on the size of the block, the size of the search window, and the position of the sample in the search window. For instance, a sample on the superior left corner of a search window is not shared by other candidates blocks, a single candidate block of a single search window have has sample, while a sample on the center of a search window is shared by many blocks of many search windows. Typically a sample can be shared by as many candidate blocks as the number of samples in a candidate blocks.

The regular pattern of FS algorithm allows the exploration of data reuse along with the exploration of parallelism in high degrees. The data reuse approach provides a way to

reduce the bandwidth at the same time that the complexity of FS similarity calculation is reduced to the calculation of the similarity of a pair of block. In this context, data reuse is essential to reduce the bandwidth and the high parallelism is essential to achieve high performance.

As higher is the required video quality and definition, as higher is the required external memory bandwidth. The bandwidth increases with the frame size increase, with the search window increase, and with the frame rate increase. The bandwidth problem can be reduced using an efficient memory hierarchy.

As mentioned before, motion estimation uses at least two frames: one current frame and one reference frame.

The current frame is divided into several nonoverlapped $N \times N$ blocks. In the FSME, the search for the best match of one current block requires that its samples are repeatedly compared with samples from the reference frame. The current block samples lifetime is the time period of motion-estimating one current block [3]. Keeping the $N \times N$ samples from the current block in a local memory during the search reduces the data access from the current frame to the maximum possible, minimizing currant frame bandwidth. Doing this, each sample of the current frame will be fetched from the main memory just once in the whole motion estimation process.

Although adjacent current blocks do not overlap, adjacent search windows are no longer independent and overlap. Each search window in the reference frame is a rectangle $(SW_W * SW_H)$ centered on the current block. This generally means that the search window of the current block shares data with the search window of the neighboring block.

In [3], four data reuse levels in the reference frame were defined according to the degree of data reuse: from level A to level D, where level A is the weakest reuse degree and the level D is the strongest reuse degree. Level A and Level B cover data reuse within a single search window. Level C and Level D cover data reuse among different search windows.

The data reuse level is an important factor in dealing with memory bandwidth requirements of ME. As stronger is the reuse level, less memory bandwidth is required.

In the search window, a row of candidate blocks is called a candidate block strip. Adjacent candidate blocks in a candidate block strip only differ by a column of samples. The Level A of data reuse take advantage of this feature to reuse all data loaded from external memory to the calculation of the previously candidate block and load just the column of samples which is necessary for the next candidate block calculation.

Figure 2 shows the level A data reuse scheme, where N represents the block dimension, SW_H and SW_W represents the height and the width of the search window, respectively. At this figure, two adjacent candidate blocks are showed (candidate block 1 and candidate block 2). The gray area is all samples within the search window that can be reused from a candidate block to another.

The level B of data reuse considers that adjacent vertical strips of candidate blocks within the search window also overlap significantly, only differing by a row of samples. All

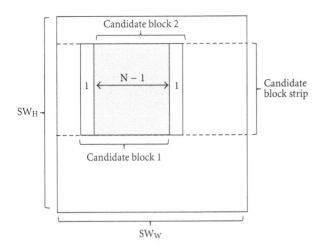

FIGURE 2: Level A data reuse scheme.

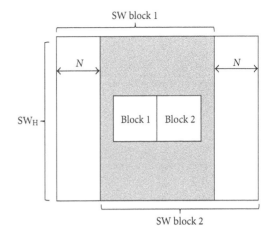

FIGURE 4: Level C on data reuse scheme.

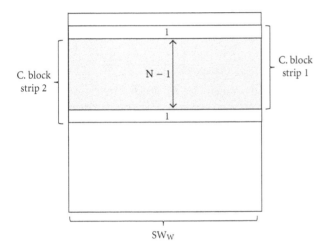

FIGURE 3: Level B data reuse scheme.

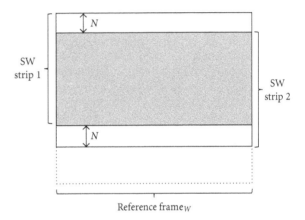

FIGURE 5: Level D data reuse scheme.

sample loaded for the previously strip of candidate blocks, with one row exception, can be reused.

Figure 3 represent two vertically adjacent candidate block strips (C. block Strip 1 and C. block strip 2). All the gray area represents data that can be reused while processing the next candidate block strip.

The level C refers to data reuse among different search windows. Search windows from neighboring blocks have several samples in common. in Figure 4, two blocks (block 1 and block 2) and their respective search windows (SW block 1 and SW block 2) are represented. The data of the two search windows differ by N columns of samples (where N represents the block dimension). All gray area is data that can be reused in the next block processing.

Finally, level D showed in Figure 5 resembles to level B of reuse data, except that it applies to reuses of samples in the entire search window strip instead of candidate blocks strip. With this level application, each sample of the reference frame is loaded just once during the entire motion estimation process.

The level A scheme uses the smallest size of on-chip memory, but it consumes more off-chip memory bandwidth.

On the other hand, the level D uses more on-chip memory but it archives minimal off-chip memory bandwidth.

This work adopts Level C on data reuse scheme to balance on-chip memory size and off-chip memory bandwidth.

4. Proposed Memory Hierarchy

Generally, a memory hierarchy is composed of registers, local memories, and external memories. External memories are cheaper and have high storage capacity. But they are also slower. Local memories are faster than external memories, and their cost is also higher. Registers are the fastest option but with the highest cost among all solutions.

Considering these features, the proposition of a memory hierarchy for the motion estimation process must provide: (i) memory capacity to store at least the data that can be reused, considering the adopted reuse level (in this paper the Level C was chosen); (ii) a combination of high-level and low level memories in the hierarchy aiming to balance memory hierarchy cost, bandwidth, and throughput.

Data that can be reused in the ME in general was previously loaded from external memory. So it must be appropriately distributed between memory modules in the memory hierarchy to meet the goals described above.

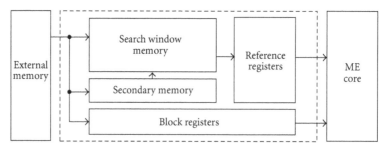

FIGURE 6: Proposed memory hierarchy model.

According to level C, data reuse scheme presented on [8] and illustrated in Figure 6 was proposed. This model aims to reduce the required memory bandwidth, while it balances cost and throughput. This way, the memory hierarchy will be able to provide the necessary data to the ME core that achieves the required high processing rates.

The external memory stores frames (current and reference frames) that will be used in the motion estimation process. The memory hierarchy levels store data that are recurrently used, avoiding redundant accesses to the external memory. These levels are composed by a search window memory, a secondary memory, and registers (block and reference registers). Each one will be described below.

In the proposed hierarchy, the block registers bank (BRB) contains $N \times N$ registers, each one storing a sample of the current block. The data from current block is used in the similarity calculation of all candidate blocks in the search window. It is important to use registers to store this block because it will be accessed continuously during all motion estimation process so the access to these data must be fast. The data at this bank is loaded just once per each block in the current frame and all values are used at each cycle during all ME process of the current block. Using this block register bank reduces to the minimum possible the external memory access of the current frame.

The reference register bank (RRB) has $N * (\mathrm{SW_W} - N)$ registers, where $\mathrm{SW_W}$ is the search window width. It is loaded with data from search window memory. These data refers to candidate blocks in the search window which are being used in the similarity calculation in relation to the current block. This bank in the way it was designed is sufficient to provide a high throughput to the ME core process. A fast access to these data is required to allow a high throughput in the ME core; thus, registers are also needed to store them.

At the reference register bank, three types of data shifts are allowed: shift right, shift left, and shift up. It was planned to minimize local memory access when the procedure of full search scan is performed as proposed in Figure 7.

In the proposed scheme, the data in RRB are shifted N times left until reaching the search window right border. One shift down is made when borders are reached and N shifts right are done to reach the left border of the search window. In each shift, only one column or row of new data must be stored in the RRB. Each shift is performed in one clock cycle. Every time a search window border (left or right) is reached, a complete data of candidate blocks strip has been provided to the ME core.

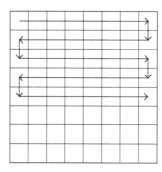

FIGURE 7: Proposed full-search scanning order.

The search window memory stores the complete search window of the current block. Sets of data from this memory are accessed at each moment from the motion estimation process. Since these data do not need to be simultaneously accessed, it can be stored in a local memory (on-chip memory). So the search window memory has a storage limit of $\mathrm{SR_W} * \mathrm{SR_H}$ samples. This is the memory that provides data to the RRB. After the initial RRB fill, at each clock cycle, the search window memory provides to the RRB on row or column of data.

Together, the RRB and the search window memory cover data reuse within a single search window, which represents level A and level B on the data reuse scheme.

The secondary memory stores the difference of search window data from two adjacent current blocks. So the size of this memory is $N * \mathrm{SR_H}$. These data are loaded from external memory, while the full search scan is being done. Once immediate accesses to them are not required, they can be stored in the local memory. When it is time to process a new current block, no extra clock cycle is expended to request data from external memory. The search window memory keeps the data that can be reused from the search window of the previously current block, and the data at the secondary memory overwrites the data that are no longer needed in the search window memory. So the complete search window from the next current block is available in the memory hierarchy modules.

The search window memory and secondary memory cover the level C on the data reuse scheme that refers to data that can be reused among different search windows.

A complete search window of a current block just need to be loaded from external memory when the current block is the first one in the strip of current blocks in the current frame.

5. Experimental Results

Table 1 presents the experimental results using the proposed memory hierarchy for three sizes of search window (32×32, 64×64, and 96×96) and two block sizes (8×8 and 16×16).

The first and second columns on the table present the search windows and block sizes, respectively, used in this evaluation. The third column presents the number of candidate blocks existent in the search window. The number of candidate blocks in a $k \times k$ search window can be calculated by the formula $(k - n + 1)^2$, where n represents the block dimension.

The fourth column presents the bandwidth required (in megabytes) to bring data from external memory to process 30 frames in 1080 HD using our memory hierarchy model. The fifth column shows the bandwidth per second (in gigabytes) provided, using the proposed model, to the ME Core. The presented numbers consider the way of our memory hierarchy reuse data, keeping data previously loaded into local memories and registers.

The sixth column presents the number of cycles needed to fill a complete local memory with data from a whole search window. The next one shows the size (in Kbytes) of on-chip memory needed for each pair "search window/block size." This number is the sum of search window memory size and the secondary memory size. The eighth column presents the size (in Kbytes) of used registers (block registers and reference registers).

Finally, the last column shows the PSNR (Peak Signal Noise Rate) reached using the specific parameters of search window and block size. The PSRN results were obtained by software evaluations, using the H.264/AVC reference software [9], testing 10 video sequences (blue sky, man in Car, pedestrian area, riverbed, rolling tomatoes, rush hour, station, sunflower, traffic, and tractor). The PSNR values presented are the average of the values of all 10 video sequences because the values of PSNR may vary according to the video characteristics, like the amount of movement present in each video sequence.

An important relation that must be observed is the increase in the number of candidate blocks. A smaller block size, for a same search window, implies in a higher number of candidate blocks. Considering the search window variation, the number of candidate blocks increases proportionally with the search window increase. These aspects affect directly the computation necessary to the ME, and, consequently, the properly amount of data must be provided to ME core.

Using the proposed memory hierarchy, the external memory bandwidth to the ME is reduced, as shown in Figure 8. While the number of candidate blocks increases exponentially, the bandwidth maintains a linear growth. Comparing the best and the worst case presented on Table 1, while the number of candidate blocks increases approximately 27 times, the bandwidth required is only 4.4 times bigger. Without the proposed hierarchy, both curves

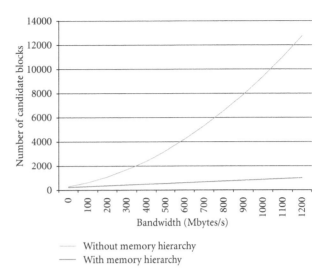

FIGURE 8: Candidate blocks versus bandwidth required.

presented on Figure 6 would have the same exponential behavior.

According to a DDR SDRAM behavior, the number of clock cycles needed to fill the complete memory hierarchy with data from external memory was estimated.

A complete search window must be loaded from external memory only when the current block is the first one in a strip of current blocks. Considering a 1080 HD frame and a block size 8×8, there are 135 strips of current blocks. Using a 32×32 search window, 74 clock cycles are needed to fill the local memory. So only 9.990 clock cycles are expended with external memory accesses per frame. The fill of secondary memory can be done without introducing any extra clock cycles in the critical path, since this filling is done in parallel with the ME core process.

The on-chip memory presented in Table 1 is the sum of search window memory size and secondary memory size. The search window memory has a fixed size according to the size of search window. Once motion estimation uses only luminance samples (the motion vector to chrominance blocks are calculated based on the luminance ones), with a 32×32 search window and using 1 byte per luminance sample, the size of local memory is exactly 1 Kbyte. But the size of secondary memory depends on the block width and on the search window height. So using an 8×8 block size and the same 32×32 search window, the secondary memory uses 0.25 Kbytes of on-chip memory, totalizing 1.25 Kbytes. This way, the increase of search window memory is proportional to the square size of search window, when the secondary memory increase is proportional to both, the search window and the block size. When comparing the size of secondary memory with search window memory, the search window memory size increases 9 times between the best and worst case, and the secondary memory increases only 1.5 times.

The number of registers used is proportional to the block size and the search window. As bigger is the block size, as bigger is the block register size. Analogously, bigger search windows imply in bigger reference registers banks.

TABLE 1: Experimental results.

Search window	Block size	Candidate blocks	Bandwidth Ext. mem. (Mbytes/sec)	Bandwidth ME core (Gbytes/sec)	Clock cycles	On-chip memory (Kbytes)	Registers (Kbytes)	PSNR (dB)
32×32	16×16	289	179.0	15.8	74	1.50	0.5	34.00
	8×8	625	299.6	34.8		1.25	0.25	35.90
64×64	16×16	2,401	302.6	136.3	266	5.00	1	35.41
	8×8	3,249	547.8	184.9		4.50	0.5	37.64
96×96	16×16	6,561	430.1	375.4	586	10.50	1.5	35.90
	8×8	7,921	803.9	453.8		9.75	0.75	38.26

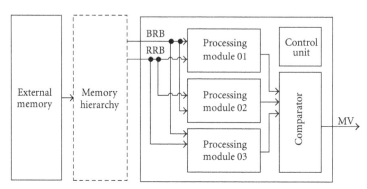

FIGURE 9: ME core block diagram.

6. Case Study

So, according to Table 1, the configuration that spends more registers is that considering a 96×96 search window and a 16×16 block size.

One important factor that must also be considered when the parameters presented Table 1 in are evaluated is the quality of generated matches. The PSNR (peak signal noise rate) is one of the most used parameters to compare the video quality [6]. It is a quantitative measure that evaluates how much noise exists in the encoded video when compared to the original one. As biggest the PSNR value is, smaller is the noise and better is the video quality.

The PSNR results presented on Table 1 are the average of PSNR results from ten 1080 HD video sequences. As larger is the size of the search window, as higher is the ME chance to find a best match and a best motion vector. On the other hand, as smaller is block size, as higher is the ME chance to find a best match. Analyzing the PSNR results, the variation between worst and best case is more than 4 dB.

Furthermore, as bigger is the search window size and as smaller is the block size, as bigger is the number of computation needed to process the ME and also higher is the memory bandwidth required, as shown on Table 1.

Motion estimation architecture decisions always imply in a tradeoff between the numbers of needed calculations, the quality of ME results, the chip area, and the required external memory bandwidth. So it is important to balance all these criteria when designing a new architecture for motion estimation. But, in all cases, the use of the proposed memory hierarchy will decrease a lot the external memory bandwidth, allowing the ME to reach high throughputs, even for high-definition videos.

The proposed memory hierarchy model and a functional motion estimation core were implemented and coupled as shown, in Figure 9 to demonstrate the qualities of the proposed memory hierarchy. The complete architecture, including the memory hierarchy and the ME core, was described in VHDL and synthesized to a Xilinx Virtex 4 XC4VLX25 FPGA [10].

The local memories (search window memory and secondary memory) were mapped to FPGA BRAMs.

A module to control the accesses to memory hierarchy was designed. It was designed to make read and write requests at the right moment: write data from external memory into the search window memory, secondary memory or block register; read data from search window memory, and writes in the reference register bank; also read data from secondary memory and writes into the search window memory.

These ME core was implemented using a fixed 8×8 block size and the 32×32 search window. This parameters were defined after analyzing some of the criteria presented in Table 1, and it is realized that these parameters presents good tradeoff between numbers of needed calculations, the quality of ME results, the chip area, and the required external memory bandwidth.

The ME core uses SAD [4] as similarity criterion. This is the most used criteria for hardware implementations because it executes simple calculations and it offers a good quality answer. It performs the absolute difference between samples from current block and samples from candidate block. The ME core was implemented intending to achieve

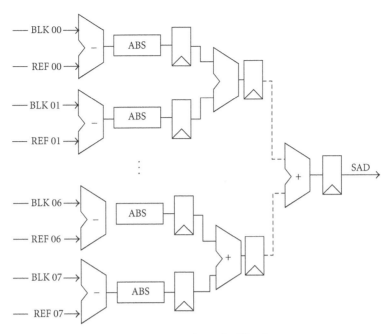

FIGURE 10: Processing unit RTL scheme.

high processing rates. So it takes all bandwidth provided by the memory hierarchy.

The ME architecture is composed by three processing modules (PMs), each one including units responsible for arithmetic operations; a comparator to decide which block represents the best match; a control unit that is responsible to manage the data flow with control signals.

Each PM is composed by eight processing units (PUs). The processing units (PUs) are responsible to give the results of similarity calculation between the current block and candidate block. Figure 10 presents the PU RTL scheme.

Once there are eight processing units per PM, each PU calculates the absolute difference between one row of the current block and one row of the candidate block. The data of the current block are obtained from the BRB, and the data from the candidate block are obtained from the RRB. In the PM there are pipelined adders that sum the results of the eight PUs and compute the complete SAD for a candidate block.

The comparator (Figure 11) receives the three SAD values and their respective motion vectors (MVs), each one generated for one PM. The three values are compared and the small one is stored in best motion vector register (best vector in Figure 11).

Once the PMs generate SAD values in pipeline, three SAD values are received for the comparator module at each clock cycle. After the comparator's pipeline is full, the comparison of these three values is delivered at each clock cycle. The best value of the three SADs is compared with the SAD stored at the best SAD register. At the end of the ME process, the best motion vector referent to the best SAD will be available at the best vector register.

The architecture control was developed in a decentralized way. Each module has its own manager, and the control unit sends signals for all the modules managers. The control unit

TABLE 2: Synthesis results.

	Used	Available	Percent of usage
Slices	6,895	10,752	64%
Slice flip flops	6,469	21,504	30%
4 input LUTs	11,893	21,504	55%
BRAMs	1	72	1%

has signals to initialize the complete architecture and output signals that signalize when the process of ME has finished.

The synthesized results of the complete architecture to the Virtex 4 XC4VLX25 FPGA are showed on Table 2.

As shown in Table 2 the complete architecture spends 64% of available slices, 30% of flip-flop slices, and 55% of LUTs. Once this device is not a huge one, these values are acceptable for ME cores.

Focusing on BRAM results showed in Table 2, it is possible to realize that, from the total of BRAMs available on the target FPGA device, only 1% was used for the complete architecture. This means that the proposed memory hierarchy is very efficient to reduce the external bandwidth, to feed a high throughput ME core, and presents all these features using a very low amount of hardware resources. This result is also a stimulus to design a new hierarchy model considering the level D of data reuse, as proposed in [3].

Table 3 presents information about the minimum operation frequency required to achieve real time for different video resolutions, considering this implementations. The achieved frequency in this case study using a Virtex 4 was 292 MHz. The complete architecture is capable to process, in real time, since small resolution videos until high-definition videos. With this frequency, the architecture is able to process more than 86 720 HD frames per second and 38 1080 HD frames per second. Considering 1080 HD resolution at a

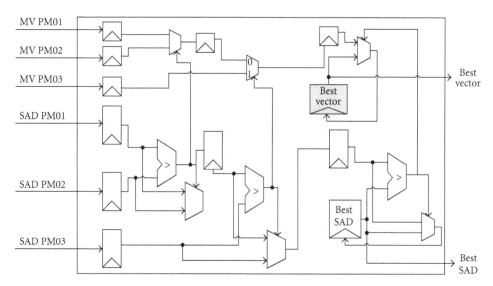

FIGURE 11: RTL scheme for the comparator module.

TABLE 3: Frequency and bandwidth required.

Resolution	Min. freq. (MHz)	Max. frames/sec.	Bandwidth (Mbytes/s)
CIF (352 × 288)	11.20	784.10	15.29
VGA (640 × 480)	33.83	259.59	45.26
SD (720 × 480)	38.04	230.84	50.75
720 HD (1280 × 720)	101.29	86.70	133.81
1080 HD (1920 × 1080)	227.75	38.56	299.59

TABLE 4: Comparison with related works.

	[11]	[12]	[13]	This work
Block size	4 × 4 to 16 × 16	4 × 4 to 16 × 16	4 × 4 to 16 × 16	8 × 8
Search window	19 × 19	16 × 16	65 × 65	32 × 32
Level of data reuse	B	B	C	C
Memory (Kbytes)	—	0.25	7.75	1.25
Register (Kbytes)	0.08	0.06	0.5	0.25
Bandwidth (MB/s)	1,397.8	1,008.5	1,054.0	299.5

frame rate of 30 fps, the required bandwidth is 299 Mbytes per second.

Using the proposed memory hierarchy, it is possible to develop a functional architecture for motion estimation with good quality results, high processing rates, and mainly with a reduced bandwidth.

7. Related Works

There are many works that focus on motion estimation architectures. But few of them focus on the memory bandwidth reduction. All works presented in this section uses full search as block matching algorithm. Table 4 presents a comparison with this related works.

The work presented in [11] uses variable block size, doing the SAD calculation for 4 × 4 blocks, and reusing these data to generate the SAD for the other block sizes. The architecture stores just the current block and the 4 lines of the search window. No local memory are used, only registers. This architecture attends to the level B data reuse scheme. Besides the use of small amount of registers and no local memory, it requires more external memory bandwidth than our solution.

In [12] is presented an architecture that allows variable block size and uses a 16 × 16 search window. It has a computation mechanism that processes the search window line per line, processing the first line of all candidate blocks in

that line, and then, starting the next line, and so on, until the last line of the search window is reached. This architecture attends to the level B data reuse scheme. Although using a small size of search window, this architecture requires a high bandwidth because it does not reuse search window data from neighboring blocks.

The work presented in [13] attends to the level C data reuse scheme. It uses a 65 × 65 search window and variable block size. The size of the used search window is higher but the architecture attends to level C data reuse scheme, and then, this work also requires a very high bandwidth with external memory.

The architecture presented in this work using the proposed memory hierarchy model, presents a great tradeoff between search window size, block size and external memory bandwidth requirement.

Considering the external memory bandwidth required to process 30 frames per second, this work presents best result. Even using small search windows, the solutions presented in [11, 12] need a higher bandwidth to process 1080 HD videos in real time. This is because these architectures do not use a high level of data reuse. The work presented in [13] in spite of using level C of reuse of data uses a large search window, requiring a higher bandwidth than our work.

Develop hardware architecture for motion estimation implies always in a tradeoff between several parameters. So it is necessary to verify if the application priority is a better quality, a low cost in on-chip area, a reduction on external memory bandwidth or, an increase in the processing rate, for example. But, balancing all these criteria it is possible to develop efficient motion estimation architectures.

8. Conclusions and Future Works

This paper presented a memory hierarchy model for full-search motion estimation aiming to reduce the external memory bandwidth requirement. The proposed model, besides reducing memory bandwidth, it is also able to provide a high throughput to the ME core allowing the ME to process high-definition videos.

Considering the highest search window and the lowest block size evaluated, this architecture can reduce the external memory bandwidth in 578 times when compared to a solution without hierarchy.

The ME core designed and coupled to the memory hierarchy model proposed in this paper was described in detail. The complete architecture formed by the memory hierarchy and ME core can reach more than 38 frames per second when processing a 1080 HD video using only 299 Mb of external memory bandwidth.

As future works, we plan to evolve the memory hierarchy model to support motion estimation with multiple reference frames. It is also a future work to adopt the level D of data reuse, In this case, more on-chip memory will be necessary, but also the memory bandwidth requirement will be lower.

References

[1] J. V. Team, Draft ITU-T Rec. and Final Draft Int. Standard of Joint Video Spec. ITU-T Rec. H.264 and ISO/IEC 14496-10 AVC, May 2003.

[2] A. Bovik, *Handbook of Image and Video Processing*, Academic Press, 2000.

[3] J. C. Tuan, T. S. Chang, and C. W. Jen, "On the data reuse and memory bandwidth analysis for full-search block-matching VLSI architecture," *IEEE Transactions on Circuits and Systems for Video Technology*, vol. 12, no. 1, pp. 61–72, 2002.

[4] Y. Q. Shi and H. Sun, *Image and Video Compression for Multimedia Engineering*, CRC Press, 2nd edition, 2008.

[5] P. A. Kuhn, *Complexity Analysis and VLSI Architectures for MPEG-4 Motion Estimation*, Kluwe Academic Plubisher, Boston, Mass, USA, 1999.

[6] I. Richardson, *H.264 and MPEG-4 Video Compression: Video Coding for Next-Generation Multimedia*, John Wiley & Sons, Chichester, UK, 2003.

[7] Y. H. Hu and S.-Y. Kung, *Handbook of Signal Processing Systems*, Springer, New York, NY, USA, 2010.

[8] A. S. B. Lopes, I. S. Silva, and L. V. Agostini, "An efficient memory hierarchy for full search motion estimation on high definition digital videos," in *Proceedings of the 24th Symposium on Integrated Circuits and Systems Design*, pp. 131–136, Joao Pessoa, Brazil, September 2011.

[9] JM15.1, "H.264/AVC JM Reference Software," 2011, http://iphome.hhi.de/suehring/tml/.

[10] Xilinx, "FPGA and CPLD Solutions from Xilinx, Inc," http://www.xilinx.com/.

[11] R. S. S. Dornelles, F. M. Sampaio, and L. V. Agostini, "Variable block size motion estimation architecture with a fast bottom-up Decision Mode and an integrated motion compensation targeting the H.264/AVC video coding standard," in *Proceedings of the 23rd Symposium on Integrated Circuits and Systems Design (SBCCI '10)*, pp. 186–191, September 2010.

[12] R. Porto, L. Agostini, and S. Bampi, "Hardware design of the H.264/AVC variable block size motion estimation for real-time 1080HD video encoding," in *Proceedings of the IEEE Computer Society Annual Symposium on VLSI (ISVLSI '09)*, pp. 115–120, May 2009.

[13] L. Deng, W. Gao, M. Z. Hu, and Z. Z. Ji, "An efficient hardware implementation for motion estimation of AVC standard," *IEEE Transactions on Consumer Electronics*, vol. 51, no. 4, pp. 1360–1366, 2005.

12

Combining SDM-Based Circuit Switching with Packet Switching in a Router for On-Chip Networks

Angelo Kuti Lusala and Jean-Didier Legat

Institute of Information and Communication Technologies, Electronics and Applied Mathematics,
Université Catholique de Louvain, 1348 Louvain-la-Neuve, Belgium

Correspondence should be addressed to Angelo Kuti Lusala, angelo.kutilusala@uclouvain.be

Academic Editor: Marco D. Santambrogio

A Hybrid router architecture for Networks-on-Chip "NoC" is presented, it combines Spatial Division Multiplexing "SDM" based circuit switching and packet switching in order to efficiently and separately handle both streaming and best-effort traffic generated in real-time applications. Furthermore the SDM technique is combined with Time Division Multiplexing "TDM" technique in the circuit switching part in order to increase path diversity, thus improving throughput while sharing communication resources among multiple connections. Combining these two techniques allows mitigating the poor resource usage inherent to circuit switching. In this way Quality of Service "QoS" is easily provided for the streaming traffic through the circuit-switched sub-router while the packet-switched sub-router handles best-effort traffic. The proposed hybrid router architectures were synthesized, placed and routed on an FPGA. Results show that a practicable Network-on-Chip "NoC" can be built using the proposed router architectures. 7×7 mesh NoCs were simulated in SystemC. Simulation results show that the probability of establishing paths through the NoC increases with the number of sub-channels and has its highest value when combining SDM with TDM, thereby significantly reducing contention in the NoC.

1. Introduction

Real-time applications have grown in complexity and require more and higher-power computing resources. These applications are then suitable to be run on parallel environments such as MultiProcessor Systems-on-Chip "MPSoC" platforms. However, application performance in an MPSoC platform strongly depends on the on-chip interconnection network used to carry communications between cores in the platform. Since Real-time applications generate both streaming and best-effort traffics, there is then a need for the on-chip interconnection network to provide QoS for the streaming traffic and data completion for the best-effort traffic.

Streaming traffic is best handled in circuit-switched network. Since communication resources are prereserved before any data transfer, QoS is thereby intrinsically supported. Circuit switching often leads to a poor usage of communication resources, since reserved resources for a transaction

are exclusively used by that transaction. For that reason, it is not suitable for best-effort traffic. Best-effort traffic is well handled in packet-switched network, however, because of its nondeterministic behavior; packet switching is not suitable for streaming traffic. To improve resource utilization in circuit-switched networks, time division multiplexing "TDM" is often used in order to share resources among multiple connections. TDM consists in dividing a channel in time intervals called time slots; multiple connections can therefore use a given channel by assigning a time slot to each connection. In TDM-based circuit-switched networks, consecutive time slots are reserved in consecutive links along the path between a source node and a destination node. Using TDM, a circuit-switched network can then handle both streaming and best-effort traffic. Reserved time slots are used to carry streaming traffic, while unreserved time slots are used to carry best-effort traffic [1]. However, providing QoS and sharing resources between streaming and best-effort traffic are hard and often lead to a complex design with huge hardware and power consumption overhead [2]. In packet-switched network, streaming and best-effort traffics are handled by either assigning priorities to each type of traffic, with streaming traffic having the highest priority, [3] or by reserving buffers or virtual channels "VCs" for carrying the streaming traffic, while the unreserved buffers are used to carry the best-effort traffic [4]. The first approach, while providing interesting results for varying traffic, cannot provide strong guarantees denoted "Hard QoS" for real-time applications. The second approach also leads to a complex design, with huge area and power consumption overhead depending on the number of buffers per input port.

In order to efficiently handle both streaming and best-effort traffic in an NoC, we propose a hybrid router which combines circuit switching with packet switching in order to separately and independently handle each type of traffic. The hybrid router then consists of two subrouters: a circuit switched subrouter and a packet switched subrouter. The circuit switched subrouter is responsible for handling streaming traffic, while the packet-switched subrouter is responsible for handling best-effort traffic. In this way, we ensure that each type of traffic is efficiently and suitably handled. In order to improve low resources usage inherent to circuit switching, the circuit-switched subrouter uses SDM and TDM techniques. The SDM technique that we use consists in having more than one link between two adjacent routers. In this way, concurrent data streams are physically separated, thereby increasing path diversity in the router and improving throughput. The TDM technique allows sharing physically separate links among multiple connections. We then define an SDM Channel as a set of links. Each link or subchannel is identified by a number. When the SDM-Channel is shared following the TDM technique, the SDM-Channel is thereby denoted SDM-TDM Channel.

Since circuit-switched subrouters are used to carry the streaming traffic, a path which consists of successive links between a source node and a destination node must first be established before transferring streaming traffic. This task is performed by the packet-switched subrouters by reserving an available subchannel in an SDM-Channel or by reserving a requested time slot at any subchannel in an SDM-TDM channel along the path between the source and the destination nodes. The packet-switched subrouter then configures the attached circuit-switched subrouter by indicating the subchannel to use in an SDM-Channel or by indicating the subchannel and the time slots to use in the SDM-TDM Channel for the concerned connection. When the transfer of the streaming traffic is completed, the circuit-switched subrouter notifies the attached packet-switched subrouter to release reserved resources used to carry the concerned streaming traffic.

In the proposed router architecture, each subrouter independently handles traffic. A node or tile, which can be a processing element "PE" or a storage element "SE", is connected to each subrouter as shown in Figures 1 and 2. When a PE needs to transfer best-effort traffic, it directly sends its "normal or data payload" best-effort packet to the attached packet-switched subrouter for routing through the network

hop by hop. When the PE needs to transfer streaming traffic, it first sends a "set-up" best-effort packet to the attached packet-switched subrouter. The set-up best-effort packet is responsible for reserving resources, thereby establishing a path between a source and destination nodes. When a set-up packet reaches its destination, an acknowledgment best-effort packet is generated and routed from destination to source through the packet-switched subnetwork. Upon receiving the acknowledgment packet, the source node then starts transferring streaming traffic, which is segmented in packets like cells in asynchronous transfer mode "ATM" networks. When the transfer of the streaming traffic is completed, the source node sends a teardown streaming packet along the established path whose purpose is to release reserved resources used for the concerned streaming traffic.

Since the circuit-switched subrouters and the packet-switched subrouters do not share links, and avoiding the use of the store-and-forwardstrategy, there is then no need to use FIFO buffers in the circuit-switched subrouter to store streaming packets unlike in [5]. This significantly reduces the area and power consumption of the router. Combining SDM and TDM techniques in a router allows taking advantages of the abundance of wires resulting from the increased level of CMOS circuits. We then have two degrees of freedom to optimize the router; one can increase either the number of subchannels in an SDM-TDM Channel or the number of time slots per subchannel. In both cases, the number of available channels increases in the network, thereby increasing the possibilities of establishing paths through the network.

The proposed hybrid router architectures were implemented in Verilog and synthesized on FPGA with different number of subchannels in an SDM-Channel and for different numbers of subchannels and time slots in an SDM-TDM Channel. Synthesis results show that increasing the number of subchannels in an SDM-Channel does not significantly impact the size of the router, while the clock frequency is only slightly reduced. When combining SDM and TDM techniques, increasing the number of subchannels, while maintaining fixed the number of time slots significantly impacts the size of the router, while the maximum clock frequency remains almost constant; increasing the number of time slots while maintaining fixed the number of subchannels does not significantly impact the size of the router while it significantly reduces the clock frequency. In order to evaluate the performance of the proposed architectures in terms of established paths through the network according to the number of set-up requests packets, three 7×7 2D meshes NoCs were simulated in SystemC under random uniform traffic and compared: an SDM-based hybrid NoC, a TDM-based hybrid NoC, and an SDM-TDM-based hybrid NoC. Simulation results show that combining SDM and TDM techniques in a router substantially increases the probability of establishing paths through the network, while this probability is appreciable in the SDM-based NoC and small in the TDM-based NoC.

The rest of the paper is organized as follows. Related work is reviewed in Section 2. Section 3 introduces the proposed router architectures. Section 4 discusses simulation

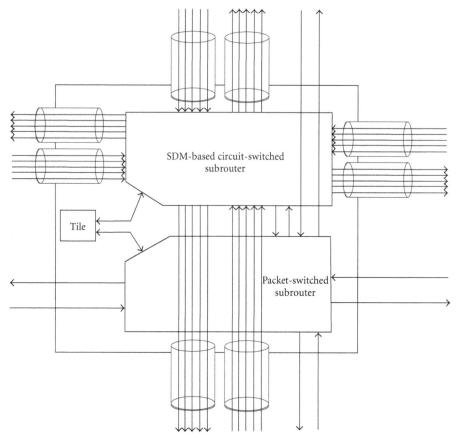

FIGURE 1: Hybrid SDM-based router architecture.

and synthesis results of the proposed router architectures. Finally, Conclusions are drawn in Section 5.

2. Related Work

Many hybrid NoCs have been proposed in the literature. Some of them deal with topological aspects by combining several topologies in a single NoC [6]; others combine different switching techniques in order to either provide "QoS" for streaming traffic while supporting best-effort traffic or reduce average packet latency in the network [5, 7, 8]. In this paper, we focus on hybrid NoCs which combine different switching techniques.

In [5], ÆTHEREAL NoC is presented. It consists of two disjoint subnetworks: a guaranteed service "GS" subnetwork and a best-effort "BE" subnetwork. The GS subnetwork is circuit-switched, while the BE network is packet-switched. TDM is used in order to share the same links between the BE and the GS subnetworks. Reserved time slots are used to carry the streaming traffic, while the unreserved time slots are used to carry the best-effort traffic. The BE subnetwork is responsible for establishing paths for the streaming traffic through the GS subnetwork by reserving time slots and thus configuring the GS subnetwork. For this purpose, four types of best-effort packets are used: a set-up packet which is responsible for establishing paths through the network by reserving time slots; an ACK packet which

is generated when a set-up packet reaches its destination; an NACK packet which is generated when a set-up packet fails and is responsible for releasing reserved time slots in the previous crossed packet-switched subrouters; a teardown packet which is responsible for releasing reserved resources when the streaming traffic transfer is completed. The GS subrouter uses the store-and-forward strategy, while the BE subnetwork uses the wormhole strategy. Despite the fact that TDM is simple to implement, the use of buffers in both GS and BE subrouters and the necessity of a memory device to store the configuration of the shared resources lead to a complex design with a huge area and power consumption overhead [9]. Our proposed hybrid router architecture uses a similar approach by having two distinct subrouters; however, our proposed circuit-switched subrouter is SDM or SDM-TDM based; by avoiding the use of the store and forward strategy, there is therefore no need to use FIFO buffers in the circuit-switched subrouter. However, when combining SDM with TDM, simple registers are required in order to schedule streaming packets to travels through the network in pipeline fashion at the reserved time slots. Furthermore, the two subrouters do not share links; this makes it easy to separately design and optimize each part of the router.

In [7], a hybrid NoC which uses a technique called hybrid circuit switching "HCS" is presented. It consists of a network design which removes the set-up time overhead in circuit-switched network by intermingling packet-switched

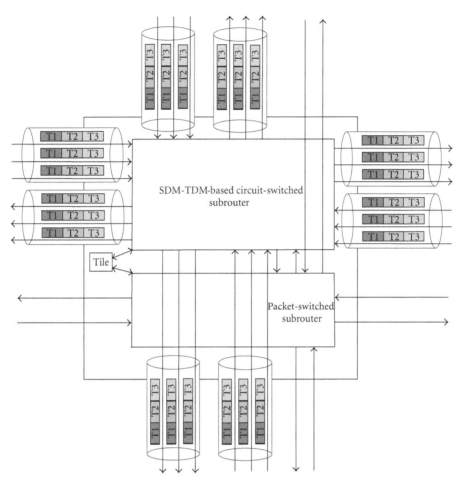

FIGURE 2: Hybrid SDM-TDM router architecture.

flits with circuit-switched flits. In this architecture, there is no need to wait for an acknowledgment that a circuit has been successfully established; data can then be injected immediately behind the circuit set-up request. If there is no unused resource, then the circuit-switched packet is transformed to a packet-switched packet and buffered; it will then keep its new state until it is delivered. With this approach, it is still difficult to provide hard "QoS" for streaming traffic.

The work presented in [8] is similar to the one presented in [7]. Since in packet switching it is very difficult to predict latency and throughput, sharing the same resource between packet-switched and circuit-switched networks makes it difficult to provide QoS for streaming traffic. In [9] is presented one of the first works using SDM in NoC in order to provide QoS for streaming traffic; however, this NoC does not handle best-effort traffic. In this work, a subset of links constituting an SDM-Channel are allocated to connections according to their bandwidth needs. The authors claim a gain in area and power consumption compared to the TDM approach but with the cost of a huge delay in the SDM switch which significantly limits the scalability of the approach. In the SDM variant that we propose, a connection can only acquire one link among links constituting the SDM-Channel. This significantly reduces the complexity of the

switch. Furthermore, we combine SDM with TDM in the circuit-switched subrouter while handling best-effort traffic in a packet-switched subrouter.

3. Proposed Router Architecture

3.1. Router Architecture. The proposed router architecture consists of two major components as illustrated in Figure 1: a packet-switched subrouter and an SDM-based circuit-switched subrouter. The two subrouters are distinct and independently handle traffic. The SDM-based circuit-switched subrouter is responsible for carrying streaming traffic and is configured by the packet-switched subrouter. The SDM-based circuit-switched subrouter notifies the packet-switched, when the transfer of the streaming traffic transfer is completed in order to release reserved resources. The packet-switched subrouter carries best-effort traffic.

The use of SDM technique, by allowing multiple simultaneous connections, mitigates the impact of the poor usage of resources in circuit switching, however the reserved resource (subchannel) is only used by one connection. To improve resource utilization, the SDM technique is combined with the TDM technique as shown in Figure 2. Therefore, a subchannel can be used by multiple connections. As seen previously, an SDM-Channel consists of a set of a given

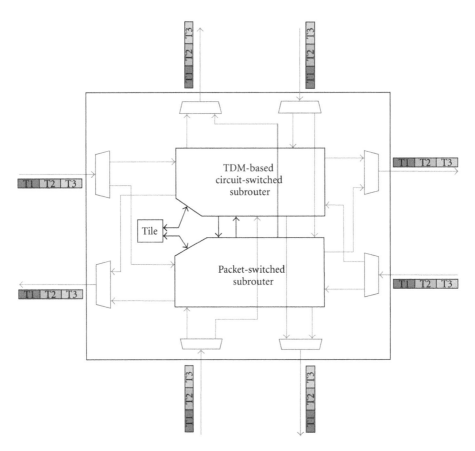

FIGURE 3: Hybrid TDM-based router architecture.

number of subchannels, while an SDM-TDM Channel is an SDM-Channel shared in time. Each subchannel is n-bits wide. In the SDM-based router, a connection can only acquire one subchannel and exclusively uses it until the end of the transaction, while in SDM-TDM-based router a connection can only acquire one subchannel but uses it at a specific time slot which is assigned to that connection; in the remaining time slots, the subchannel can be used by other connections.

The use of TDM allows sharing links between a circuit-switched subrouter and a packet-switched subrouter as shown in Figure 3. However, the scheduling constraint on time slots reservation which imposes that when a time slot T_i is reserved in a router the time slot $(T_i + 1)$ *modulo S* must be reserved in the next router along the path between a source and destination, and S is the number of time slots, constitutes a bottleneck in TDM-based network since it can limit significantly the number of established paths through the network and best-effort packets can experience a huge delay in the network when all time slots are reserved. Increasing the number of time slots does not solve efficiently this problem while increasing the size of the router. Since SDM allows increasing the probability of establishing paths through the network [10], therefore combining SDM with TDM can efficiently solve the problem of the scheduling on time slots reservation.

To illustrate the benefits of combining SDM and TDM techniques, let us consider the hybrid routers shown above. For the hybrid TDM-based router represented in Figure 3 with 3 time slots, a set-up request packet in any direction should have three possibilities to reserve a time slot; however, the scheduling constraint on time slot reservation imposes the time slot to reserve, thereby reducing the possibilities to choose a time slot from three to one. Let us now consider the SDM-based hybrid router shown in Figure 1 with 3 subchannels. Since there is no constraint on choosing a subchannel, a set-up request packet has three possibilities to choose a subchannel. Finally, let us consider the SDM-TDM-based hybrid router shown in Figure 2 with 3 subchannels in an SDM-Channel and each subchannel shared with 3 time slots. In this case taking in account the scheduling constraint on time slot reservation, there are three possibilities for the set-up request packet to choose the requested time slot. This means that, for the three considered cases, at a given time slot, the probability to establish a path in an SDM, and SDM-TDM-based hybrid NoC is three times greater than in the TDM-based router. However, the SDM-Channel can support up to 3 connections, while the SDM-TDM Channel can support up to fifteen connections.

3.2. Packet-Switched Subrouter. The packet-switched subrouter is responsible for routing best-effort traffic and

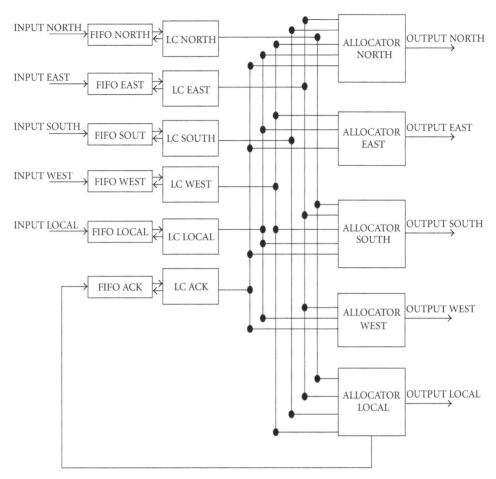

FIGURE 4: Packet-switched subrouter.

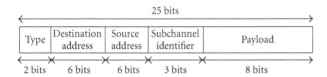

FIGURE 5: Best-effort packet format SDM-based router.

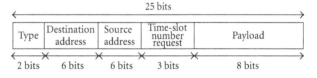

FIGURE 7: Best-effort packet format TDM-based router.

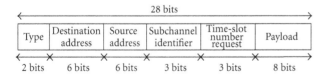

FIGURE 6: Best-effort packet format SDM-TDM router.

configuring the attached SDM- or SDM-TDM-based circuit-switched subrouter as shown in Figures 1 and 2. It uses *XY* deterministic routing algorithm with cutthrough as control flow strategy. Routing is distributed so that up to five packets can simultaneously be routed when they request different output channels.

The packet-switched subrouter consists of input FIFO buffers, link controllers, and allocators as shown in Figure 4.

The input FIFO buffers store the incoming best-effort packets. The link controllers are responsible for routing the best-effort. Depending to the destination address, they decide to which allocator the fetched packet should be sent. The link controller keeps the fetched packet in a register until it receives a signal from the allocator which indicates that the packet is successfully sent to the output port. This strategy ensures that no packet is lost in the network.

A best-effort packet consists of five fields for SDM- and TDM-based hybrid routers and six fields for the SDM-TDM-based router as shown in Figures 5, 6, and 7, respectively. Two bits indicating the type of the best-effort packet, the destination, and the source addresses are 6-bit wide, allowing building a 7×7 2D mesh NoC, the subchannel identifier and the requested time slot are 3-bit wide, and the payload is 8-bit wide. We define three types of best-effort packets in the

Type	Destination address	Source address	Subchannel identifier	Payload
2	(2, 3)	(2, 1)	0	0

FIGURE 8: Set-up packet node source (2,1).

Type	Destination address	Source address	Subchannel identifier	Payload
2	(2, 3)	(2, 1)	1	0

FIGURE 9: Incoming set-up packet allocator EAST (2,2).

proposed hybrid router.

(i) Set-up request best-effort packet.

(ii) ACK best-effort packet.

(iii) Normal best-effort packet.

The set-up request packet is responsible for reserving resources which are subchannels for the SDM-based router, subchannels and requested time slots for the SDM-TDM-based router, and requested time slots for the TDM-based router. The set-up request packet thereby establishes a path between a source node and a destination node. Its payload is zero and its type is 2. The ACK packet, which is generated when a set-up request packet reaches its destination, is responsible for notifying the source node that the path is successfully established. Its type is 1and its subchannel identifier, time slot request number, and payload fields are zero, respectively. The Normal best-effort packet carries the best-effort payload. Its type is 3and its subchannel identifier and time lot number request fields are zero respectively.

The allocators are responsible for forwarding best-effort packets to the output ports, reserving resources and configuring the attached circuit-switched subrouter. They first check the type of the best-effort packet. If the packet is an ACK or a normal packet, the allocator directly sends it to the output link without modifying it. If the best-effort packet is a set-up request packet, then the SDM-TDM-based router, allocator reserves an available requested time slot at any available subchannel in the SDM-TDM Channel in the concerned direction and builds a new set-up packet by replacing the fields subchannel number and time slot number request of the incoming packet by the number identifier of the reserved subchannel and the time slot number to request in the next hop. For the SDM-based router, the allocator only reserves a subchannel in the SDM-Channel and builds a new set-up packet by replacing the field subchannel identifier of the incoming set-up request packet by the number identifier of the reserved subchannel. In both cases, the value of the subchannel identifier in the incoming set-up request packet and the value of the subchannel in the outgoing set-up request packet are concatenated, and the result is stored in a register which is denoted "reg_identifier". Its MSB is the incoming subchannel and its LSB is the outgoing subchannel. Each subchannel has its own

Type	Destination address	Source address	Subchannel identifier	Payload
2	(2, 3)	(2, 1)	2	0

FIGURE 10: Outgoing set-up packet allocator EAST (2,2).

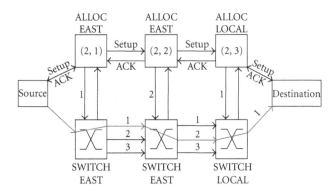

FIGURE 11: SDM path between source (2,1) and destination (2,3).

reg_identifier. This register helps to retrieve the subchannel to release when a NACK signal is received.

3.2.1. Set-up Path Phase in SDM-Based Router. To illustrate the process of path establishment in the SDM-based router, let us consider an SDM-channel consisting of 3 subchannels; the subchannel identifiers are 1, 2, and 3, respectively. Let us consider a set-up path phase between a source node attached to the router with coordinates (2,1) and a destination node attached to the router with coordinates (2,3) as shown in Figure 11. The set-up request packet from the source node is given in Figure 8; the fields subchannel identifier and payload are zero.

At the router (2,1), the allocator EAST, reserves an available subchannel in the SDM-Channel output port. Suppose that the reserved subchannel is the subchannel 1, the allocator then builds the outgoing set-up request packet with the identifier of the reserved subchannel and concatenates the value of the subchannel identifier in the incoming set-up request packet with the value of the channel identifier in the outgoing set-up request packet. It then stores this value in the *register identifier* of subchannel 1 which is the outgoing subchannel. At the router (2,2), let us assume that subchannel 1 in this allocator is already reserved by another set-up request packet and the remaining subchannels are available. The allocator will then reserve for example subchannel 3. It builds the outgoing set-up request packet (Figure 10) and concatenates the value of subchannel identifier in the incoming set-up packet (Figure 9) with the value of the subchannel identifier in the outgoing set-up request packet and stores this value in the *register identifier* of subchannel identifier 2.

At the router (2,3), the allocator LOCAL reserves the subchannel if it is free. It then generates an ACK packet, which is routed through the packet-switched subnetwork from the destination to the source. Upon reception of

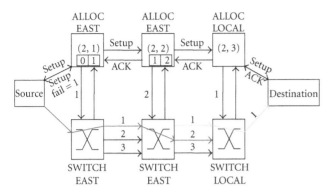

FIGURE 12: Failed path establishment in SDM-based router.

Type	Dest addr	Src addr	Subchannel identifier	Time-slot number request	Payload
1	(2, 3)	(2, 1)	0	0	0

FIGURE 13: SDM-TDM set-up packet node source (2,1).

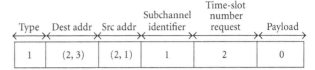

Type	Dest addr	Src addr	Subchannel identifier	Time-slot number request	Payload
1	(2, 3)	(2, 1)	1	2	0

FIGURE 14: SDM-RDM outgoing set-up packet allocator EAST (2,1).

Type	Dest addr	Src addr	Subchannel identifier	Time-slot number request	Payload
1	(2, 3)	(2, 1)	3	3	0

FIGURE 15: SEM-TDM outgoing set-up packet allocator EAST (2,2).

the ACK packet, the source node then starts transferring streaming traffic. For simplicity, we represent in Figure 11 this process with only the concerned allocators and switches.

When a set-up request packet fails to reserve a subchannel in a hop, the NACK signal is generated and propagates to all previous crossed packet subrouter in order to release the reserved subchannels by the failed set-up request packet. The NACK signal at the router where it fails is equal to the subchannel value contained in the incoming set-up request packet; it indicates the subchannel to release in the previous packet-switched subrouter. At the previous subrouter, the value of the NACK to propagate is the MSB of the register identifier associated to the subchannel indicated by the NACK value. Figure 12 shows the NACK signals for the considered example when the set-up request packet fails at the allocator LOCAL at router (2,3).

3.2.2. Set-up Path Phase in SDM-TDM-Based Router. Let us now consider an SDM-TDM Channel consisting of 3 subchannels and 3 time slots. The subchannel identifiers are 1, 2, and 3, respectively, and the time slots numbers are also 1, 2, and 3, respectively. We considerm as in the previous example, a set-up path phase between a source node attached to the router with coordinates (2,1) and a destination node attached to the router with coordinates (2,3). The set-up request packet from the source node is given in Figure 13; the fields' subchannel identifier, time slot number request, and payload are set to zero, respectively.

At the router (2,1), the allocator EAST reserves an available time slot in any available subchannel in the SDM-TDM Channel output port and indicates to the source the time slot from which to transfer streaming packet following the relationship $(T_i - 1)$ *modulo S*, where T_i is the reserved time slot and S the number of time slots. Let us suppose that time slot 1 is reserved at the subchannel

1, the allocator then builds the outgoing set-up request packet with the reserved subchannel identifier and the time slot to request in the next hop (Figure 14), therefore the time slot number 3 is the time slot at which the source node injects streaming packets in the network. The allocator concatenates the incoming subchannel with the outgoing subchannel in a register denoted "reg_identifier_time1". Since there are three time slots per sub-subchannel, we thereby define reg_identifier_time1, reg_identifier_time2, and reg_identifier_time3 for each subchannel. These registers allow easy retrieval of the subchannel where the specified time slot must be released if a NACK signal is received.

At the router (2,2), let us assume that time slot number 2 at subchannel 1 and time slot number 2 at subchannel 2 are already reserved by other set-up request packets; the allocator will then reserve the time slot number 2 at the subchannel 3. The outgoing set-up request packet is shown in Figure 15. It concatenates the incoming subchannel and the outgoing subchannel in the reg_identifier_time2 associated to the subchannel identifier 3.

At the router (2,3), the allocator LOCAL reserves the requested time slot at the unique subchannel; in this case, it is the time slot number 3. The ACK packet is then generated and routed through the packet-switched subrouter from the destination to the source. Upon reception of the ACK packet, the source node then starts transferring streaming data at the time slot specified by the allocator EAST at router (2,1). Figure 16 shows the established path and the scheduling of time slots.

When a set-up request packet failed to reserve time slot at any subchannel, the NACK signal is sent back and propagated to all previous packet-switched subrouters crossed by the failed set-up request packet. The NACK indicates the subchannel in which the specified time slot number has to be released. For illustration purposes, let us suppose for the considered example that the set-up request packet fails to reserve the time slot number 3 at the allocator LOCAL (2,3). The allocator LOCAL will then issue the NACK signal indicating to the router (2,2) to release time slot number 2 at the subchannel value contained in the incoming set-up packet, which is 3 in our case. At the router (2,2),

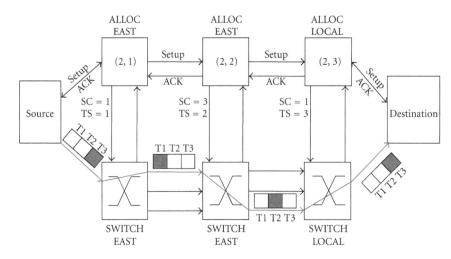

FIGURE 16: SDM-TDM path between source (2,1) and destination (2,3).

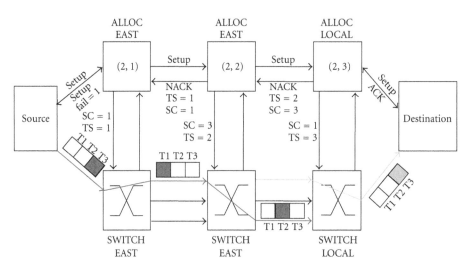

FIGURE 17: Failed path establishment in SDM-TDM-based NoC.

upon reception of the NACK, it releases specified resources and computes the NACK to send back to the router using the MSB of the reg_identifier_time2 of the subchannel 3. According to this register, the NACK to router (2,1) directs to release the time slot number 1 at the subchannel 1. At router (2,1), the allocator releases the reserved resources and notifies the source node that the set-up request packet failed. This process is shown in Figure 17.

3.3. SDM-Based Circuit-Switched Subrouter. The SDM-based circuit-switched subrouter is responsible for carrying streaming traffic. It has five bidirectional ports. Four bidirectional ports are SDM-based and are used to connect the circuit-switched subrouter to the four adjacent circuit-switched subrouters, and the fifth bidirectional port, which consists of a subchannel, is used to connect the SDM-based circuit-switched subrouter to the local tile as shown in Figure 18. This port is a subchannel since we assume that the local tile cannot receive more than one packet simulta-

neously. The SDM-Channel consists of a given number of subchannels. Each subchannel is N-bit wide. The streaming traffic is organized in packets like cells in ATM networks. The streaming packet format is shown in Figure 19.

The header indicates the validity of the carried payload. A header value 1 indicates that the carried payload is valid, and a header value 2 indicates that the payload is not valid. The header is used in order to release or maintain reserved resources. When the value of the header is zero, no action is taken. When this value is 1, it means that the transfer of the streaming traffic is ongoing. When a header value 2 is detected, a signal is sent to the attached packet-switched allocator to release the reserved resources. The SDM-based circuit-switched subrouter consists of five switches and header detectors. The switch consists of multiplexers. Since switches are configured by the packet-switched allocators, the use of an *XY* deterministic routing algorithm in the packet-switched subrouter which prevents best-effort packets to return in the direction where they come from determines the number of input ports of each switch.

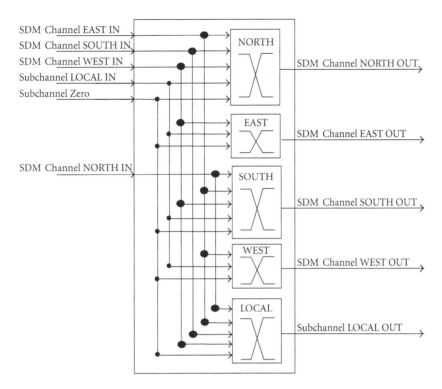

FIGURE 18: SDM-based circuit-switched subrouter.

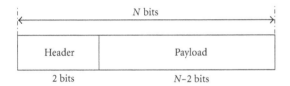

FIGURE 19: Streaming packet format.

In *XY* deterministic routing algorithm, a packet is routed first in the X dimension until it reaches its X-coordinate destination, then it begins to be routed in Y dimension until it reaches its Y-coordinate destination. Since we impose that packets coming from a given direction cannot return in the same direction, following the *XY* deterministic routing algorithm packets coming from EAST direction can only be routed either towards WEST, NORTH, SOUTH, or LOCAL directions, while packets from NORTH can only be routed either towards SOUTH or LOCAL directions. Thus, packets travelling in X-direction (From EAST or WEST) and packets from local tile can be routed in four possible directions, while packets travelling in Y-direction (From NORTH or SOUTH) can only be routed in two possible directions. This implies that the allocator in EAST direction (Figure 4) can only route packets coming from Input WEST and from input local. The switch attached to this allocator can then carry streaming packets either from the "SDM Channel WEST IN" or from the "subchannel LOCAL IN" as shown in Figure 18. The input port "Subchannel Zero" is used by default for all unreserved output subchannels.

For illustration purposes, let us consider the switch in direction EAST. According to Figure 18, it has three input ports; these are "SDM-Channel WEST IN", "subchannel LOCAL IN", and "Subchannel Zero". We consider an SDM-Channel consisting of 3 subchannels. The bloc diagram of such switch is shown in Figure 20, and its implementation is shown in Figure 21.

The signals "Sel1", "Sel2", and "Sel3" are provided by the allocator EAST of the attached packet-switched subrouter. The signals "Rel1", "Rel2", and "Rel3" are provided by the header extractor which is attached to the three subchannels.

The SDM-based circuit-switched subrouter is entirely combinational. Once a path is established, communication latency is only determined by the serialization time to send the entire streaming message. QoS is then easily provided. Latency and throughput can be configured by inserting pipelines between circuit-switched subrouters. However, each reserved subchannel is only used by one connection; this limits the scalability of the proposed approach. We then combine SDM with TDM in order to share each subchannel among multiple connections.

3.4. SDM-TDM-Based Circuit-Switched Subrouter. The SDM-TDM based circuit-switched subrouter has the same configuration as the SDM-based circuit-switched subrouter, however it contains additional input registers which allow scheduling the streaming packets in their trip through the network as illustrated in Figure 16. The scheduling of time slots reservation ensures that streaming packets are injected in the network in such way that they do not

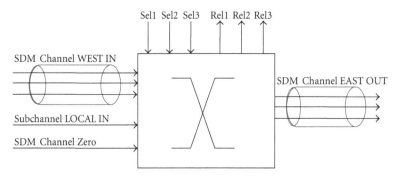

FIGURE 20: Block diagram SDM switch EAST.

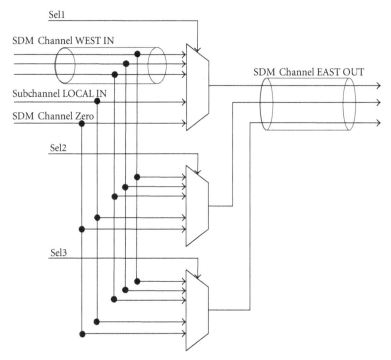

FIGURE 21: SDM switch EAST implementation.

collide. Figure 22 shows the bloc diagram of the SDM-TDM circuit-switched subrouter, and Figure 23 shows the bloc diagram of the switch in direction NORTH and the attached packet-switched allocator.

4. Results

4.1. Simulation Results. The proposed hybrid routers were implemented in SystemC RTL. 7×7 2D mesh NoCs were built and simulated in SystemC under synthetic traffic. We evaluate the performance of the NoCs in terms of number of simultaneous established connections (paths) through the network when all tiles in the network attempt to establish a path in the network. This worst case scenario leads to a high level of contention to occur in the network. The number of established paths in the network reflects the capacity of the network to face congestion. The fraction of set-up request

packets which reach their destination reflects the probability of establishing a path in the network. A higher probability of establishing paths implies a higher number of applications to be run simultaneously in the network, thereby significantly improving the performances of the applications.

Three NoC platforms are compared; the SDM-based hybrid NoC, the SDM-TDM-based hybrid NoC, and the TDM-based hybrid NoC. These platforms are evaluated with the same traffic pattern in order to objectively compare them in terms of established paths according to the number of set-up request packets sent through the network. The destination nodes are generated using a uniform distribution. These simulations were performed with 4-packet deep FIFO buffer per input port for the packet-switched subrouter, while a different number of channels in an SDM-Channel, an SDM-TDM Channel, and TDM Channel are considered.

For the SDM-based NoC, the number of established paths through the network for 3, 4, and 5 subchannels in

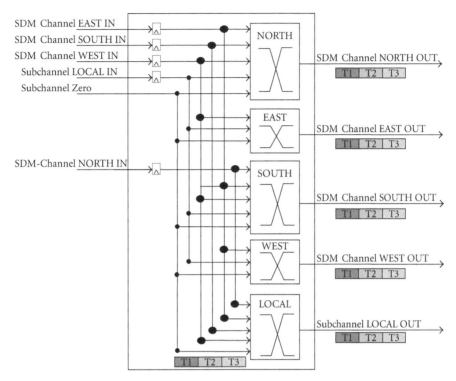

FIGURE 22: SDM-TDM circuit-switched subrouter.

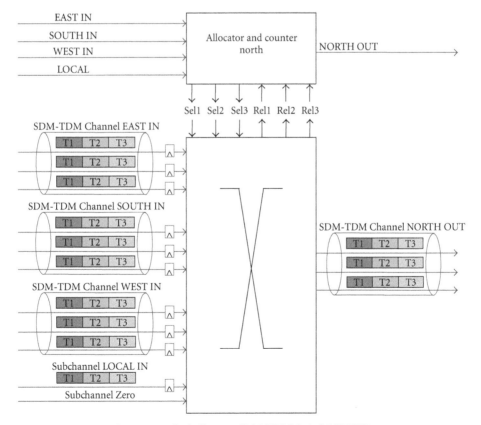

FIGURE 23: Block diagram SDM-TDM Switch NORTH.

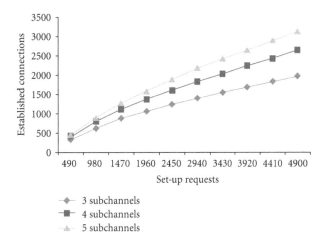

FIGURE 24: Established connections in 7×7 SDM-NoC.

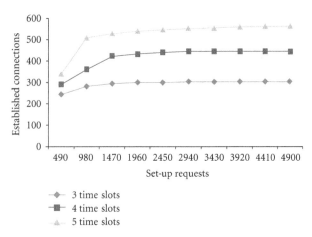

FIGURE 26: Established connections in 7×7 TDM NoC.

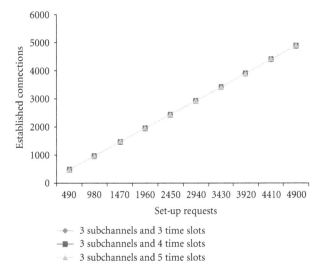

FIGURE 25: Established connections in 7×7 SDM-TDM NoC.

an SDM-Channel is given in Figure 24. For the SDM-TDM-based NoC, the number of established connections for 3 subchannels and 3, 4, and 5 time slots is given in Figure 25. Figure 26 gives the number of established connections in an TDM-based NoC for 3, 4, and 5 time slots in a channel.

For the SDM-based NoC, simulation results show that the number of established connections increases with the number of subchannels in an SDM-Channel. For 3 subchannels in an SDM-Channel, up to 46% of the set-up request packets sent in the network successfully reach their destination; for 4 and 5 subchannels in a SDM-Channel, up to 61% and 72% of set-up request packets sent in the network reach their destination, respectively.

For the SDM-TDM-based NoC, considering only 3 subchannels and 3, 4, and 5 time slots, Figure 25 shows that up to 98% of set-up request packets sent in the network successfully reach their destination in the three cases. For the TDM-based NoC, simulation results in Figure 26 show that for 3, 4, and 5 time slots up to 17%, 22%, and 27%, respectively, of the set-up request sent in the network

reach their destination. The poor performance of the TDM-based NoC related to the number of established paths is essentially due to the scheduling constraint on time slot reservation, which is a bottleneck for TDM-based NoC. Increasing the number of time slots does not efficiently solve the problem while increasing the size of the router. Since there is no constraint on resource reservation in the SDM-based NoC and by offering an increased path diversity, the SDM-based NoC has an appreciable probability of establishing connections through the network, however since each reserved resource is exclusively used by one connection until the end of the transaction, there is still a poor usage of subchannel, although overall the poor usage of resource is mitigated by the number of subchannels in the SDM-Channel. The SDM-TDM NoC solves this problem by allowing increased path diversity, while sharing subchannels among multiple connections, thereby performing the highest probability of path establishment in the network.

The ability of the proposed hybrid routers to handle best-effort traffic is evaluated by means of the average latency and average throughput according to the injection best-effort traffic rate. To evaluate the average latency for the best-effort traffic, we consider that 25 tiles are injecting best-effort traffic, while 24 tiles are transferring streaming traffic.

Figure 27 shows the average latency of the best-effort traffic for the three hybrid NoCs. The TDM-based NoC has the smallest average latency compared to the SDM- and SDM-TDM-based NoCs. This is due to the fact that the TDM-based NoC has the smallest probability of path establishment; it in results a small number of established paths, therefore a small number of ACK best-effort packets, thereby impacting weakly the total number of the best-effort packets in the network. Whereas the SDM-TDM-based NoC allows the highest number of established paths, it results in a higher number of ACK best-effort packets, which significantly impact the total number of best-effort packets in the network, thereby increasing the average latency. However, the three hybrid routers begin to saturate beyond an injection traffic rate of 0.1.

The average time to establish paths through the SDM-based NoC is reported in Table 1. As noticed previously, we

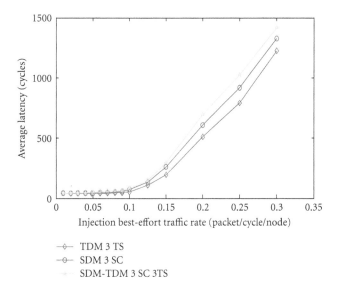

FIGURE 27: Average latency.

TABLE 1: Average time to set up a path in a 7×7 SDM-based NoC.

Injection best-effort traffic rate [Packet/Cycle/Node]	Average establishment path time in an SDM-based NoC [Cycles] Number of subchannels		
	3	4	5
0.01	96.18	96.43	96.44
0.02	96.28	96.36	96.48
0.03	96.33	96.42	96.46
0.04	96.47	96.48	96.61
0.05	96.64	96.68	96.77
0.06	96.98	97.11	97.14
0.08	97.47	97.67	97.47
0.1	98.41	98.56	98.59

consider for this experiment that 25 tiles are transferring best-effort traffic, while 24 are transferring streaming traffic. Table 1 shows that the average time to establish paths, which is the average latency before a tile starts to transfer the streaming traffic, is not greatly impacted by the best-effort traffic load. By imposing a minimum Manhattan distance of 5 hops between a given pair of source and destination, the average time to establish paths through an SDM-based NoC is around 96 cycles and does not depend on the number of subchannels in an SDM-Channel.

4.2. Synthesis Results. The proposed hybrid router architectures have also been implemented in Verilog HDL and synthesized in FPGA from Altera. For the SDM- and the SDM-TDM-based routers, the packet-switched subrouter has a 4-packet deep FIFO buffer per input port. For the SDM-based router, the packet-switched ports are 25-bit wide and the subchannels in SDM-Channels are 18-bit wide (2 control bits + 16 bits payload).

TABLE 2: Synthesis results SDM router (18 bits per subchannel).

SDM Number of channels	STRATIX III EP3SL340F	
	Total logic element utilization	Frequency [MHz]
3 subchannels	4590	200
4 subchannels	5307	190
5 subchannels	6432	186

TABLE 3: Synthesis results SDM router (10 bits per subchannel).

SDM Number of channels	STRATIX III EP3SL340F	
	Total logic element utilization	Frequency [MHz]
3 subchannels	3867	200
4 subchannels	4648	190
5 subchannels	5392	186

TABLE 4: Synthesis results TDM router.

TDM Number of channels	STRATIX III EP3SL340F	
	Total logic element utilization	Frequency [MHz]
3 time slots	5934	152
4 time slots	6381	123
5 time slots	6895	113

TABLE 5: Synthesis results SDM-TDM router (3 SC, 3, 4, 5 TS).

SDM-TDM Number of channels	STRATIX III EP3SL340F	
	Total logic element utilization	Frequency [MHz]
3 subchannels and 3 time slots	6057	160
3 subchannels and 4 time slots	7013	150
3 subchannels and 5 time slots	7841	145

TABLE 6: Synthesis results SDM-TDM router (3 TC, 3, 4, 5 SC).

SDM-TDM Number of channels	STRATIX III EP3SL340F	
	Total logic element utilization	Frequency [MHz]
3 subchannels and 3 time slots	6057	160
4 subchannels and 3 time slots	7652	159
5 subchannels and 3 time slots	9194	158

Table 2 reports synthesis results for 3, 4, and 5 subchannels in an SDM-Channel. Since the packet-switched and the circuit-switched subrouters separately handle traffic, they can be designed and optimized separately. Thus, Table 3 shows how reducing the width of subchannels from 18 bits to 10 bits impacts the overall size of the router.

For the TDM-based router, the packet-switched router has an 8-packet deep FIFO per input port, while the circuit-switched has a 4-packet deep FIFO buffer per input port. The ports are 25-bit wide. Synthesis results for the TDM-based router are reported in Table 4 for 3, 4, and 5 time

TABLE 7: Synthesis results 4×4 SDM-based NoC.

Number of channels	4×4 SDM NoC				
Subchannels	Combinational	Combinational with register	Registers	Total logic utilization	Frequency
3	19564	29499	18696	67759/270400 (25%)	124 MHz
4	24953	33032	18978	76963/270400 (28%)	100 MHz
5	30001	36473	19036	85531/270400 (32%)	82 MHz

TABLE 8: Synthesis results 4×4 SDM-TDM based NoC.

Number of channels		4×4 SDM-TDM NoC				
Subchannels	Time Slots	Combinational	Combinational with register	Registers	Total logic utilization	Frequency
3	3	24383	38134	22771	85288/270400 (32%)	85 MHz
4	3	32996	47811	22862	103669/270400 (38%)	78 MHz
5	3	37362	55222	22942	111526/270400 (43%)	70 MHz

slots, respectively. For the SDM-TDM-based router, synthesis results are reported for a various number of subchannels and time. Packet-switched ports are 28-bit wide, and the subchannels are 18-bit wide. Synthesis results are reported in Tables 5 and 6.

Results from Tables 2, 4, 5, and 6 show that for a given number of channels (subchannels and time slots) the SDM-based router has better performances in terms of maximum clock frequency and the total logic used in the FPGA compared to the two other hybrid routers. This is due to its simplicity, since the critical path is confined in the packet-switched subrouter, while the circuit-switched subrouter is entirely combinational. Increasing by one, the number of the subchannels in an SDM-Channel results in the increase of 16% in the router size, while the clock frequency is slightly reduced.

Furthermore, results from Table 2 show the impact of reducing the width of the subchannels from 18 bits to 10 bits on the size of the router, while the clock frequency is not impacted. Thus, optimization for a high clock frequency concerns only the packet-switched subrouter, while optimization of the size of the router concerns essentially the circuit-switched subrouter.

For the TDM-based hybrid router, Table 4 shows that it has the smallest clock frequency compared to the two other hybrid routers; this is essentially due to the fact that channels are shared between the two subrouters and the use of buffers in both subrouters, which increases the complexity of the router, thereby lengthening the critical path and increasing the size of the router. Increasing by one, the number of time slots leads to an increase of 7% in the router size, while the clock frequency is significantly reduced.

However, the size of the TDM-based router grows slower than the sizes of the SDM- and SDM-TDM-based routers when increasing the number of the channels by one. It means that, compared to the SDM-based router, there is a subchannels number threshold from which the size of the SDM-based router becomes greater than the size of the TDM-based router.

For the SDM-TDM based subrouter, it has the highest overhead in the total logic used in the FPGA; this is the cost of combining the two techniques in a single router. However, it offers appreciable clock frequencies compared to the TDM-based router, since the packet-switched and the circuit-switched subrouters do not share the same channels and independently handle traffic. Furthermore, the circuit-switched subrouter has just simple registers instead of FIFO buffers. This eases the control of the critical path in the design of the router. Optimization can be done separately in order to either reduce the size or increase the clock frequency of the router. The SDM-TDM approach gives more flexibility since it allows optimization in either space or time. Table 5 shows that keeping the number of subchannel fixed while increasing the number of the time slots implies an increase by 16% in the size of the router, whereas results from Table 6 show that maintaining constant the number of time slots while increasing the number of the subchannels leads to an increase of 20% in the size of the router, while the clock frequency remains practically constant.

Thus, there is a tradeoff between an optimal number of subchannels and the number of time slots according to the constraint on the clock frequency and the area of the router.

The proposed hybrid routers were used to build complete 4×4 2D mesh NoC on the Stratix III EP3SL340F FPGA device. Synthesis results for the SDM-based NoC, SDM-TDM-based NoC, and TDM-based NoC are shown in Tables 7, 8, and 9, respectively. These results show the impact of the interconnecting links on the frequency and area.

The impact of the interconnecting links on the frequency and the area of the TDM-based NoC is small compared to the SDM- and SDM-TDM-based NoCs. This is essentially due to the fact that links in the TDM-based router are shared between the best-effort and the streaming traffic, thereby reducing the link overhead between routers. However, The SDM-based NoC and the SDM-TDM based NoC, although the interconnecting link overhead, take advantages of the abundance of wires resulting from the high-level integration of CMOS circuits. The impact of interconnecting link can be mitigated by reducing the width of subchannels as shown in Tables 2 and 3, thereby reducing the area of the complete NoC.

TABLE 9: Synthesis results 4×4 TDM-based NoC.

| Number of channels | 4×4 TDM NoC | | | | |
Time slots	Combinational	Combinational with register	Registers	Total logic utilization	Frequency
3	18733	38540	29961	87234/270400 (32%)	80 MHz
4	20604	40040	30781	91425/270400 (34%)	72 MHz
5	21881	45031	31776	98688/270400 (37%)	66 MHz

For the total logic utilization in the FPGA, the SDM-TDM-based NoC has the highest percentage of resource utilization, while the SDM-based NoC has the smallest percentage of resource utilization. The total logic utilization of the NoC is not directly proportional to the router size, since for the 4×4 2D mesh, only 4 routers, located in the center of the mesh, are fully connected, while the routers at the edges have port in either one or two directions that are not connected. These unconnected ports are removed, thereby reducing the size of these routers.

5. Conclusions

In this paper, a hybrid router architecture which combines an SDM-based circuit switching with packet switching for on-chip networks is proposed. Since real-time applications can generate both streaming and best-effort traffic, instead of handling both traffics in a complex packet-switched or circuit-switched router, we propose to separately and efficiently handle each type of traffic in a suitable subrouter. The SDM-based circuit-switched subrouter is responsible for handling streaming traffic, while a packet-switched subrouter is responsible for handling the best-effort traffic. Handling the streaming traffic in a circuit-switched subrouter, QoS in terms of minimum throughput, and maximum latency is easily guaranteed.

The SDM approach used in the circuit-switched subrouter allows increased path diversity, improving thereby throughput while mitigating the low resources usage inherent to circuit switching. To improve usage of resources in the proposed router architecture, the SDM technique is combined with TDM technique, thereby allowing shared subchannels among multiple connections. The proposed hybrid router architectures were implemented in SystemC RTL and Verilog. 7×7 2D mesh NoCs were simulated in SystemC and compared to a TDM-based NoC. Simulation results show that increasing the number of subchannels in SDM-Channel or in an SDM-TDM Channel increases the probability of establishing connections in the network. Furthermore, by combining the SDM with the TDM, the NoC offers the highest probability of establishing paths through the network. Synthesis results on an FPGA show that increasing the number of subchannels in an SDM-channel has a slight overhead in router area, but does not greatly impact the maximum clock frequency compared to the TDM-based hybrid NoC. However, when SDM and TDM techniques are combined in a single router, the size of the router significantly increases according to the number of subchannels and time slots in an SDM-TDM Channel while

reaching an appreciable clock frequency. Combining SDM and TDM in a single router offers more flexibility since optimization can be made either in space or in time. There is thus an opportunity to take advantage of partial dynamic reconfiguration in order to dynamically add additional subchannels or time slots in an SDM-TDM Channel in presence of heavy traffic and congestion.

References

[1] G. De Micheli and L. Benini, *Networks On Chips: Technology and Tools*, Morgan Kaufman, 2006.

[2] M. A. A. Faruque and J. Henkel, "QoS-supported on-chip communication for multi-processors," *International Journal of Parallel Programming*, vol. 36, no. 1, pp. 114–139, 2008.

[3] E. Bolotin, I. Cidon, R. Ginosar, and A. Kolodny, "QNoC: QoS architecture and design process for network on chip," *Journal of Systems Architecture*, vol. 50, no. 2-3, pp. 105–128, 2004.

[4] N. Kavaldjiev, G. J. M. Smit, P. G. Jansen, and P. T. Wolkotte, "A virtual channel network-on-chip for GT and BE traffic," in *Proceedings of the IEEE Computer Society Annual Symposium on Emerging VLSI Technologies and Architectures*, pp. 211–216, March 2006.

[5] K. Goossens, J. Dielissen, and A. Radulescu, "ÆTHEREAL network-on-chip concepts," *IEEE Design and Test of computers*, vol. 22, no. 5, pp. 414–421, 2005.

[6] S. Bourduas and Z. Zilic, "A hybrid ring/mesh interconnect for network-on-chip using hierarchical rings for global routing," in *Proceedings of the 1st International Symposium on Networks-on-Chip (NOCS '07)*, pp. 195–202, May 2007.

[7] N. E. Jerger, M. Lipasti, and L. S. Peh, "Circuit-switched coherence," *IEEE Computer Architecture Letters*, vol. 6, no. 1, pp. 5–8, 2007.

[8] M. Modarressi, H. Sarbazi-Azad, and M. Arjomand, "A hybrid packet-circuit switched on-chip network based on SDM," in *Proceedings of the Design, Automation and Test in Europe Conference and Exhibition (DATE '09)*, pp. 566–569, April 2009.

[9] A. Leroy, P. Marchal, A. Shickova, F. Catthoor, F. Robert, and D. Verkest, "Spatial division multiplexing: a novel approach for guaranteed throughput on NoCs," in *Proceedings of the 3rd IEEE/ACM/IFIP International Conference on Hardware/Software Codesign and Systems Synthesis (CODES+ISSS '05)*, pp. 81–86, September 2005.

[10] A. K. Lusala and J.-D. Legat, "A hybrid router combining SDM-based circuit switching with packet switching for On-Chip networks," in *Proceedings of the International conference on Reconfigurable Computing and FPGAs (ReConFig '10)*, pp. 340–345, Quintano Roo, Mexico, December 2010.

13

Fully Pipelined Implementation of Tree-Search Algorithms for Vector Precoding

Maitane Barrenechea, Mikel Mendicute, and Egoitz Arruti

Department of Electronics and Computer Science, University of Mondragon, 20500 Mondragon, Spain

Correspondence should be addressed to Maitane Barrenechea; mbarrenetxea@mondragon.edu

Academic Editor: João Cardoso

The nonlinear vector precoding (VP) technique has been proven to achieve close-to-capacity performance in multiuser multiple-input multiple-output (MIMO) downlink channels. The performance benefit with respect to its linear counterparts stems from the incorporation of a perturbation signal that reduces the power of the precoded signal. The computation of this perturbation element, which is known to belong in the class of NP-hard problems, is the main aspect that hinders the hardware implementation of VP systems. To this respect, several tree-search algorithms have been proposed for the closest-point lattice search problem in VP systems hitherto. Nevertheless, the optimality of these algorithms has been assessed mainly in terms of error-rate performance and computational complexity, leaving the hardware cost of their implementation an open issue. The parallel data-processing capabilities of field-programmable gate arrays (FPGA) and the loopless nature of the proposed tree-search algorithms have enabled an efficient hardware implementation of a VP system that provides a very high data-processing throughput.

1. Introduction

Since the presentation of the vector precoding (VP) technique [1] for data transmission over the multiuser broadcast channel, many algorithms have been proposed in the literature to replace the computationally intractable exhaustive search defined in the original description of the algorithm. To this respect, lattice reduction approaches have been widely used as a means to compute a suboptimum perturbation vector with a moderate complexity. The key idea of lattice-reduction techniques relies on the usage of an equivalent and more advantageous set of basis vectors to allow for the suboptimal resolution of the exhaustive search problem by means of a simple rounding operation. This method is used in [2], where the Lenstra-Lenstra-Lovász (LLL) reduction algorithm [3] is used to yield the Babai's approximate closest-point solution [4]. Similar approaches can be found in [5–7]. Despite achieving full diversity order in VP systems [8, 9], the performance degradation caused by the quantization error due to the rounding operation still remains. Moreover, many lattice reduction algorithms have a considerable computational complexity, which poses many challenges to a prospective hardware implementation.

An appropriate perturbation vector can also be found by searching for the optimum solution within a subset of candidate vectors. These approaches, also known as tree-search techniques, perform a traversal through a tree of hypotheses with the aim of finding a suitable perturbation vector.

In spite of the high volume of research work published around the topic of precoding algorithms, the issues raised by their implementation have not been given the same attention. Some of the few publications on this area, such as [10–12], describe precoding systems that either have a considerable complexity in terms of allocated hardware resources or provide a rather low data transmission rate.

Despite the lack of published research in the area of hardware architectures for precoding algorithms, the implementation issues of tree-search schemes in MIMO detection scenarios have been widely studied. For example, the field programmable gate array (FPGA) implementation of the fixed-complexity sphere decoder (FSD) detector has been analyzed in [13–15], whereas the hardware architecture of the K-best tree search considering a real equivalent model was researched in [16–21]. Moreover, the implementation of a K-best detector with suboptimum complex-plane enumeration was performed in [22, 23]. A thorough review of K-best tree-search implementation techniques was carried out in [24]. The adaptation of these tree-search schemes to precoding systems implies many variations with respect to the original description of the algorithms. Even if many lessons can be learned from the hardware architecture of tree-search techniues for point-to-point MIMO systems, the peculiarities of the precoding scenario render the results of the aforementioned publications inadequate for the current research topic.

Consequently, this contribution addresses the high-throughput implementation of fixed-complexity tree-search algorithms for VP systems. More specifically, two state-of-the-art tree-search algorithms that allow for the parallel processing of the tree branches have been implemented on a Xilinx Virtex VI FPGA following a rapid-prototyping methodology. In order to achieve a high throughput, both schemes operate in the complex plane and have been implemented in a fully-pipelined fashion providing one output per cycle.

This contribution is organized as follows: in Section 2 the system model is introduced, followed by a short review provided in Section 3 on the noniterative tree-search algorithms to be implemented. Next, the general hardware architecture of the data perturbation process is outlined in Section 4 whereas the specific features of the K-best and FSE modules are analyzed in Sections 5 and 6, respectively. An analysis on the tree-search parameters for both techniques is performed in Section 7 and the hardware implementation results are shown in Section 8. Finally, some concluding remarks are drawn in Section 9.

Notation. In the remainder of the paper the matrix transpose and conjugate transpose are represented by $(\cdot)^T$ and $(\cdot)^H$, respectively. We use $\mathbf{I}_N$ to represent the $N \times N$ identity matrix and $\text{Mod}(\cdot)$ to denote the modulo operator. The set of Gaussian integers of dimension N, namely, $\mathbb{Z}^N + j\mathbb{Z}^N$, is represented by $\mathbb{CZ}^N$.

2. System Model

Consider the multiuser broadcast channel with M_T antennas at the transmitter and N single-antenna users, denoted as $M_T \times N$ where $M_T \geq N$. We assume that the channel between the base station and the N users is represented by a complex-valued matrix $\mathbf{H} \in \mathbb{C}^{N \times M_T}$, whose element $h_{n,m}$ represents the channel gain between transmit antenna m and user n. For all simulations, the entries of the channel matrix are assumed independent and identically distributed with zero-mean circularly symmetric complex Gaussian distribution and $E[|h_{n,m}|^2] = 1$.

The precoding system under study is shown in Figure 1. According to the aforementioned model, the data received at

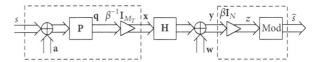

FIGURE 1: Block diagram of a VP system.

the N user terminals can be collected in the vector $\mathbf{y} \in \mathbb{C}^N$, which is given by

$$\mathbf{y} = \mathbf{Hx} + \mathbf{w}, \tag{1}$$

where $\mathbf{w} \in \mathbb{C}^N$ represents the additive white Gaussian noise vector with covariance matrix $E[\mathbf{ww}^H] = \sigma^2 \mathbf{I}_N$.

In precoding systems such as the one depicted in Figure 1, the independent data acquisition at the receivers is enabled by a preequalization stage at the base station. This procedure, which is carried out by means of a precoding filter $\mathbf{P}$, anticipates the distortion caused by the channel matrix in such a way that the received signal is (ideally) fully equalized at the receive terminals. However, the precoding process causes variations in the power of the user data streams, and therefore, a power scaling factor $\beta^{-1} = \sqrt{E_{\text{Tr}}/E[\|\mathbf{q}\|^2]} \in \mathbb{R}_+$ is applied to the vector of precoded symbols $\mathbf{q}$ prior to transmission to ensure a certain transmit power E_{Tr}. At the user terminals, the received signal is scaled by β again to allow for an appropriate detection of the data symbols. Hence, the signal prior to the detection stage reads as

$$\mathbf{z} = \mathbf{Hq} + \beta\mathbf{w}. \tag{2}$$

From this equation, one can notice that in the event of $E[\|\mathbf{q}\|^2] > E_{\text{Tr}}$, or equivalently $\beta > 1$, an increase in the power of the noise vector is experienced at the receivers, which greatly deteriorates the error-rate performance of the system. To this respect, nonlinear signal processing approaches aim at reducing the power of the linearly precoded symbols, in such a way that a considerable performance enhancement can be attained. In VP systems, this objective is achieved by incorporating a perturbation signal prior to the linear precoding stage.

The data perturbation process is supported by the modulo operator at the receivers, which provides the transmitter with additional degrees of freedom to choose the perturbation vector that is most suitable. Note that the perturbation signal must be composed of integer multiples of the modulo constant τ, namely, $\mathbf{a} \in Q$ with $Q = \tau\mathbb{CZ}^N$, so that it can be easily removed at the receivers by means of a simple modulo operation.

The VP system model that achieves the best error-rate performance targets the minimization of the mean square error (MSE) instead of the traditional goal of reducing the average power of the transmitted symbols [25]. In this model, the precoding matrix is designed as $\mathbf{P} = \mathbf{H}^H \mathbf{\Psi}$, with $\mathbf{\Psi} = (\mathbf{HH}^H + N\sigma^2/E_{\text{Tr}}\mathbf{I}_N)^{-1}$, and the triangular matrix used for the computation of the perturbation signal is computed as

$\mathbf{U}^H\mathbf{U} = \mathbf{\Psi}$. Finally, the optimum perturbation vector is obtained by evaluating the following cost function:

$$\mathbf{a} = \arg\min_{\hat{\mathbf{a}}\in\tau\,\mathbb{C}\mathbb{Z}^N}\|\mathbf{U}\,(\mathbf{s} + \hat{\mathbf{a}})\,\|_2^2. \tag{3}$$

The computation of the perturbing signal in (3) entails a search for the closest point in a lattice. Several techniques to efficiently obtain the perturbation signal will be analyzed in the following section.

3. Tree-Search Techniques for Vector Precoding

The triangular structure of the matrix $\mathbf{U}$ in (3) enables the gathering of all the solution vector hypotheses in an organized structure which resembles the shape of a tree. Following the analogy with the tree structure, the concatenation of $\psi < N$ lattice elements or nodes is referred to as a branch, where a branch of length N represents a candidate solution vector. The search for the perturbation vector is then performed by traversing a tree of N levels (each one representing a user) starting from the root level $i = N$, and working backwards until $i = 1$.

Since the elements of the solution vector belong to the expanded search space $\mathcal{Q}$, the amount of nodes that originate from each parent node in the tree equals $|\mathcal{Q}| = \infty$ in theory. However, depending on the tree-traversal strategy to be followed, the cardinality of this set can be reduced either artificially, by limiting the search space to the group $\mathcal{L}$ of closest points to the origin, or by identifying the set of eligible nodes following a distance control policy (also known as the sphere constraint). Note that, as opposed to the point-to-point MIMO detection scenario, the amount of child nodes that stem from the same parent node does not depend on the modulation constellation in use. This way, the computation of the (squared) Euclidean distances in (3) can be distributed across multiple stages as follows:

$$D_i = u_{ii}^2\left|a_i + z_i\right|^2 + \sum_{j=i+1}^{N} u_{jj}^2\left|a_j + z_j\right|^2 = d_i + D_{i+1}, \tag{4}$$

where

$$z_i = s_i + \sum_{j=1}^{i-1}\frac{u_{ij}}{u_{ii}}\left(a_j + s_j\right). \tag{5}$$

The partial Euclidean distance (PED) associated with a certain node at level i is denoted as d_i, while the accumulated Euclidean distance (AED) down to level i is given by $D_i = \sum_{j=i}^{N} d_j$. Since the elements of the solution vector belong to the expanded search space $\mathcal{Q}$, the amount of nodes that originate from each parent node in the tree equals $|\mathcal{Q}| = \infty$ in theory. However, depending on the tree-traversal strategy to be followed, the cardinality of this set can be reduced either artificially, by limiting the search space to the group $\mathcal{L}$ of $|\mathcal{L}|$ closest points to the origin, or by identifying the set of eligible nodes following a distance control policy (also known as the sphere constraint).

The traversal of the search tree is usually performed following either a depth-first or breadth-first strategy.

3.1. Depth-First Tree-Search Techniques. Depth-first tree-search techniques traverse the tree in both forward and backward directions enabling the implementation of a sphere constraint for pruning of unnecessary nodes based on, for example, the Euclidean distance associated with the first computed branch. The pruning criterion, which is updated every time a leaf node at level $i = 1$ with a smaller AED is reached, does not impose a per-level run-time constraint, and therefore, the complexity of these algorithms is of variable nature.

One of the most noteworthy depth-first techniques is the SE algorithm [26, 27], which restricts the search for the perturbation vector to the set of nodes with $D_i \leq R$ that lie within a hypersphere of radius R centered around a reference signal. The good performance of the algorithm is a consequence of the identification and management of the admissible set of nodes at each stage of the tree search. Every time a forward iteration is performed ($i \rightarrow i - 1$) the algorithm selects and computes the distance increments of the nodes that fulfil the sphere constraint and continues the tree search with the most favorable node according to the Schnorr-Euchner enumeration [28] (the node resulting in the smallest d_i). This process is repeated until a leaf node is reached (which will result in a radius update) or no nodes that satisfy the sphere constraint are found. In any case, the SE will proceed with a backward iteration ($i \rightarrow i + 1$) where a radius check will be performed among the previously computed set of candidate points. If a node with $D_i < R$ is found, the tree traversal is resumed with a forward iteration. The optimum solution has been found when the hypersphere with the updated radius contains no further nodes.

The radius reduction strategy along with the tracking of potentially valid nodes at each level of the algorithm prevents unnecessary distance computations but ultimately results in a rather complex tree-search hardware architecture.

3.2. Breadth-First Tree-Search Techniques. Breadth-first tree-search algorithms with upper-bounded complexity traverse the tree in only forward direction, identifying a set of potentially promising nodes and expanding only these in the subsequent tree-levels. These algorithms benefit from a fixed and high data-processing throughput that stems from the parallel processing of the branches. Nevertheless, the speculative pruning carried out during the tree search prevents bounded breadth-first algorithms from achieving an optimum performance.

As one can guess from its name, the K-best precoder [29, 30] selects the K best branches at each level of the tree regardless of the sphere constraint or any other distance control policy. At each stage i of the K-best tree search, an ordering procedure has to be performed on the eligible $K|\mathcal{L}|$ candidate branches based on their AEDs down to level i. After the sorting procedure, the K paths with the minimum accumulated distances are passed on to the next level of the tree. Once the final stage of the tree has been

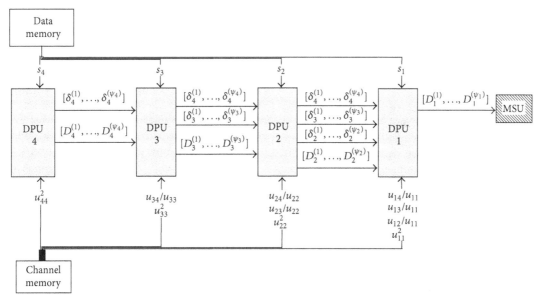

FIGURE 2: General hardware architecture of the fixed-complexity tree-search techniques for an $N = 4$ user system.

reached, the branch with the minimum Euclidean distance is selected as the K-best solution. Clearly, the main bottleneck in this scheme stems from the node ordering and selection procedures performed at every level of the tree search.

The fixed-complexity sphere encoder (FSE) was presented in [31] as a sort-free alternative to the aforementioned K-best precoder. The proposed scheme avoids the intricate sorting stages required by the K-best by defining a node selection procedure based on a tree configuration vector $\mathbf{n} = [n_1, \ldots, n_N]$. This vector specifies the number of child nodes to be evaluated at each level (n_i) following the Schnorr-Euchner enumeration. Therefore, only n_i PEDs are computed per parent node at each level, yielding a total candidate branch count of $n_T = \prod_{i=1}^{N} n_i$.

Both fixed-complexity algorithms achieve a high data-processing throughput due to their capability of parallel branch computation. This high-speed data-processing feature will be assessed by carrying out the hardware implementation of a 4×4 vector precoder based on the fixed-complexity algorithms under study. The main objectives of this study are twofold: on one hand, the quantification of the data-transmission throughput of the proposed architectures, and on the other hand, the assessment of the hardware resource allocation required for their implementation.

4. General Architecture Overview

Both tree-search schemes share the same general distance computation structure, as can be seen in Figure 2. The lack of loops in the hardware architecture of the fixed-complexity tree-search techniques enables a high throughput and fully-pipelined implementation of the data perturbation process, thus being its implementation specially suitable for a target FPGA device.

The AEDs of the candidate branches are computed by accumulating the PEDs calculated at the local distance

processing units (DPUs) to the AEDs of the previous level. This way, the AEDs down to level i corresponding to the considered candidate branches, namely, $[D_i^{(1)}, \ldots, D_i^{(\psi_i)}]$, are passed on from DPU i to DPU $i - 1$. The parameter ψ_i stands for the number of candidate branches at each level of the tree search, being it $\psi_i = K$ for all i for the K-best and $\psi_i = \prod_{j=i}^{N} n_j$ for the FSE model.

Two input memory blocks, named Data Memory and Channel Memory, have been included to store the data symbols and the values of the triangular matrix $\mathbf{U}$, respectively. The off-diagonal matrix coefficients are stored as u_{ij}/u_{ii}, whereas the diagonal values are in the form of u_{ii}^2 to simplify the calculation of (4) and (8). Note that the matrix preprocessing stage required by the FSE and K-best approaches has not been included in the hardware design. The computation of the intermediate points z_i requires the values of all previous $\delta_j = a_j + s_j$. To avoid redundant calculations, the set of values $[\delta_j^{(1)}, \ldots, \delta_j^{(\psi_j)}]$ for all $j > i$ is transferred to DPU i, as is shown in Figure 2.

The hardware structure of the first DPU is common in both schemes. The computation of the Euclidean distances in this level does not involve any data from previous levels, and therefore, the only operation to be performed is to select the ψ_N lattice values closest to s_N and to compute the corresponding PEDs. Given that the position of the modulation's constellation within the complex lattice is known beforehand, and considering the symmetries of the complex lattice, it is possible to select the nodes to be passed on to the next level without performing any extra distance calculations and sorting procedures. Additionally, the hardware structure of the last DPU is also equal for both algorithms, as only the most favorable child node that stems from each one of the ψ_2 parent nodes needs to be expanded at this level. Such a task can be performed by simply rounding the value of z_1 to the position of the nearest lattice point.

The main and crucial differences between the FSE and K-best tree-search algorithms rely on the DPUs of levels $1 < i < N$.

5. DPU for the K-Best

The difficulty of performing the sorting procedure in the complex plane, where the amount of nodes to be considered is higher, and the intricacy of complex-plane enumeration have led to the dominance of real-valued decomposition (RVD) as the preferred technique when implementing the K-best tree search. Nevertheless, direct operation on the complex signals is preferred from an implementation point of view as the length of the search tree is halved, and hence, the latency and critical path of the design can be shortened.

5.1. Structure of the Sorting Stage. Regardless of the domain of the signals to be used, the bottleneck in this type of systems is usually the sorting stage performed at each tree level. The number of child nodes that stem from the same parent node will be defined as B, being its value $B = |\mathscr{L}|$ for the complex-plane model, whereas $B = \sqrt{|\mathscr{L}|}$ will be required for the RVD scheme. The PED calculation and subsequent sorting procedure on the KB child nodes at each level is a computationally expensive process that compromises the throughput of the whole system. With the aim of alleviating the burden of the sorting stage, the use of the Schnorr-Euchner ordered sequence of child nodes and the subsequent merging of the sorted sublists is proposed in [17]. Even if the proposed scheme is implemented on an RVD model due to the simplicity of the local enumeration, it is possible to extend it to the complex plane if a low-complexity enumerator, such as the puzzle enumerator presented in [32], is utilized. Additionally, a fully-pipelined RVD architecture of the sorted sublists algorithm is proposed in [33] for high-throughput systems. By dividing the real axis into $2B$ regions and storing the corresponding enumeration sequences in look-up tables (LUTs), the algorithm is able to determine the child node order by means of a simple slicing procedure. Nevertheless, this technique is advantageous only when operating with RVD symbols as the amount of data to be stored and the quantity of nonoverlapping regions grow remarkably when complex-valued symbols are utilized. In any case, the use of any of the aforementioned sublist merging approaches reduces the amount of PED computations to be performed at each level to $K^2 \le KB$.

5.1.1. The Winnersec Path Extension Algorithm. The number of costly distance computations can be further reduced by implementing the winner path extension (WPE) selection approach presented in [34] and incorporated into the RVD hardware architecture of the K-best tree search in [35, 36]. The proposed scheme selects the K most favorable branches in K iterations by performing just $2K - 1$ PED computations. An illustrative example of the WPE algorithm is depicted in Figure 3 for a system with $B = 4$ and $K = 3$. The child nodes at a certain tree level i are tagged as $a_i^{(x,y)}$, where x represents the

index of the parent node and y denotes the position of that certain node within the ordered Schnorr-Euchner sequence of child nodes.

The WPE sorting procedure is based on the generation and management of a node candidate list $\mathscr{A}$. This way, the child node corresponding to the kth most favorable branch is extracted from the candidate list of the kth sorting stage $\mathscr{A}_k$. The initial values in the candidate list are comprised of the AEDs down to level i of the best child nodes that stem from each one of the K parent nodes, which gives $\mathscr{A}_1 = \{a_i^{(1,1)}, \ldots, a_i^{(K,1)}\}$. The winner branch in the initial sorting stage, or equivalently the first of the K most favorable branches, is selected as the branch with the smallest AED within $\mathscr{A}_1$. The PED of the second most favorable child node that stems from the same parent node as the latest appointed winner branch is computed ($a_i^{(3,2)}$ in the example illustrated in Figure 3) and the AED of the resulting tree branch is added to the candidate list $\mathscr{A}_2$. The algorithm proceeds accordingly until the K required branches have been identified.

Additionally note that, according to the complexity analysis based on the amount of comparisons in a WPE-enabled K-best tree search published in [35], the complexity of an RVD-based tree traversal doubles that of its complex-plane counterpart.

5.2. Structure of the K-best DPU. The structure of the proposed K-best DPU is depicted in Figure 4 for a system with $K = 3$. The branch selection procedure is carried out in K fully-pipelined sorting stages following a modified version of the WPE algorithm presented in [33, 34]. First of all, the computation of the intermediate points is performed for each one of the K branches that are passed on from the previous level. The set of best child nodes that stem from each parent node can be computed by simply rounding off the value of the intermediate point to the nearest lattice point. The distance increments (d_i in (4)) for those K-best children are computed by K metric computation unit (MCU) and are accumulated with their corresponding D_{i-1} values. These distance values and their corresponding branches comprise the candidate list Λ_1. The minimum AED within Λ_1 is found at the minimum-search unit (MSU) by simple concatenation of compare-and-select blocks. The MSU also outputs the index of the first winner branch $\alpha_1 \in \{1, \ldots, K\}$ so that the appropriate value of z_i can be selected for the local enumeration procedure.

At the second stage of the sorting procedure, the $a_i^{(\alpha_1,2)}$ node needs to be identified for any parent node index α_1. This task is performed by the E_2 block, which comprises a puzzle enumerator that outputs the second most favorable node given a certain value of z_i. However, in the subsequent stages of the algorithm, the enumeration procedure will depend on the index of the previously appointed winner branches. Hence, if $\alpha_1 = \alpha_2$, the third most promising child node will need to be expanded, namely, $a_i^{(\alpha_1,3)}$, whereas the second most favorable node in the α_2 branch ($a_i^{(\alpha_2,2)}$) will be required if $\alpha_1 \ne \alpha_2$. Consequently, the new candidate branch to be included in the $\mathscr{A}_k$ candidate list at the kth sorting stage will

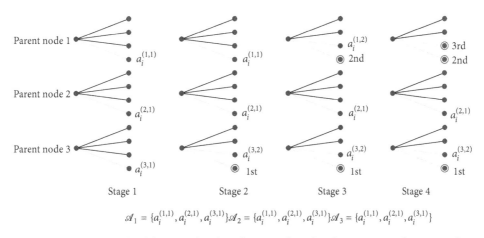

FIGURE 3: Illustrative example of the WPE distributed sorting algorithm for a system with $K = 3$ and $B = 4$.

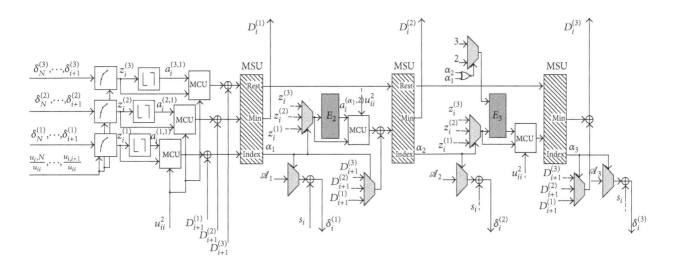

FIGURE 4: Block diagram of the K-best DPU.

require the expansion of the ρth most favorable child node, where ρ may take any value within the set $\{2, 3, \ldots, k\}$.

The enumeration approach at each sorting stage k has been carried out by means of a puzzle enumerator unit capable of ascertaining the optimum ordered sequence of the first k child nodes in a nonsequential fashion. The node order determination in the puzzle enumerator can be carried out without performing any costly distance computations. For each sorting stage k any node in the ordered sequence of best k child nodes can be selected for expansion. This way, the desired child node in the ordered sequence is determined by an additional input variable which keeps track of the amount of already expanded child nodes for each parent node. The puzzle enumerator has been selected as the enumeration scheme to be used along with the WPE due to its lower hardware resource demand and nonsequential nature, as discussed in [32]. Note that, there are no feedback loops in the structure of the K-best DPU, and therefore, it is possible to implement it following a fully-pipelined scheme.

6. DPU for the FSE

The intricate node ordering and selection procedure required by the K-best algorithm is replaced by a simple Schnorr-Euchner enumerator in the FSE tree-search model. This derives in a considerably simpler DPU architecture of the FSE scheme.

Figure 5 depicts the structure of the FSE DPU, where the block diagram for $n_T^{(i)} = \prod_{j=1}^{i-1} n_j = 3$ and $n_i = 1$ is represented. First of all, the data of the $\{\delta_{i+1}, \ldots, \delta_n\}$ values transferred from level $i + 1$ are used to compute intermediate values z_i for each one of the parent nodes. Afterwards, the node selection procedure is performed by means of a simple rounding operation when $n_i = 1$, as depicted in the illustrative example in Figure 5, or by means of the unordered puzzle enumerator [32] for the cases where $n_i > 1$. The PEDs of the selected nodes are then computed by $n_T^{(i)}$ MCUs and accumulated to the AEDs from the previous level. Finally, as was the case with the K-best DPU, the

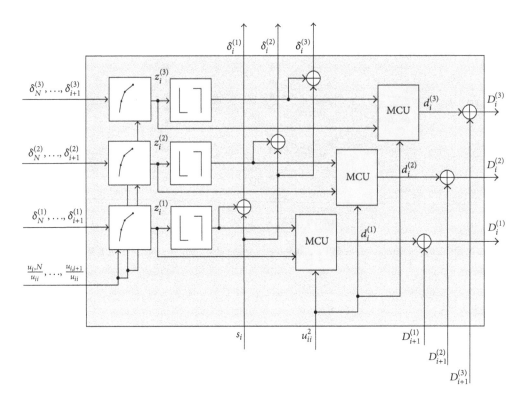

FIGURE 5: Block diagram of the FSE DPU.

FSE DPU does not have any feedback paths in its design, and hence, it can be easily implemented following a fully-pipelined scheme.

7. Design Considerations

This section addresses the design parameter selection for the fixed-complexity algorithms to be implemented in hardware. Additionally, the impact of applying an approximate norm for the computation of the distance increments is studied from an error-rate-performance point of view.

7.1. Choice of the Design Parameters. The configurable parameters K and n_T offer a flexible trade-off between performance and complexity for the K-best and FSE encoders, respectively. These configuration parameters establish the shape of the search tree, which in turn determines the amount of hardware multipliers required for its implementation. Embedded multipliers are scarce in FPGA devices and are considered an expensive resource in application-specific integrated circuit (ASIC) designs. Thus, the number of multiplication units required by the tree-search algorithm has been regarded as the critical factor in the current hardware architecture design. For the sake of a fair comparison, the configuration parameters of the fixed-complexity tree-search methods have been selected so as to yield a similar amount of allocated embedded multipliers.

Considering that 3 multipliers are used for the multiplication of two complex terms, the number of multiplication units required for the K-best tree-search structure can be computed as

$$N_{\mathrm{MUL},KB} = 6K + 3(N-2)(2K-1) + 3K\left[\frac{N(N-1)}{2}\right],$$
(6)

whereas the total amount of embedded multipliers for an FSE tree structure is given by

$$N_{\mathrm{MUL,FSE}} = 3\sum_{i=1}^{N} in_T^{(i)}.$$
(7)

The number of required embedded multipliers for the K-best and FSE tree-search techniques is shown in Figure 6 for a system with $N = 4$ single-antenna users. The amount of multiplier units is given as a function of the number of candidate branches, namely, K and n_T for the K-best and FSE approaches, respectively. As one can notice, the amount of hardware resources in the K-best tree-search model grows linearly with the number of considered candidate branches. However, this constant growth rate does not apply for the FSE case. This is due to the n_i values being differently distributed through the tree configuration vector depending on the divisibility of n_T. As proved in [37], among all possible tree configuration vectors that yield the same value of n_T, the one with the most dispersedly distributed values of n_i achieves the best error-rate performance and requires the lowest amount of allocated embedded multipliers.

In order to assess the hardware resource occupation required for the the implementation of the different tree-search algorithms, the design parameter values $K = 7$

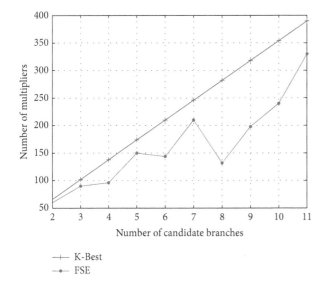

FIGURE 6: Number of required multipliers for the K-best and FSE tree-search techniques as a function of the number of candidate branches.

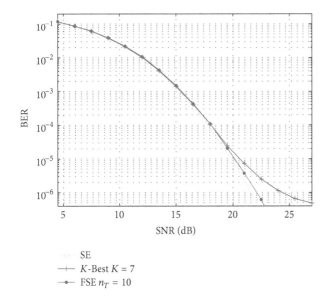

FIGURE 7: BER performance of the implemented FSE and K-best tree-search structures.

and $n_T = 10$ have been selected for the K-best and FSE models, respectively. This choice of parameters ensures a similar multiplier occupation for both schemes and offers a significantly better error-rate performance than other lower K and n_T pairs, for example, $K = 6$ and $n_T = 9$.

The BER versus SNR curves of the implemented fixed-complexity schemes are depicted in Figure 7. As one can notice, the error-rate performance of the implemented models is close to the optimum set by the SE in the low-to-mid SNR range. However, a performance degradation of 0.5 dBs is noticeable for the FSE model at high-SNRs, whereas the

performance gap of the K-best structure increases with the SNR, reaching up to 3 dBs at a BER of 10^{-6}.

7.2. Implementation of an Approximate Norm. A significant portion of the hardware resources in the implementation of any tree-search algorithm is dedicated to computing the ℓ^2 norms required by the cost function in (3). Additionally, the long delays associated with squaring operations required to compute the PEDs account for a significant portion of the latency of the fixed-complexity tree-search architectures. It is possible to overcome these problems by using an approximate norm that prevents the use of the computationally expensive squaring operations.

The application of the modified-norm algorithm (MNA) [38] entails two main benefits: on one hand, a simplified distance computation scheme that immediately reduces silicon area and delay of the arithmetic units can be performed, and on the other hand, a smaller dynamic range of the PEDs is achieved. The key point of the MNA is to compute the square root of the accumulated and partial distance increments, namely, $E_i = \sqrt{D_i}$ and $e_i = \sqrt{d_i}$, respectively. Hence, the accumulation of the distance increments in this equivalent model gives $E_i = \sqrt{E_{i+1}^2 + e_i^2}$. An approximate norm can now be applied to get rid of the computationally expensive squaring and square root operations, such that $E_i \approx f(|E_{i+1}|, |e_i|)$. This way, the accumulated distance computation in (4) can be reformulated as

$$E_i = E_{i+1} + e_i, \tag{8}$$

with

$$e_i = u_{i,i} \left(\left| \Re \left(a_i + z_i \right) \right| + \left| \Im \left(a_i + z_i \right) \right| \right) \tag{9}$$

for the $\ell^{\bar{1}}$-norm variant of the algorithm. The norm approximation can also be performed following the $\ell^{\widetilde{\infty}}$-norm simplified model, in which case the following expressions should be considered

$$E_i = \max \left(E_{i+1}, e_i \right), \tag{10}$$

with

$$e_i = u_{i,i} \left[\max \left(\left| \Re \left(a_i + z_i \right) \right|, \left| \Im \left(a_i + z_i \right) \right| \right) \right]. \tag{11}$$

The implementation of an approximate norm impacts the error-rate performance of the VP system differently depending on the tree-search strategy used in the perturbation process. This fact is shown in Figure 8, where the BER performance degradation introduced when approximating the ℓ^2 norm by the suboptimum $\ell^{\bar{1}}$ and $\ell^{\widetilde{\infty}}$ norms is depicted for the FSE and K-best tree-search approaches. For the FSE case depicted in Figure 8(a), the use of an approximate norm only affects the accumulated distances related to the candidate branches, but not the branches themselves. This is due to the fact that the nodes expanded at each level where $n_i \leq 2$ are the same regardless of the norm used to compute the distance increments to z_i. In the K-best model, on the other hand, the node selection procedure is solely

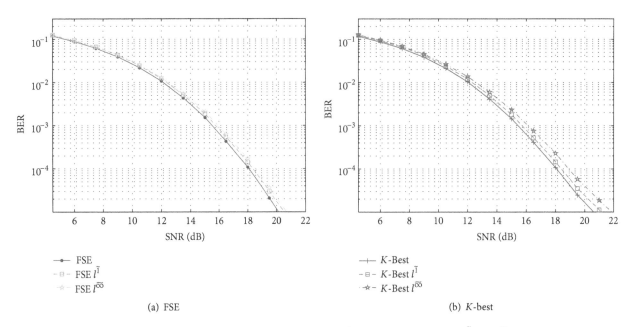

(a) FSE   (b) K-best

FIGURE 8: BER performance degradation introduced by approximating the ℓ^2 norm by the simplified $\ell^{\tilde{1}}$ and $\ell^{\widetilde{\infty}}$ norms in the FSE ($n_T = 10$) (a) and K-best ($K = 7$) (b) tree-search approaches.

TABLE 1: Hardware resource occupation and throughput of the tree-search architectures under study.

	K-Best $K = 7$	FSE $n_T = 10$	K-Best $\ell^{\tilde{1}}$ $K = 7$	FSE $\ell^{\tilde{1}}$ $n_T = 10$
Number of occupied slices (39,360)	25%	10%	26%	10%
Number of slice registers (314,880)	10%	5%	10%	4%
Number of slice LUTs (157,440)	20%	7%	20%	7%
Used as logic	11%	6%	11%	6%
Used as memory	27%	2%	27%	2%
Number of DSP48els (576)	40%	40%	31%	29%
Q (Gbps)	5.52	5.63	5.34	5.62

based on previously computed distances, and therefore, the introduction of an approximate norm will noticeably alter the structure of the candidate branches. Consequently, a higher error-rate performance degradation of the K-best algorithm with an approximate norm can be expected when compared to the norm-simplified FSE model.

The implementation of the approximate $\ell^{\tilde{1}}$ norm yields a high-SNR performance loss of 0.22 dB and 0.25 dB for the FSE and K-best fixed-complexity algorithms, respectively. Due to the worse approximation of the Euclidean distances performed by the suboptimum $\ell^{\widetilde{\infty}}$ norm, the performance gap with respect to the optimum FSE and K-best structures is widened in this case. This way, a performance loss of 0.45 dBs is experienced by the simplified $\ell^{\widetilde{\infty}}$-FSE model, whereas an error-rate degradation of 0.85 dBs is suffered by the K-best in

the high-SNR regime. In any case, the implementation of an alternative norm does not alter the diversity order of the VP scheme.

The computational complexity reduction yielded by both norm approximation approaches is similar, whereas the performance is slightly better for the $\ell^{\tilde{1}}$ norm. Consequently, the $\ell^{\tilde{1}}$ norm-simplified model will be considered for hardware implementation.

8. Implementation Results

The proposed tree-search architectures have been implemented on a Xilinx Virtex VI FPGA (XC6VHX250T-3). The occupation results have been obtained by means of the place and route tool included in the System Generator for DSP software.

Table 1 depicts the device occupation summary of the implemented vector precoders for an $N = 4$ users system with $B = 25$ eligible lattice points. Even if the FSE and K-best models use a similar amount of embedded multipliers (DSP48e1), the device occupation in terms of slices is considerably higher for the latter. This is due to the longer latency of the K-best architecture caused by the distributed sorting procedure, which ultimately results in a great amount of data being stored in several pipeline stages. As a consequence to this, around 27% of the slice LUTs are used as memory in the K-best implementation, as opposed to the 2% utilized by the FSE for the same purpose. Other than the higher occupation due to pipeline registers, the difference in latency between the two designs is of minor importance as both structures are fully-pipelined and therefore output a processed data vector at every clock-cycle. As already anticipated, the utilization of the approximate $\ell^{\tilde{1}}$ norm yields a notable reduction in the

TABLE 2: Throughput, area occupation and BER loss with respect to the optimum for the K-Best applied to MIMO detection and the proposed K-Best and FSE approaches for VP.

	[16]	[19]	[17]	[22]	[36]	K-Best (proposed)	FSE (proposed)
Systems	4×4 16-QAM $K = 10$	4×4 16-QAM $K = 5$	4×4 16-QAM $K = 5$	4×4 64-QAM $K = 64$	4×4 64-QAM $K = 64$	4×4 16-QAM $K = 7$	4×4 16-QAM $n_T = 10$
Throughput (Mbps)	10	53.3	424	75	100	5520	5630
Area (kGE)	52	91	68	1790	1760	1732	374
Mbps/kGE	0.19	0.58	6.23	0.04	0.056	3.18	15.05
BER loss at 20 dB	<0.5 dB	<0.5 dB	~0.75 dB	~0.5 dB	<0.5 dB	0.7 dB	0.3 dB

amount of allocated embedded multipliers for both fixed-complexity tree-search models.

The maximum throughput of the implemented architectures in terms of processed gigabits per second is also shown in Table 1 for a 16-QAM modulation constellation. For a system with N users and a constellation of P elements, the throughput for fully-pipelined architectures can be computed as

$$Q = N f_{\mathrm{clock}} \log_2 (P), \qquad (12)$$

where f_{clock} represents the maximum working frequency of the design as given by the *Post-Place and Route Static Timing Report*. Both tree-search algorithms achieve a very high data-processing throughput (in the range of 5 Gbps) due to the loopless parallel structure that enables the processing of a new data vector at every clock cycle. Note that the maximum working frequency of the designs presented in this contribution can be obtained by using (12) and the results in Table 1.

Additionally note that a higher throughput can be achieved by increasing the order of the modulation in use. In such a case, the modifications to be performed in the proposed architecture are minimal. These include an update of the considered lattice values ($|\mathscr{L}|$) and the adaptation of the first DPU where the straightforward node sequencing is performed. Furthermore, given the low hardware resource occupation required by the proposed FSE tree-search architectures, a higher data processing throughput can be easily obtained by running several tree-search instances in parallel.

Table 2 compares the area and throughput of the proposed K-best and FSE hardware architectures with similar structures used in point-to-point MIMO detection. Even if a direct comparison should be done carefully due to the already described differences between multiuser precoding and MIMO detection scenarios, it is worth noting the high Mbps/kGE ratio of the presented FSE approach.

9. Conclusion

This paper has addressed the issues of a fully-pipelined implementation of the FSE and K-best tree-search approaches for a 4×4 VP system. The sorting stages required by the K-best scheme have been performed by means of the WPE distributed sorting strategy along with a nonsequential complex-plane enumerator, which has also been incorporated into the FSE structure to determine the child nodes to be expanded in those tree levels $i < N$ where $n_i > 1$. The design parameters that establish the performance-complexity trade-off of these nonrecursive tree-search approaches have been set so as to yield a similar count of allocated embedded multipliers. Additionally, the use of an approximate norm to reduce the computational complexity of the PED calculations has been contemplated.

Provided performance results have shown a close-to-optimal performance and a very high achievable throughput in the range of 5 Gbps for both techniques. Nevertheless, the error-rate performance of the FSE has been shown to considerably outperform the K-best in the high-SNR range. Additionally, the provided FPGA resource occupation results have demonstrated the greater efficiency of the FSE architecture when compared to the K-best fixed-complexity structure.

Due to the good performance, occupation results, and simplicity of implementation, it is concluded that the FSE is best suited for the practical implementation of fixed-complexity and high-throughput vector precoders.

Acknowledgments

The authors would like to thank the Department of Education, Universities and Research and the Department of Industry, Trade and Tourism of the Basque Government.

References

[1] B. M. Hochwald, C. B. Peel, and A. L. Swindlehurst, "A vector-perturbation technique for near-capacity multiantenna multiuser communication, part II: perturbation," *IEEE Transactions on Communications*, vol. 53, no. 3, pp. 537–544, 2005.

[2] C. Windpassinger, R. F. H. Fischer, and J. B. Huber, "Lattice-reduction-aided broadcast precoding," *IEEE Transactions on Communications*, vol. 52, no. 12, pp. 2057–2060, 2004.

[3] A. K. Lenstra, H. W. Lenstra, and L. Lovász, "Factoring polynomials with rational coefficients," *Mathematische Annalen*, vol. 261, no. 4, pp. 515–534, 1982.

[4] L. Babai, "On lovász' lattice reduction and the nearest lattice point problem," *Combinatorica*, vol. 6, no. 1, pp. 1–13, 1986.

[5] D. Seethaler and G. Matz, "Efficient vector perturbation in multi-antenna multi-user systems based on approximate integer relations," in *Proceedings of the EURASIP European Signal Processing Conference (EUSIPCO '06)*, pp. 1–5, September 2006.

[6] S. Hur, N. Kim, H. Park, and J. Kang, "Enhanced lattice-reduction-based precoder with list quantizer in broadcast channel," in *Proceedings of the IEEE 66th Vehicular Technology Conference (VTC '07)*, pp. 611–615, October 2007.

[7] F. Liu, L. Jiang, and C. He, "Low complexity MMSE vector precoding using lattice reduction for MIMO systems," in *Proceedings of the IEEE International Conference on Communications (ICC '07)*, pp. 2598–2603, June 2007.

[8] M. Taherzadeh, A. Mobasher, and A. K. Khandani, "LLL lattice-basis reduction achieves the maximum diversity in MIMO systems," in *Proceedings of the IEEE International Symposium on Information Theory (ISIT '05)*, pp. 1300–1304, September 2005, maximum diversity; MIMO fading channels; MIMO broadcast systems; lattice-reductionaided decoding; point-to-point system;multiple-access system.

[9] M. Taherzadeh, A. Mobasher, and A. K. Khandani, "Communication over MIMO broadcast channels using lattice-basis reduction," *IEEE Transactions on Information Theory*, vol. 53, no. 12, pp. 4567–4582, 2007.

[10] K. H. Lin, H. L. Lin, R. C. Chang, and C. F. Wu, "Hardware architecture of improved Tomlinson-Harashima Precoding for downlink MC-CDMA," in *Proceedings of the IEEE Asia Pacific Conference on Circuits and Systems (APCCAS '06)*, pp. 1200–1203, December 2006.

[11] A. Burg, D. Seethaler, and G. Matz, "VLSI implementation of a lattice-reduction algorithm for multi-antenna broadcast precoding," in *Proceedings of the IEEE International Symposium on Circuits and Systems (ISCAS 07)*, pp. 673–676, May 2007.

[12] P. Bhagawat, W. Wang, M. Uppal et al., "An FPGA implementation of dirty paper precoder," in *Proceedings of the IEEE International Conference on Communications (ICC '07)*, pp. 2761–2766, June 2008.

[13] L. G. Barbero and J. S. Thompson, "Rapid prototyping of a fixed-throughput sphere decoder for MIMO systems," in *Proceedings of the IEEE International Conference on Communications (ICC '06)*, vol. 7, pp. 3082–3087, June 2006.

[14] L. G. Barbero and J. S. Thompson, "FPGA design considerations in the implementation of a fixed-throughput sphere decoder for MIMO systems," in *Proceedings of the International Conference on Field Programmable Logic and Applications (FPL '00)*, pp. 1–6, August 2006.

[15] L. G. Barbero and J. S. Thompson, "Extending a fixed-complexity sphere decoder to obtain likelihood information for turbo-MIMO systems," *IEEE Transactions on Vehicular Technology*, vol. 57, no. 5, pp. 2804–2814, 2008.

[16] K. W. Wong, C. Y. Tsui, R. S. K. Cheng, and W. H. Mow, "A VLSI architecture of a k-best lattice decoding algorithm for MIMO channels," in *Proceedings of the IEEE International Symposium on Circuits and Systems (ISCAS '02)*, vol. 3, pp. 273–276, May 2002.

[17] M. Wenk, M. Zellweger, A. Burg, N. Felber, and W. Fichtner, "K-best MIMO detection VLSI architectures achieving up to 424 Mbps," in *Proceedings of the IEEE International Symposium on Circuits and Systems (ISCAS '06)*, pp. 1151–1154, September 2006.

[18] Q. Li and Z. Wang, "Improved k-best sphere decoding algorithms for MIMO systems," in *Proceedings of the IEEE International Symposium on Circuits and Systems (ISCAS '06)*, pp. 1159–1162, May 2006.

[19] Z. Guo and P. Nilsson, "Algorithm and implementation of the k-best sphere decoding for MIMO detection," *IEEE Journal on Selected Areas in Communications*, vol. 24, no. 3, pp. 491–503, 2006.

[20] M. Shabany and P. G. Gulak, "Scalable VLSI architecture for k-best lattice decoders," in *Proceedings of the IEEE International Symposium on Circuits and Systems (ISCAS '08)*, pp. 940–943, May 2008.

[21] C. A. Shen and A. M. Eltawil, "A radius adaptive k-best decoder with early termination: algorithm and VLSI architecture," *IEEE Transactions on Circuits and Systems I*, vol. 57, no. 9, pp. 2476–2486, 2010.

[22] S. Chen, T. Zhang, and Y. Xin, "Relaxed k-best MIMO signal detector design and VLSI implementation," *IEEE Transactions on Very Large Scale Integration (VLSI) Systems*, vol. 15, no. 3, pp. 328–337, 2007.

[23] M. Mahdavi, M. Shabany, and B. V. Vahdat, "A modified complex k-best scheme for high-speed hard-output MIMO detectors," in *Proceedings of the 53rd IEEE International Midwest Symposium on Circuits and Systems (MWSCAS '10)*, pp. 845–848, August 2010.

[24] C. A. Shen, A. M. Eltawil, and K. N. Salama, "Evaluation framework for k-best sphere decoders," *Journal of Circuits, Systems and Computers*, vol. 19, no. 5, pp. 975–995, 2010.

[25] D. A. Schmidt, M. Joham, and W. Utschick, "Minimum mean square error vector precoding," in *Proceedings of the IEEE 16th International Symposium on Personal, Indoor and Mobile Radio Communications (PIMRC '05)*, vol. 1, pp. 107–111, September 2005.

[26] E. Viterbo and J. Boutros, "A universal lattice code decoder for fading channels," *IEEE Transactions on Information Theory*, vol. 45, no. 5, pp. 1639–1642, 1999.

[27] M. O. Damen, H. El Gamal, and G. Caire, "On maximum-likelihood detection and the search for the closest lattice point," *IEEE Transactions on Information Theory*, vol. 49, no. 10, pp. 2389–2402, 2003.

[28] C. P. Schnorr and M. Euchner, "Lattice basis reduction: improved practical algorithms and solving subset sum problems," in *Proceedings of the International Symposium on Fundamentals of Computation Theory (FCT '91)*, vol. 529, pp. 68–85, September 1991.

[29] J. Zhang and K. J. Kim, "Near-capacity MIMO multiuser precoding with QRD-M algorithm," in *Proceedings of the 39th Asilomar Conference on Signals, Systems and Computers (ACSSC '05)*, vol. 1, pp. 1498–1502, November 2005.

[30] R. Habendorf and G. Fettweis, "Vector precoding with bounded complexity," in *Proceedings of the 8th IEEE Signal Processing Advances in Wireless Communications (SPAWC '07)*, pp. 1–5, June 2007.

[31] M. Barrenechea, M. Mendicute, J. Del Ser, and J. S. Thompson, "Wiener filter-based fixed-complexity vector precoding for the MIMO downlink channel," in *Proceedings of the IEEE 10th Workshop on Signal Processing Advances in Wireless Communications (SPAWC '09)*, pp. 216–220, ita, June 2009.

[32] M. Barrenechea, M. Mendicute, I. Jimenez, and E. Arruti, "Implementation of complex enumeration for multiuser mimo

vector precoding," in *Proceedings of the EURASIP European Signal Processing Conference (EUSIPCO '11)*, pp. 739–743, August 2011.

[33] P. Y. Tsai, W. T. Chen, X. C. Lin, and M. Y. Huang, "A 4 × 4 64-QAM reduced-complexity k-best MIMO detector up to 1.5 Gbps," in *Proceedings of the IEEE International Symposium on Circuits and Systems (ISCAS '10)*, pp. 3953–3956, May 2010.

[34] S. Mondal, W. H. Ali, and K. N. Salama, "A novel approach for k-best MIMO detection and its VLSI implementation," in *Proceedings of the IEEE International Symposium on Circuits and Systems (ISCAS '08)*, pp. 936–939, May 2008.

[35] S. Mondal, A. M. Eltawil, and K. N. Salama, "Architectural optimizations for low-power k-best MIMO decoders," *IEEE Transactions on Vehicular Technology*, vol. 58, no. 7, pp. 3145–3153, 2009.

[36] S. Mondal, A. Eltawil, C. A. Shen, and K. N. Salama, "Design and implementation of a sort-free K-best sphere decoder," *IEEE Transactions on Very Large Scale Integration (VLSI) Systems*, vol. 18, no. 10, pp. 1497–1501, 2010.

[37] M. Barrenechea, *Design and implementation of multi-user mimo precoding algorithms [Ph.D. dissertation]*, University of Mondragon, Mondragon, Spain, 2012.

[38] A. Burg, M. Wenk, M. Zellweger, M. Wegmueller, N. Felber, and W. Fichtner, "VLSI implementation of the sphere decoding algorithm," in *Proceedings of the 30th European Solid-State Circuits Conference (ESSCIRC '04)*, pp. 303–306, September 2004.

14

Occam-pi for Programming of Massively Parallel Reconfigurable Architectures

Zain-ul-Abdin and Bertil Svensson

Centre for Research on Embedded Systems (CERES), Halmstad University, 301 18 Halmstad, Sweden

Correspondence should be addressed to Zain-ul-Abdin, zain-ul-abdin@hh.se

Academic Editor: João Cardoso

Massively parallel reconfigurable architectures, which offer massive parallelism coupled with the capability of undergoing run-time reconfiguration, are gaining attention in order to meet the increased computational demands of high-performance embedded systems. We propose that the `occam-pi` language is used for programming of the category of massively parallel reconfigurable architectures. The salient properties of the `occam-pi` language are explicit concurrency with built-in mechanisms for interprocessor communication, provision for expressing dynamic parallelism, support for the expression of dynamic reconfigurations, and placement attributes. To evaluate the programming approach, a compiler framework was extended to support the language extensions in the `occam-pi` language and a backend was developed to target the Ambric array of processors. We present two case-studies; DCT implementation exploiting the reconfigurability feature of `occam-pi` and a significantly large autofocus criterion calculation based on the dynamic parallelism capability of the `occam-pi` language. The results of the implemented case studies suggest that the `occam-pi`-language-based approach simplifies the development of applications employing run-time reconfigurable devices without compromising the performance benefits.

1. Introduction and Motivation

The computational requirements of high-performance embedded applications, such as video processing in HDTV, baseband processing in telecommunication systems, and radar signal processing, have reached a level where they cannot be met with traditional computing systems based on general-purpose digital signal processors. Massively parallel reconfigurable processor arrays are made up of highly optimized functional blocks or even program-controlled processing elements composed in a reconfigurable interconnect. The coarse-grained composition leads to less reconfiguration data than in their more fine-grained counterparts, which improves the reconfiguration time, while the communication overhead is also decreased. The ability of coarse-grained reconfigurable architectures to undergo partial and run-time reconfiguration makes them suitable for implementing hardware acceleration of streaming applications.

However, developing applications that employ such architectures poses several other challenging tasks. The procedural models of high-level programming languages, such as C, rely on sequential control flow, procedures, and recursion, which are difficult to adapt for reconfigurable arrays. The focus of these sequential languages is to provide abstractions for algorithm specification, but the abstractions, intentionally, do not say much about how they are mapped to underlying hardware. Furthermore, because these languages were originally designed for sequential computers with unified memory system, applying them for arrays of reconfigurable processing units with distributed memories results in inefficient use of available hardware, leading to increased power consumption and increased communication delays. The development challenges include the need to learn multiple low-level languages, the requirement of partitioning and decomposing the application into several independent subtasks that can execute concurrently, and the need for expressing reconfigurations in order to cope with the adaptability requirements. Clearly, all these challenges need to be taken care of by using an appropriate programming model.

We propose to use the concurrent programming model of occam-pi [1], combining Communicating Sequential Processes (CSP) [2] with pi-calculus [3]. This model allows the programmer to express computations in a productive manner by matching them to the target hardware using high-level constructs. Occam-pi, with its minimal run-time overhead, has built in semantics for concurrency and interprocess communication. The explicit expression of concurrency in occam-pi, with its ability to describe computations that reside in different memory spaces, together with the facility of expressing dynamic parallelism, dynamic process invocation mechanisms, and the language support for placement attributes, makes it suitable for mapping applications to a wide class of coarse-grained reconfigurable architectures. These are based on tiles of processing units which have nearest neighbour links, no shared memory, and which are reconfigurable. The compiler that we have developed provides portability across different hardware architectures.

In earlier work, we have demonstrated the feasibility of using the occam-pi language to program an emerging massively parallel reconfigurable architecture by implementing a 1D-DCT algorithm [4]. We have also previously demonstrated the applicability of the approach on another reconfigurable architecture, namely, PACT XPP [5]. The contributions of this paper are as follows.

(i) Identification of a CSP-based programming model and language extensions to express reconfigurability.

(ii) Implementation of a compiler framework to support language extensions of the occam-pi language, such as channel direction specifiers, mobile data and channels, dynamic process invocation, and process placement attributes. These can be used to express run-time reconfiguration in the underlying hardware and for development of the Ambric backend.

(iii) Evaluation of the approach by implementing a reconfigurable version of the 1D-DCT algorithm and by programming compute-intensive parts of Synthetic Aperture Radar (SAR) systems [6]. In particular, we have used the dynamic process invocation mechanism of occam-pi to implement the reconfigurable version of the DCT algorithm and the dynamic parallelism feature of occam-pi in the form of replicated parallel processes to implement autofocus criterion calculations on the Ambric array of processors.

The rest of the paper is organized as follows. Section 2 presents some related work, and Section 3 presents the Ambric architecture and its programming environment. Section 4 describes the occam-pi language basics, in particular extensions for supporting reconfigurability. Section 5 provides an overview of the compiler framework. Section 6 describes a component framework that is used to implement the dynamic reconfigurability features of occam-pi. Section 7 presents the 1D-DCT case study. Section 8 describes the SAR system and the significance of the autofocus algorithm. Section 9 presents the autofocus criterion case study and the two design approaches. Section 10 discusses the implementation results of the two case studies, and the paper is concluded with some remarks and future work in Section 11.

2. Related Work

There has been a number of initiatives in both industry and academia to address the requirement of high-level languages for reconfigurable silicon devices. The related work presented here covers a range of prominent programming languages and compilers based on their relevance to the field of reconfigurable computing.

Handel-C is a high-level language with ANSI-C like syntax used to program gate level reconfigurable hardware [7]. It supports behavioral descriptions with parallel processing statements (par) and constructs to offer communication between parallel elements. Handel-C is being used for compilation to synchronous hardware and inherit sequential behaviors.

Streams-C [8], a project initiated by Los Alamos National Laboratory, is based on the CSP model for communication between processes and is used for stream-oriented FPGA applications. The Streams-C implementation consists of annotations and library function calls for stream modules. The annotations define the process, stream, and signal.

Mobius is a tiny, domain specific, concurrent, recently emerging programming language with CSP-based interprocess communication and synchronization methodologies using handshaking [9]. It has a Pascal-like syntax with bit specific control and occam-like extensions suitable for fine-grained architectures. The hierarchical modules in Mobius are composed of procedures and functions. The processes execute concurrently and communicate with each other through message passing unidirectional channels.

Pebble [10] has been developed at Imperial College London to facilitate development of hardware circuits and support modeling of run-time reconfigurations. The language has a block-structured syntax, with the primitive block describing bit-level logic gates. The reconfigurability is supported by introducing control blocks consisting of either a multiplexer or a demultiplexer around the logic block that needs to be reconfigured.

Apart from the above-mentioned languages, there have been attempts to exploit the dynamic reconfiguration capabilities of reconfigurable architectures by implementing a library of custom hardware modules each supporting a specific instruction. These custom-instruction modules are reconfigured onto the FPGA under the control of a global controller which resides on the FPGA [11]. Burns et. al. [12] have proposed a similar approach in which the reconfiguration process is controlled by a run-time system that is executed on a host processor.

To summarize, although most of the discussed languages are based on the CSP computation model, they differ from each other in the way they expose parallelism. For instance, while Handel-C and Streams-C both have C-like syntax, Streams-C relies entirely on the compiler to expose parallelism, whereas Handel-C offers extensions. These extensions allow statement level parallel constructs to identify collection of instructions to be executed in parallel. The latter is similar to the approach taken in Mobius. All of the above-mentioned languages have been implemented for fine-grained architectures, whereas we are interested in targeting coarse-grained architectures. Another important feature lacking in these languages, except Pebble, is the ability to express run-time reconfiguration. With Pebble, the reconfigurability support is provided at a very low level, describing individual logic blocks mainly intended for fine-grained architectures, whereas we are interested in exploring the abstractions to support reconfigurability at task and process level, which is more suitable for coarse-grained architectures. These limitations of the above-mentioned languages have motivated us to suggest using the occam-pi language, which provides platform-independent abstractions that enable the programmer to target a variety of coarse-grained architectures. Occam-pi can also be adopted for fine-grained architectures, and, in that case, it will closely resemble the Mobius language.

In addition, there are also compiler frameworks such as Riverside Optimizing Compiler for Configurable Computing (ROCCC) [13] for fine-grained architectures and Dynamically Reconfigurable Embedded System Compiler (DRESC) [14] for coarse-grained architectures. Both of these frameworks use C language for application description and perform aggressive program analysis to identify loops in the source code that can then be transformed into pipelines. The loop-based transformations are limited to innermost loops that do not involve function calls. Furthermore, since the C language was originally designed for sequential computers with unified memory system, applying it for arrays of reconfigurable processing units with distributed memories results in inefficient use of available hardware. In contrast to the C language approach, the occam-pi language allows the programmer to explicitly describe the statements to be executed in parallel by using the PAR construct. Thus, our compiler framework does not require the loop-level transformations that both ROCCC and DRESC rely on for extracting parallelism, but we do incorporate other optimizations similar to ROCCC such as function inlining, floating-point to fixed-point conversion, and division and multiplication elimination.

3. Ambric Architecture and Programming Model

Ambric, being an example of a massively parallel processor array, is an asynchronous array of so called brics based on the globally asynchronous locally synchronous (GALS) principle. Each bric is composed of two pairs of Compute Unit (CU) and RAM Unit (RU) [15]. The CU consists of two 32-bit Streaming RISC (SR) processors, two 32-bit Streaming RISC processors with DSP extensions (SRD), and a 32-bit reconfigurable channel interconnect for interprocessor and inter-CU communications. The RU consists of four banks of RAM along with a dynamic channel interconnect to facilitate communication with these memories. The Am2045 device has a total of 336 processors in 42 brics, as shown in Figure 1.

The Ambric architecture supports a structured object programming model, as shown in Figure 2. The individual objects are programmed in a sequential manner in a subset of the java language, called aJava, or in assembly language [16]. The individual software objects are then linked together using a proprietary language called aStruct. The primitive objects contain the functionality of the component and can be combined together to form a composite software object. Each primitive software object is mapped to an individual processor, and objects communicate with each other using hardware channels without using any shared memory. Each channel is unidirectional, point-to-point, and has a data path width of a single word. The channels are used for both data and control traffic.

Thus, when designing an application in the Ambric environment, the programmer needs to partition the application into a structured graph of objects and define the functions of the individual objects. It is then up to the proprietary tools to compile or assemble the source code and to generate the final configuration after completing placement and routing.

4. Occam-pi Language Overview

Occam [17] is a programming language based on the Communicating Sequential Processes (CSP) concurrent model of computation and was developed by Inmos for their microprocessor chip Transputer. However, CSP can only express a static model of the application, where processes synchronize communication over fixed channels. In contrast, the pi-calculus allows modeling of dynamic constructions of channels and processes, which enables the dynamic connectivity of networks of processes. Occam-pi [1] can be regarded as an extension of classical occam to include the mobility feature of the pi-calculus. The mobility feature is provided by the dynamic asynchronous communication capability of the pi-calculus. It is this property of occam-pi that is useful when creating a network of processes in which the functionality of processes and their communication network change at run time. The occam-pi language is based on well-defined semantics and is suitable because of its simplicity, static compilation properties, minimal runtime overhead, and its power to express parallelism and reconfigurability. The communication between the processes is handled via channels using message passing, which helps in avoiding interference problems. The dynamic parallelism features of the language make it possible for the compiler to perform resource-aware compilation in accordance with the application requirements.

4.1. Basic Constructs. The hierarchical modules in occam are composed of processes and functions. The primitive processes provided by occam include assignment, input process (?), and output process (!). In addition to these, there are also structural processes such as sequential processes (SEQ), parallel processes (PAR), WHILE, IF/ELSE, and replicated processes [17].

A process in occam contains both the data and the operations required to be performed on the data. The data

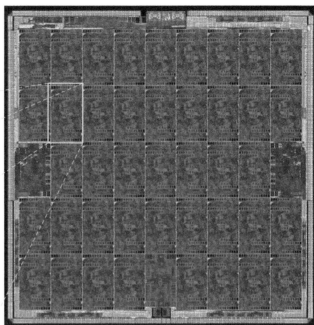

FIGURE 1: Ambric architecture.

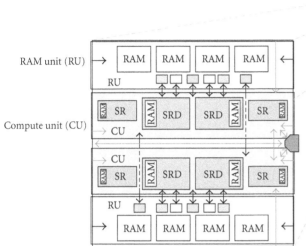

FIGURE 2: Ambric structured object programming model.

in a process is strictly private and can be observed and modified by the owner process only. In contrast, in occam-pi, the data can be declared as MOBILE, which means that the ownership of the data can be passed between different processes. Occam-pi also supports the REAL data type to express floating-point computations. Compared to the channel definition in classical occam, the channel type definition in occam-pi has been extended to include the direction specifiers, Input (?) and Output (!). Thus, a variable of channel type refers to only one end of a channel. The channel types added to occam are considered as first class citizens in the type system, allowing the channel ends of that type to be declared and communicated to other processes. A channel direction specifier is added to the type of a channel definition and not to its name. Based on the direction specification, the compiler performs its usage checking both outside and within the body of the process. Channel direction specifiers are also used when referring to channel variables as parameters of a process call.

Let us now take a look at an occam-pi program that computes raise to the power 8 of integers. The main process invokes three instantiations of a process, square, which are executed in parallel, as shown in Code Example 1. The inputs to the main process are passed through the input channel-end in, and the results are retrieved from the output channel-end out. The square process contains a sequential block that takes one input value, computes its square, and passes the resulting value to its output channel.

4.2. Language Extensions to Support Reconfigurability. In this section, we will describe the semantics of the extensions in the occam-pi language, such as mobile data and channels, dynamic process invocation, and process placement attributes. These extensions are used to express the different configurations of hardware resources in the programming model. The reconfiguration of the hardware resources at run-time can be controlled by using dynamic process invocation and process placement attributes.

4.2.1. Mobile Data and Channels. The assignment and communication in classical occam follow the copy semantics, that is, for transferring data from the sender process to the receiver both the sender and the receiver, maintain separate copies of the communicated data. The mobility concept of the pi-calculus enables the movement semantics during assignment and communication, which means that the respective data has moved from the source to the target and afterwards the source loses the possession of the data. In case the source and the target reside in the same memory space, then the movement is realized by swapping of pointers, which is secure, and no aliasing is introduced.

In order to incorporate mobile semantics into the occam-pi language, the keyword MOBILE has been introduced as a qualifier for data types [18]. The definition of the MOBILE types is consistent with how ordinary types

```
PROC main (CHAN INT in?,  out!)          PROC square (CHAN INT c?,  d!)
  CHAN INT a, b:                         INT x,y:
  PAR                                    SEQ
    square (in?, a!)                       c ? x
    square (a?, b!)                        y = x * x
    square (b?, out!)                      d ! y
:                                        :
```

CODE EXAMPLE 1: An occam-pi program.

are defined when considered in the context of defining expressions, procedures, and functions. However, the mobility concept of MOBILE types is applied in assignment and communication. The syntax of mobile data variables and channels of mobile data is given as

    MOBILE INT x:

    CHAN OF MOBILE INT c:

The modeling of mobile channels is independent of the data types and structures of the messages that they carry.

Mobile Assignment. Having defined the syntax of mobile types, we now illustrate the movement semantics as applied in the case of the assignment operation. Let us consider the assignment of a variable y to x, where x initially has a value $v0$ and y has an initial value of $v1$. According to the copy semantics of occam, x will acquire the value $v1$ after the assignment has taken place and y will retain its copy of the value $v1$. Instead, applying the movement semantics for mobile assignment, x will acquire the value $v1$ after the assignment has taken place but the value of y will become undefined.

Mobile Communication. Mobile communication is introduced in the form of mobile channel types, and the data communicated on mobile channels has to be of the mobile data type. Channel type variables behave similarly to the other mobile variables. Once they are allocated, communicating them means moving the channel-ends around the network. In terms of pi-calculus, it has the same effect as if passing the channel-end names as messages. Let us explain the mobility concept of pi-calculus by considering a composition of three processes, A, B, and C, such that all of them are executing concurrently as shown in Figure 3, where u and o are the names for input channel-ends and $\bar{u}$ and $\bar{o}$ represent output channel-ends.

Now, in order to undergo a dynamic change of communication topology between processes, process A acquires a channel-end, whereas process B loses its channel-end. The realization of the transfer of channel-end is performed by transmitting the name of the channel-end as the value of the communication between the two processes. Thus, the transmitting process loses the possession of the communicated channel-end. In the case of Figure 3, a mobile channel-end named $\bar{o}$ is sent along the channel u from process B to process A, where $\bar{o}$ becomes undefined in the sending process B

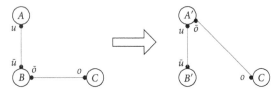

FIGURE 3: Mobile channel-end communication flow graph.

afterwards. The receiving process A receives the channel-end named $\bar{o}$ and later uses it for communicating with process C.

MOBILE Parameter. Passing parameters in an ordinary PROC call consisting of mobile types do not introduce any new semantics implications and are treated as renaming when mobile variables are passed to either functions or processes.

Dynamic Process Invocation. For run-time reconfiguration, dynamic invocation of processes is necessary. In occam-pi, concurrency can be introduced not only by using the classical PAR construct but also by dynamic parallel process creation using forking. Forking is used whenever there is any requirement of dynamically invoking a new process which can either execute concurrently with the dispatching process or replace the previously executing processes. In order to implement dynamic process creation in occam-pi, two new keywords, FORK and FORKING, are introduced [19]. The scope of the forked process is controlled by the FORKING block in which it is being invoked, as shown in Code Example 2.

The parameters that are allowed for a forked process are

(i) VAL data type: whose value is copied to the forked process;

(ii) MOBILE data type and channels of MOBILE data type: which are moved to the forked process.

The parameters of a forked process follow the communication semantics instead of the renaming semantics adopted by parameters of ordinary processes.

Process Placement Attribute. Having presented the extensions in the occam-pi language, we now introduce the placement attribute, which is inspired by the *placed parallel* concept of occam. The placement attribute is essential in order to identify the location of the components that will

```
FORKING
  MOBILE INT x:
  SEQ
     x := 42
     FORK P(x)
:
```

CODE EXAMPLE 2: An example illustrating a forking process.

be reconfigured in the reconfiguration process. The qualifier PLACED is introduced in the language followed by two integers to identify the location of the hardware resource where the associated process will be mapped. The identifying integers are logical numbers which are translated by the compiler to the physical address of the resource.

5. Compiler Framework

In this section, we will give a brief overview of a method for compiling occam-pi programs to reconfigurable processor arrays. The method is based on implementing a compiler backend for generating native code for the target architecture.

5.1. Compiler for Ambric. When developing a compiler targeting coarse-grained reconfigurable arrays, we have made use of the frontend of an existing *Translator from Occam to C from Kent* (Tock) [20]. As shown in Figure 4, the compiler is divided into frontend, which consists of phases up to machine independent optimization, and backend, which includes the remaining phases that are dependent upon the target machine architecture. We have extended the frontend for supporting occam-pi and developed two new backends, targeting Ambric and PACT XPP, thus generating native code in the proprietary languages aJava, assembly, aStruct, and Native Mapping Language (NML). In this paper, we are only going to describe the Ambric backend, whereas the details of the XPP backend can be found in [5].

In the following, we give a brief description of the modifications that are incorporated in the compiler to support the language extensions of occam-pi, introduced to express reconfigurability, and the backend to support the two target architectures.

Frontend. The frontend of the compiler, which analyzes the occam-pi source code, consists of several modules for parsing and syntax and semantic analysis. We have extended the parser and the lexical analyzer to take into account the additional constructs for introducing mobile data and channel types, dynamic process invocation, and process placement attributes. We have also introduced new grammar rules corresponding to these additional constructs to create Abstract Syntax Trees (AST) from tokens generated at the lexical analysis stage. Steps for resolving names and type checking are performed at this stage. The frontend also tests the scope of the forking block, and whether or not the data

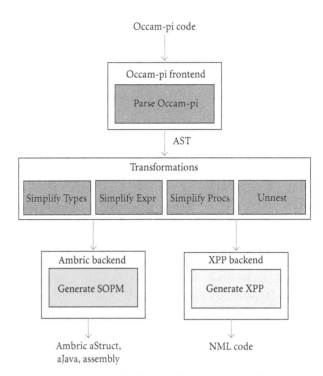

FIGURE 4: Block diagram of occam-pi compiler.

passed to a forked process is of MOBILE data type, thus fulfilling the requirement for communication semantics.

In order to support the channel end definition, we have extended the definition of channel type to include the direction whenever a channel name is found followed by a direction token, that is, "?" for input and "!" for output. In order to implement the channel-end definition for a procedure call, we have used the *DirectedVariable* constructor to be passed to the AST whenever a channel-end definition is found in the procedure call.

The transformation stage, which follows the front end, consists of a number of passes either to simplify its input to reduce complexity in the AST for subsequent phases or to convert the input program to a form which is accepted by the backend or to implement different optimizations required by some specific backend. As mentioned, Tock relies heavily on the use of monad transformers, and we describe here the monad transformer that is used for implementing the target-specific transformations. The PassM monad is used to transform the function definition in occam-pi to a method in aJava and to avoid wrap-up of PARs to PROCs during the transformation phase.

Ambric Backend. The Ambric backend is further divided into two main passes. The first pass generates declarations of aStruct code, including the top-level design and the interface and binding declarations for each of the composite as well as primitive objects corresponding to the different processes specified in the occam-pi source code. Thus, each process in occam-pi is translated to a primitive object, which can then be executed on either an SR or an SRD processor of Ambric. Before generating the aStruct code, the backend traverses the AST to collect a list of all the parameters passed

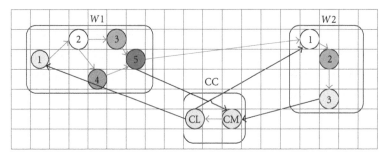

FIGURE 5: Reconfigurable components mapping.

in procedure calls specified for processes to be executed in parallel. This list of parameters, along with the list of names of procedures called, is used to generate the structural interface and binding code for each of the parallel objects.

The next pass makes use of the structured composition of the occam-pi constructs, such as SEQ, PAR, and CASE, which allows intermingling processes as well as declarations and replication of the constructs like (SEQ, PAR, IF). The backend uses the *genStructured* function from the generate C module to generate the aJava class code corresponding to processes which do not have the PAR construction. In case of the FORK construct, the backend generates the background code for managing the loading of the successive configuration from the local storage and communicating it to the concerned processing elements.

Floating-point representation is supported in the occam-pi language (in the form of REAL data types); however, it is not supported by the Ambric architecture. Thus, a transformation from floating-point numbers to fixed-point numbers has been developed and added to this pass of the Ambric backend. The supported arithmetic operations are explained as follows.

(i) The assignment operation converts the constant value on the right side of the operator to the selected fixed-point format. If the selected format of the left-side variable does not have enough precision for representing the constant value, then functions such as saturation, overflow, and rounding are performed on the constant.

(ii) The add and subtract operations are applied directly without any loss of accuracy during the operation.

(iii) The multiply operation is implemented as an assembly module, and each instance of the multiply operator is replaced by a function call to the assembly module.

(iv) The division operation is also implemented as an assembly module. The divider module consists of shift operations to align the decimal part of the result.

6. Implementing the Reconfiguration Framework

Let us explain how the occam-pi language can be applied for the realization of dynamic reconfiguration of hardware

resources. The reconfiguration process based on its specification in the occam-pi language can be performed by taking into account a work farm design approach [21, 22].

A worker is a particular function mapped onto a specific processor or group of processors. The functionality of an individual worker is described either by one process, or it can be a composition of a number of processes which are interconnected according to their communication requirements. A worker can either occupy one processing element or it can be mapped to a collection of processing elements together performing a particular function as shown in Figure 5. Each worker (indicated as W1 and W2) can have multiple inputs and outputs. The reconfiguration process for the whole application consisting of multiple functions is controlled by a configuration controller (CC), which is composed of a configuration loader (CL) and a configuration monitor (CM). In Ambric, both the loader and the monitor processes are mapped to some of the processors in the array, but, in other cases, the reconfiguration management processes can instead be mapped to dedicated hardware. The configuration loader has a local storage of all the configurations in the form of precompiled object codes, which can then be loaded successively. The order of the reconfigurations is explicitly defined in the configuration loader. The communication channels within each worker are established by taking into account the communication requirements of all the configurations to be mapped on a given set of resources.

Two types of packets are communicated between the configuration loader and different workers, that is, work packets and configuration packets, as shown in Figure 6. The work packets can also be communicated directly to the workers from the external stimuli in case they have multiple inputs. The work packets consist of the data to be processed, and the configuration packets contain the configuration data. Both types of packets are routed to different workers based on either the worker ID or some other identifier. Each worker executes a small kernel to differentiate between the incoming packets based on their header information. Whenever a worker finishes its function, it returns control to its internal kernel after sending a reconfiguration request packet indicating that the particular worker has completed its function and the corresponding hardware resources are ready to be reconfigured to a new configuration. The configuration monitor keeps track of the current state of each worker

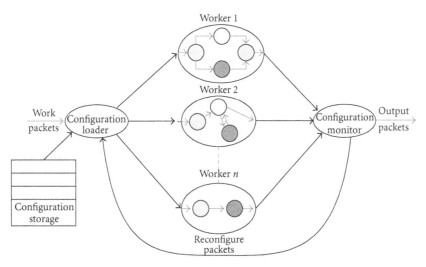

FIGURE 6: Communication within the framework of reconfigurable components.

and receives the reconfiguration request from the particular worker once it has completed its specific task and issues it to the configuration loader, which forks a new worker process to be reconfigured in place of the existing worker. The location of the worker is specified by the placement attribute, which consists of two integers. The first integer relates to the identification of the worker, and the second integer identifies the individual processing element within the worker. The placement attributes are logical integers, and they are translated to the physical address of the target architecture by the compiler. The configuration data is communicated in the form of a configuration packet that includes the instruction code for the individual processing elements. The configuration packet is passed around all the processing elements within the worker, where each processing element extracts its own configuration data and passes the rest to its adjacent neighbors.

7. 1D-DCT Case Study

In this section, we present and discuss the reconfigurable implementation of the one-dimensional discrete cosine Transform (1D-DCT), which is developed in occam-pi and then ported to Ambric using our compilation platform. DCT is a compression technique used in video compression encoders, such as MPEG encoding, to transform an $N \times N$ image block from the spatial domain to the DCT domain [23]. Since DCT is one part of the overall MPEG encoders, it becomes feasible to implement a reconfigurable version of DCT in order to conserve the hardware resources, so that these resources can be used for implementing other parts of the compression encoders. The mathematics for the 1D-DCT algorithm is described by the following equations:

$$X(k) = C(k) \sum_{n=0}^{N-1} \cos \frac{(2n+1)k\pi}{2N}, \quad 1 \le k \le N-1,$$

$$C(0) = \sqrt{\frac{1}{N}}, \qquad C(k) = \sqrt{\frac{2}{N}}. \tag{1}$$

We have used a streaming approach to implement the 1D-DCT algorithm, and the dataflow diagram of an 8-point 1D-DCT algorithm is shown in Figure 7. When computing the forward DCT, an 8×8 samples block is input on the left and the forward DCT vector is received as output on the right. The implementation is based on a set of filters which operate in four stages, and two of these stages are reconfigured at run-time based on the framework presented in Section 5. The reconfiguration process is applied between these stages in such a way that when the first two stages are completed, the next two stages of the pipeline are configured on the same physical resources, thus reusing the same processors. The function of "worker1" is described by a process named "worker1," which consists of the first two stages of the DCT algorithm and which are mapped to two individual SRD processors of "compute-unit 1," as they are invoked in a parallel block. The implementation of the configuration loader as expressed in the occam-pi program is shown in Code Example 3(a), which has one output channel-end "cnf" of mobile type because it is used to communicate the configuration data. (Note that Code Example 3 only shows the code related to configuration management, not the complete code.) The implementation of the configuration monitor is shown in Code Example 3(b). The configuration monitor will wait until it receives a "RECONFIG" message from the worker, which indicates that the worker has finished performing its functions and the corresponding hardware resource is ready to be reconfigured. The monitor will generate a reconfiguration request message along with the logical address of the resource to be reconfigured to the configuration loader. The configuration loader, upon receipt of a reconfiguration request, will issue a FORK statement, as shown in Code Example 3(a), which includes the name of the process to be configured in place of "worker1," its corresponding configuration data, and its associated channels. The configuration data is defined as a mobile data type, meaning that the configuration loader loses the possession of the configuration data after it has been passed to the forked process. The new forked "worker2" process has

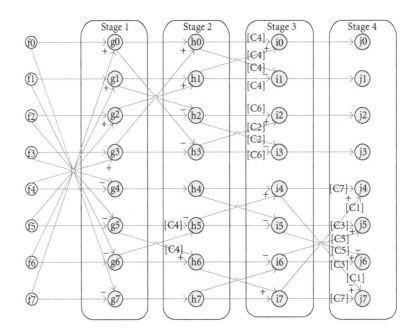

FIGURE 7: Dataflow diagram for 1D-DCT.

```
PROC loader (CHAN INT inp?, CHAN MOBILE INT cnf!,          PROC monitor (CHAN INT res?, CHAN INT ack!,
             CHAN INT ack?)                                              CHAN INT outp!)
INT cstatus, value, id:                                       INT status:
MOBILE [100] INT config:                                     VAL RECONFIG IS 255:
CHAN MOBILE INT cnf:                                          WHILE TRUE
CHAN INT res:                                                   SEQ
VAL RECONFIG IS 255:                                              res ? status
SEQ                                                               IF
  FORKING                                                           status = RECONFIG
    WHILE TRUE                                                        ack ! RECONFIG
      SEQ                                                           status <> RECONFIG
        inp ? value                                                  outp ! status
        cnf ! value                                       :
        ack ? cstatus
        IF                                                              (b)
          cstatus = RECONFIG
            SEQ                                            PROC worker2 (MOBILE [100] INT config,
              ack ? id                                                 CHAN MOBILE INT cnf?, CHAN INT res!)
              IF                                             CHAN INT ch:
                id = 1                                       PLACED PAR
                  FORK worker2 (config, cnf?, res!)            PROCESSOR 1,1
                Id = 2                                            stage3 (config, cnf?, ch!)
                ...                                           PROCESSOR 1,2
  :                                                              stage4 (config, ch?, res!)
                                                          :
                (a)                                                     (c)
```

CODE EXAMPLE 3: Source code illustrating (a) Configuration loader, (b) configuration monitor, and (c) worker process.

the same placement attributes as those of "*worker1*," as shown in Code Example 3(c), meaning that the "*worker2*" process will be mapped to the same processing element as that of the "*worker1*" process. The newly configured "*worker2*" process consists of the last two stages of the DCT algorithm. The computed results of "*worker1*" are also passed

from the monitor to the configuration loader and are fed into the "*worker2*" process along the same channel that is used for communicating configuration data. The computations of different stages of the DCT algorithm are described in the form of expressions in separate processes that are invoked in a parallel block in the individual worker processes.

8. SAR and Autofocus

In this section, we illustrate our approach on a larger application example, part of a synthetic aperture radar (SAR). SAR systems can be used to create high-resolution radar images from low-resolution aperture data. A SAR system produces a map of the ground while the platform is flying past it. The radar transmits a relatively wide beam to the ground, illuminating each resolution cell over a long period of time. The effect of this movement is that the distance between a point on the ground and the antenna varies over the data collection interval. This variation in distance is unique for each point in the area of interest. This is illustrated in Figure 8 where the area to be mapped is represented by $M \times N$ resolution cells and L represents the number of pulses. The cells correspond to paths in the collected radar data. The task for the signal processor is to integrate, for each resolution cell in the output image, the responses along the corresponding path. The flight path is assumed to be linear.

8.1. Image Forming. A computationally efficient method for creating the image is the Fast Factorized Back-Projection (FFBP) [24]. In FFBP, the whole image initially consists of a large number of small subimages with low angular resolution. These subimages are iteratively merged into larger ones with higher and higher angular resolution, until the final image with full angular resolution is obtained. The autofocus method used here assumes a merge base of two subimages.

8.2. Autofocus. In reality, the flight path is not perfectly linear. This can, however, be compensated for in the processing. In the FFBP, the compensations typically are based on positioning information from GPS. If this information is insufficient or even missing, autofocus can instead be used. The autofocus calculations use the image data itself and are done before each subaperture merge. One autofocus method, which assumes a merge base of two, relies on finding the flight path compensation that results in the best possible match between the images of the contributing subapertures in a merge. Several flight path compensations are thus tested before a merge. The image match is evaluated according to a selected focus criterion, as shown in Figure 9. The criterion assumed in this study is maximization of correlation of image data. As the criterion calculations are carried out many times for each merge, it is important that these are done efficiently. Here, the effect of a path error is approximated to a linear shift in the data set. Thus, a number of correlations between subimages that are slightly shifted in data are to be carried out. Interpolation is performed in order to compute the value from samples in the contributing data set of the subimages. More details about the calculations are given in the next section. Autofocus in FFBP for SAR is further discussed in [25].

8.3. Performance Requirements. The integration time may be several minutes. The computational performance demands are tens or hundreds of GFLOPS. The large data sets themselves represent a challenge but also the complicated

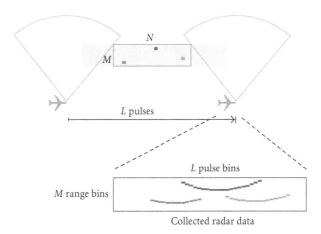

FIGURE 8: Simplified illustration of stripmap SAR.

memory addressing scheme due to, for example, changing geometric proportions during the processing. The exact computational requirements are dependent on the chosen detailed algorithms and radar system parameters.

9. Autofocus Criterion Case Study

In order to realize the autofocus algorithm on the Ambric platform, the first step in the development process is to determine the dataflow patterns of the algorithm and estimate an approximate amount of resources to be used. The next step is to write the occam-pi application code in terms of processes based on the dataflow diagram and compose these processes to be executed either in sequence or in parallel to each other. The occam-pi application is tested for functional correctness by using the Kent Retargetable occam Compiler (KRoC) [26] run-time system, and finally the occam-pi application code is compiled by our compiler to the native languages of Ambric. The generated code can then be compiled to generate binaries for the Ambric platform using its proprietary design environment.

We have implemented two versions of the same algorithm, with a different degree of parallelism exploited by the two approaches. We have used a parameterized approach for both of the designs, so the amount of parallelism can be varied easily by using the construct of replicated PAR of occam-pi based on parameters such as area of interest (A) and number of pixels processed per interpolation kernel (P). In addition, there are the other parameters of degree of shift and degree of tilt which are to be passed to the algorithm. Both design approaches take as an input two 6×6 blocks of image pixels from the area of interest of the contributing images. Cubic interpolation based on Neville's algorithm [27] is performed in the range direction followed by the beam direction to estimate the value of the contributing pixels along the tilted lines, and the resulting subimages are to be correlated according to the autofocus criterion. Figure 10(a) illustrates how an interpolated value is computed from samples in the contributing data set, and Figure 10(b) indicates how the intermediate interpolated results in the range direction are reused in order to calculate several

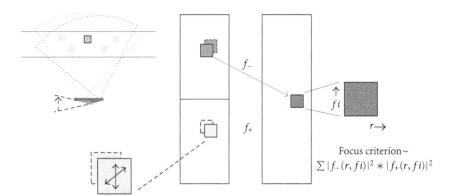

Figure 9: Illustration of autofocus and focus criterion.

interpolated values in the beam direction. Each pixel data comprises two 32-bit floating-point numbers corresponding to the real and imaginary components. These floating-point numbers are represented by the REAL data type in occam-pi, and the REAL data values are translated to Q16 format fixed-point representation. For fixed-point arithmetics, specialized assembly language code is inserted in place of arithmetic operations in the generated code by the compiler backend. Following is a description of the two design approaches.

9.1. Design-I. In the first design, we have used six-range interpolators to calculate the cubic interpolation along the six rows of pixel data in one of the two input pixel blocks, as shown in Figure 11. The input pixel data is fed to the range interpolators through two splitters, which route the pixel data values received from the source distributor block. Since there are no arithmetic computations performed by the source and splitter blocks, when mapped on the Ambric array, these blocks are implemented on SR processors.

The range interpolators perform the same operation on different rows of pixel data. During the first iteration, each range interpolator takes data values corresponding to four pixels from their inputs and performs the cubic interpolation; then the resultant interpolated pixel data values are passed to the beam interpolation stage. Each range interpolator is implemented on a set of three SRD processors which are connected in a pipeline manner. Since the computed results of the different range interpolators are to be used by multiple beam interpolators, some of the range interpolator blocks have multiple outputs and the resulting interpolated data is copied to these multiple outputs.

The next stage in the dataflow diagram is to perform the cubic interpolation in the beam direction. Three beam interpolators are implemented to perform the beam interpolation on the resulting output of the range interpolation stage. Similar to the range interpolator, each beam interpolator block is also composed of three SRD processors connected in a pipeline. Each beam interpolator takes four inputs from four different range interpolators, and it receives its input data values corresponding to four-range interpolated pixels on these input ports. The resulting data values of the beam interpolation stage is passed to the three correlators. Each correlator is implemented on one SRD processor and takes

pixel data values from each of the pixel data blocks, calculates their correlation, and passes the result to the summation block to calculate the final autofocus criterion. The summation block is implemented on a single SRD processor. Three iterations of the range interpolation, beam interpolation, correlation, and summation stages are performed in order to compute the autofocus criterion for the entire 6×6 image block.

The parameters of area of interest (A) and number of pixels processed per interpolation kernel (P) have been used in the construct of replicated PAR of occam-pi to control the resource usage as shown in Code Example 4. The values of these parameters determine how many instances of processes invoked in the replicated PAR block will be generated, that is, how many split, rangeintp, beamintp, and so forth processes will be instantiated. The parameters of an invoked process define the input and output channelends used by the said process. Based on the definition of the input and output channel-ends required by each process, the compiler generates the static interconnections between different processes.

9.2. Design-II. The second design uses three times as many range and beam interpolators as the first design, as shown in Figure 12, so that only one iteration of execution of each of the stages will result in computation of the autofocus criterion for the complete 6×6 pixel block. However, due to the limitation of the maximum number of SRD processors available on the Am2045 chip that we are using as a target for realization, we have to reduce the number of pipelined processors within each of the range and beam interpolation blocks to two.

The increase in the number of range interpolators is also reflected in the increase in the number of splitters, so there are six splitters used to feed the 18-range interpolators performing the cubic interpolation in the range direction of one of the input 6×6 pixel blocks. The six splitters are fed by a single source through two source distributors, because the number of output ports on an SR processor cannot exceed five. As in the first design, the source and source distributors are executed on SR processors. The dataflow patterns from the range interpolators to the beam interpolators, from the beam interpolators to the correlators, and further on to

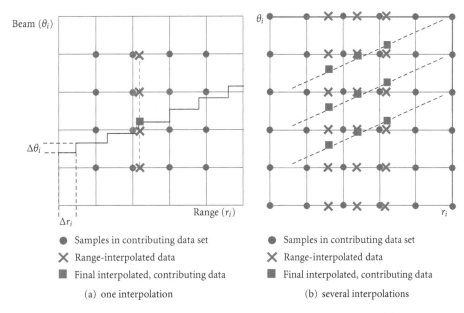

$$\text{Beam } (\theta_i)$$

$$\Delta\theta_i$$

$$\text{Range } (r_i)$$

$$\Delta r_i$$

● Samples in contributing data set
✕ Range-interpolated data
■ Final interpolated, contributing data

(a) one interpolation

$$\theta_i$$

$$r_i$$

● Samples in contributing data set
✕ Range-interpolated data
■ Final interpolated, contributing data

(b) several interpolations

FIGURE 10: Usage of cubic interpolation kernel to calculate contributing pixel data points.

the summation stage are similar to those in the previous design except that we now have separate resources for each iteration of interpolation and correlation stages.

10. Implementation Results and Discussion

10.1. ID-DCT Case Study. We now present the results of the reconfigurable 1D-DCT which is implemented by using the framework presented in Section 4. Our aim in this case study is to demonstrate the applicability of the programming model of occam-pi, together with the proposed framework for expressing reconfigurability, thus we do not claim to achieve efficient implementations with respect to performance. The application case studies to prove the performance benefit of carrying out reconfigurations using our proposed methodology is part of our future work.

The coarse-grained parallelized DCT is implemented in a four stage pipeline. Earlier results reveal that an implementation using four SRD processors takes 1340 cycles to compute 64 samples of 1D-DCT [4]. This time includes the time consumed during communication stalls between different stages. We compared this implementation with a reconfigurable one that uses only two SRD processors, which are reconfigured to perform the different stages successively. The computation of the same amount of samples now takes 2612 cycles, which includes the cycle count for the reconfiguration process, which is 550 cycles. The number of instruction words to be stored in the local memory of each individual processor is 97. The SRD processor takes 2 cycles to write one memory word in its local memory, thus the memory writing time is a significant part of the overall reconfiguration time. The reconfiguration process is controlled in such a way that the time taken by the two processors to update their instruction memories is partially overlapped, meaning that the first processor will be performing computations while the second one is being reconfigured.

In the two-processor reconfigurable implementation, most of the communication stalls that appeared in the four processor implementation are eliminated, and time is instead used for the reconfiguration management. The results also show that the reconfiguration time is one fifth of the overall time of computation, indicating reasonable feasibility of the approach.

10.2. Autofocus Criterion Case Study. For the autofocus application, the implementation results are achieved by realizing both the designs on the Ambric Am2045 architecture and executing them on a GT board containing one Am2045 chip being operated at 300 MHz clock. We have used the performance harness library provided by Nethra Imaging Inc. to obtain cycle accurate performance measurements. We have also obtained results of a sequential version of the same algorithm by executing it as a single threaded application on an Intel i7-M620 CPU operating at 2.67 GHz. Table 1 presents the resources consumed in terms of number of used SRD processors, SR processors, and RU banks, alongwith the percentage of total amount of available resources.

The greater number of SRD processors used as compared to the SR processors is due to the fact that most of the blocks involve complex arithmetics which cannot be performed on SR processors, and also due to the limited instruction memories of the SR processors, which in this case makes them useful only for data distribution. A significant number of RU banks are used to store the additional instructions for SRD processors that exceed the internal memory of 256 words. Some of the RU bank memory is also used in implementing FIFO buffers on the channels between different processors to reduce the effect of communication stalls. When going from the first design to the second one, the number of SRD processors should be three times the number of SRD processors used in Design-I, but, due to the limited number of available SRD processors, we have to reduce

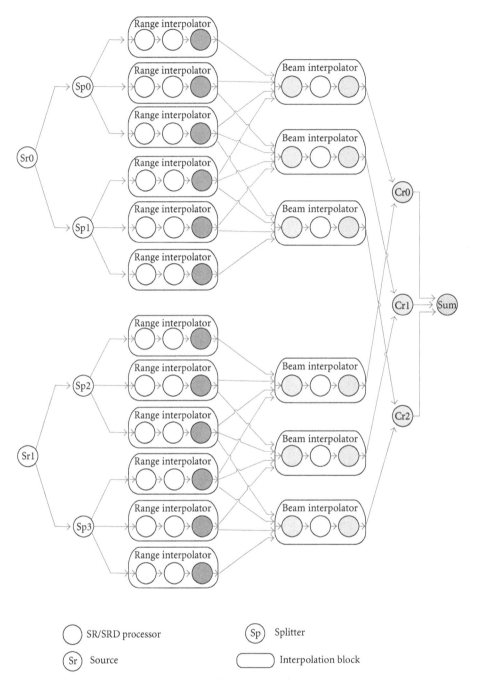

FIGURE 11: Dataflow diagram of Design-I.

TABLE 1: Resources consumed for autofocus criterion calculation.

	SRDs	SRs	RU Banks
Am2045 full capacity	168	168	336
Design-I on Ambric	70 (42%)	24 (14%)	113 (34%)
Design-II on Ambric	141 (84%)	28 (17%)	208 (62%)

the pipelined processors within each interpolator to two. The use of the performance harness library results in the use of one additional SR and one additional SRD processor, as well as six additional RU banks.

Table 2 shows performance and power results: the latency, in cycle count, for producing first correlation output,

the throughput, in terms of number of pixels per second on which the given autofocus criterion is computed, and the speedup figures for the design realized on Ambric compared to a sequential implementation executed on Intel i7-M620 CPU. It also shows the estimated power consumed by the two parallel and one sequential implementation based on the figures obtained from Am2045 [28] and Intel i7-M620 processor [29] data sheets.

The latency results of the design-II depict an improvement in terms of 30% less cycles as compared to design-I. The throughput of the second design is 2.1x times the throughput of the first design, and the throughput speedup with respect to the sequential implementation is 11x and 23x,

```
PROC autofocus(VAL INT A, P, VAL REAL xintr, xinti, CHAN REAL dinp0?, dinp1?, CHAN REAL res!)
  [(A/P)*2] CHAN REAL doutp:
  [A*2] CHAN REAL32 soutp:
  [A*4] CHAN REAL routp:
  [A] CHAN REAL boutp:
  [A/2] CHAN REAL coutp:
  PAR
    datadist(A,dinp0?,doutp[0]!,doutp[]!)
    PAR i=0 FOR ((A/P)-1)
      PAR j=0 FOR ((A/P)-1)
        PAR
          split(A,doutp[(i*2)+j]?,soutp[(i*3)+(j*3)]!,soutp[((i*3)+(j*3))+1]!,
            soutp[((i*3)+(j*3))+2]!)
          rangeintp1(xintr,xinti,soutp[(i*6)+(j*5)]?,routp[(i*12)+(j*11)]!)
          rangeintp2(xintr,xinti,soutp[((i*6)+(j*3))+1]?,routp[((i*12)+(j*8))+1]!,
            routp[((i*12)+(j*8))+2]!)
          rangeintp3(xintr,xinti,soutp[((i*6)+(j*1))+2]?,routp[((i*12)+(j*3))+3]!,
            routp[((i*12)+(j*3))+4]!,routp[((i*12)+(j*3))+5]!)
        PAR j=0 FOR (A/P)
          beamintp(xintr,xinti,routp[(i*12)+(j*4)]?,routp[((i*12)+(j*4))+1]!,
            routp[((i*12)+(j*4))+2]!,boutp[(i*3)+j]!)
      PAR j=0 FOR (A/P)
        corr(boutp[i]?,boutp[i+3]?,coutp[i]!)
    corrsum(coutp[0]?,coutp[1]?,coutp[2]?,res!)
:
```

CODE EXAMPLE 4: Simplified illustration of Design-I implementation of autofocus criterion calculation in occam-pi.

TABLE 2: Performance and estimated power results of autofocus criterion calculation.

Implementations	Latency (cycles)	Throughput (pixels/sec.)	Speedup throughput	Power (watts)
Sequential on Intel i7 @ 2.67 GHz	—	21,600	1	17.5
Design-I on Ambric @ 300 MHz	16,497	236,386	11	6.52
Design-II on Ambric @ 300 MHz	12,793	486,224	23	9.8

respectively, for the two designs. With 94 processors which are clocked 9 times slower, a speedup of 11 shows that the design programmed in occam-pi is indeed efficient. Ideally, the throughput of design-II should have been three times that of design-I, but the use of almost twice the number of processors results in some communication stalls in between the data distribution and interpolation stages. Also, the effects of the reduced number of pipelined processors within individual interpolators is reflected in the reduction of the throughput. The two designs realized on Ambric consume much less power than the traditional one, and they provide 29x and 40x, respectively, more throughput per watt as compared to the sequential implementation.

We have experienced that the program code for the different stages of the cubic interpolation kernel to be executed on the pipelined processors have to be optimized to be able to fit into at most two RU banks of memory for each SRD processor. Otherwise, if it exceeds the size of two RU banks, the placement tool cannot make use of the second SRD processor available in the same compute unit of the Ambric architecture. The optimization is achieved by generating the assembly code for the fixed-point arithmetics used in the cubic interpolation kernel by the compiler backend. Other optimizations implemented in the compiler include scalarization of array variables and exploitation of instruction level parallelism by using the mac_32_32 instruction in place of successive multiplication and addition instructions.

11. Conclusions and Future Work

We have presented an approach of using a CSP-based language for programming the emerging class of processor array architectures. We have also described the mobility features of the occam-pi language and the extensions in language constructs that are used to express run-time reconfigurability. The ideas are demonstrated by a working compiler, which compiles occam-pi programs to native code for an array of processors, Ambric. The presented approach is evaluated by implementing one common signal processing algorithm and one more complex case study which is part of a radar signal processing algorithm.

In terms of performance, the two implementations of Autofocus criterion calculation targeted on ambric outperform the CPU implementation by factors of 11–23, despite operating at a clock frequency of 300 MHz as compared to 2.67 GHz. This shows that the designs programmed in occam-pi are indeed efficient. The use of a much lower clock

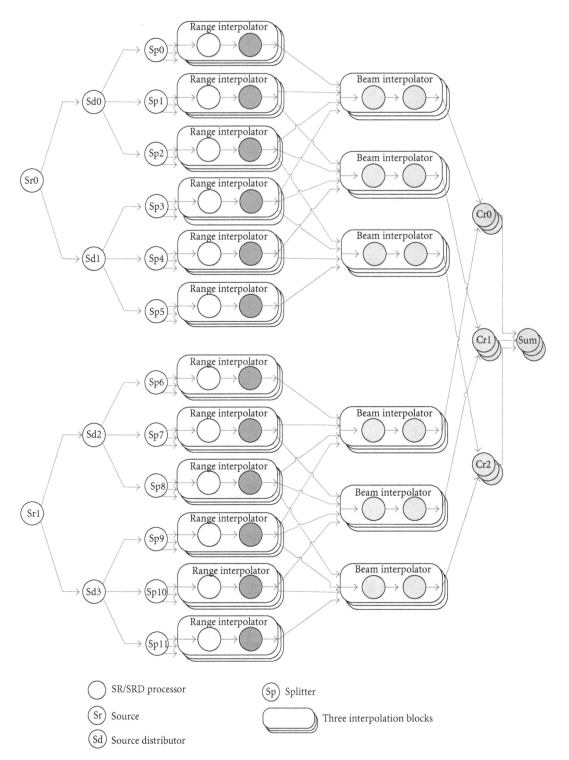

FIGURE 12: Dataflow diagram of Design-II.

frequency together with the switching off of unused cores in the Ambric architecture provides the side advantage of a significant reduction in energy consumption of the two parallel implementations, which is an important factor to consider for embedded systems. The reconfigurable versions of the benchmark algorithms prove that the occam-pi language allows expression of different configurations of the

algorithm which can be used successively to implement a particular algorithm within limited resources.

From the programmability point of view, it is observed that the explicit concurrency of occam-pi with the ability to describe computations that reside in different memory spaces, together with the dynamic process invocation mechanism, makes it suitable for mapping applications to massively parallel reconfigurable architectures. The `occam-pi` language is based on well-defined semantics, and its simplicity, static compilation properties, minimal run-time overhead, and power to express parallelism help in the task of parallelization. The existence of the `REAL` data type in `occam-pi` and the introduced conversion of the floating-point arithmetics to fixed-point by the compiler backend also reduces the overall burden on the programmer, compared to manually implementing the fixed-point arithmetics. Furthermore, the support for expressing dynamic parallelism in the form of replicated `PAR` constructs enables the compiler to perform resource-aware compilation in accordance with the application requirements. The reconfigurability support allows effective reuse of resources, and the placement attributes allow processes to be colocated, which gives a potential to avoid unnecessarily expensive communication. In addition to the language features, our proposed methodology of testing the functionality of the application in `occam-pi` before compiling the generated native code using the Ambric design environment reduces the turnaround time for implementing various design alternatives quite significantly.

In conclusion, using the `occam-pi` language is a practical and flexible approach to enable mapping of applications to massively parallel reconfigurable architectures that are based on globally asynchronous locally synchronous (GALS) principle and distributed memory model. The success of the approach stems from the well-defined semantics of the language that allows the expression of concurrent computations, interprocess communication, and reconfigurations with a formal basis. By simplifying these tasks, the problem of efficiently mapping applications to the massively parallel reconfigurable architectures is more readily addressed, as demonstrated in this work.

Future work will focus on developing more complex applications in the `occam-pi` language to exploit the run-time reconfiguration capability of the target hardware and on extending the compiler framework to target other reconfigurable architectures such as picoArray and Element CXI.

Acknowledgments

The authors would like to thank Nethra Imaging Inc. for giving access to their software development suite and hardware board. They would also like to acknowledge the support from Saab AB for the SAR application. This research is part of the CERES research program funded by the Knowledge Foundation and the ELLIIT strategic research initiative funded by the Swedish government.

References

[1] P. H. Welch and F. R. M. Barnes, "Communicating mobile processes introducing occam-pi," in *Proceedings of the Symposium on the Occasion of 25 Years of CSP—Communicating Sequential Processes*, Lecture Notes in Computer Science, pp. 175–210, Springer, July 2004.

[2] C. A. R Hoare, *Communicating Sequential Processes*, Prentice-Hall, 1985.

[3] R. Milner, J. Parrow, and D. Walker, "A calculus of mobile processes, I," *Information and Computation*, vol. 100, no. 1, pp. 1–40, 1992.

[4] Zain-ul-Abdin and B. Svensson, "Using a CSP based programming model for reconfigurable processor arrays," in *Proceedings of the International Conference on Reconfigurable Computing and FPGAs (ReConFig '08)*, pp. 343–348, December 2008.

[5] Zain-ul-Abdin and B. Svensson, "Occam-pi as a high-level language for coarsegrained reconfigurable architectures," in *Proceedings of the 18th International Reconfigurable Architectures Workshop held in Conjunction with International Parallel and Distributed Processing Symposium (IPDPS/RAW '11)*, Anchorage, Alaska, USA, May 2011.

[6] A. Åhlander, H. Hellsten, K. Lind, J. Lindgren, and B. Svensson, "Architectural challenges in memory-intensive, real-time image forming," in *Proceedings of the 36th International Conference on Parallel Processing in Xi'an (ICPP '07)*, September 2007.

[7] "Handel-C language reference manual," Version 3.1, Celoxica, 2002.

[8] J. Frigo, M. Gokhale, and D. Lavenier, "Evaluation of the streams-C C-to-FPGA compiler: an applications perspective," in *Proceedings of the ACM/SIGDA 9th International Sysmposium on Field Programmable Gate Arrays (FPGA '01)*, pp. 134–140, February 2001.

[9] "Mobius Language Manual," Codetronix LLC, 2006.

[10] W. Luk and S. Mckeever, "Pebble: a language for parametrised and reconfigurable hardware design," in *Proceedings of the 8th International Workshop on Field-Programmable Logic and Applications*, vol. 1482 of *Lecture Notes in Computer Science*, pp. 9–18, Springer, 1998.

[11] M. J. Wirthlin and B. L. Hutchings, "Dynamic instruction set computer," in *Proceedings of the IEEE Symposium on FPGAs for Custom Computing Machines*, pp. 99–107, April 1995.

[12] J. Burns, A. Donlin, J. Hogg, S. Singh, and M. D. Wit, " A dynamic reconfiguration run-time system," in *Proceedings of the Annual IEEE Symposium on Field-Programmable Custom Computing Machines*, 1997.

[13] J. Villarreal, A. Park, W. Najjar, and R. Halstead, "Designing modular hardware accelerators in C with ROCCC 2.0," in *Proceedings of the 18th IEEE International Symposium on Field-Programmable Custom Computing Machines (FCCM '10)*, pp. 127–134, May 2010.

[14] M. Bingfeng, S. Vernalde, D. Verkest, H. De Man, and R. Lauwereins, "DRESC: a retargetable compiler for coarse-grained reconfigurable architectures," in *Proceedings of the IEEE International Conference on Field-Programmable Technology*, 2002.

[15] A. M. Jones and M. Butts, "TeraOPS hardware: a new massively-parallel MIMD computing fabric IC," in *Proceedings of IEEE Hot Chips Symposium*, 2006.

[16] M. Butts, A. M. Jones, and P. Wasson, "A structural object programming model, architecture, chip and tools for reconfigurable computing," in *Proceedings of the 15th Annual IEEE Symposium on Field-Programmable Custom Computing Machines (FCCM '07)*, pp. 55–64, April 2007.

[17] "Occam® 2.1 reference manual, SGS-Thomson Microelectronics Limited," 1995.

[18] P. H. Welch and F. R. M. Barnes, "Prioritised dynamic communicating processes: part I," in *Communicating Process Architectures*, pp. 321–352, IOS Press, 2002.

[19] P. H. Welch and F. R. M. Barnes, "Prioritised dynamic communicating processes—part II," in *Communicating Process Architectures*, pp. 353–370, IOS Press, 2002.

[20] Tock, "Translator from Occam to C by Kent," http://projects.cs.kent.ac.uk/projects/tock/trac, 2011.

[21] M. Butts, B. Budlong, P. Wasson, and E. White, "Reconfigurable work farms on a massively parallel processor array," in *Proceedings of the 16th IEEE Symposium on Field-Programmable Custom Computing Machines (FCCM '08)*, pp. 206–215, April 2008.

[22] N. Shirazi, W. Luk, and P. Cheung, "Run-time management of dynamically reconfigurable designs," in *Proceedings of the 8th International Workshop on Field Programmable Logic and Applications (FPL '98)*, vol. 1482 of *Lecture Notes in Computer Science*, Springer, 1998.

[23] Xilinx, "Video compression using DCT," http://direct.xilinx.com/bvdocs/appnotes/xapp610.pdf, 2006.

[24] L. M. H. Ulander, H. Hellsten, and G. Stenström, "Synthetic-aperture radar processing using fast factorized back-projection," *IEEE Transactions on Aerospace and Electronic Systems*, vol. 39, no. 3, pp. 760–776, 2003.

[25] H. Hellsten, P. Dammert, and A. Åhlander, "Autofocus in fast factorized backprojection for processing of SAR images when geometry parameters are unknown," in *Proceedings of the IEEE International Radar Conference (RADAR '10)*, pp. 603–608, May 2010.

[26] "KRoC: Kent Retargetable Occam Compiler," http://www.cs.kent.ac.uk/projects/ofa/kroc/, 2010.

[27] E. H. Neville, "Iterative interpolation," *Journal of Indian Mathematical Society*, vol. 20, pp. 87–120, 1934.

[28] *Am2045 Data Book*, Ambric, 2007.

[29] Intel® Core™ i7-600, i5-500, i5-400, and i3-300 Mobile processor series datasheet, Intel Corporation, 2010.

Permissions

The contributors of this book come from diverse backgrounds, making this book a truly international effort. This book will bring forth new frontiers with its revolutionizing research information and detailed analysis of the nascent developments around the world.

We would like to thank all the contributing authors for lending their expertise to make the book truly unique. They have played a crucial role in the development of this book. Without their invaluable contributions this book wouldn't have been possible. They have made vital efforts to compile up to date information on the varied aspects of this subject to make this book a valuable addition to the collection of many professionals and students.

This book was conceptualized with the vision of imparting up-to-date information and advanced data in this field. To ensure the same, a matchless editorial board was set up. Every individual on the board went through rigorous rounds of assessment to prove their worth. After which they invested a large part of their time researching and compiling the most relevant data for our readers. Conferences and sessions were held from time to time between the editorial board and the contributing authors to present the data in the most comprehensible form. The editorial team has worked tirelessly to provide valuable and valid information to help people across the globe.

Every chapter published in this book has been scrutinized by our experts. Their significance has been extensively debated. The topics covered herein carry significant findings which will fuel the growth of the discipline. They may even be implemented as practical applications or may be referred to as a beginning point for another development. Chapters in this book were first published by Hindawi Publishing Corporation; hereby published with permission under the Creative Commons Attribution License or equivalent.

The editorial board has been involved in producing this book since its inception. They have spent rigorous hours researching and exploring the diverse topics which have resulted in the successful publishing of this book. They have passed on their knowledge of decades through this book. To expedite this challenging task, the publisher supported the team at every step. A small team of assistant editors was also appointed to further simplify the editing procedure and attain best results for the readers.

Our editorial team has been hand-picked from every corner of the world. Their multi-ethnicity adds dynamic inputs to the discussions which result in innovative outcomes. These outcomes are then further discussed with the researchers and contributors who give their valuable feedback and opinion regarding the same. The feedback is then collaborated with the researches and they are edited in a comprehensive manner to aid the understanding of the subject.

Apart from the editorial board, the designing team has also invested a significant amount of their time in understanding the subject and creating the most relevant covers. They scrutinized every image to scout for the most suitable representation of the subject and create an appropriate cover for the book.

The publishing team has been involved in this book since its early stages. They were actively engaged in every process, be it collecting the data, connecting with the contributors or procuring relevant information. The team has been an ardent support to the editorial, designing and production team. Their endless efforts to recruit the best for this project, has resulted in the accomplishment of this book. They are a veteran in the field of academics and their pool of knowledge is as vast as their experience in printing. Their expertise and guidance has proved useful at every step. Their uncompromising quality standards have made this book an exceptional effort. Their encouragement from time to time has been an inspiration for everyone.

The publisher and the editorial board hope that this book will prove to be a valuable piece of knowledge for researchers, students, practitioners and scholars across the globe.

List of Contributors

Diana Gohringer
Institute for Data Processing and Electronics, Karlsruhe Institute of Technology, 76344 Eggenstein-Leopoldshafen, Germany
Object Recognition Department, Fraunhofer IOSB, 76275 Ettlingen, Germany

Lukas Meder, Stephan Werner, Oliver Oey and Jurgen Becker
Institute for Information Processing Technology, Karlsruhe Institute of Technology, 76128 Karlsruhe, Germany

Michael Hubner
Chair for Embedded Systems in Information Technology, Ruhr-University of Bochum, 44780 Bochum, Germany

João Bispo and João M. P. Cardoso
Departmento de Engenharia Informática, Faculdade de Engenharia, Universidade do Porto, Rua Dr. Roberto Frias s/n, 4200-465 Porto, Portugal

João Canas Ferreira and Nuno Paulino
INESC TEC, Faculdade de Engenharia, Universidade do Porto, Rua Dr. Roberto Frias s/n, 4200-465 Porto, Portugal

Sascha Muhlbach
Secure Things Group, Center for Advanced Security Research Darmstadt, Mornewegstr. 32, 64293 Darmstadt, Germany

Andreas Koch
Department of Computer Science, Embedded Systems and Applications Group, Technische Universitat Darmstadt, Hochschulstr. 10, 64289 Darmstadt, Germany

Laurent Sauvage, Sylvain Guilley, Florent Flament, Jean-Luc Danger and Yves Mathieu
Telecom ParisTech, Institut Telecom CNRS LTCI, 46 rue Barrault, F-75634 Paris Cedex 13, France

Michael Schaeferling, Ulrich Hornung and Gundolf Kiefer
Department of Computer Science, Augsburg University of Applied Sciences, An der Hochschule 1, 86161 Augsburg, Germany

Mariusz Grad and Christian Plessl
Paderborn Center for Parallel Computing, University of Paderborn, 33098 Paderborn, Germany

Lyndon Judge, Suvarna Mane and Patrick Schaumont
Bradley Department of Electrical and Computer Engineering, Center for Embedded Systems for Critical Applications (CESCA), Virginia Tech, Blacksburg, VA 24061, USA

Ilia Lebedev and Christopher Fletcher
CSAIL, Massachusetts Institute of Technology, Cambridge, MA 02139, USA

Shaoyi Cheng, JamesMartin, Austin Doupnik, Daniel Burke, Mingjie Lin and John Wawrzynek
Department of EECS, University of California at Berkeley, CA 94704, USA

Matthias Kuehnle, Andre Wagner and Juergen Becker
Institute for Information Processing Technology, KIT, 7602 Karlsruhe, Germany

Alisson V. Brito
Department of Informatics, Federal University of Paraiba (UFPB), 58051-900 Joao Pessoa, PB, Brazil

Malte Baesler and Sven-Ole Voigt
Institute for Reliable Computing, Hamburg University of Technology, Schwarzenbergstraße 95, 21073 Hamburg, Germany

Alba Sandyra Bezerra Lopes
Federal Institute of Education, Science and Technology of Rio Grande do Norte, Campus Joao Camara, 59550-000 Joao Camara, RN, Brazil

Ivan Saraiva Silva
Department of Computer Science and Statistics, Campus Ministro Petronio Portela, Federal University of Piauı, 64049-550 Teresina, PI, Brazil

Luciano Volcan Agostini
Group of Architectures and Integrated Circuits-GACI, Federal University of Pelotas Pelotas, RS, Brazil

Angelo Kuti Lusala and Jean-Didier Legat
Institute of Information and Communication Technologies, Electronics and Applied Mathematics, Universite Catholique de Louvain, 1348 Louvain-la-Neuve, Belgium

Maitane Barrenechea, Mikel Mendicute and Egoitz Arruti
Department of Electronics and Computer Science, University of Mondragon, 20500 Mondragon, Spain

Zain-ul-Abdin and Bertil Svensson
Centre for Research on Embedded Systems (CERES), Halmstad University, 301 18 Halmstad, Sweden

Printed in the USA
CPSIA information can be obtained
at www.ICGtesting.com
JSHW051438221024
72173JS00006B/1512